HMH |  **into Math**™

Grade 8

Dear Students and Families,

Welcome to *Into Math*, Grade 8! In this program, you will develop skills and make sense of mathematics by solving real-world problems, using hands-on tools and strategies, and collaborating with your classmates.

With the support of your teacher and by engaging with meaningful practice you will learn to persevere when solving problems. *Into Math* will not only help you deepen your understanding of mathematics, but also build your confidence as a learner of mathematics.

Even more exciting, you will write all your ideas and solutions right in your book. In your *Into Math* book, writing and drawing on the pages will help you think deeply about what you are learning, help you truly understand math, and most important, you will become a confident user of mathematics!

Sincerely,
The Authors

Authors

Edward B. Burger, PhD
President, Southwestern University
Georgetown, Texas

Matthew R. Larson, PhD
Past-President, National Council
of Teachers of Mathematics
Lincoln Public Schools
Lincoln, Nebraska

Juli K. Dixon, PhD
Professor, Mathematics Education
University of Central Florida
Orlando, Florida

Steven J. Leinwand
Principal Research Analyst
American Institutes for Research
Washington, DC

Timothy D. Kanold, PhD
Mathematics Educator
Chicago, Illinois

Consultants

English Language Development Consultant

Harold Asturias
Director, Center for Mathematics
Excellence and Equity
Lawrence Hall of Science, University of California
Berkeley, California

Program Consultant

David Dockterman, EdD
Lecturer, Harvard Graduate School of Education
Cambridge, Massachusetts

Blended Learning Consultant

Weston Kiercshneck
Senior Fellow
International Center for Leadership in Education
Littleton, Colorado

STEM Consultants

Michael A. DiSpezio
Global Educator
North Falmouth, Massachusetts

Marjorie Frank
Science Writer and
Content-Area Reading Specialist
Brooklyn, New York

Bernadine Okoro
Access and Equity and
STEM Learning Advocate and Consultant
Washington, DC

Cary I. Sneider, PhD
Associate Research Professor
Portland State University
Portland, Oregon

Build Conceptual Understanding   Connect Concepts and Skills   Apply and Practice

Unit 2

Linear Equations and Applications

MODULE 3 Solve Linear Equations

MODULE 4 Angle Relationships

Unit 3
Relationships and Functions

MODULE 5 Proportional Relationships

Build Conceptual Understanding   Connect Concepts and Skills   Apply and Practice

MODULE 6 Understand and Analyze Functions

MODULE 7 Systems of Linear Equations

Build Conceptual Understanding   Connect Concepts and Skills   Apply and Practice

© Houghton Mifflin Harcourt Publishing Company • **Image Credits:** ©Tetra Images/Getty Images

Unit
4
Statistics and Probability

© Houghton Mifflin Harcourt Publishing Company • Image Credits: (t) ©Rawpixel.com/Shutterstock (b) ©VladyslavDanilin/Shutterstock

Build Conceptual Understanding   Connect Concepts and Skills   Apply and Practice

© Houghton Mifflin Harcourt Publishing Company • Image Credits: ©Betsy Hansen/Houghton Mifflin Harcourt

Build Conceptual Understanding   Connect Concepts and Skills   Apply and Practice

My Progress on Mathematics Standards

The lessons in your *Into Math* book provide instruction for Mathematics Standards for Grade 8. You can use the following pages to reflect on your learning and record your progress through the standards.

As you learn new concepts, reflect on this learning. Consider inserting a checkmark if you understand the concepts or inserting a question mark if you have questions or need help.

	Student Edition Lessons	My Progress
Domain: THE NUMBER SYSTEM		
Cluster: Know that there are numbers that are not rational, and approximate them by rational numbers.		
Know that numbers that are not rational are called irrational. Understand informally that every number has a decimal expansion; for rational numbers show that the decimal expansion repeats eventually, and convert a decimal expansion which repeats eventually into a rational number.	10.1	
Use rational approximations of irrational numbers to compare the size of irrational numbers, locate them approximately on a number line diagram, and estimate the value of expressions (e.g., π^2).	10.3	
Domain: EXPRESSIONS & EQUATIONS		
Cluster: Work with radicals and integer exponents.		
Know and apply the properties of integer exponents to generate equivalent numerical expressions.	12.1	
Use square root and cube root symbols to represent solutions to equations of the form $x^2 = p$ and $x^3 = p$, where p is a positive rational number. Evaluate square roots of small perfect squares and cube roots of small perfect cubes. Know that $\sqrt{2}$ is irrational.	10.2	
Use numbers expressed in the form of a single digit times an integer power of 10 to estimate very large or very small quantities, and to express how many times as much one is than the other.	12.2	

Perform operations with numbers expressed in scientific notation, including problems where both decimal and scientific notation are used. Use scientific notation and choose units of appropriate size for measurements of very large or very small quantities (e.g., use millimeters per year for seafloor spreading). Interpret scientific notation that has been generated by technology.	12.3	
Cluster: Understand the connections between proportional relationships, lines, and linear equations.		
Graph proportional relationships, interpreting the unit rate as the slope of the graph. Compare two different proportional relationships represented in different ways.	5.2, 5.3, 5.4	
Use similar triangles to explain why the slope m is the same between any two distinct points on a non-vertical line in the coordinate plane; derive the equation $y = mx$ for a line through the origin and the equation $y = mx + b$ for a line intercepting the vertical axis at b.	5.1, 5.2, 6.2	
Cluster: Analyze and solve linear equations and pairs of simultaneous linear equations.		
Solve linear equations in one variable.	3.1, 3.2, 3.3 *See also below.*	
• Give examples of linear equations in one variable with one solution, infinitely many solutions, or no solutions. Show which of these possibilities is the case by successively transforming the given equation into simpler forms, until an equivalent equation of the form $x = a$, $a = a$, or $a = b$ results (where a and b are different numbers).	3.2, 3.3	

• Solve linear equations with rational number coefficients, including equations whose solutions require expanding expressions using the distributive property and collecting like terms.	3.1, 3.2, 3.3	
Analyze and solve pairs of simultaneous linear equations.	7.1, 7.2, 7.3, 7.4, 7.5, 7.6 *See also below.*	
• Understand that solutions to a system of two linear equations in two variables correspond to points of intersection of their graphs, because points of intersection satisfy both equations simultaneously.	7.2	
• Solve systems of two linear equations in two variables algebraically, and estimate solutions by graphing the equations. Solve simple cases by inspection.	7.3, 7.4, 7.5	
• Solve real-world and mathematical problems leading to two linear equations in two variables.	7.6	

Domain: FUNCTIONS		
Cluster: Define, evaluate, and compare functions.		
Understand that a function is a rule that assigns to each input exactly one output. The graph of a function is the set of ordered pairs consisting of an input and the corresponding output.	6.1	
Compare properties of two functions each represented in a different way (algebraically, graphically, numerically in tables, or by verbal descriptions).	6.5	
Interpret the equation $y = mx + b$ as defining a linear function, whose graph is a straight line; give examples of functions that are not linear.	6.2	
Cluster: Use functions to model relationships between quantities.		
Construct a function to model a linear relationship between two quantities. Determine the rate of change and initial value of the function from a description of a relationship or from two (x, y) values, including reading these from a table or from a graph. Interpret the rate of change and initial value of a linear function in terms of the situation it models, and in terms of its graph or a table of values.	6.3, 6.4, 8.3	
Describe qualitatively the functional relationship between two quantities by analyzing a graph (e.g., where the function is increasing or decreasing, linear or nonlinear). Sketch a graph that exhibits the qualitative features of a function that has been described verbally.	6.6	

Domain: GEOMETRY		
Cluster: Understand congruence and similarity using physical models, transparencies, or geometry software.		
Verify experimentally the properties of rotations, reflections, and translations:	1.1, 1.2, 1.3, 1.4 *See also below.*	
• Lines are taken to lines, and line segments to line segments of the same length.	1.1, 1.2, 1.3, 1.4	
• Angles are taken to angles of the same measure.	1.1, 1.2, 1.3, 1.4	
• Parallel lines are taken to parallel lines.	1.1, 1.2, 1.3, 1.4	
Understand that a two-dimensional figure is congruent to another if the second can be obtained from the first by a sequence of rotations, reflections, and translations; given two congruent figures, describe a sequence that exhibits the congruence between them.	1.5	
Describe the effect of dilations, translations, rotations, and reflections on two-dimensional figures using coordinates.	1.2, 1.3, 1.4, 1.5, 2.1, 2.2	
Understand that a two-dimensional figure is similar to another if the second can be obtained from the first by a sequence of rotations, reflections, translations, and dilations; given two similar two-dimensional figures, describe a sequence that exhibits the similarity between them.	2.3	
Use informal arguments to establish facts about the angle sum and exterior angle of triangles, about the angles created when parallel lines are cut by a transversal, and the angle-angle criterion for similarity of triangles.	4.1, 4.2, 4.3	
Cluster: Understand and apply the Pythagorean Theorem.		
Explain a proof of the Pythagorean Theorem and its converse.	11.1, 11.2	
Apply the Pythagorean Theorem to determine unknown side lengths in right triangles in real-world and mathematical problems in two and three dimensions.	11.1, 11.2, 11.3	
Apply the Pythagorean Theorem to find the distance between two points in a coordinate system.	11.4	
Cluster: Solve real-world and mathematical problems involving volume of cylinders, cones, and spheres.		
Know the formulas for the volumes of cones, cylinders, and spheres and use them to solve real-world and mathematical problems.	13.1, 13.2, 13.3, 13.4	

Domain: STATISTICS & PROBABILITY		
Cluster: Investigate patterns of association in bivariate data.		
Construct and interpret scatter plots for bivariate measurement data to investigate patterns of association between two quantities. Describe patterns such as clustering, outliers, positive or negative association, linear association, and nonlinear association.	8.1	
Know that straight lines are widely used to model relationships between two quantitative variables. For scatter plots that suggest a linear association, informally fit a straight line, and informally assess the model fit by judging the closeness of the data points to the line.	8.2	
Use the equation of a linear model to solve problems in the context of bivariate measurement data, interpreting the slope and intercept.	8.3	
Understand that patterns of association can also be seen in bivariate categorical data by displaying frequencies and relative frequencies in a two-way table. Construct and interpret a two-way table summarizing data on two categorical variables collected from the same subjects. Use relative frequencies calculated for rows or columns to describe possible association between the two variables.	9.1, 9.2, 9.3	

Transformational Geometry

Puzzle Designer

A puzzle designer combines creativity and imagination with logical reasoning to make challenging and entertaining puzzles. From three-dimensional puzzles to jigsaw puzzles to mazes to crossword puzzles, puzzle designers have something to intrigue just about everyone.

STEM Task:

Starting with 12 toothpicks arranged as shown, perform each task:

- Remove 4 toothpicks to form exactly 1 square.
- Remove 4 toothpicks to form exactly 2 squares.
- Move 3 toothpicks to form exactly 3 squares.

Learning Mindset

Challenge-Seeking Builds Confidence

Have you ever been asked to do something that you didn't know how to do? This happens to everyone at one time or another. Sometimes, people back away from a challenge because they are afraid of making a mistake. But taking on a challenge can be a rewarding growth experience. Here are two suggestions that can help you overcome a challenge when your confidence is fading.

- Build your confidence by trying simpler versions of the task. Think of learning to draw, dance, or build furniture. Succeeding at simple skills when you start gives you confidence to take on advanced challenges.

- Don't give up. Remember, you are learning and growing through this process. A positive attitude will make this and future challenges easier to meet.

Reflect

Q Did you feel confident as you worked on the STEM Task?

Q How does self-confidence affect your ability to complete tasks or meet challenges?

Transformations and Congruence

TREASURE Hunt

A treasure is on a remote island represented by the coordinate plane.

Graph the following polygons.

A. *ABCD* with *A*(1, 6), *B*(7, 6), *C*(7, −5), *D*(−4, −5)

B. *FGHJ* with *F*(−1, 3), *G*(6, 3), *H*(6, −4), *J*(−1, −4)

C. *KLMN* with *K*(−6, −3), *L*(3, −3), *M*(0, −9), *N*(−9, −9)

D. *STUV* with *S*(−9, 2), *T*(−3, 2), *U*(−3, −6), *V*(−9, −6)

E. Clues: The treasure is at a point with integer coordinates. The treasure is buried inside a trapezoid that is not a parallelogram, outside any squares or rectangles, and inside a parallelogram.

Where is the treasure buried? Explain how you know.

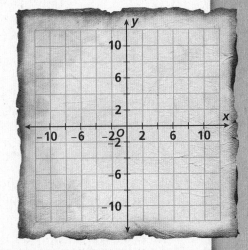

_____

_____

_____

_____

 Turn and Talk

How did you use the clues to find the treasure?

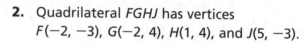
Are You Ready?

Complete these problems to review prior concepts and skills you will need for this module.

Polygons in the Coordinate Plane

Draw each polygon in the coordinate plane.

1. Triangle *ABC* has vertices *A*(−4, 3), *B*(3, 1), and *C*(1, −3).

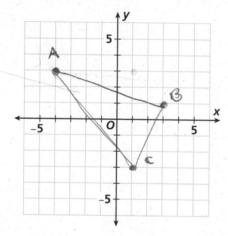

2. Quadrilateral *FGHJ* has vertices *F*(−2, −3), *G*(−2, 4), *H*(1, 4), and *J*(5, −3).

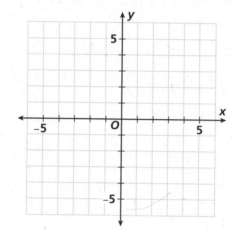

Draw Shapes with Given Conditions

Use a ruler and protractor to draw a quadrilateral that matches each description. Label the sides or angles described.

3. a square with a side length of 2 centimeters

4. a parallelogram with two angles that measure 65° and two angles that measure 115°

Use a ruler and protractor to draw a triangle that matches each description. Label the sides or angles described.

5. a right triangle with sides that measure 3 centimeters, 4 centimeters, and 5 centimeters

6. a triangle with two angles measuring 70° and the side between them measuring 3 centimeters

Name _____

Investigate Transformations

(I Can) describe what happens to the sides and angles of a figure when it is transformed.

Spark Your Learning

Rachel is tiling a rectangular floor using triangles. Draw a triangle and cut it out. Move the triangle in different ways, and trace those shapes to draw a rectangular pattern using triangular tiles. Experiment with different shapes of triangles and different ways of moving the triangle to tile the whole floor with no gaps or overlapping tiles.

Turn and Talk Describe multiple ways you could move the original triangle to tile the floor.

Build Understanding

1 On graph paper, draw a quadrilateral that has exactly one pair of parallel sides. Remember, parallel sides are sides that would not intersect even if extended indefinitely. Cut out the shape and trace it in the center of the box.

A. Slide the quadrilateral to a new location in the box and trace it. Describe the direction and length you slid the shape.

_____

B. Use a ruler to measure the sides of each quadrilateral. Use a protractor to measure the angles of the original shape and the new shape. What has happened to the lengths of the sides, the measures of the angles, and the relationship between the parallel sides of the two shapes?

_____

_____

_____

_____

C. When you slid the shape, did anything change besides its position?

_____

D. Draw a horizontal line near, but outside, your second quadrilateral. Flip the second quadrilateral in Part A over the horizontal line and trace it in the box as your third shape. Measure the lengths of the sides and the angles of both quadrilaterals. Have the relationships between the sides and angles of the original shape changed or stayed the same compared to the flipped shape?

_____

_____

Turn and Talk Describe a way to move the third quadrilateral back to the original location of the first quadrilateral.

2 ▸ On graph paper, draw a polygon that has at least six sides and one pair of parallel sides. Cut out the shape and trace it in the center of the box.

A. Place the tip of your pencil on the center of the shape and turn the shape. Trace the shape in its new location.

B. How do the sides and angles of the original polygon compare to the polygon you drew after turning the original?

_____

_____

_____

C. Trace the shape again. Then, place the tip of your pencil on one corner of the shape and turn it. Trace the shape in its new location.

D. Draw an X on one angle of the original shape and on the same angle of the turned shape. Describe how the angle has been moved.

_____

_____

_____

E. Based on these two examples, what do you think stays the same and what changes when a shape is turned?

_____

_____

_____

 Turn and Talk Two students use two different transformations on the same shape. One student slides it up. The other student flips it. What is true about the side lengths and angle measures of both transformed shapes?

3 Dakota has a mirror in the shape of a trapezoid. She started by hanging the mirror in one location. Then she decided to hang the mirror in a different location.

A. Complete the drawing of the mirror in its new location.

B. How could Dakota move the mirror from the first location to the second location?

_____

_____

_____

C. How have the parallel sides of the mirror changed?

_____

_____

D. Describe how the side lengths and angle measures were affected when Dakota moved the mirror. How do you know?

_____

_____

Check Understanding

1. Darby hung a kite on the wall. Then she slid the kite higher on the wall to a better position. What is true about the size and shape of her kite? Explain what happened to the side lengths and angle measures after she made the move.

_____

_____

_____

2. Marlon cuts a label in the shape of a capital letter V. He turns the label one-quarter turn clockwise to place it on a package. Which way is the open part of the V facing after the rotation?

_____

3. Rachel tells Jonah that she can turn a square, but he won't be able to tell that it was turned after she is finished. How can she do this?

_____

_____

_____

On Your Own

4. Tarik is working on a photo album and moved a photo as shown. What transformation did he use?

_____

_____

_____

Before   After

Use the information to answer Problems 5–6.

Ryan lays a pentagonal pattern on a piece of fabric.

5. If Ryan slides the pattern two inches to the right, what happens to the measure of the angles of the pentagon?

_____

6. Ryan decides to rotate the pattern one-fourth turn clockwise. What happens to the lengths of the sides of the pattern?

_____

7. (MP) **Reason** Beckie cuts out a piece of paper in the shape of a trapezoid with only one pair of parallel sides. The parallel sides are 2 inches apart. Then she flips the shape over. What is the distance between the parallel sides of the flipped shape? Explain how you know.

_____

_____

_____

8. (MP) **Reason** Is Figure B a transformation of Figure A? Why or why not?

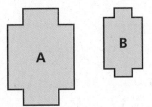

9. (MP) **Reason** Is Figure Y a transformation of Figure X? Why or why not?

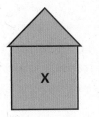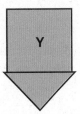

_____

_____

_____

10. Bailey has a sheet of plywood with four right angles. She saws off one of the angles and turns the plywood one-half turn clockwise. How many right angles are there on the plywood now?

_____

Use the information to answer Problems 11–12.

Margot draws a shape with one pair of parallel lines that are four centimeters apart. She then flips the shape across a horizontal line.

11. How many pairs of parallel lines are on the flipped shape?

_____

12. How far apart are the parallel lines on the flipped shape? How do you know?

_____

_____

13. Complete each transformation of the given figure.

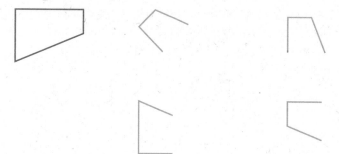

14. Complete the drawing of the parallelogram after a slide to the right.

15. Open Ended Perform a transformation on the shape. Draw the result and describe the transformation you performed.

_____

 I'm in a Learning Mindset!

Did I have confidence in my answer to Problem 15? What specific evidence do I have that I performed a transformation correctly?

_____

_____

© Houghton Mifflin Harcourt Publishing Company

Name _____

Explore Translations

(I Can) translate figures, describe the translations using words and mapping notation, and determine an algebraic rule for translating a figure on a coordinate plane.

Spark Your Learning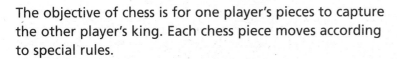

The objective of chess is for one player's pieces to capture the other player's king. Each chess piece moves according to special rules.

Piece	Movement
♟ ♙	Pawns can move forward 1 or 2 squares on the first move and 1 square thereafter. They can also move diagonally to capture another piece.
♞ ♘	Knights can move 2 squares horizontally and 1 square vertically, or 2 squares vertically and 1 square horizontally.

Which move(s) will get any piece to land on a yellow, a blue, or a red dot? Two of the dots?

Turn and Talk Move the black knight 1 space right and 2 spaces up. Then return the knight to its original location and move it 2 spaces up and 1 space right. What do you notice? Is this always true? Explain.

Build Understanding

The figure that results from a transformation, such as a translation, is called the **image**. The original figure is called the **preimage**.

Connect to Vocabulary

A **translation** is the movement of a figure along a straight line.

preimage   translation   image

1   Aran says that if the pawn shown below is translated 2 inches right, the preimage and the image will have the same parallel line **segments** and will be the same height and width. Hiro says the parallel line segments will remain parallel but the height and width will not be the same. Who is correct?

A. Fill in the dimensions and angle measures. Are the dashed segments parallel? _____

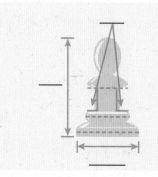 

B. Trace the pawn. Translate your tracing 2 inches right. What is the relationship between the dimensions, angle measures, and parallel segments of the preimage and image?

_____

_____

_____

C. Which student is correct? _____

D. What translation must Aran perform on the image so that it returns to the exact location of the preimage?

_____

 Turn and Talk Does the direction or distance a figure is translated affect the side lengths, relationships between sides, or angle measures of the figure? Explain.

Step It Out

2 Hiro draws a sketch of a game piece on a **coordinate plane**. Then he translates it 3 units right and 3 units up.

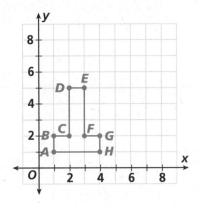

A. Draw the image of Figure *ABCDEFGH* on the coordinate plane after it is translated 3 units right and 3 units up.

B. **Prime notation**, adding apostrophes to each letter label, is used to label images. For instance, Point *A* in the preimage is labeled *A'* in the image and read as "A prime." Label the image you drew using prime notation.

C. Complete the table of ordered pairs.

Preimage	$A(1, 1)$	$B(1, 2)$	$C(2, 2)$					
Image	$A'(4, 4)$							

D. What do you notice about the relationship between the *x*- and *y*-values of each **vertex** of the preimage compared to the *x*- and *y*-values of each vertex of the image?

_____

_____

_____

_____

E. Translations in the coordinate plane can be described in **mapping notation** as $(x, y) \rightarrow (x \pm a, y \pm b)$ where *a* is the number of units the figure is translated horizontally and *b* is the number of units the figure is translated vertically. You read this notation as, "The ordered pair *x, y* is mapped to the ordered pair *x* plus or minus *a*, *y* plus or minus *b*."

Describe the translation of Figure *ABCDEFGH* using mapping notation.

$(x, y) \rightarrow (x + \underline{\quad}, y + \underline{\quad})$

F. What do you notice about the size, shape, angle measures, and relationship between the sides in the preimage and image?

_____

_____

_____

Turn and Talk If Figure *ABCDEFGH* is translated using the rule $(x, y) \rightarrow (x - 2, y - 4)$, how does the image of this translation compare to the image of the translation described in Task 2?

3 Triangle *DEF* is translated using the rule $(x, y) \rightarrow (x + 3, y - 4)$.

A. Use words to describe the distance and direction Triangle *DEF* is translated.

_____

B. Draw the image. Label it using prime notation.

C. Complete the table.

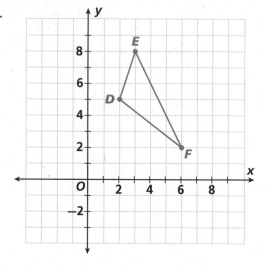

Triangle *DEF*	Triangle *D'E'F'*
D(2, 5)	

Check Understanding

1. The coordinates of a triangle's vertices are (2, 2), (4, 5), and (6, 1).

A. If the triangle is translated using the rule $(x, y) \rightarrow (x + 3, y - 5)$, by how many units and in what direction was the preimage translated?

_____

B. What are the coordinates of the image's vertices?

_____

C. Write a true statement about the relationship of the line segments and angle measures when a translation is applied to a preimage.

_____

_____

D. Will the line segment between (2, 2) and (4, 5) be parallel to its image?

_____

2. The coordinates of the vertices of the preimage of a parallelogram are (1, 5), (3, 3), (3, 7), and (5, 5). The coordinates of the vertices of the image are (−5, 3), (−3, 1), (−3, 5), and (−1, 3). How far and in what direction was the parallelogram translated? Write your answer using mapping notation and practice reading your answer aloud.

_____

On Your Own

Solve Problems 3–5 using the graph of Buildings *A*, *B*, *C*, *D*, and *E*.

3. Shana translates Building *B* three units right and three units up. Draw the image of Building *B* in the new location.

4. (MP) **Model with Mathematics** Shana translates Building *C* to the location of Building *E*. Use mapping notation to describe the translation of Building *C*.

   _____

5. (MP) **Construct Arguments** The coordinates of the vertices of the image of Building *D* are (−7, 3), (−1, 3), (−1, −5), and (−7, −5). The coordinates of the vertices of the image of Building *A* are (1, 1), (3, 1), (3, 3), and (1, 3). Which of these is not a translation of the preimage? Explain by using the definition of a translation.

   _____

   _____

   _____

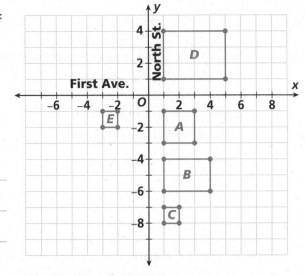

Use the triangles shown to answer Problems 6–7. Triangle 2 is a translation of Triangle 1.

6. All the sides of Triangle 1 have a length of 3 inches. What is the length of each side of Triangle 2? _____

7. All the angles of Triangle 1 have a measure of 60°. What is the measure of each angle of Triangle 2? _____

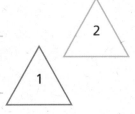

Use the description shown to answer Problems 8–9.

Square *P′Q′R′S′* is a translation of Square *PQRS*.

8. What is true about the angles of Square *PQRS* and Square *P′Q′R′S′*?

   _____

9. Opposite sides of Square *PQRS* are parallel and the same length. What is true about opposite sides of Square *P′Q′R′S′*?

   _____

Solve Problems 10–13 using the graph of Houses B, C, D, and E.

10. (MP) **Attend to Precision** House B is translated using the rule $(x, y) \rightarrow (x - 3, y + 2)$. Draw House B in its new location.

11. (MP) **Model with Mathematics** The builder adds House A to her plan first with vertices at $(-1, 1)$, $(-5, 1)$, $(-5, 7)$, and $(-1, 7)$. Then she moves it so it has vertices at $(6, 2)$, $(2, 2)$, $(2, 8)$, and $(6, 8)$. Use mapping notation to describe how far and in what direction she translated the house.

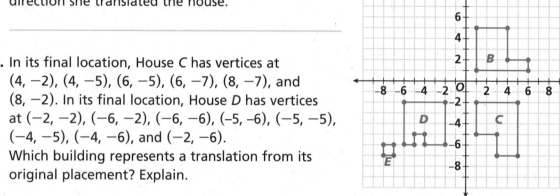

12. In its final location, House C has vertices at $(4, -2)$, $(4, -5)$, $(6, -5)$, $(6, -7)$, $(8, -7)$, and $(8, -2)$. In its final location, House D has vertices at $(-2, -2)$, $(-6, -2)$, $(-6, -6)$, $(-5, -6)$, $(-5, -5)$, $(-4, -5)$, $(-4, -6)$, and $(-2, -6)$.
    Which building represents a translation from its original placement? Explain.

13. Building E is a shed. It is translated 1 unit left and 2 units up. Draw Building E in its new location.

14. Is Figure B a translation of Figure A? Explain.

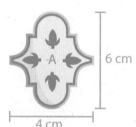

4 cm

6 cm

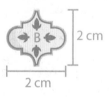

2 cm

2 cm

How does my mindset affect my ability to successfully translate figures?

Image Credit: ©William Britten/iStock · © Houghton Mifflin Harcourt Publishing Company

Name

Explore Reflections

(I Can) reflect a figure over either axis in the coordinate plane and describe the reflection algebraically.

Spark Your Learning

The word "AMBULANCE" is often written backward on the front of ambulances, so that it will appear forward in the rear-view mirrors of cars.

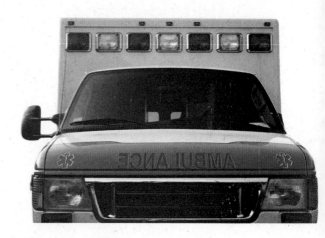

ƎƆИA⅃UꓭMA

Use tracing paper to trace the word as it is shown above. What can you do with your result to make the word readable?

What effect do your actions have on the order of the letters, and what effect do your actions have on the individual letters themselves?

Turn and Talk As you change the word "AMBULANCE" so that it is readable, which letters change their appearance and which do not? What is different about the letters that remain the same after the transition, as opposed to the letters that change?

Build Understanding

1 How can you reflect a figure using tracing paper? Draw the letter "N" on a piece of tracing paper, then fold the paper over the diagonal and trace the "N". Unfold the paper, and you should see the original "N" and its reflection:

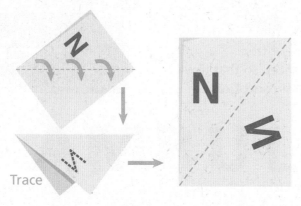

Trace

A. Find two line segments for the letter "N" that are parallel in the preimage. Are the corresponding segments in the image also parallel?

_____

B. Use a ruler to measure the length of a line segment in the preimage. Then measure the length of the corresponding line segment in the image. What do you notice about the lengths of the two segments?

_____

C. Use a protractor to measure an angle in the preimage and the corresponding angle in the image. What do you notice?

_____

D. What can you conclude about the way reflecting a figure affects side length, angle measure, and parallel line segments?

_____

_____

E. Look again at the "N" and its image on the paper. Why do you think the word _reflection_ is used to describe such an image?

_____

_____

 Turn and Talk Two students perform a reflection of the same shape. One reflects over a vertical line. The other reflects over a horizontal line. How are their reflections the same? How are they different?

Step It Out

2 How can you reflect a figure over the **x-axis** or **y-axis**?

A. Reflect the image shown over the *x*-axis. Remember to keep each point of the image the same distance from the *x*-axis as the corresponding preimage point. For instance, Point *C* is 12 units from the *x*-axis, so Point *C'* in the image must also be 12 units from the *x*-axis. Label the points using prime notation.

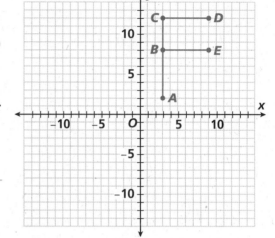

B. The preimage is upright. Is the image also upright, or has it changed?

_____

C. Find the length of $\overline{AC}$ in the preimage (in units). What do you expect the length of $\overline{A'C'}$ to be? Find this length.

_____

D. The original letter "F" faces to the right. Reflect the original image over the *y*-axis. Does the new image face the same direction? If not, how is it different? Label the points using double-prime notation ('').

_____

E. What are the coordinates of the points on the images corresponding to the labeled points on the preimage? Complete the table.

Point	Preimage	Image after reflection over *x*-axis	Image after reflection over *y*-axis
A	(3, 2)	(3, −2)	
B	(3, 8)		
C	(3, 12)		(−3, 12)
D	(9, 12)	(9, −12)	
E	(9, 8)		

F. Look at your table. In general:

A point (*a*, *b*) reflected over the *x*-axis has the coordinates (☐ , ☐).

A point (*a*, *b*) reflected over the *y*-axis has the coordinates (☐ , ☐).

 Turn and Talk On the grid, draw $\overline{DE}$ and $\overline{D'E'}$. Find the areas of Rectangle *BCDE* and Rectangle *B'C'D'E'*. What do you notice about these areas?

3 ▸ On a piece of graph paper, draw a parallelogram in the third **quadrant** of the coordinate plane as shown.

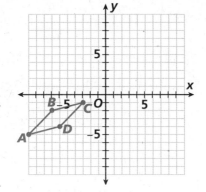

A. Reflect this preimage over the *x*-axis and describe the location of the image after reflection.

_____

B. Reflect the preimage over the *y*-axis and describe the location of the image after reflection.

_____

C. Fill in the table with the coordinates of the vertices.

Point	Preimage	Image after reflection over *x*-axis	Image after reflection over *y*-axis
A	(−10, −5)		
B	(−7, −2)		
C	(−3, −1)		
D	(−6, −4)		
Any point	(*a, b*)		

Check Understanding

1. The coordinates of the vertices of a triangle are (2, 3), (5, 1), and (6, 4). After one reflection, the coordinates of the vertices of the triangle's image are (2, −3), (5, −1), and (6, −4). Over what line has the triangle been reflected?

_____

2. The coordinates of the vertices of a square are (−10, −2), (−5, −2), (−5, −7), and (−10, −7). The square is reflected over the *y*–axis.

A. What are the coordinates of the vertices of the image?

_____

B. Show that the image still has parallel sides and has the same angles as the preimage: The image's sides are segments of the lines $y =$ _____ ,

$y =$ _____ , $x =$ _____ , and $x =$ _____ , which meet at _____ angles.

C. Does the image have the same side lengths as the preimage? Explain.

_____

_____

3. In your own words, describe the meaning of a reflection.

_____

On Your Own

Use the figures to answer Problems 4–7.

Figure *Y* is a reflection of Figure *X*.

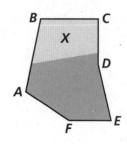

4. $\overline{AB}$ is 3 centimeters long. What is the length of the corresponding side of Figure *Y*? How do you know?

   _____

   _____

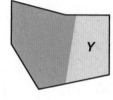

5. Angle *A* measures 115°. What is the measure of the corresponding angle in Figure *Y*?

   _____

6. $\overline{FE}$ is parallel to $\overline{BC}$. Are the corresponding sides in Figure *Y* also parallel?

   _____

7. (MP) **Use Tools** Draw the line of reflection between Figures *X* and *Y*.

8. (MP) **Use Tools** Draw a reflection of the preimage over the line shown.

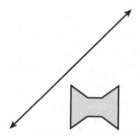

9. Marie is practicing her reflections on graph paper.

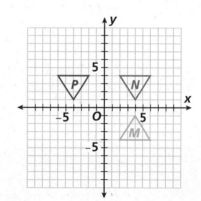

   A. Is Figure *P* a reflection of Figure *N* over the *y*-axis?

   _____

   B. Is Figure *P* a reflection of Figure *M* over the *y*-axis and then over the *x*-axis?

   _____

   C. Is Figure *P* a reflection of Figure *M* over the *x*-axis and then over the *y*-axis?

   _____

10. Figure *ABCD* is a trapezoid in the second quadrant.

A. (MP) **Attend to Precision** On the given graph, draw the image of Figure *ABCD* reflected across the *y*-axis. What are the coordinates of the vertices of *ABCD* and *A′B′C′D′*?

ABCD	A′B′C′D′

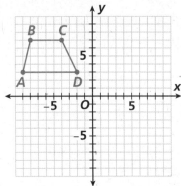

B. Given any point (x, y) on *ABCD*, what are the coordinates of the corresponding point on *A′B′C′D′*?

$(x, y) \rightarrow ($ ☐ , ☐ $)$

C. Is *A′B′C′D′* facing the same direction as *ABCD*? Explain.

_____

11. (MP) **Use Tools** Draw a square with sides that are horizontal and vertical on a piece of paper.

A. If you reflect the square over a vertical line, does it look any different? If you reflect the square over a horizontal line, does it look any different?

_____

B. In your original square, draw a right-angle mark in one corner. Reflect this square over a horizontal line. Does it look any different? If so, what is different?

_____

C. If you reflect the square from Part B over a vertical line, does it look any different? If so, what is different?

_____

 I'm in a Learning Mindset!

How does my mindset affect my confidence with performing reflections?

_____

_____

Name _____

Explore Rotations

(I Can) identify and perform rotations, and describe a rotation on a coordinate plane algebraically.

Spark Your Learning PAIRS

Use tracing paper to trace a copy of this recycling symbol.

Place the tip of your pencil in the center of the symbol and turn the paper about that point. You'll see that the original design reappears three times in every full turn.

In the space provided, sketch a design that reappears every quarter of a full turn. Trace the shape on tracing paper, then turn it to check your work.

 Turn and Talk If the preimage and image of a figure look identical after being turned one-fourth turn clockwise or one-fourth turn counterclockwise, what must be true about the figure?

Build Understanding

1 Trace the hexagon and Points *P*, *Q*, and *R* on tracing paper.

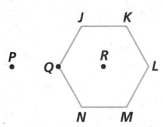

Connect to Vocabulary

A **rotation** is a transformation in which a figure is turned around a point. That point is called the **center of rotation**.

A. Use a ruler and protractor to complete the table.

Length of $\overline{JK}$	_____ mm
Measure of ∠*JQN*	_____ °

B. Place the tip of a pencil on Point *R* and rotate the hexagon 90° (one-fourth turn) clockwise about that point.

- What happens to the measure of ∠*JQN*?

  _____

- What happens to the length of $\overline{JK}$?

  _____

- Name a pair of parallel sides in the shape. What happens to the pair when the shape is rotated?

  _____

C. Move the center of rotation by placing the tip of your pencil on Point *P*. Rotate the shape about Point *P*. Describe the rotation. How is it different from the rotation in Part B?

  _____

  _____

  _____

D. Draw an arrow inside your hexagon that points to the top of the shape. When you rotate the shape 180° (one-half turn), what happens to the direction of the arrow in the image, and why?

  _____

  _____

 Turn and Talk Can you make your hexagon change its shape using a rotation? Why or why not?

© Houghton Mifflin Harcourt Publishing Company

Step It Out

2 ▶ You can rotate the letter "N" and get the letter "Z." Figure 2 was formed by rotating Figure 1 90° clockwise about the **origin**.

A. Use a ruler and protractor to measure the line segments and angles of both figures. What is the relationship between the side lengths and angle measures of the image and preimage?

_____

B. In Figure 1, $\overline{AB}$ is parallel to $\overline{DC}$. What is the relationship between $\overline{A'B'}$ and $\overline{D'C'}$ in Figure 2?

_____

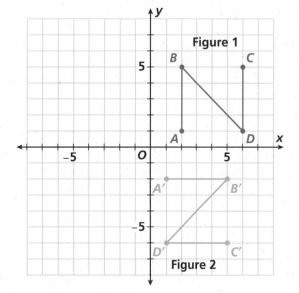

C. Fill in the coordinates for each point.

Figure 1	A(2, 1)			
Figure 2	A′(1, −2)			

D. Look at the relationship between the coordinates of the vertices of Figure 1 and Figure 2. Write a rule to find the coordinates of the vertices of any figure rotated 90° clockwise about the origin.

$(x, y) \rightarrow (\boxed{} , \boxed{})$

E. Rotate Figure 2 180° counterclockwise about the origin. Label the result as Figure 3. Then fill in the table.

Figure 2	A′(1, −2)			
Figure 3	A″(−1, 2)			

F. Write a rule that represents the change in coordinates of any figure rotated 180° counterclockwise about the origin.

$(x, y) \rightarrow (\boxed{} , \boxed{})$

G. If you rotate the letter "W" 180° clockwise, what letter does it resemble? _____

 Turn and Talk Identify which uppercase letters look the same after a 180° rotation.

3 Figure 1 is rotated to form Figure 2.

A. Describe the rotation.

_____

B. Fill in the table of vertex coordinates.

Q(1, 4)			
Q'(−1, −4)			

C. Write a rule that represents the change in coordinates of any figure rotated 180° about the origin.

$(x, y) \rightarrow (\boxed{} , \boxed{})$

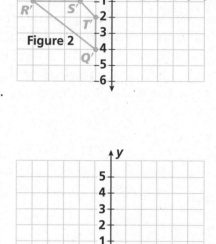

4 A triangle has vertices (2, 4), (5, 1), and (1, 2).

A. Graph the triangle and label it *Figure 1*.

B. Rotate Figure 1 by the rule $(x, y) \rightarrow (y, -x)$ and label the image *Figure 2*. Complete the sentence about the rotation:
To form Figure 2, Figure 1 underwent a rotation of 90° _____ about the origin.

C. Rotate Figure 1 by the rule $(x, y) \rightarrow (-y, x)$ and label the image *Figure 3*. Complete the sentence about the rotation:
To form Figure 3, Figure 1 underwent a rotation of _____ counterclockwise about the origin.

Check Understanding

1. Antoine and Bobby each rotated a pentagon about Point *P*, but they each got a different image. Which rotation is correct? Why?

_____

_____

_____

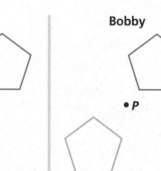

2. A. Draw rotations of Rectangle *STUV* 90°, 180°, and 270° clockwise about the origin.

B. What do all four figures have in common? They all have _____ side lengths and _____ angle measures, and their _____ sides are parallel.

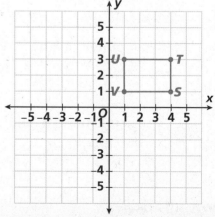

On Your Own

3. Victor rotated his initial, V, about Point *P*. What stayed the same between the preimage and image? What changed?

    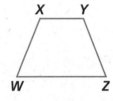

    _____

    _____

4. (MP) **Use Tools** Sketch a rotation of the Figure *WXYZ*. Use Point *W* as the center of rotation.

    A. What is the same about the two images?

       _____

       _____

    B. What is different about the two images?

       _____

5. (MP) **Model with Mathematics** Elias graphed the movement of one quarter-turn of a ceiling fan.

    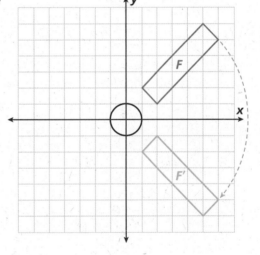

    A. Continue the rotation and draw the fan blade in the third and second quadrants after two more rotations of 90° each.

    B. Describe the rotation of the fan blade from *F* to *F'*.

       _____

       _____

       _____

    C. Describe the rotation from *F* to *F'* in mapping notation.

       _____

6. (MP) **Attend to Precision** Rotate each figure 180° about the origin.

    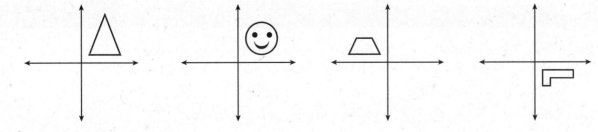

7. Describe the transformation of Figure 1 to Figure 2 using mapping notation.

_____

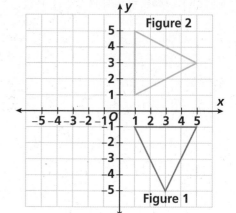

8. △*JKL* has an area of 3.25 square units. What happens to its area when it is rotated 180° about Point *J*?

_____

_____

9. The vertices of the preimage of a triangle are (−2, 1), (−5, 2), and (−3, 6). The triangle is rotated and its image has vertices at (1, 2), (2, 5), and (6, 3).

    A. Describe the rotation that resulted in the image.

    _____

    B. If the image is then rotated 90° clockwise, what are the coordinates of the new image?

    _____

10. **Attend to Precision** Rotate the shape by the rule $(x, y) \rightarrow (y, -x)$. Then rotate the new image according to the rule $(x, y) \rightarrow (-x, -y)$.

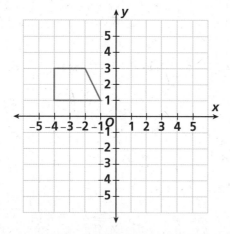

© Houghton Mifflin Harcourt Publishing Company

I'm in a **Learning Mindset!**

Do I have a fixed-mindset voice or growth-mindset voice in my head when I'm working with rotations? How can I tap into my growth-mindset voice?

_____

_____

Name _____

Understand and Recognize Congruent Figures

 I Can determine congruence by performing or describing a sequence of transformations that maps one figure onto another.

Spark Your Learning

Maribel wants to make a quilt like this one. She has quilt pieces that are triangles and quilt pieces that are parallelograms. Describe ways she can transform the shapes to match the pattern in the quilt.

 Turn and Talk Design a second quilt using parallelograms and triangles. Exchange your design with a partner and have him or her describe the transformations you used to design your quilt.

© Houghton Mifflin Harcourt Publishing Company

Build Understanding

1 ▸ Maribel needs to cut shapes out of fabric to prepare for a different quilt. Trace Figure 1 on a piece of paper and cut it out. Lay your cut-out on top of Figure 1 to make sure it is the same size and shape.

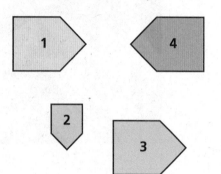

A. Experiment with transformations to move the cut-out shape on top of Figure 2. What transformations did you use? Explain how the figures are the same and how they are different.

_____

_____

_____

B. Experiment with transformations to move the cut-out shape over Figures 3 and 4. What transformations did you use?

_____

_____

C. What do you notice when you compare Figure 1 to Figures 3 and 4?

_____

_____

D. A figure is congruent to another figure if and only if a series of rotations, reflections, and translations can map one onto the other. Which figures are congruent?

_____

Connect to Vocabulary

Congruent figures are the same size and shape.

 Turn and Talk Is there a series of rotations, reflections, or translations you can perform on Figure 2 to produce Figure 1, 3, or 4? Explain.

Step It Out

2 While preparing fabric for quilting, Maribel lays a grid over her fabric. She wants to cut out five congruent triangles. She draws the triangles on the coordinate grid below.

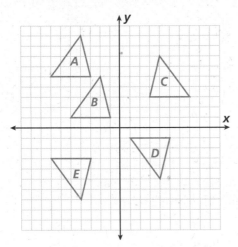

A. Triangle A is translated 2 units down and then reflected across the y-axis. Which triangle is the image of this sequence of transformations?

_____

B. Are the two triangles congruent? Explain how you know.

_____

_____

_____

C. Which two transformations can you perform on Triangle B to show that it is congruent to Triangle D?

_____

_____

D. Record the vertices of Triangle A and Triangle B. Use mapping notation to show how the vertices of Triangle A changed, and read the mapping notation aloud to another student. Explain how you know the shapes are congruent.

Triangle A → Triangle B

$$(x, y) \rightarrow \left(x + \boxed{}, y - \boxed{} \right)$$

_____

_____

_____

3 Maribel wants to cut a new shape. She will reflect Figure A across the x-axis and translate the image 5 units left. She claims that the order in which she performs the transformations matters. Is she correct?

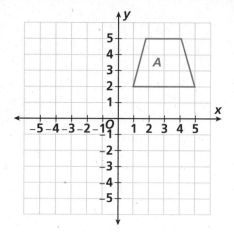

A. Reflect Figure A across the x-axis and then translate the figure 5 units left. Draw the final image.

Reverse the order of the transformations and draw the image again. How did the order you performed the transformations change the final image?

_____

_____

B. The vertices of Figure B have coordinates shown in the table. Figure B is rotated 90° clockwise about the origin and then reflected across the x-axis to form Figure C. Figure B is also reflected across the x-axis and then rotated 90° clockwise about the origin to form Figure D. Complete the table.

Figure B	(0, 0)	(0, −3)	(2, −3)	(1, −1)	(2, 0)
Figure C		(−3, 0)			
Figure D		(3, 0)			

C. How did the order you performed the transformations on the figure change the final images, Figures C and D?

_____

_____

Check Understanding

Use the figures to answer Problems 1–2.

1. Which of these figures are not congruent to Figure 1? Why?

_____

_____

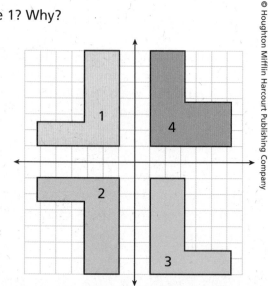

2. A. What sequence of transformations can you perform on Figure 1 to produce Figure 3?

_____

_____

B. Write a mapping notation to show the result of this sequence of transformations.

_____

© Houghton Mifflin Harcourt Publishing Company

On Your Own

3. Can a square ever be congruent to a pentagon? Explain.

_____

_____

Use the graph to answer Problems 4–10.

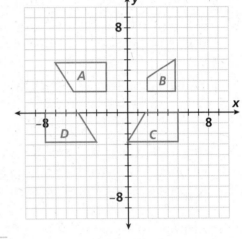

4. **Open Ended** What sequence of transformations can you perform on Figure _C_ to produce Figure _A_?

_____

_____

_____

5. Figure _D_ is translated 3 units right and reflected across the _y_-axis. Which figure will this sequence of transformations produce?

_____

6. Which figures are congruent to Figure _A_? How do you know?

_____

_____

_____

_____

7. Figure _B_ is translated 3 units up and then reflected across the _y_-axis to form Figure _E_. Draw Figure _E_ on the coordinate grid.

8. (MP) **Critique Reasoning** Nathan claims Figure _B_ is congruent to Figure _A_. Is he correct? Explain.

_____

_____

9. Without performing a transformation on Figure _A_, how can you use tools to be sure it is congruent to Figure _D_?

_____

_____

_____

10. Without performing a transformation on Figure _A_, how can you use tools to be sure that it is not congruent to Figure _B_?

_____

_____

Use the figures to answer Problems 11–13.

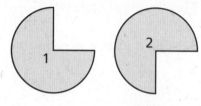

11. Which figures are congruent to Figure 1? Which are not congruent to Figure 1?

_____

_____

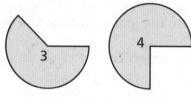

12. What sequence of transformations can be performed on Figure 4 to produce Figure 1?

_____

_____

_____

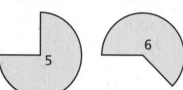

13. Kailee reflected Figure 5 across a vertical line and then translated it up. Which figure is the result?

_____

Use the graph to answer Problems 14–17.

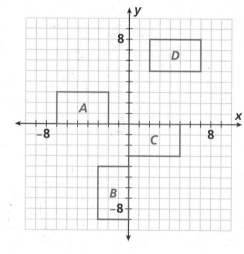

14. (MP) **Critique Reasoning** Henrietta claims that Figure *B* can be transformed into Figure *A* by translating it 2 units right and rotating it 90° clockwise about the origin. Is she correct? If not, find and correct her error.

_____

_____

15. Figure *C* is rotated 90° clockwise about the origin and translated 4 units down. Which figure will this sequence of transformations produce?

_____

16. How can you prove that Figure *A* is congruent to Figure *C*?

_____

_____

17. Figure *B* is translated 5 units left and then reflected across the *x*-axis to form Figure *E*. Draw Figure *E* on the coordinate grid.

 I'm in a Learning Mindset!

How does my mindset affect my confidence with performing reflections?

_____

_____

Review

Vocabulary

For Problems 1–5, choose the correct term from the vocabulary box.

Vocabulary
image
preimage
reflection
rotation
translation

1. A(n) _____ is a transformation that slides a figure.

2. A(n) _____ is a transformation that flips a figure across a line.

3. A(n) _____ is a transformation that turns a figure about a point.

4. A(n) _____ is the original figure in a transformation.

5. A(n) _____ is the resulting figure in a transformation.

Concepts and Skills

6. Figure *ABCD* and its image, Figure *FGHJ*, are shown. Which transformation of Figure *ABCD* produced Figure *FGHJ*?

    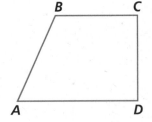

    (A) vertical translation

    (B) horizontal translation

    (C) reflection across a vertical line

    (D) reflection across a horizontal line

7. (MP) **Use Tools** Describe a sequence of transformations you could use to show that Triangle *DEF* is congruent to Triangle *JKL*. State what strategy and tool you will use to answer the question, explain your choice, and then find the answer.

    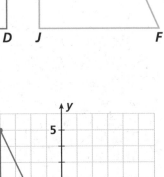

    _____

    _____

    _____

    _____

8. Triangle *PQR* has vertices $P(2, -4)$, $Q(4, -5)$, and $R(7, -2)$. It is translated 6 units left and 3 units up to produce Triangle *P'Q'R'*. Complete the table.

Vertex	x-coordinate	y-coordinate
P'		
Q'		
R'		

For Problems 9–10, draw the image of each transformation.

9. Rotate Triangle *RST* 180° about the origin.

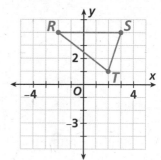

10. Translate Quadrilateral *WXYZ* 5 units right and 2 units down.

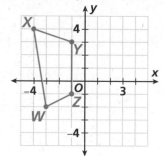

11. Side *KN* of Figure *KLMN* is parallel to Side *LM*. Figure *KLMN* is rotated 90° clockwise about Point *P* to produce Figure *RSTU*. Based on this information, select all statements that are true.

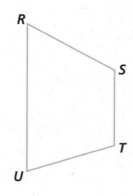

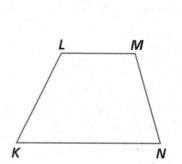

Ⓐ $\overline{ST}$ is parallel to $\overline{RU}$.

Ⓑ ∠R has the same measure as ∠N.

Ⓒ $\overline{RS}$ is the same length as $\overline{MN}$.

Ⓓ Figure *RSTU* is congruent to Figure *KLMN*.

Ⓔ ∠T has the same measure as ∠M.

12. An artist is designing a logo for a new company by reflecting Triangle *ABC* across a vertical line and then translating it up and to the right to produce Triangle *DEF*. Find each measure.

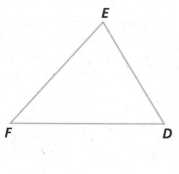

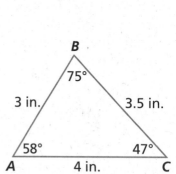

measure of ∠D: _____ °

length of $\overline{EF}$: _____ in.

length of $\overline{DF}$: _____ in.

13. The point (*a*, *b*) is reflected across the *x*-axis and then translated 4 units to the right. What are the coordinates of the image of the point?

Ⓐ (−*a*, *b* + 4)   Ⓑ (−*a* + 4, *b*)   Ⓒ (*a*, −*b* + 4)   Ⓓ (*a* + 4, −*b*)

14. How many types of transformations did you study in this module? Name and define each of them.

_____

_____

Transformations and Similarity

DO YOU HAUL BONES?

A museum received a crate containing a set of dinosaur bones. You need to move the crate from its current location to the location marked on the grid. Each unit on the grid represents 1 meter.

How could you use a sequence of transformations to haul the crate to its new location?

_____

_____

_____

_____

_____

 Turn and Talk

Why might the museum not want you to use a reflection to move the crate?

Are You Ready?

Complete these problems to review prior concepts and skills you will need for this module.

Polygons in the Coordinate Plane

Determine the length, in units, of each side of the figure on the coordinate plane.

1. $\overline{LM}$ _7_

2. $\overline{MN}$ _3_

3. $\overline{NP}$ _3_

4. $\overline{PQ}$ _6_

5. $\overline{QR}$ _4_

6. $\overline{LR}$ _9_

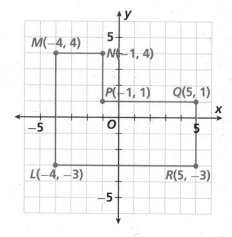

Scale Drawings

A scale drawing of a school cafeteria has a scale of 1 inch : 4 feet. Use this information to answer each question.

7. In the drawing, the cafeteria dining room has a length of 18 inches. What is the actual length of the dining room?

   _72 ft_

8. The actual width of the cafeteria kitchen is 42 feet. What is the width of the kitchen in the scale drawing?

   10.5 inch

Translations, Reflections, and Rotations

Draw the image of each transformation on the coordinate plane.

9. Rotate Triangle *ABC* 180° about the origin.

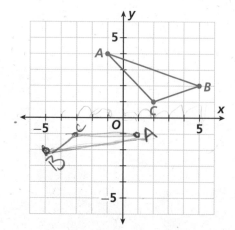

10. Reflect Triangle *DEF* across the *y*-axis, and then translate it 4 units down.

On Your Own

3. Identify whether the transformation from each blue Figure *A* to green Figure *B* is an enlargement or a reduction.

 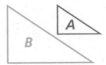 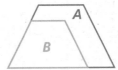

_____   _____   _____

4. Use the coordinate plane to sketch an enlargement with side lengths twice those in the figure shown.

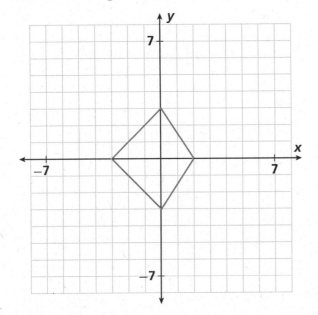

5. (MP) **Reason** Fredrick drew a reduction of a phone. Is the reduction accurate? Why or why not?

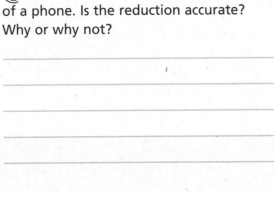 

_____

_____

_____

_____

6. (MP) **Use Tools** Draw a reduction of the figure with dimensions half those of the original figure.

7. (MP) **Use Tools** Use the coordinate plane to reduce the side lengths of the figure shown by half.

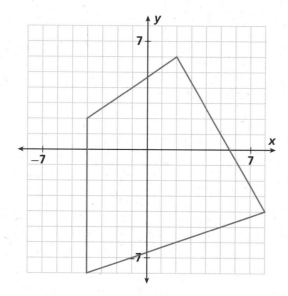

8. For each figure, determine if it is a reduction of Figure *S*.

 I'm in a Learning Mindset!

How does my mindset affect my confidence with reducing and enlarging figures?

_____

_____

Name _____

Explore Dilations

 I Can identify and perform dilations given a scale factor and center of dilation, perform a dilation on a coordinate plane, and identify an algebraic rule for the dilation.

Spark Your Learning

On a computer, Raquel uses polygons and a circle to make a model of the top of London's Big Ben clock tower. Then she reduces it.

Compare Raquel's image and reduction. What do you find?

 Turn and Talk What is the relationship between the perimeter of Raquel's original image and her reduction? How does this relate to the relationship between the side lengths?

Build Understanding

1 ▸ Rectangle *R′S′T′U′* is a dilation of Rectangle *RSTU*.

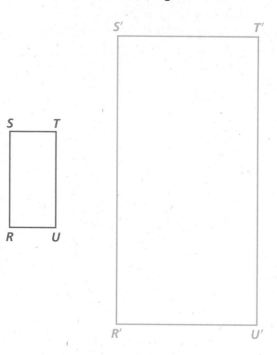

A. Measure the sides of the figures, then fill in the table.

	RSTU	*R′S′T′U′*
Height (in.)		
Width (in.)		

What is the relationship between the measurements of the two rectangles?

_____

_____

B. What is the scale factor of this dilation?

_____

C. Points *R* and *R′* are an example of corresponding vertices. Use a ruler or straight edge to draw four rays, each extending from a vertex of the image to the corresponding vertex of the preimage, and continuing through to the left. What do you notice?

_____

D. Label the center of dilation for Rectangles *RSTU* and *R′S′T′U′* as Point *P*.

Step It Out

2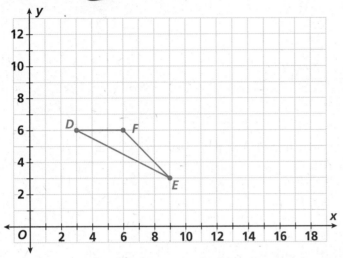

A. In order to dilate △DEF to form △D'E'F' with a scale factor of 2 and center of dilation (0, 0), first draw a ray from the center of dilation through Vertex D.

B. Find a point on the ray that is twice the distance from the center of dilation as Vertex D. Label it D'.

C. Give the ordered pairs for Vertices D and D'. How are these values related to the scale factor?

_____

_____

D. Predict the ordered pairs for Vertices E' and F'. Explain your reasoning.

_____

_____

_____

E. Draw △D'E'F' on the graph. Use rays from the center of dilation to draw your dilation.

F. Using the ordered pairs of △DEF, how would you make a dilation △D"E"F" with a scale factor of $\frac{1}{3}$ and center (0, 0)?

_____

_____

G. Draw △D"E"F" on the graph. Use rays from the center of dilation to check your dilation. What are the coordinates of the vertices of △D"E"F"?

_____

 Turn and Talk What happens when you dilate △DEF with a scale factor of 1? Describe the resulting image.

3 △G′H′J′ is a dilation of △GHJ. Find the scale factor and center of dilation. Represent the dilation algebraically.

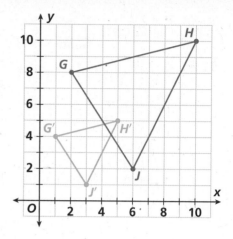

A. Complete the table.

G(2, 8)	→	G′(1, 4)
H	→	H′
J	→	J′

B. How are the corresponding coordinates for the image and the preimage related?

_____

_____

C. What is the scale factor of the dilation? _____

D. Circle the algebraic representation that best describes this dilation. Explain your reasoning.

$(x, y) \rightarrow \left(x + \frac{1}{2}, y + \frac{1}{2}\right)$ $(x, y) \rightarrow \left(x - \frac{1}{2}, y - \frac{1}{2}\right)$

$(x, y) \rightarrow \left(\frac{1}{2}x, \frac{1}{2}y\right)$ $(x, y) \rightarrow (2x, 2y)$

_____

_____

E. Draw rays through corresponding vertices of both figures to find the center of dilation. What is the center of dilation?

_____

Check Understanding

1. Polygon BCDE has vertices B(5, 1), C(5, 6), D(10, 6), and E(10, 1). If B′C′D′E′ is a dilation of BCDE with scale factor 4 and center (0, 0), give the coordinates of B′C′D′E′.

_____

2. Does the pair of figures show a dilation with scale factor 4?

A.

B.

On Your Own

3. (MP) **Reason** Figure *S'* is a dilation of Figure *S*.

S

S'

    A. Is the scale factor greater than 1 or less than 1? _____

    B. Is Figure *S* congruent to Figure *S'*? _____

    C. Is the dilation a reduction? _____

4. (MP) **Use Tools** Dilate △*DEF* with scale factor $\frac{3}{2}$ and center (0, 0).

    A. Find the coordinates of vertices *D*, *E*, and *F*.

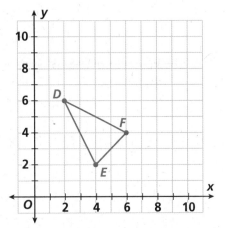

    _____

    B. Multiply each coordinate of each vertex by the scale factor to find the coordinates of vertices *D'*, *E'*, and *F'*.

    _____

    C. Graph and label the vertices *D'*, *E'*, and *F'*. Draw rays to connect each corresponding vertex with the center of dilation.

    D. Represent the dilation algebraically.

    _____

5. Figure *J'K'L'M'* is a dilation of Figure *JKLM*. The center of dilation is the origin, (0, 0).

J(3, 2)	→	J'(9, 6)
K(7, 4)	→	K'(21, 12)
L(7, 9)	→	L'
M(2, 5)	→	M'

    A. Given the coordinates of *J*, *J'*, *K*, and *K'*, what is the scale factor of the dilation?

    _____

    B. Use the scale factor to complete the table for points *L'* and *M'*.

    C. Represent the dilation algebraically.

    _____

6. Graph △*TUV* with vertices *T*(4, 2), *U*(2, 0), and *V*(2, 4). Dilate the figure by a scale factor of $\frac{5}{2}$ with a center of dilation of (0, 0). Graph △*T'U'V'*.

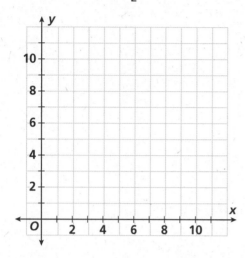

7. **STEM** An ophthalmologist is a doctor who studies the eye. The ophthalmologist records the effect of changes in lighting on the size of the pupil of an eye and graphs the results on a coordinate plane.

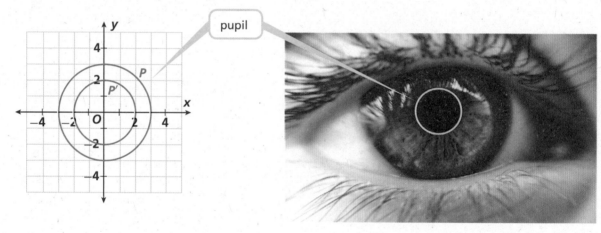

pupil

A. What is the scale factor of the dilation from *P* to *P'*? _____

B. Graph a dilation of *P* using scale factor $\frac{1}{3}$.

 I'm in a Learning Mindset!

Did I have confidence in my answer? What specific evidence do I have that I found a scale factor of a dilation correctly?

_____

_____

© Houghton Mifflin Harcourt Publishing Company • Image Credit: ©Miroslav Kyosev/EyeEm/Getty Images

Name _____

Understand and Recognize Similar Figures

(I Can) describe a sequence of transformations that exhibits the similarity between two figures.

Spark Your Learning

To make a design for a phone case, start with Parallelogram *ABCD*. Then dilate the parallelogram using a vertex as the center of dilation. Finally, translate the dilated parallelogram. Draw a possible final image for the figure and label it *A'B'C'D'*. Show your work.

How are the sides and angles of *ABCD* and *A'B'C'D'* the same? How are they different?

_____

_____

 Turn and Talk Use the same translation first, followed by the same dilation. Would the answers to the above questions be different? Explain.

© Houghton Mifflin Harcourt Publishing Company

Build Understanding

1 Use the shapes shown to make a customized phone case.

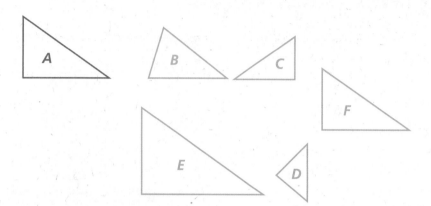

A. Which triangles are similar to Triangle *A*? You can use tracing paper, a protractor, and/or a ruler to help you decide which triangles are similar.

_____

Connect to Vocabulary

Two figures are **similar** if one can be obtained from the other by a transformation or sequence of transformations that may include a dilation.

B. For each of the similar triangles you identified, describe a transformation or sequence of transformations that takes Triangle *A* to the other triangle.

_____

_____

_____

_____

C. Is Triangle *A* similar to Triangle *B*? Why or why not?

_____

D. Add another triangle to your design. Dilate Triangle *B* using a scale factor of 1 and then rotate the image to form Triangle *G*. How are Triangle *B* and Triangle *G* related? Explain.

_____

_____

_____

_____

 Turn and Talk If two figures are congruent can you always conclude that they are similar? Why or why not?

© Houghton Mifflin Harcourt Publishing Company

Step It Out

2 Use a coordinate plane to draw figures for a custom phone case. Include several similar figures in the design, as shown on the graph.

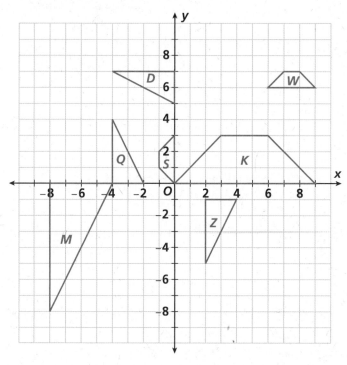 

A. For each pair of similar figures, describe a sequence of transformations that can be used to map the first figure to the second figure.

Figure *K* to Figure *W*

_____

_____

Figure *S* to Figure *K*

_____

_____

B. Which pair of similar figures can be mapped from one to the other by the given sequence of transformations?

a dilation with scale factor $\frac{1}{2}$ and center of dilation (0, 0), followed by a reflection across the *x*-axis

_____

the dilation $(x, y) \rightarrow (2x, 2y)$ with a center of dilation (0, 0), followed by a translation 12 units left and 2 units up

_____

3 For the phone case, make an additional shape △*ABC*. Dilate the triangle using a dilation with a scale factor of $\frac{1}{2}$ and center of dilation (0, 0). Then reflect the image across the *y*-axis.

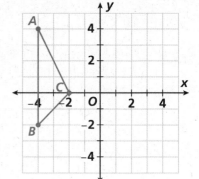

A. Draw the image of △*ABC* after the dilation.

B. Draw the final image after the reflection. Label the final image △*A'B'C'*.

C. What can you conclude about △*ABC* and △*A'B'C'*? Why?

_____

_____

D. Use a dilation with a scale factor of 1 instead of a scale factor of $\frac{1}{2}$. What can you conclude about △*ABC* and △*A'B'C'* in this case? Explain.

_____

_____

Check Understanding

1. Doretta is choosing tiles for a mosaic in a kitchen. She wants to choose two tiles that are similar but not congruent. Which pair of tiles could she use? Explain why she can choose only those tiles.

  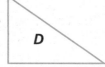

_____

_____

_____

2. Identify all pairs of similar figures on the coordinate plane. For each pair, describe the sequence of transformations that maps one figure to the other.

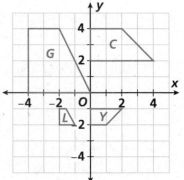

_____

_____

_____

_____

_____

Name _____

On Your Own

3. Ryan is a landscape architect. He uses the coordinate plane shown to design flower beds at a mall.

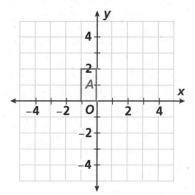

   A. To draw flower bed *B*, Ryan reflects flower bed *A* across the *x*-axis. Then he applies the dilation $(x, y) \rightarrow (2x, 2y)$. Draw and label flower bed *B*.

   B. To draw flower bed *C*, Ryan rotates flower bed *A* by 180° about the origin. Then he applies the dilation $(x, y) \rightarrow (2.5x, 2.5y)$. Draw and label flower bed *C*.

   C. What can you conclude about the three flower beds?

_____

4. **Art** A car show has advertising posters in different shapes and sizes. They are shown as they appear next to each other on a wall at the car show.

   A. Circle all of the posters that are similar.

   B. For the posters you identified, describe a sequence of transformations that takes one poster to the other.

_____

Use the graph to solve Problems 5–7.

5. Which pair of similar triangles can be mapped from one to the other by a dilation with scale factor $\frac{1}{3}$ and center of dilation (0, 0), followed by a rotation of 180° clockwise around the origin?

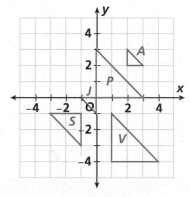

_____

6. Which pair of similar triangles can be mapped from one to the other by a dilation with scale factor 3 and center of dilation (0, 0), followed by the translation $(x, y) \rightarrow (x - 6, y - 6)$?

_____

7. Describe a sequence of transformations that can be used to map Triangle *J* to Triangle *S*.

_____

_____

8. Glass laboratory flasks come in a variety of shapes and sizes. Different flasks have different purposes, such as heating, measuring, and mixing. Are any of the flasks shown similar? Explain why or why not.

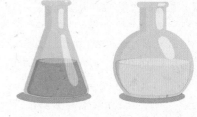

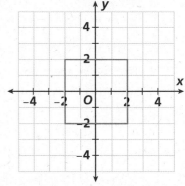

_____

9. Describe a sequence of transformations that can be used to map △RST with vertices R(−1, 0), S(0, 1), and T(1, 0) to △JKL with vertices J(−4, 0), K(0, −4), and L(4, 0).

_____

_____

10. **Open Ended** The coordinates of the vertices of △ABC are A(0, 0), B(0, 4), and C(−2, 0). Give the coordinates of the vertices of a triangle, △DEF, that is similar to △ABC but not congruent to △ABC. Then describe a sequence of transformations that maps △ABC to △DEF.

_____

_____

_____

11. (MP) **Use Repeated Reasoning** Jaycee draws a sequence of squares on the coordinate plane. First she draws the square shown and dilates it using $(x, y) \rightarrow (3x, 3y)$. Then she uses this same transformation to dilate the image. She continues dilating each image in this way to draw a total of six squares. What dilation could she use to map the first square she draws directly to the last square she draws?

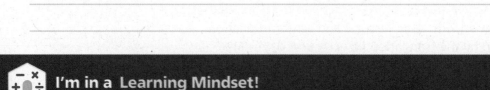

_____

12. If Figure X is similar to Figure Y, and Figure Y is similar to Figure Z, can you conclude that Figure X is similar to Figure Z? Explain.

_____

_____

_____

_____

I'm in a Learning Mindset!

Do I have a fixed-mindset voice or a growth-mindset voice in my head when I'm working with finding similar figures? How can I tap into my growth-mindset voice?

_____

_____

Linear Equations and Applications

Entrepreneur

An entrepreneur is a person who starts and operates a business. Entrepreneurs recognize the need or desire for a product or service that is not currently available and then set out to provide it. An entrepreneur's skills may vary depending on the business, but all entrepreneurs need resilience and perseverance—a new business is bound to have ups and downs. Entrepreneurs must expect setbacks and be prepared to keep going in spite of them.

STEM Task:

Gina's part-time computer repair business is growing. The table shows her approximate earnings each month. Predict when her monthly earnings will reach $1000 if her earnings continue to increase at a constant rate. Explain your thinking.

Month	1	2	3	4
Earnings	$600	$640	$680	$720

Learning Mindset

Perseverance

Perseverance is a quality that allows you to keep working toward a goal, even when you are faced with difficulties or delays. Projects and tasks that are long or complex can challenge your perseverance. Here are some tips to help you persevere and not give up on your goal.

- Check your progress often to be sure you're on the right path. Identify steps and milestones that will let you track your progress. Are you moving closer to your goal?

- Before moving forward from a setback, look back. What caused the setback? What can you learn from it? Is there anything you can do differently in the future to prevent the setback from happening again?

- Don't give up, but don't be afraid to adjust your goals or plans either. Your situation may change, or you may encounter new and interesting ideas that you weren't aware of when you started.

Reflect

Q What strategies did you use to complete the STEM Task? Did you try any strategies that did not work? If so, how did you adjust?

Q What can you learn by describing your strategies for completing a task or solving a problem? What can you learn by listening to others' strategies?

Solve Linear Equations

Rent a Tent

Four friends went camping but they couldn't stay the same number of days. They each rented different types of tents, but each paid a total of $27. The cost of each tent rental is represented by an equation.

Solve for *d* to find the number of days each person camped. The constant represents the company's charge to clean the tent.

Kate's rental: $8d + 3 = 27$

Days spent camping _____

Andrea's rental: $11d + 5 = 27$

Days spent camping _____

Manuel's rental: $7.5d + 4.5 = 27$

Days spent camping _____

Peter's rental: $8.5d + 1.5 = 27$

Days spent camping _____

 Turn and Talk

• Explain how to solve each equation to find the number of days.

• If you rent a tent for 5 days the cleaning fee is not charged. Which tent costs the least to rent for 5 days? Explain.

Are You Ready?

Complete these problems to review prior concepts and skills you will need for this module.

Solve One-Step Equations

For Problems 1–3, solve each equation.

1. $x + 24 = 70$

$$x = 64$$

2. $b - 3.5 = 6.8$

$$b = 10.3$$

3. $\frac{t}{8} = 4$

$$t = 32$$

4. It costs $0.80 to download a song from an online music store. Maxine has $6.00 to spend on songs. The equation $0.80s = 6.00$ can be used to determine the number of songs s that she can afford to download. Solve the equation, and interpret the solution.

Write and Solve Two-Step Equations

For Problems 5–10, solve each equation.

5. $4a - 12 = -8$

$$A = 1$$

6. $\frac{n}{4} + 15 = 38$

$$5.75$$

7. $2r + 10 = 14$

$$r = 2$$

8. $\frac{x}{3} - 5 = -3$

$$x = 6$$

9. $2p = 47 - 17$

$$p = 15$$

10. $\frac{z}{2} = 13 + 3$

$$z = 31$$

11. A one-year membership to a swim club is $170. This cost includes a $20 registration fee and 12 monthly payments. The equation $12m + 20 = 170$ can be used to find the amount m of each monthly payment. Solve the equation, and interpret the solution.

12. A group of friends bought 6 movie tickets. They used a coupon for $2.00 off the cost of one of the tickets, and their total cost with the coupon was $50.50. Write an equation that can be used to determine the regular cost c of each movie ticket.

13. Shaun keeps his baseball card collection in an album. The album has 25 pages, and each page can hold 9 cards. Four pages are empty, and the rest are full. Write an equation that can be used to determine the number of baseball cards b in Shaun's collection.

Solve Multi-step Linear Equations

(I Can) solve linear equations with integer and rational number coefficients.

Spark Your Learning

$44

Jordan buys 2 new jerseys and a glove for softball. She pays the price shown for the glove and gives the clerk two fifty-dollar bills to pay the exact amount. How much does Jordan pay for each jersey? Write and solve an equation.

What would the equation and solution be if Jordan gives the clerk a single hundred-dollar bill? How are the equations alike or different? How is the process of solving the equations alike or different?

Turn and Talk Is there another equation that will solve the same problem? Explain.

Build Understanding

1 ▶ A batting machine uses an automatic baseball feeder. During baseball practice the feeder is $\frac{1}{6}$ full. An attendant fills it with 15 baseballs so that the feeder is now $\frac{2}{3}$ full. How many baseballs does the feeder hold when full?

A. Write an equation to represent the problem.

$\frac{1}{6}x + \boxed{} = \boxed{}\, x$

B. In order to **isolate the variable**, all terms containing x need to be on one side of the equation. How can you isolate the variable in the equation? What is the resulting equation before simplifying?

_____

_____

C. Solve the equation for x.

D. Look back at the original equation. How could you use the **least common denominator** of the fractions to rewrite the equation with integer coefficients? A **coefficient** is the number multiplied by the variable.

_____

E. What is the new equation? Solve this new equation. Do you get the same solution?

This is an example of a linear equation with only one solution.

 Turn and Talk Which equation did you prefer to work with? Why?

Step It Out

2 ▶ Lanie and Jen buy the same number of books at the used book sale. Lanie buys paperback books and Jen buys hardcover books. Lanie spends $1.50 less than Jen. Solve the equation to find the number of books each of them buys.

$1.20
Hard Cover

Paperback
$0.45

$$1.2n - 1.5 = 0.45n$$

$$1.2n = 0.45n + \boxed{}$$

$$1.2n - \boxed{} = \boxed{}$$

$$\boxed{} = \boxed{}$$

$$n = \boxed{}$$

A. Look at the decimals in the equation and think about how you could rewrite the equation with integer coefficients. What is the least power of 10 you could multiply each term by to eliminate all the decimals?

_____

B. Multiply each term of the original equation to eliminate all the decimals. Solve the equation.

$$1.2n - 1.5 = 0.45n$$

$$\boxed{}(1.2n) - \boxed{}(1.5) = \boxed{}(0.45n)$$

$$\boxed{}n - \boxed{} = \boxed{}n$$

$$\boxed{}n = \boxed{}$$

$$n = \boxed{}$$

C. Do you get the same solution?

_____

D. Which equation was easier to solve? Why?

_____

_____

Turn and Talk How is solving an equation that involves fractions similar to solving an equation with decimals? What methods can you use to solve each type of equation?

© Houghton Mifflin Harcourt Publishing Company • **Image Credits:** (tl) ©Kirsten Hinte/Shutterstock; (tr) ©JakeWalk/Alamy

3 Jackie has a coupon for $8 off the price of a jacket. Then the clerk takes 25% off the discounted price, so she saves an additional $10. Determine the original price of the jacket.

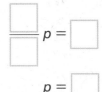
SALE 25% OFF

A. Write an equation using the **Distributive Property**, which states that for all real numbers a, b, and c, $a(b + c) = ab + ac$, and $a(b - c) = ab - ac$. Convert the percentage to a fraction. Solve the equation.

$$\frac{1}{4}(p - 8) = 10$$

$$\frac{\square}{\square}\, p - \square = 10$$

$$\frac{\square}{\square}\, p = \square$$

$$p = \square$$

B. Write the original equation, eliminate the fractions, and solve.

$$\frac{1}{4}(p - 8) = 10$$

$$4\left[\frac{1}{4}(p - 8)\right] = 4(10)$$

$$p - \square = \square$$

$$p = \square$$

4 Solve the equation $4(2.5x + 2) - x = 26.9$.

A. Use the Distributive Property to write an equivalent equation.

_____

B. Combine **like terms**, terms that have the same variable raised to the same exponent, and solve.

_____

Check Understanding

1. Anna spent $2.75 at the school store. She bought two erasers and some pencils. How many pencils did she buy? Write and solve an equation.

_____

2. Solve the equation. Check your solution.

$$\frac{1}{5}(n - 10) = 6 - 3\frac{1}{2}$$

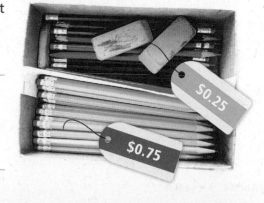
$0.25
$0.75

_____

© Houghton Mifflin Harcourt Publishing Company • **Image Credits:** (tr) ©Brook Chen/Shutterstock; (br) ©Lane V. Erickson/Alamy

Name _____

On Your Own

3. The sum of the measures of the angles in the triangle is 180°. What is the measure of each angle? Write and solve an equation.

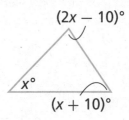

4. (MP) **Reason** Jamie solved the equation $\frac{2}{3}x + 4 = 2 + \frac{1}{2}x$. Is his solution correct? Explain.

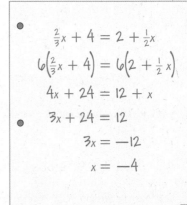

$$\frac{2}{3}x + 4 = 2 + \frac{1}{2}x$$
$$6\left(\frac{2}{3}x + 4\right) = 6\left(2 + \frac{1}{2}x\right)$$
$$4x + 24 = 12 + x$$
$$3x + 24 = 12$$
$$3x = -12$$
$$x = -4$$

5. Karinne hit 4 more home runs than half the number of home runs Lu hit. Together they hit 10 home runs. Let x represent the number of home runs Lu hit.

A. Write an equation to represent the situation.

B. Solve for x.

C. How many home runs did Lu hit?

D. How many home runs did Karinne hit?

E. How can you check your answer?

6. (MP) **Construct Arguments** Max and Corey solve the same equation but they use different methods. Which method would you use? Explain your answer.

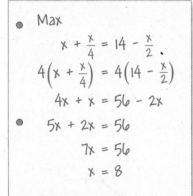

Max

$$x + \frac{x}{4} = 14 - \frac{x}{2}$$
$$4\left(x + \frac{x}{4}\right) = 4\left(14 - \frac{x}{2}\right)$$
$$4x + x = 56 - 2x$$
$$5x + 2x = 56$$
$$7x = 56$$
$$x = 8$$

Corey

$$x + \frac{x}{4} = 14 - \frac{x}{2}$$
$$x + \frac{x}{4} + \frac{x}{2} = 14$$
$$\frac{4x}{4} + \frac{x}{4} + \frac{2x}{4} = 14$$
$$\frac{7x}{4} = 14$$
$$7x = 56$$
$$x = 8$$

7. What is a first step to solve the equation $0.3n - 15 = 0.2n - 5$?

Solve each equation. Check your solution.

8. $3(x - 2) + 6 = 5(x + 4)$

9. $2.2(4p + 2) = 13.2$

10. $\frac{m + 3}{2} = m - 5$

11. $2(11t + 1.5t) = 12 - 5t$

12. $\frac{7}{8}m - \frac{1}{2} = \frac{3}{16}m + 5$

13. $9(n + 1) = 2(n - 1)$

14. $\frac{4}{5}x - 3 = \frac{3}{10}x + 7$

15. $-4(-5 - b) = \frac{1}{3}(b + 16)$

16. $3.6w = 2(0.8w + 12)$

◧×
┼◉÷ **I'm in a Learning Mindset!**

How is the first step in solving a multi-step linear equation different from the first step in solving a multi-step word problem?

Name _____

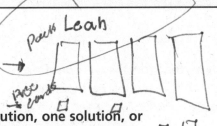

Examine Special Cases

(I Can) recognize linear equations that have no solution, one solution, or infinitely many solutions. I can determine if all the solutions of an equation with infinitely many solutions make sense in a real-world context. I can interpret the meaning of an equation with no solution in a real-world context.

Spark Your Learning SMALL GROUPS

Leah and Mai are taking a card-making class. The teacher has 4 packs of blank cards and an additional 8 cards. Leah buys 4 packs of cards that each come with an additional 3 free cards in the pack. Mai buys 4 packs of cards that each come with an additional 2 free cards in the pack.

How many cards would need to be in each pack of cards so that the teacher had the same number of cards as Leah? as Mai?

Leah and Teacher

$4(x + 3) = 4x + 8$

Mai and Teacher

$4(x + 2) = 4x + 8$

What do you notice when you solve each equation? What do you think this means?

Teacher = 4x+8

Leah = 4(x+3)

$4(x+3) = 4x+8$

$4x+12 = 4x+8$
$\quad -12 \quad\quad -12$
$4x = 4x - 4$

$4(x+2) = 4x+8 \quad 4x = 4x$

$4x+8 = 4x+8$

Teacher = 4 packs of cards
+ 8 cards

Leah = 4 packs
+ 3 cards

Mai = 4 packs
+ 2 cards.

Turn and Talk What do you think it means when an equation simplifies to an equation that is not true? Why?

Build Understanding

You know that to solve an equation means to find the values for the variable that make a true statement. Sometimes an equation may have **no solution** or may not have a unique solution.

Just like a detective, you can gather clues to help you discover what will happen in each equation. Then you can gather clues in a table.

Solution	Meaning	Number of solutions
$x = a$	Only one value of x makes the equation true.	1

1 ▶ Solve the equation $2\left(\frac{x}{8} + 3\right) = 7 + \frac{1}{4}x$.

$$2\left(\frac{x}{8}\right) + 3) = 7 + \frac{1}{4}x$$

$$\frac{4}{4}\left(\frac{x}{4} + 6\right) = \left(7 + \frac{1}{4}x\right)4$$

$$x + 24 = 28 + x$$
$$-x \qquad\qquad -x$$
$$24 = 28$$

False Statement

A. What do you notice about the final equation?

_____

B. **Substitute** several different values for x into the original equation. Simplify. Explain what happens.

_____

_____

C. How many solutions does the equation have? Use what you have discovered to fill in the table.

Solution	Meaning	Number of solutions
$a = b$, where $a \neq b$		

 Turn and Talk Write an equation with a variable x so that the equation is never true. Use addition on both sides of the equation.

2 ▶ Solve the equation $x + 8 = 2(0.5x + 4)$.

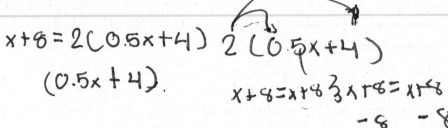

$$x + 8 = 2(0.5x + 4)$$
$$(0.5x + 4).$$

$$2(0.5x + 4)$$
$$x + 8 = x + 8 \quad \{ 3x + 8 = x + 8$$
$$\qquad\qquad -8 \quad -8$$
$$-x \quad -x$$
$$\boxed{8 = 8}$$
$$\boxed{x = x}$$

A. What do you notice about the final equation?

_____

Connect to Vocabulary

An equation that is true for all values of the variable has **infinitely many solutions.**

B. Substitute several different values for x into the original equation. Simplify. Explain what happens.

_____

_____

_____

C. How many solutions does the equation have? Use what you have discovered to fill in the table.

Solution	Meaning	Number of solutions
$a = a$ or $x = x$		

D. Collect your information into one table.

Solution	Meaning	Number of solutions
$x = a$	Only one value of x makes the equation true.	1
$a = b$, where $a \neq b$		
$a = a$ or $x = x$		

Möbius Strip

 Turn and Talk What do you notice about equations that have no solution and equations that have infinitely many solutions? How are they alike or different?

Step It Out

3 ▶ Use the simplified version of an equation to show how many solutions the equation has.

A. Jose draws an equilateral triangle with side length x. Marin draws an equilateral triangle with sides 2 inches longer. Marin writes an equation to show that her triangle has a perimeter that is 6 inches greater than Jose's triangle. Solve the equation.

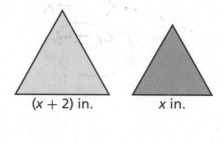

$$3(x + 2) - 6 = 3x$$

$$3x + \boxed{2} - 6 = 3x$$

$$\boxed{} = 3x$$

$$\boxed{0} = 0$$

(x + 2) in.   x in.

How many solutions does the equation have? Since the equation is always true, does it make sense that x could be a negative number?

_____

_____

_____

B. Simplify the equation.

$$5.5x - 2.1 = 3 + 5.5x$$

$$5.5x - 2.1 - \boxed{5.5}\; x = 3 + 5.5x - \boxed{-5.5}\; x$$

$$\boxed{-2.1} = \boxed{\cancel{2}\,3}$$

How many solutions does the equation have? What does the simplified equation mean?

_____

_____

Check Understanding

1. Brynne simplifies an equation and gets $2 = 3$. What does this tell you about the equation?

_____

2. Simplify the equation and tell whether the equation has one solution, no solution, or infinitely many solutions.

$$9(x + 5) = 20 + 9x + 25$$

_____

On Your Own

3. Lilly starts hiking along a trail at 3 miles per hour. Dave starts hiking the same trail from the same starting point at 3.5 miles per hour. If Lilly walked 2 miles before Dave started hiking, will he catch up to her? Write an equation to represent the situation and determine how many solutions the equation has.

3 miles

$3x+2 = 3.5x$ Well depending what x is he will get

$3x+2 = 3.5x$
$2 hrs$ $17 = 17.5$
$6+12$
$8 = 7$

4. Maria pays a yearly fee of $3 to her swimming club and $2 per lesson. Carmen pays a yearly fee of $5 and $2 per lesson. After how many lessons will Maria and Carmen have paid the same amount? Write an equation and explain your answer.

$3 + 2x = 5 + 2x$

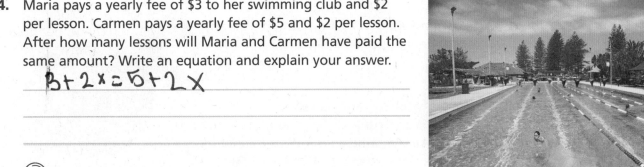

5. (MP) **Construct Arguments** Alex says that $3.2x - 5 = 3.2(x - 5)$ has infinitely many solutions. Is Alex correct? Explain why or why not.

6. Complete the equation so that it has infinitely many solutions.

$2(2x + 1) = 2 + \underline{\hspace{2cm}}$

For Problems 7–11, determine whether each equation has one solution, no solution, or infinitely many solutions. If there is only one solution, find it.

7. $\frac{1}{2}x + 3 - \frac{1}{4}x = 3 + \frac{1}{4}x$

8. $4 + 3x = 3x - 7$

$4 + x = x - 7$ $4 = 7$ No solution

9. $5.4x + 12 = 2(2.7x - 9)$

$5.4x + 12 = 5.4x 18$ No solution

10. $6 + 2.5x = 0.5x - 8$

11. $2(x - 1) + 6x = 4(2x - 1) + 2$

$12x2) + 4x c^8$

12. Carlos draws a square with side lengths 2x. Vincent draws a rectangle with a length of 2x + 4 and a width of 2x. Vincent says that he can choose a value for x so that the two shapes have the same perimeter. Carlos says this cannot be done. Who is correct and why?

_____

_____

_____

13. Open Ended Write an equation that has infinitely many solutions. Prove that your equation is correct.

_____

14. Molly charges an hourly fee to watch a pet plus an initial fee of $12. Bennett charges an hourly fee, but no initial fee. Can Molly and Bennett make the same amount? Write and solve an equation to justify your answer.

_____

_____

_____

_____

Molly: $8 per hour

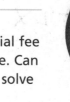

Bennett: $10 per hour

For Problems 15–18, determine whether the equation has one solution, no solution, or infinitely many solutions.

15. $\frac{1}{4}x + 7 + \frac{1}{4}x = 4 + \frac{5}{10}x + 3$ _____

16. $5(4 + x) = x + 44$ _____

17. $0.25 + 2x = 2x - 1.75$ _____

18. $3x + 1 = 6x - 8$ _____

I'm in a Learning Mindset!

What did I learn from writing an equation with infinitely many solutions that I can use in my future learning?

_____

_____

Name

Apply Linear Equations

(I Can) solve linear equations and interpret solutions in context.

Step It Out

1 ▶ A student service club is raising money through a "Loose Change" competition among the grades. Jenaya brings in 20 coins, all of which are nickels and dimes, that have a total value of $1.30 to put in her grade's bucket.

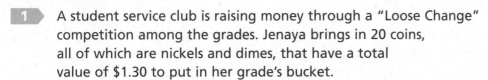

The equation $5(20 - d) + 10d = 130$ can be solved to determine the number of dimes in Jenaya's donation. How many dimes did Jenaya place in the bucket?

A. Apply the Distributive Property to the left side of the equation.

$$\boxed{} - \boxed{} + 10d = 130$$

B. Combine like terms.

$$\boxed{} + \boxed{} = 130$$

C. Solve the equation for d.

$$100 + 5d = 130$$

$$-\boxed{} \qquad -\boxed{}$$

$$\frac{\boxed{}}{\boxed{}} = \frac{\boxed{}}{\boxed{}}$$

$$d = \boxed{}$$

D. How many dimes does Jenaya place in the bucket? Write a sentence.

_____

_____

Turn and Talk Which variable or **expression** represents the number of dimes? Which variable or expression represents the number of nickels? Explain your reasoning.

2 Grant needs to construct a rectangular garden with 55 feet of fencing around the perimeter. He draws a diagram to determine the length and width of the garden. What is the side length that Grant should choose for the garden?

A. How much fencing is needed for half of the garden, one length and one width?

_____ feet

B. If the length of the garden is represented by ℓ, how can you represent the width of the garden?

_____

C. Label the sides of the garden.

D. Complete the equation that represents the perimeter of the garden.

$2\ell + 2\left(\right) = \boxed{}$

E. What should be the first step in solving the equation? Why?

_____

_____

F. Complete the first step of solving the equation.

$2\ell + \boxed{} - \boxed{} = 55$

G. Combine the like terms on the left side of the equation and simplify.

_____

H. What does this result mean about the solutions for ℓ?

_____

_____

I. What does this result mean about the length of the garden?

_____

_____

3 Pam and Rachel buy books at the bookstore where Rachel works. Each uses a coupon. As an employee Rachel pays only 75% of the advertised price after her coupon is applied. How many books could each purchase and spend the same amount for the same number of books?

A. Complete the equation to represent Rachel and Pam buying *x* books each and paying the same amount.

$$\boxed{} = 0.75 \left(\boxed{} \right)$$

> **Pam:** I bought books for $4.00 each and used a $5.00 off coupon.

B. Solve the equation.

$$x = \boxed{}$$

C. Is it possible for Pam and Rachel to purchase *x* books and pay the same amount? Explain.

_____

_____

> **Rachel:** I bought books where I work for $8.00 each and used a $4.00 off coupon.

D. What does the solution to the equation represent about the situation?

_____

_____

_____

Turn and Talk How would the solution be different if Rachel did not have a coupon?

Check Understanding

1. The equation $x + (75.3 - x) = 75.3$ represents the sum of two angle measures. How many possible combinations of angle measures satisfy these conditions?

_____

2. Two bicyclists on a 75-mile trail ride toward each other. One bicyclist begins at the 45-mile marker. The other begins at the end of the trail. The expressions shown represent the distance from the Parking Lot for each bicyclist when they meet.

   A. Write an equation to represent the bicyclists' meeting after *x* hours.

   _____

   B. After how many hours do the bicyclists meet?

   _____

   C. How far away are the bicyclists from the parking lot when they meet?

   _____

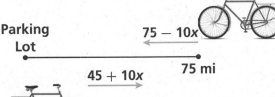

Parking Lot

$75 - 10x$

$45 + 10x$

75 mi

On Your Own

3. James rides down in an elevator that starts at a height of 120 feet. Brianne runs up the stairs from the ground floor.

   Use the equation $120 - 2.5t = 1.5t$ to represent when James and Brianne are at the same height after t seconds.

   2.5 $\frac{ft}{sec}$

   A. Solve the equation.

   _____

   B. What does the solution represent about James and Brianne's locations?

   _____

   _____

   C. What is their height above the ground floor when they are at the same height at the same time?

   _____

   1.5 $\frac{ft}{sec}$

4. The expression $100 - 2.5x$ represents the balance of Grace's account after x days. The expression $100 + 2.5(5 - x)$ represents the balance of Tim's account after x days. After how many days do the accounts have the same balance?

   _____

5. Josh is 3 years older than Lynette. The sum of their ages is 49. Write expressions for Josh's age and Lynette's age, and use the expressions to write an equation relating their ages. Use the equation to determine Josh's age and Lynette's age.

   _____

6. Zander downloads a combination of 30 games and songs. He downloads 8 more songs than games. The equation $g + (8 + g) = 30$ can be solved to determine g, the number of games Zander downloaded. How many games did Zander download? How many songs did he download?

   _____

7. **Open Ended** A business *breaks even* when its production costs are equal to its revenue. The expression $120 + 4x$ represents the cost of producing x items. Decide on a selling price for each item, and write an expression for the revenue generated by selling x items. How many items would you need to sell at your chosen price to break even? Write an equation and solve it.

   _____

8. **STEM** A scientist conducts an experiment with two trees over many years. The shorter tree has fertilizer applied to it, and the taller tree does not. The shorter tree grows at an average rate of 8 inches per year. The taller tree grows at an average rate of 6 inches per year.

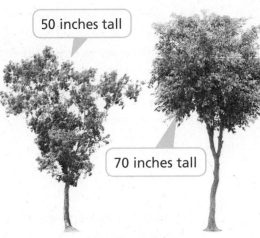

50 inches tall

70 inches tall

Starting Heights

A. Complete the equation to represent the trees having the same height after *t* years:

$$50 + 8t = \boxed{}$$

B. After how many years will the heights of the two trees be equal?

_____

C. What will be the height of the trees when they are the same height?

_____

9. Rodney opens a savings account with $75 and also deposits $40 each month. Morgan opens an account with $50 and also deposits $40 each month. Will they have the same amount in their account at any point? If so, after how many months? Explain.

_____

_____

_____

10. (MP) **Critique Reasoning** Ethan said $5x - 20 = 5(x - 20)$ has infinitely many solutions. Is he correct? Explain.

_____

_____

_____

_____

11. Abigail wants to find three consecutive even integers whose sum is four times the smallest of those integers. She lets *n* represent the smallest integer, then writes this equation: $n + (n + 2) + (n + 4) = 4n$.

A. Solve the equation.

_____

B. What are the three integers?

_____

12. Every year Aiden uses income from his job to pay for 75% of his college tuition. Next year's tuition will be $720 more than this year's, and Aiden will pay $2400. How much is this year's tuition?

_____

13. 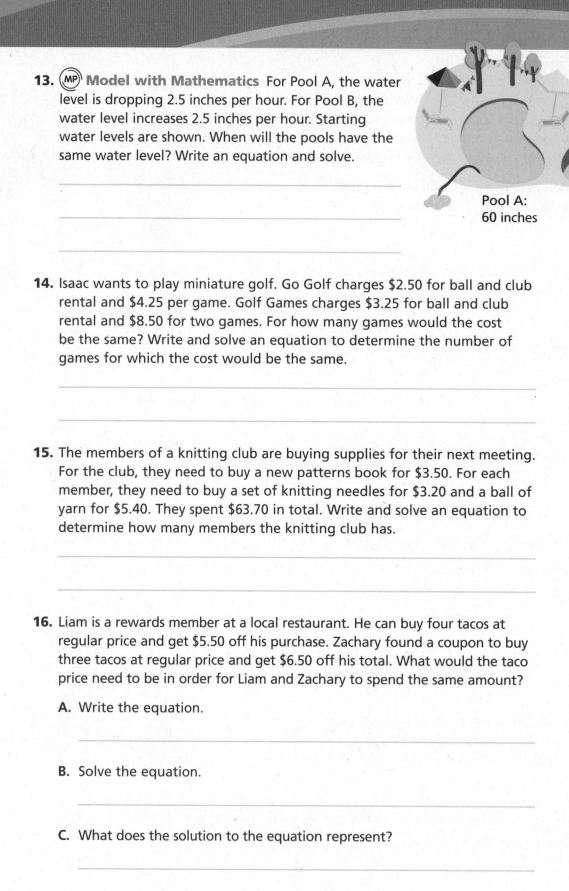 **Model with Mathematics** For Pool A, the water level is dropping 2.5 inches per hour. For Pool B, the water level increases 2.5 inches per hour. Starting water levels are shown. When will the pools have the same water level? Write an equation and solve.

Pool A:
60 inches

Pool B:
20 inches

14. Isaac wants to play miniature golf. Go Golf charges $2.50 for ball and club rental and $4.25 per game. Golf Games charges $3.25 for ball and club rental and $8.50 for two games. For how many games would the cost be the same? Write and solve an equation to determine the number of games for which the cost would be the same.

15. The members of a knitting club are buying supplies for their next meeting. For the club, they need to buy a new patterns book for $3.50. For each member, they need to buy a set of knitting needles for $3.20 and a ball of yarn for $5.40. They spent $63.70 in total. Write and solve an equation to determine how many members the knitting club has.

16. Liam is a rewards member at a local restaurant. He can buy four tacos at regular price and get $5.50 off his purchase. Zachary found a coupon to buy three tacos at regular price and get $6.50 off his total. What would the taco price need to be in order for Liam and Zachary to spend the same amount?

A. Write the equation.

B. Solve the equation.

C. What does the solution to the equation represent?

Angle Relationships

A Fox From Any Angle

The diagram shows the design for a fox made from folded paper.

Give an example of each type of angle pair in the design.

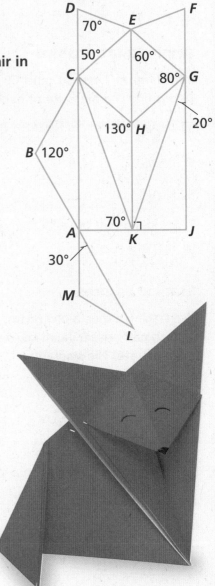

A. Vertical angles

_____

B. Adjacent supplementary angles

_____

C. Non-adjacent supplementary angles

_____

D. Adjacent complementary angles

_____

E. Non-adjacent complementary angles

_____

 Turn and Talk

How did you identify a pair of non-adjacent supplementary angles?

Are You Ready?

Complete these problems to review prior concepts and skills you will need for this module.

$(h+7) + 3n$

$q3$

Operations with Linear Expressions

Simplify each expression.

1. $x + 2x + 48$

$3x + 48$

2. $(n + 7) + 3(n + 1) + 90$

$4n + 100$

3. $180 - (68 + a)$

$112 + a$

Angle Relationships

In the figure, Lines *AD* and *CE* intersect at Point *F*. Determine the measure of each angle.

180
121°
48

4. ∠*CFD* _____

5. ∠*DFE* _____

6. ∠*AFE* _____

7. Name a pair of vertical angles in the figure.

_____

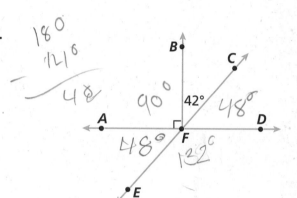

90° $42°$ 48°

48° 122°

Similar Figures

Use tracing paper, a protractor, and a ruler to determine whether the triangles in each pair are similar. If so, describe a sequence of transformations that demonstrates the similarity.

8.

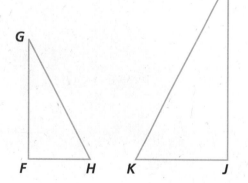

_____
_____
_____
_____

9.

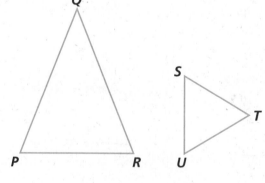

_____
_____
_____
_____

Name _____

Develop Angle Relationships for Triangles

 find an unknown angle measure in a triangle.

Spark Your Learning

The angles of a triangle have a relationship with each other. Draw three unique triangles. What do you notice about the measures of the interior angles of the triangles?

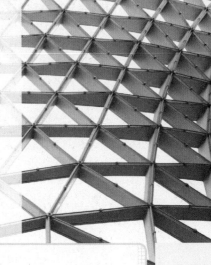

 Turn and Talk What conjecture can you make about the sum of the measures of the angles of a triangle?

Build Understanding

1 ▶ What is the sum of the measures of the three **interior angles** of a triangle?

A. Find the sum of the measures of the angles in each of the three triangles.

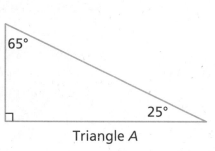
Triangle *A*

Triangle *B*

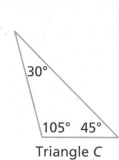
Triangle *C*

B. What do you notice about the sum of the measures of the three triangles?

_____

C. Do you think this is true for all triangles? Explain.

_____

_____

The **Triangle Sum Theorem** states that the measures of the three interior angles of a triangle sum to 180°.

D. The angles in a triangle measure 2*x*, 3*x*, and 4*x* degrees. Write and solve an equation to determine the angle measures.

_____

_____

 Turn and Talk Discuss how to find a missing measure of an angle in a triangle when the other two angle measures are given.

© Houghton Mifflin Harcourt Publishing Company

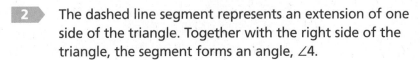

Step It Out

The Triangle Sum Theorem can be used to draw conclusions about a triangle's interior angles.

2 ▶ The dashed line segment represents an extension of one side of the triangle. Together with the right side of the triangle, the segment forms an angle, ∠4.

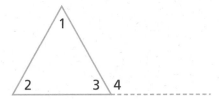

A. What is the sum of the measures of ∠3 and ∠4?

_____

B. An **exterior angle** of a polygon is an angle formed by one side of the polygon and the extension of an adjacent side. Which angle in the diagram is an exterior angle?

_____

C. If the measure of ∠3 is 60°, what is the measure of ∠4?

_____

D. If the measure of ∠3 is 60°, what is the sum of the measures of ∠1 and ∠2?

_____

E. Which angle has a measure equal to the sum of the measures of ∠1 and ∠2?

_____

F. A **remote interior angle** of an exterior angle of a polygon is an angle that is inside the polygon and is not adjacent to the exterior angle. Which two angles in the diagram are remote interior angles in relation to Angle 4?

_____

G. If the sum of the measures of ∠1 and ∠2 is 115°, what is the measure of ∠4?

_____

Turn and Talk A triangle has exterior Angle *P* with remote interior Angles *Q* and *R*. Can you determine which angle has the greatest measure? Why or why not?

© Houghton Mifflin Harcourt Publishing Company • Image Credit: ©Huntstock, Inc/Alamy

3 A machinist is drawing a triangular piece of an industrial machine.

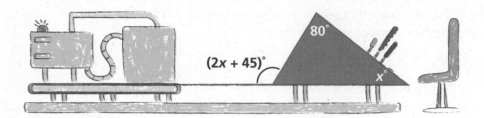

A. Write an equation and solve to find the value of x. Show your work.

$$\boxed{}x + \boxed{} = x + \boxed{}$$
$$\boxed{}x - x = 80 - \boxed{}$$
$$x = \boxed{}$$

B. What is the measure of the unknown remote interior angle?

_____

C. Use the value of x from Part A to find the measure of the exterior angle.

$$2x + 45 = 2\left(\boxed{}\right) + 45 = \boxed{} + 45 = \boxed{}$$

D. What is the measure of the exterior angle?

_____

Check Understanding

1. Two angles of a triangle have measures of 30° and 45°. What is the measure of the remaining angle?

_____

2. Dana draws a triangle with one angle that has a measure of 40°.

A. What is the measure of the angle's adjacent exterior angle?

_____

B. What is the sum of the measures of the remote interior angles for the exterior angle adjacent to the 40° angle?

_____

3. An exterior angle of a triangle has a measure of 80°, and one of the remote interior angles has a measure of 20°. Write and solve an equation to find the measure of the other remote interior angle.

_____

© Houghton Mifflin Harcourt Publishing Company

On Your Own

4. A puppeteer is making a triangular hat for a puppet. If two of the three angles of the hat both measure 30°, what is the measure of the third angle?

_____

5. (MP) **Construct Arguments** Can a triangle have two obtuse angles? Explain your answer.

_____

_____

_____

_____

6. **STEM** In engineering, equilateral triangles can support the most weight and so are commonly found in the design of bridges and buildings. Equilateral triangles are triangles with three congruent sides and three congruent angles. What are the measures of the angles of an equilateral triangle?

_____

7. A triangle has one 30° angle, an unknown angle, and an angle with a measure that is twice the measure of the unknown angle. Find the measures of the triangle's unknown angles and explain how you found the answer.

_____

_____

_____

_____

For Problems 8–10, find the measures of the unknown third angles.

8. 31.5°

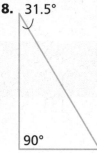

90°

9.

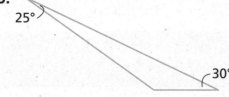

25°

30°

10.

45°   80°

11. **Open Ended** The measure of an exterior angle of a triangle is $x°$. The measure of the adjacent interior angle is at least twice $x°$. List three possible solutions for x.

_____

12. The measure of an exterior angle of a triangle is 40°. What is the sum of the measures of the corresponding remote interior angles?

_____

13. Steven is building a fin for his surfboard. In order to make the fin, he needs to know the value of x in the following diagram. Use your knowledge of triangle angle relationships to find the value of x.

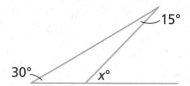

_____

14. Find the value of x in the diagram. Explain how you found the answer.

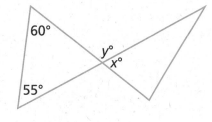

_____
_____
_____
_____
_____

I'm in a Learning Mindset!

What did I learn from applying my knowledge of interior angles of a triangle to find the missing exterior angle in Problem 13 that I can explain clearly to a classmate?

_____
_____

Name _____

Investigate Angle-Angle Similarity

(I Can) use Angle-Angle similarity to test triangles for similarity and find unknown angle measures.

Spark Your Learning

Asa is comparing the architect's model of a barn with the finished building. He looks at the triangle that forms the front of the roof in the model and in the completed barn. Are the triangles similar? Why or why not?

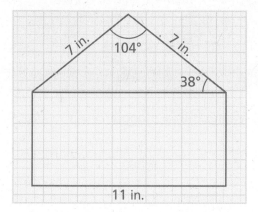

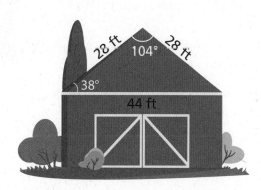

Turn and Talk Which is the easier way of deciding if the triangles are similar, comparing the angles or comparing the side lengths? Why?

Build Understanding

Two triangles are similar if all three pairs of corresponding angles are congruent. What if only two out of three pairs of corresponding angles are congruent?

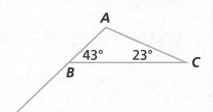

1 ▶ Using the given drawing by the set designer, Shawna is making a flag for a play. She has measured Angles *ABC* and *C* with a protractor, and they match Angles *E* and *F*, respectively, on the set designer's notes. Can she be sure that her flag is similar to the drawing without measuring the third angle?

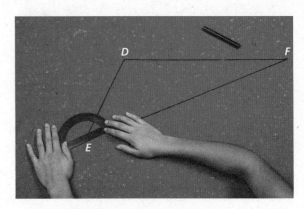

A. What do you know about the sum of the measures of the angles in a triangle?

_____

_____

B. How does knowing the sum of the measures of the angles in a triangle help you solve this problem?

_____

_____

C. Write and evaluate an expression to find the measure of the third angle of Triangle *ABC*, using the angle measures given.

_____

D. Write and evaluate an expression to find the measure of the third angle of Triangle *DEF* using the angle measures given.

_____

E. Based on your calculation of the measure of the third angle, can you now state with confidence whether Shawna's flag is similar to the drawing without measuring the third angle? Explain.

_____

_____

_____

The **Angle-Angle Similarity Postulate** states that two triangles are similar if they have two pairs of corresponding angles that are congruent.

 Turn and Talk When two triangles have two angle measures in common, will the third angle measure always be the same for both triangles? Explain.

Name _____

Step It Out

2 In the two triangles shown, m∠A = m∠D and m∠C = m∠F.

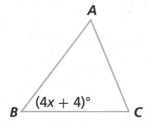

A. Do you know enough to say whether the two triangles are similar? Explain.

_____

_____

B. What does your answer to Part A imply about Angles B and E? Explain how you know.

_____

_____

C. What equation can you write relating the measures of Angles B and E?

_____

D. Solve your equation from Part C for x. What are the measures of

Angles B and E? _____

E. How can you find the measure of Angle F?

_____

_____

_____

F. How can you find the measure of Angle C?

_____

G. Fill in the measures of the six angles:

m∠A = _____   m∠B = _____   m∠C = _____

m∠D = _____   m∠E = _____   m∠F = _____

 **Turn and Talk** If you were given the measures of Angles A, C, D, and E from Part G, how could you determine whether the triangles are similar?

3 ▶ The illustration shows a wheelchair ramp from the side. The support at $\overline{BC}$ binds the ramp to the floor. Are Triangles *ABC* and *ADE* similar?

A. What do the little squares at Points *C* and *E* mean?

_____

B. Do Triangles *ABC* and *ADE* both contain the same angle? If so, name it.

_____

C. Does that mean both triangles have two pairs of corresponding congruent angles? If so, name the corresponding congruent angles.

_____

D. Are Triangles *ABC* and *ADE* similar? Explain.

_____

Check Understanding

1. Which two triangles are similar?

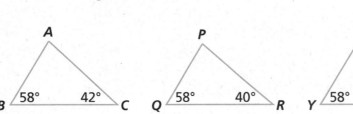

2. Explain why △*XYZ* is similar to △*LMZ*.

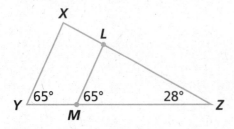

_____

_____

On Your Own

3. **(MP) Reason** A graphic designer wants to reproduce a logo of a mountain-climbing club for some club stationery. The logo is a triangle with the angles shown.

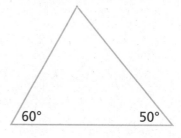

60°   50°

A. The designer wants the base to be 2 inches long. How should the triangle be drawn?

_____

_____

_____

B. How can the Angle-Angle Similarity Postulate help the graphic designer make sure the triangle is reproduced correctly?

_____

_____

_____

4. Angles *A*, *D*, and *G* are congruent, and Angles *C*, *F*, and *J* are congruent.

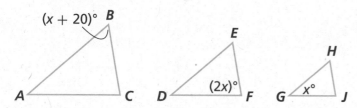

$(x + 20)°$ *B*

A   *C*   *D* $(2x)°$ *F*   *G* $x°$ *J*   *E*   *H*

A. Write an expression to find the measures of Angles *B*, *F*, and *G*.

_____

B. What is the measure of Angle *E*? _____

Use Triangles *QRS* and *TUV* to solve Problems 5–6.

5. Are Triangles *QRS* and *TUV* similar? How do you know?

_____

_____

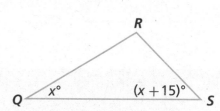

R

Q $x°$ $(x + 15)°$ *S*

6. What is the measure of Angle *R* in terms of *x*?

_____

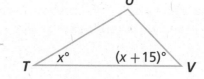

U

T $x°$ $(x + 15)°$ *V*

7. (MP) **Reason** Are the triangles shown similar? Why or why not?

_____

_____

_____

_____

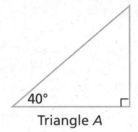

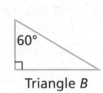

Triangle *A*   Triangle *B*

8. (MP) **Reason** Are the triangles shown similar? How do you know?

_____

_____

_____

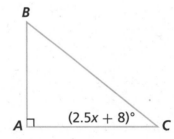   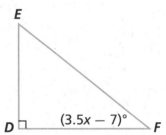

35°   35°

9. (MP) **Reason** Are the triangles similar? Explain.

_____

_____

_____

_____

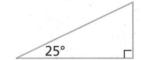

75°

25°

10. Angle *C* is congruent to Angle *F*. What is the measure of Angle *E*?

_____

B   *E*

A   (2.5x + 8)°   *C*   *D*   (3.5x − 7)°   *F*

11. Does the diagram show similar triangles? Explain.

_____

_____

_____

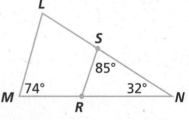

L

S

85°

74°   32°

M   *N*

R

 I'm in a Learning Mindset!

What can I apply from previous work with triangles to better understand whether two triangles are similar?

_____

_____

Name

Explore Parallel Lines Cut by a Transversal

 identify the relationship between angle pairs as either supplementary or congruent.

Spark Your Learning

A walker sees these logs on a hike and notices that they make several angles.

Draw a representation of the logs and compare the lines and the angles in your drawing. How are the angles the same and how are they different?

 Turn and Talk What pattern do you notice after measuring all the angles?

Build Understanding

When two lines are cut by a third line, the third line is called a **transversal**. The intersections of the lines form eight angles, including five special types of angle pairs. When the two lines cut by a transversal are parallel, as shown, the angles in any of the special pairs will be either congruent or supplementary.

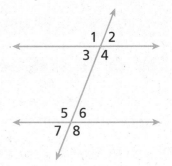

1 The term alternate means that two angles are on opposite sides of the transversal.

A. Alternate interior angles are angles on opposite sides of the transversal inside the parallel lines. Measure a pair of alternate interior angles with a protractor. Name the angles you found. Are they congruent or supplementary?

_____

_____

B. Alternate exterior angles are angles on opposite sides of the transversal outside the parallel lines. Measure a pair of alternate exterior angles with a protractor. Name the angles you found. Are they congruent or supplementary?

_____

_____

The term same-side means that two angles are on the same side of the transversal.

C. Same-side interior angles are on the same side of the transversal and between the parallel lines. Measure a pair of same-side interior angles. Name the angles you found. Are they congruent or supplementary?

_____

_____

D. Same-side exterior angles are on the same side of the transversal but outside the parallel lines. Measure a pair of same-side exterior angles. Name the angles you found. Are they congruent or supplementary?

_____

_____

E. Corresponding angles are angles in the same position formed when a third line intersects two parallel lines. Measure two pairs of corresponding angles. Name the angles you found. Are they congruent or supplementary?

_____

_____

Step It Out

2 The diagram shows two parallel lines cut by a transversal. Find the value of x.

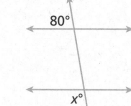

A. What kind of angle pair is formed by the two labeled angles?

_____

B. How are the two angles related to each other?

_____

C. Complete the equation to find the value of x.

$x + 80 =$ ⬜

$x =$ ⬜

3 The diagram shows two parallel lines cut by a transversal.

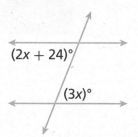

$(2x + 24)°$

$(3x)°$

A. What kind of angle pair is formed by the two labeled angles?

_____

B. What is true about the measures of the angles?

_____

C. Complete and solve the equation to find the value of x.

$3x =$ ⬜

$x =$ ⬜

D. Find the measures of the angles.

$3x = 3\left(\;\boxed{}\;\right) = 72$

$2x + 24 = 2\left(\;\boxed{}\;\right) + 24 = \boxed{} + 24 = 72$

The angles both measure _____ .

 Turn and Talk Consider the diagram in Task 3. What happens if it is rotated so the parallel lines are vertical? Explain how this affects the relationships with the angle pairs.

4 You can use what you know about the angles formed by parallel lines and a transversal to prove the Triangle Sum Theorem. For any triangle, draw a line through a vertex parallel to the opposite side (in this case, through the vertex of ∠4).

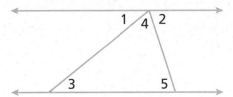

A. What is the sum of the measures of Angle 1, Angle 2, and Angle 4? How do you know?

_____

B. How would you classify the angle pairs ∠1 and ∠3, and ∠2 and ∠5?

_____

C. What does that tell you about their respective angle measures?

_____

D. Complete this statement: If m∠1 = m∠3 and m∠2 = m∠5, then

m∠3 + m∠4 + m∠5 = m∠ ☐ + m∠4 + m∠ ☐ = ☐ .

E. Make three copies of the triangle and arrange them so the three angles form a line. Use parallel lines and transversals to explain how your figure proves the Triangle Sum Theorem.

_____

Check Understanding

Problems 1–2 show two parallel lines and a transversal. Find the values of x.

1.

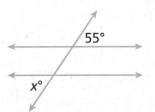

55°

x°

2.

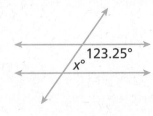

123.25°

x°

_____

On Your Own

3. The picture shows a bridge between two parallel river banks. What angle does the driver's right turn make with the river after crossing the bridge to continue on Northbridge Road?

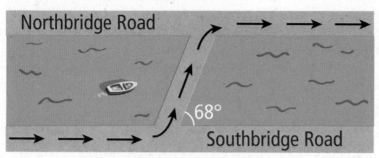

_____

Use the diagram showing two parallel lines and a transversal to answer Problems 4–6.

4. Which angle forms a pair of alternate interior angles with ∠ACB?

_____

5. Which angle forms a pair of corresponding angles with the 41° angle?

_____

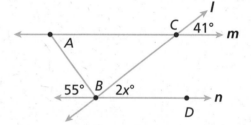

6. Solve for x.

_____

7. (MP) **Reason** The diagram shows two parallel lines cut by a transversal. Clarissa measured ∠1 and ∠2 with her protractor. She says the angles measure 43° and 142°, respectively. Is she correct? Explain.

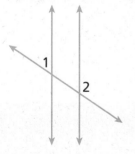

_____

_____

_____

8. In the diagram, two parallel lines are cut by a transversal. Which of the numbered angles measures 152°?

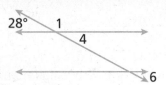

_____

9. (MP) **Reason** You're not sure whether a pair of angles formed by two parallel lines and a transversal are same-side exterior angles or alternate exterior angles. Both angles measure 53°. Which of the two types must they be? Explain.

_____

_____

10. Which two angles have the same measure?

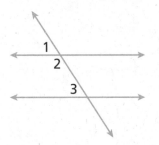

_____

11. Lines *m* and *n* are parallel. Find the following angle pairs in the diagram. If you can't find any, write *none*.

alternate exterior _____

corresponding angles _____

same-side exterior _____

alternate interior _____

same-side interior _____

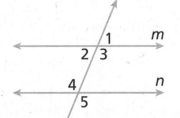

12. Two angles are same-side interior angles. The measures of the angles are represented by the expressions $7x + 18$ and $10x + 9$. What are the two angle measures? _____

 I'm in a Learning Mindset!

How can I apply previous understanding of supplementary and vertical angles to find missing angles formed by parallel lines cut by a transversal?

_____

_____

Unit 3 Relationships and Functions

Auto Engineer

Auto engineers design new vehicles and improve existing vehicles. Some auto engineers work on improving a car's performance, fuel efficiency, or safety. Others specialize in certain components, such as brakes or electrical systems. Auto engineers must understand how some quantities, such as a car's braking distance, depend on other quantities, such as the car's speed.

STEM Task:

Three quantities related to a car engine's performance are torque, horsepower, and revolutions per minute (RPM). These quantities are related by the equation

$$\text{torque} = \frac{\text{horsepower}}{\text{RPM}} \cdot 5252,$$

where torque is measured in pound-feet. How much torque is required to produce 300 horsepower at 2500 RPM? At 5000 RPM? How are the two torques related?

Learning Mindset

Challenge-Seeking Defines Own Challenges

As you grow, you discover the pleasure of setting your own goals and challenges, and designing ways to meet them. Maybe you want to learn a new language, write a book, or become more successful academically. Here are some things to keep in mind as you seek and define new challenges.

■ Believe in your ability to improve skills which are challenges for you now. Use positive self-talk to address any fixed-mindset voices telling you that you can't reach your goal. Believe in the power of "yet."

■ Think about how you will handle unexpected difficulties. Don't become discouraged. Every failure can help you get closer the next time.

■ Be flexible. You may find it necessary to adjust your plan or even redefine the end goal.

■ Don't be afraid to ask for advice and assistance from content resources or people with more experience than you have currently.

Reflect

Q How do you know whether a task is the right level of challenge for you?

Q Was the STEM Task an appropriate challenge for you? If not, what reasonable challenge would you set for yourself?

Proportional Relationships

Proportional Smoothies

The owners of a smoothie shop want the price of each size of smoothie to be proportional to the amount of liquid it contains. A small smoothie will be 16 fluid ounces and sell for $3.52.

Complete the shop's price chart by deciding how many fluid ounces the other smoothie sizes will have and then determine the price of each smoothie.

Smoothies		
Size	Fluid ounces	Price ($)
Kid-size	8	
Small	16	3.52
Medium	24	
Large	32	

 Turn and Talk

- Explain how you know that the prices of the smoothies are proportional to their volumes.

- The shop owners decide to charge $0.99 for each smoothie add-in. For smoothies with a single add-in, is the total price proportional to the fluid ounces? Explain.

Are You Ready?

Complete these problems to review prior concepts and skills you will need for this module.

Tables and Graphs of Equivalent Ratios

Complete each table to represent the relationship.

1. Collette runs 6.5 kilometers each week. Let d represent the total distance, in kilometers, she runs in w weeks.

w	2	3	5
d	13	19.5	32

2. A theater charges a service fee of $0.95 per ticket bought online. Let t represent the total fee paid for ordering n tickets.

n	1	3	6
t	95¢	2.85	$5.70

Identify Proportional Relationships

Tell whether each relationship is proportional. Explain your reasoning.

3.

x	6	8	12	15
y	48	64	96	120

8   8   8   8

yes

4.

x	9	15	18	36
y	18	24	27	45

2   $\frac{9}{8}$ $\frac{5}{3}$

No

Similar Triangles

Tell whether each pair of triangles is similar. Explain your reasoning.

5.

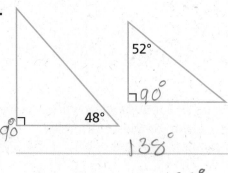

52°   90°   90°   48°

138°

180°

6.

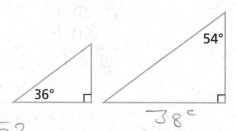

54°   36°   38°

52
+90

142

Name _____

Explain Slope with Similar Triangles

(**I Can**) determine the slope of a line and use it to find additional points on the line.

Spark Your Learning

A line passes through the origin. Two right triangles each have one side along the line and another side on the *x*-axis. How is △*OAC* related to △*OBD*?

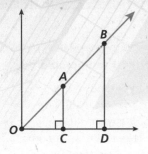

Turn and Talk Amie drew a different line through the origin and drew two new right triangles that have one side along the *x*-axis. How are her triangles different from the ones shown above? How are they the same?

© Houghton Mifflin Harcourt Publishing Company • **Image Credit:** ©Hendra Su/EyeEm/Getty Images

Build Understanding

1 ▶ Points on the line represent the vertical and horizontal distances a person would travel while climbing the path before steps were built to make the climb easier.

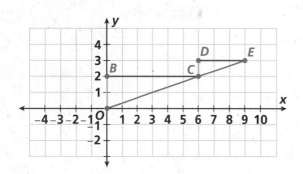

A. Write a sequence of transformations that maps one triangle onto the other to show that △*OBC* is similar to △*CDE*.

_____

_____

_____

B. Complete the following based on △*OBC* and △*CDE*.

$$\frac{\text{length of } \overline{OB}}{\text{length of } \overline{CD}} = \frac{\text{length of } \overline{BC}}{\text{length of } \overline{DE}}$$

Corresponding sides of similar triangles are proportional.

$$\frac{\boxed{}}{1} = \frac{\boxed{}}{3}$$

Substitute.

$$\frac{\boxed{}}{1} \cdot \frac{1}{6} = \frac{\boxed{}}{3} \cdot \frac{1}{6}$$

_____

$$\frac{\boxed{}}{6} = \frac{\boxed{}}{3} \quad \begin{matrix} \leftarrow \text{rise} \\ \leftarrow \text{run} \end{matrix}$$

Multiply.

C. When moving from one point to another along a line, the change in the *y*-coordinates is the **rise** and the change in the *x*-coordinates is the **run**. The legs of △*OBC* and △*CDE* can help you visualize the rise and run. What does Part B show you about the rise-to-run ratios in △*OBC* and △*CDE*?

_____

Step It Out

2 ▸ A skateboard ramp is shown on a coordinate plane.

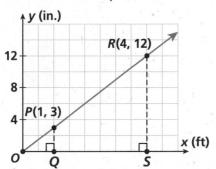

A. Line *OP* passes through the origin, Point *P*, and Point *R*.

The coordinates of Point *Q* are ($\boxed{1}$, $\boxed{0}$), and the coordinates

of Point *S* are ($\boxed{4}$, $\boxed{0}$).

B. Does this line represent a proportional relationship? Explain.

It's a line cuz it goes even.

C. Since the run between the origin and Point *P* is 1, the unit rate is equal to the rise-over-run ratio. Find the unit rate of the relationship modeled by the line. Complete the equation using the coordinates of Point *P* and the origin.

> **Connect to Vocabulary**
>
> A **rate** is a comparison of two quantities that have different units. A **unit rate** is a rate with a denominator of one unit.

unit rate $= \frac{\text{rise}}{\text{run}} = \dfrac{\boxed{3} - \boxed{0}}{\boxed{1} - \boxed{0}} = \dfrac{3}{1} = \boxed{3}$ in./ft

D. A vertical line segment from Point *R* to the *x*-axis forms a right triangle, △*ORS*. Complete the statements to show △*OPQ* is similar to △*ORS*.

m∠*POQ* is equal to m∠ $\boxed{}$. ∠*OQP* and ∠ $\boxed{}$ are right

angles, so they are also $\boxed{\text{congruent / similar}}$. By the AA Similarity

Postulate, △*OPQ* is similar to △ $\boxed{}$.

E. Find the rise-over-run relationship modeled by the line, using the coordinates of Point *R* and the origin.

$\dfrac{\text{rise}}{\text{run}} = \dfrac{\boxed{12} - \boxed{0}}{\boxed{4} - \boxed{0}} = \dfrac{12}{4\frac{3}{1}} = \boxed{3}$ in./ft

F. Describe the slope of the line.

> **Connect to Vocabulary**
>
> **Slope** is a measure of the steepness of a line and is described by the ratio of the line's rise to its run. A horizontal line has slope 0, and a vertical line's slope is undefined.

The rise-over-run ratio, or slope, between the origin and

Point *P* is $\boxed{\text{equal to / not equal to}}$ the rise-over-run ratio,

or slope, between the origin and Point *R*. The slope of

the line is $\boxed{\text{constant /not constant}}$.

3 Points $M(2, 3)$ and $N(x, -6)$ lie on the same line. The line also passes through the origin.

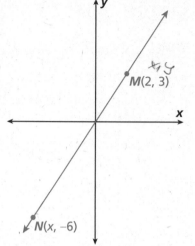

A. For a line passing through the origin, what do you notice about measuring rise over run from the origin to another point on the line?

_____

_____

B. Find the rise over run from the origin to Point M.

$$\frac{\text{rise}\,^y}{\text{run}\,_x} = \frac{\boxed{3} - \boxed{0}}{\boxed{2} - \boxed{0}} = \frac{\boxed{3}}{\boxed{2}}$$

C. The rise-over-run ratio, or slope, of any line is constant. Use this ratio to write an equation that can help you find the x-coordinate of Point N.

$$\frac{\boxed{-6} - 0}{x - 0} = \frac{\boxed{6}}{\boxed{x}}$$

$$\overset{2}{y} - \overset{1}{y} = \text{Shape}$$
$$x \overset{2}{} - x \overset{1}{}$$

D. Use proportional reasoning to solve for x.

$$x = \boxed{6}$$

 Turn and Talk Explain, using the rise and the run, why the slope of a horizontal line is 0.

Check Understanding

1. Explain how dilation scale factors can help you identify points on a line passing through the origin given one additional point.

_____

_____

_____

_____

2. A line passes through the origin and (5, 3). Identify two additional points on this line.

_____

140

On Your Own

3. A road sign is posted showing a road has a 10% grade, meaning the ratio of vertical to horizontal distance is 10%, or $\frac{1}{10}$. If a car driving on the road rises from an elevation of 543 feet above sea level to an elevation of 768 feet above sea level, how far has the car traveled horizontally?

_____

4. (MP) **Attend to Precision** Line ℓ passes through the origin and the point (4, 5). Suppose point (x, y) also lies on Line ℓ.

A. The slope of Line ℓ from the origin to (4, 5) is _____.

B. Why is the slope of Line ℓ from the origin to (x, y) the same as the slope from the origin to (4, 5)?

_____

_____

_____

_____

5. Are Triangles *OPQ* and *ORS* similar? If so, give a sequence of transformations that maps △*OPQ* onto △*ORS*.

_____

_____

_____

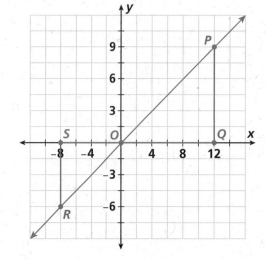

For Problems 6–9, find the value of k given that both points lie on a line passing through the origin.

6. (5, 10) and (−3, k)

_____

7. (−12, −2) and (k, 8)

_____

8. (k, 7) and (−81, −9)

_____

9. (k, −24) and (5, 40)

_____

10. At the bottom of a mountain, a ski lift starts four feet above the ground. At the top of the mountain, the lift is 1356 feet higher. If the lift ascends one foot for every four feet it travels west, how far west of the starting position is the lift at the top of the mountain?

_____

For Problems 11–13, use the given information.

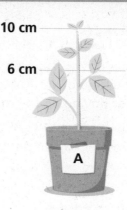

10 cm

6 cm

A

STEM Kylie is preparing for the science fair which will take place in six weeks. She has three plants that she has grown from seeds, which she considers to have height 0 centimeters, and she is measuring their heights as she applies different treatments to each.

11. The first plant is receiving Plant Food A. After 4 weeks, it is 10 centimeters tall, as shown. If it continues growing at this rate, how tall will it be after 6 weeks?

_____

12. The second plant is receiving Plant Food B. After 3 weeks, it is 10 centimeters tall. If it continues growing at this rate, how tall will it be after 6 weeks?

_____

13. The third plant is planted in the same soil as the others, but it receives only light and water. After 2 weeks, it is 6 centimeters tall. If it continues growing at this rate, how tall will it be after 6 weeks?

_____

(MP) **Use Repeated Reasoning** In Problems 14–16, a point is given that lies on a line passing through the origin. Identify four additional points that lie on the line. Include two points with positive coordinates and two points with negative coordinates.

14. (17, 51) _____

15. (72, 18) _____

16. (−8, −5) _____

17. A line passes through (6, 3), (8, 4), and $(n, -2)$. Find the value of n.

_____

18. A line passes through (−2, 4), (−4, 8), and $(n, -4)$. Find the value of n.

_____

 I'm in a Learning Mindset!

How was finding additional points that lie on a line an appropriate challenge for me?

_____

_____

Explain Slope with Similar Triangles

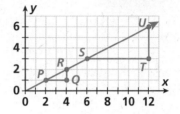
Use the graph to answer Problems 1–4.

1. How is △PQR related to △STU?

_____

2. Describe a sequence of transformations that maps △PQR onto △STU.

_____

_____

3. Identify one pair of corresponding angles and describe what you know about them.

_____

4. What is the ratio of the length of the vertical side to the length of the horizontal side of each triangle? What is the slope of the line?

_____

5. (MP) **Model with Mathematics** A person casts a shadow that aligns with the shadow of a tree. The person is 5.5 feet tall, and casts a shadow 8.25 feet long. The tree's shadow measures 22.5 feet long.

   A. Write an equation you can use to find the tree's height.

   _____

   B. How tall is the tree? How far is the person standing from the tree?

   _____

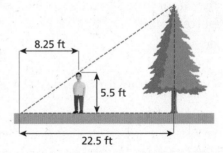

8.25 ft

5.5 ft

22.5 ft

6. **Open Ended** Explain how it is possible to find the slope of a line given any two points on the line.

_____

_____

_____

_____

_____

_____

Test Prep

7. A line passes through the origin, (3, 5), and (−12, b). What is the value of b?

  (A) −20　　　　　　　　　　(C) −7

  (B) −10　　　　　　　　　　(D) 20

8. A line passes through the origin and (8, 2). Select all points that lie on this line.

  (A) (−8, −2)　　　　　　　(D) (−1, 1)

  (B) (−4, −1)　　　　　　　(E) (16, 4)

  (C) (−2, −8)　　　　　　　(F) (40, 10)

9. A line passes through the origin, (−1, 1), and (4, n). Find the value of n.

  n = ☐

Spiral Review

10. Find the value of x. Then find the measure of each angle.

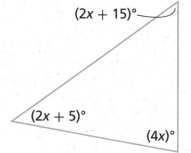

11. Ben can buy 5 notebooks for $6.75 at Store A or 3 notebooks for $4.50 at Store B. Which store offers the better value?

12. Describe a transformation that maps ABCD onto A′B′C′D′.

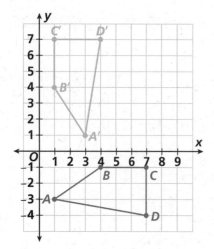

Name _____

Derive $y = mx$

(I Can) write the equation of a line given a graph or a table of values.

Spark Your Learning

Asiah's literature class is studying a new book. To complete the assigned reading on time, she has made a schedule. Asiah records her progress in a graph. What can you interpret from the graph?

Asiah's Reading Progress

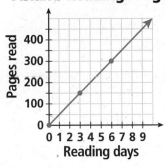

 Turn and Talk How would the graph look differently if she read more pages per day?

Build Understanding

 Use the graph of Asiah's reading to answer the following questions.

A. The number of pages that Asiah has cumulatively read increases by

$\boxed{}\dfrac{\text{pages}}{1\text{ day}}$.

B. The graph shows the number of pages that Asiah has read at the end of each day. Complete the table, including a general expression for the number of pages Asiah will read in *x* days.

Asiah's Reading Progress	
Reading days	**Pages read**
1	
2	
4	
7	
x	

C. Use the variable *y* to stand for the number of pages that Asiah has read. Write an equation to model the number of pages read after *x* days.

_____

D. From the point at 1 day to the point at 2 days, how much does the graph rise?

_____

E. What is the slope, or rise over run, for Asiah's graph? Explain your reasoning.

_____

F. How is the slope related to the unit rate of this proportional relationship?

_____

G. Look at the equation from Part C. What do you notice about the equation when you compare it to the slope from Part E?

_____

_____

H. Asiah decides she wants to adjust her schedule so she will finish the book earlier than the due date. How will this change the slope? Explain your reasoning.

_____

_____

_____

Name _____

Step It Out

2   Don is a gifted wood carver, and he has started selling his wood carvings online. He tracks the total number of carvings sold.

Months in business	Carvings sold
2	5
6	15
8	20

A. The ratios of carvings sold to months in business are / are not equal for each row in the table. The relationship between the number of months in business and the number of carvings sold is / is not a proportional relationship.

B. Sketch a graph of the relationship described by the table. Explain how the line supports your conclusion from Part A.

The graph of the relationship is / is not a straight line passing through the origin, so the relationship is / is not proportional.

Don's Carving Business

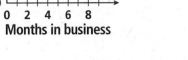

C. Complete the rise over run to find the slope of the line.

The slope is $\dfrac{}{}$.

D. Complete the linear equation to model Don's sales.

$y = \dfrac{}{} x$

> **Connect to Vocabulary**
>
> A **linear equation** is an equation whose solutions form a straight line on a coordinate plane.

E. Use the graph to predict the number of carvings sold after being in business for 10 months.

_____

F. Use the equation to predict the number of months needed for Don to sell 30 carvings online.

_____

© Houghton Mifflin Harcourt Publishing Company

Module 5 • Lesson 2

147

3   A digital thermometer records the temperature each hour. The graph shows how the temperature T has been changing each hour h.

Temperature Readings

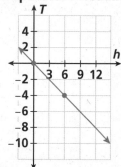

A. Describe how the temperature changes from midnight, $h = 0$, to 3 AM.

The temperature drops ☐ °C.

B. Between $h = 0$ and $h = 3$, describe the rise and run of the graph.

The rise is ☐ and the run is ☐.

C. Use the rise over run to write the slope of the graph.

The slope is _____.

D. Write an equation of the line in the form $T = mh$.

Turn and Talk A line is modeled by the equation $y = mx$. Explain how the value of m affects the graph of the line.

Check Understanding

1. The Nguyen family is traveling cross-country, driving 300 miles each day. Let x represent the number of days in the trip and let y represent the total number of miles driven. Write an equation to model their trip.

2. Write the equation for the line passing through points (0, 0), (4, 5), and (8, 10).

148

On Your Own

3. (MP) **Reason** A clothing store is going out of business. To sell their remaining inventory, the managers drop the price of each item $5 at the end of each week until the item sells.

   A. After 5 weeks, how will the price of an item have changed?

   _____

   B. A line is drawn to model the relationship between the number of weeks and the change in price. Is the slope of this line positive or negative? Explain.

   _____

   C. Write the equation of the line.

   _____

4. A line passes through the origin, (5, −15), and (−1, 3).

   A. Explain how to find the slope of the line.

   _____

   _____

   _____

   B. What happens to the *y*-values on the line as *x* increases?

   _____

For Problems 5–8, write the equation of the line shown.

5.

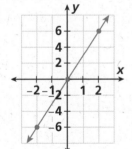

6.

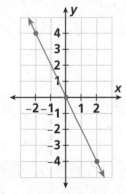

7.

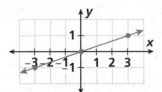

8.

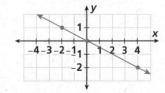

For Problems 9–10, sketch the graph of the line represented by the equation. Plot and label three points on each line.

9. $y = \frac{5}{3}x$

10. $y = -\frac{1}{4}x$

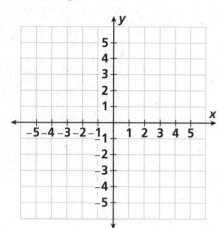

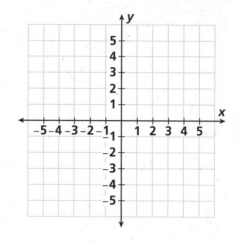

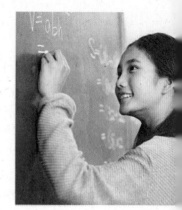

For Problems 11–12, write an equation that models the relationship shown in the table.

11.

x	y
−6	14
−3	7
3	−7
6	−14

12.

x	y
−8	−4
−4	−2
6	3
10	5

For Problems 13–14, write an equation for the line described.

13. a line passing through the origin and (−2.5, 5)

14. a line passing through the origin and (3*a*, 5*g*)

 I'm in a Learning Mindset!

What challenge did I face when writing an equation that modeled the relationship in the table for Problem 12?

Derive $y = mx$

1. Sean tutors math students to earn extra money.

   A. How much would Sean earn from 4 hours of tutoring?

   _____

   B. Write an equation to model Sean's earnings, y, after x hours.

   _____

> Sean charges $20 per hour.

2. (MP) **Attend to Precision** An inch is exactly 2.54 centimeters. Write an equation to convert the number of inches x to the corresponding length in centimeters.

   _____

3. Write an equation of the line passing through the points $(-5, -25)$, $(0, 0)$, and $(3, 15)$.

   _____

4. **Math on the Spot** The graph shows the distance Caleb runs over time.

   A. Identify four points on the line.

   _____

   B. Determine the slope of the line.

   _____

   C. Write an equation of the line.

   _____

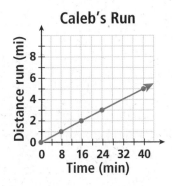

Caleb's Run

5. Sketch the graph of the line $y = 4x$.

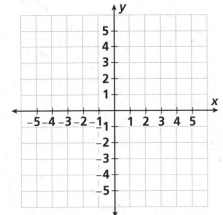

6. Write an equation that models the relationship shown in the table.

x	y
12	-9
8	-6
20	-15
32	-24

_____

Test Prep

7. What is the equation of the line passing through the points $(-2, 5)$, $(0, 0)$, and $(4, -10)$?

Ⓐ $y = -\frac{5}{2}x$

Ⓒ $y = \frac{2}{5}x$

Ⓑ $y = -\frac{2}{5}x$

Ⓓ $y = \frac{5}{2}x$

8. Write the equation of the line passing through the points $(0, 0)$, $(2, 1)$, and $(-2, -1)$.

$y = \boxed{} x$

9. The value of a house has been increasing by $5000 each year. Write an equation to show how the value will have changed x years from now.

$y = \boxed{} x$

10. Graph $y = \frac{2}{3}x$.

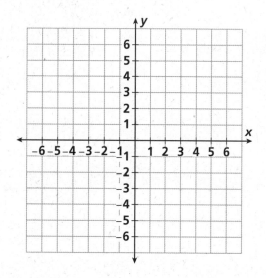

Spiral Review

11. Triangle ABC has vertices $(1, 4)$, $(5, 6)$, and $(3, 10)$. It is reflected across the y-axis, forming Triangle $A'B'C'$. What are the vertices of the new triangle?

_____

12. Quadrilateral $ABCD$ is dilated by a scale factor of 2, with the center of dilation at the origin. The vertices of $ABCD$ are $A(0, 0)$, $B(5, 0)$, $C(5, 3)$, and $D(0, 3)$. What are the coordinates of the image of Vertex C under the dilation?

_____

13. Solve the equation $3x - 2(x + 1) = 2x - 7$.

_____

Name _____

Interpret and Graph Proportional Relationships

I Can graph proportional relationships from a table or equation, calculate the unit rate, and determine whether the graph should be continuous or discrete.

Spark Your Learning

An airplane is traveling toward its destination at a constant speed. The distance that the airplane has traveled at different points in time is shown in the table. How can you find the speed of the airplane?

Commercial Plane	
Time (h)	Distance (mi)
0	0
1	400
2	800
3	1200

Turn and Talk Discuss how you found the speed of the airplane. How were the tools helpful?

Build Understanding

1 ▸ The Commercial Plane table in Spark Your Learning shows data that can be graphed on a coordinate plane, where *x* is the time passed and *y* is the distance traveled.

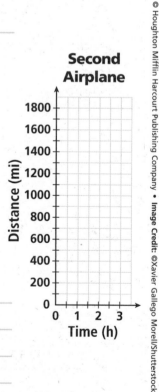

A. One of the points is (4, 1600). Describe what this point represents.

_____

_____

B. The airplane travels at a constant rate, so the relationship between distance and time is proportional. You already know that the unit rate of a proportional relationship can be calculated from any point on a graph of the relationship.

Use the point (3, 1200) to calculate the number of miles that the airplane travels per hour. Show your work.

_____

C. A second airplane starts from the same airport and is traveling at a different constant speed. After 4 hours the second airplane has flown 2100 miles from the airport. Calculate the number of miles that the second airplane traveled per hour. Show your work.

_____

D. Complete the table to show the distance that the second airplane has traveled at different points in time. Graph the points on the coordinate plane.

Second Airplane	
Time (h)	**Distance (mi)**
0	
1	
3	

E. What can you conclude about the distance that the two airplanes will have traveled after 8 hours?

_____

_____

_____

 Turn and Talk Predict how the graph of the second airplane's travel will compare to the graph of the first. What will be the same and what will be different?

Step It Out

2 A fish tank is filling at a constant rate. The equation modeling the amount of water in the tank is $y = 5x$, where y represents the amount of water in gallons and x represents the amount of time passed in minutes. Use the equation to complete the table.

Time passed: 0 minutes   Time passed: 4 minutes

A. Substitute 1 for x in the equation to find the amount of water in the tank after 1 minute.

$y = 5 \left(\boxed{} \right)$

$y = \boxed{}$

Enter your answer in the table.

Fish Tank	
Time (min)	Water (gal)
0	
1	
2.5	
5	

B. Substitute the remaining values for x in the equation and complete the table.

C. Graph the points from the table.

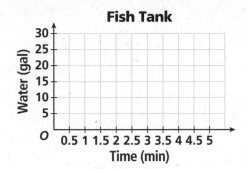

Fish Tank

D. Describe what the point (4.5, 22.5) represents.

After _____ minutes, the tank contains _____ gallons.

© Houghton Mifflin Harcourt Publishing Company

You have used a continuous graph to represent situations, such as an airplane's distance traveled. A **discrete graph** is a graph made of unconnected points. It represents data that only make sense at certain points.

> **Connect to Vocabulary**
>
> A **continuous graph** is a graph made up of connected points or curves.

3 The table shows how much a tailor charges to hem different numbers of shirts.

Tailor	
Shirts	Cost ($)
0	0
1	20
2	40
3	60

A. Would it make sense for the table to include the cost of hemming 2.5 shirts? Explain.

_____

_____

B. Graph the ordered pairs from the table. Decide whether or not to connect the points with a solid line. Should the graph be discrete or continuous? Why?

_____

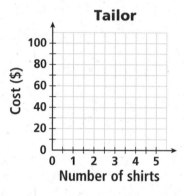

C. How many shirts can a customer have hemmed with $10? With $50?

_____

Check Understanding

A grain silo is filling at a constant rate. The amount of grain in the silo is given in the following table. Use the table to answer Problems 1–2.

Grain Silo	
Time (min)	Grain (T)
0	0
10	50
30	150
40	200
55	275

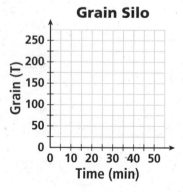

Grain Silos

1. A. Graph the points in the table. Connect the points with a line if appropriate.

B. Should the graph be discrete or continuous? Why?

_____

_____

2. What is the unit rate per minute at which the grain silo fills?

_____

On Your Own

3. (MP) **Attend to Precision** A printer is printing pages at a constant rate. The table shows the time the printer takes to print different numbers of pages.

Printer	
Complete pages printed	Time (s)
0	0
1	2
3	6
4	8

A. Graph the ordered pairs from the table.

B. Did you represent the situation with a discrete graph or a continuous graph? Why?

_____

_____

_____

C. What does the point (3, 6) represent on the graph?

_____

D. Why are the complete pages printed the independent variable?

_____

_____

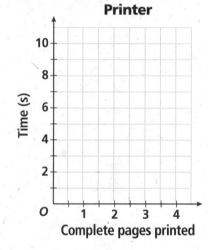

(MP) **Construct Arguments** For each relationship, decide whether you would represent it with a discrete graph or a continuous graph. Explain your reasoning.

4. a graph of the cost of shipping different numbers of identical packages

_____

5. a graph of the amount of fuel remaining in a car's gas tank while driving

_____

6. a graph of how many students can be transported by different numbers of buses

_____

7. **Model with Mathematics** An elevator is ascending at a constant rate. The height of the elevator from the ground over time is given by $y = 4x$, where x represents the amount of time passed in seconds and y represents the height of the elevator in feet.

A. Use the equation to complete the following table.

Elevator	
Time (sec)	**Height (ft)**
0	
1	
3	
4	

B. Graph the height of the elevator in terms of the amount of time that has passed.

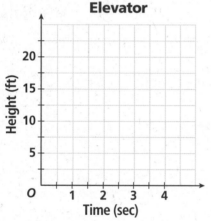

C. Did you draw a discrete graph or a continuous graph?

_____

D. Look at the point on the graph at (1, 4). Describe what this point represents.

_____

_____

 I'm in a Learning Mindset!

How can I modify the task of interpreting and graphing proportional relationships to maintain an appropriate level of challenge?

_____

_____

LESSON 5.3
**More Practice/
Homework**

ONLINE
Ⓔ Ed Video Tutorials and
Interactive Examples

Interpret and Graph Proportional Relationships

1. (MP) **Attend to Precision** A faucet is dripping water at a constant rate. The number of drops that the faucet has produced is given in the table:

Faucet	
Drops	**Time (sec)**
0	0
1	30
2	60
3	90

A. Graph the number of drops that drip over time.

B. Is your graph discrete or continuous? Explain.

_____

_____

_____

C. How long does it take for 12 drops to fall?

_____

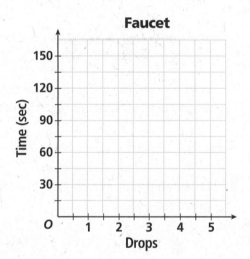

2. **Open Ended** Explain how the unit rate of a proportional relationship relates to the slope of its graph. Give a quantitative example.

_____

_____

_____

3. **STEM** The mass of a substance is equal to its density times its volume. The volume that a mass of water occupies is shown in the given table. Graph the relationship.

Water	
Mass (g)	**Volume (cm³)**
0	0
1	1
2	2
3	3
4	4

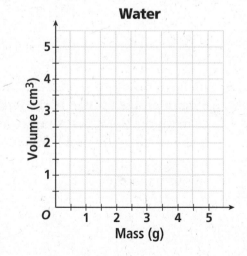

Test Prep

4. The cost of gas on a particular day is given by the equation $y = 3x$, where x is the amount of gas purchased in gallons and y represents the cost in dollars. Use the equation to complete the table and to graph the cost versus gallons purchased.

Cost of Gas	
Gas (gallons)	Cost ($)
0	
1	
2	
3	
4	

Cost of Gas

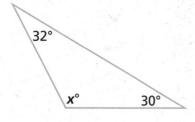

5. A graph showing the distance a person has walked over time is an example of a continuous / discrete graph.

Spiral Review

6. In the diagram, which two pairs of angles are alternate interior angles?

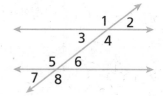

_____

7. Write and solve an equation to find the value of x.

32°

$x°$ 30°

_____

8. Juana and Andy completed 20 math problems total. Juana completed 6 more problems than Andy. Write an equation to determine the number of math problems that Andy completed, then solve the equation. How many of the math problems did Andy complete?

_____

_____

Name _____

Compare Proportional Relationships

Lincoln	
Time (h)	Distance (mi)
0	0
0.5	4.5
1	9

(I Can) identify and compare proportional
relationships presented in different ways.

Step It Out

1 ▷ Three friends, Brooklyn, Lincoln, and Taylor,
competed in a race over the weekend.
Which runner ran the fastest?

A. Choose a point in the table and use it to
calculate the pace, in miles per hour, at
which Lincoln ran.

_____

_____

_____

Brooklyn
Brooklyn ran at
a rate of 7 miles
per hour.

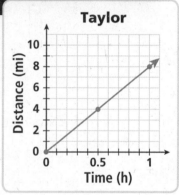

B. Taylor's pace is the same as the unit rate,
which can be calculated by dividing the
y-coordinate by the *x*-coordinate. Find a
point on the graph and use it to calculate
the pace, in miles per hour, at which
Taylor ran.

_____

_____

_____

C. The unit rates you found can now be compared to the rate at which
Brooklyn ran. Which runner ran the fastest? Complete the following
sentences.

Brooklyn ran at a rate of _____ miles per hour.

_____ ran the fastest because his/her rate is the fastest at _____
miles per hour.

 Turn and Talk If you were going to present each runner's rate in the same
way for 3 hours, which representation—graph, table, or verbal description—
would you choose? Why?

2 A sailboat and a motorboat each are traveling at a constant rate. The sailboat's speed is summarized in the graph. The motorboat's distance in terms of time is represented by the equation $y = 60x$, where x is the time in hours and y is the distance traveled in miles. Compare the speeds of the two boats.

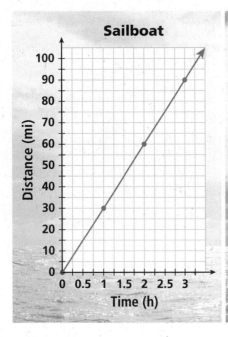

Sailboat

A. Determine the unit rate for the sailboat.

After traveling 1 hour, the sailboat has gone _____ miles, so the

unit rate of the sailboat is _____ miles per hour.

B. Determine the unit rate for the motorboat. Substitute 1 hour into the equation $y = 60x$ and solve for the distance traveled.

$y = 60\ ($_____$)$

$y =$ _____

The unit rate of the motorboat is _____ miles per hour.

C. Which boat traveled faster? How do you know?

_____

D. If you were to graph the motorboat's progress on the same axes as the sailboat's progress, would the motorboat's line be steeper or less steep than the sailboat's line? Why?

_____

 Turn and Talk How would you need to change the graph if you wanted to represent the progress of both boats over 3 hours on the same graph?

3 ▶ A grocery store and a street vendor are each selling bananas by the pound. You can buy 2 pounds of bananas from a street vendor for $1.62. The cost of bananas at a grocery store is shown in the photo.

A. Complete the table.

$0.79
PER POUND

Grocery Store	
Bananas (lb)	Cost ($)
1	$0.79
2	
3	
5	
8	

B. Find the cost of a pound of bananas from the street vendor.

$$\frac{\$\boxed{}}{\boxed{}\ \text{pounds}} = \frac{\$x}{1\ \text{pound}}$$

The unit rate is $ _____ per pound.

C. Five pounds of bananas cost $5\left(\$\boxed{}\right)$, or $ $\boxed{}$.

D. The ⬚ grocery store / street vendor ⬚ is selling bananas at the lower price.

If you purchase 5 pounds of bananas, you save _____ purchasing bananas for the lower price.

Check Understanding

Use the information to answer Problems 1–2.

The height of a hot air balloon over time is given in the following table.

Hot Air Balloon	
Time (min)	Height (ft)
0	0
2	1200
3	1800
6	3600

The height of a blimp over time is given by $y = 250x$, where y represents the height in feet and x represents the time in minutes.

1. How fast is the hot air balloon rising? How fast is the blimp rising?

_____

2. Is the hot air balloon or the blimp rising faster? By how much?

_____

_____

On Your Own

Use the information to answer Problems 3–8.

A researcher recorded facts about the flight of a duck, a crow, and a seagull. The duck's rate of flight was 20 miles per hour.

Duck

Crow

Seagull

Crow	
Time (h)	**Distance (mi)**
0	0
0.5	12
1	24

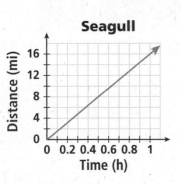

Seagull

3. Did the crow fly at a constant rate? How do you know?

_____

4. Did the seagull fly at a constant rate? How do you know?

_____

5. How fast did the crow fly? How fast did the seagull fly?

_____

6. **A.** Complete the following sentences.

   The duck flew at a rate of _____ miles per hour.

   Did the seagull or the duck fly at a faster rate? _____

   Did the crow or the duck fly at a faster rate? _____

   B. The _____ flew the fastest.

7. After 5 hours of flight, how much farther would the fastest bird have traveled than the slowest bird?

_____

8. What does (0, 0) represent for each of the birds?

_____

© Houghton Mifflin Harcourt Publishing Company • **Image Credits:** (tr) ©Justin Lo/Moment/Getty Images; (cr) ©Mark Miller Photos/Oxford Scientific/Getty Images; (br) ©Seleznov Oleksandr/Shutterstock

9. (MP) **Reason** A rain barrel and a cistern are filling at constant rates. The amount of water in the rain barrel over time is shown in the graph. The amount of water in the cistern is given by $y = 200x$, where x is the time in hours and y is gallons of water.

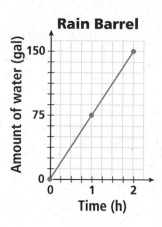

Rain Barrel

A. How fast is the rain barrel filling? How fast is the cistern filling?

_____

B. If both the barrel and the cistern were empty at $t = 0$, which would completely fill first? Explain.

_____

_____

_____

10. A video downloads at a constant rate given by $y = 5x$, where y represents the percent of the file downloaded and x represents the time in seconds. A game's download progress is shown in the table.

Game Progress	
Time (sec)	Percent downloaded
0	0%
2	40%
3	60%

A. At what rate is the game downloading? How long does it take to download the game?

_____

B. At what rate is the video downloading? How long does it take to download the video?

_____

C. The size of a digital file can be measured in megabytes ("MB"). If the video is 200 MB and the game is 100 MB, what are the download speeds of the two files?

_____

_____

11. The graph shows Peg's progress on a walking trail, showing the distance from the start of the trail she has walked over time. Her friend Raj travels along the same walking trail.

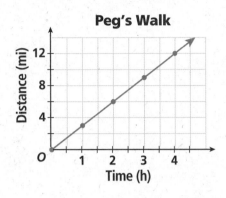

Peg's Walk

Raj walks at 2.5 miles per hour.

A. How fast is Peg walking?

_____

B. (MP) **Use Structure** Complete the table.

Time (h)	Raj's distance (mi)	Peg's distance (mi)
0		
1		
2		
3		

C. If Peg and Raj started at the same time from the same place on the

trail, they are _____ miles apart after 3 hours.

D. After how many hours will Peg and Raj be 2 miles apart?

_____

12. Financial Literacy Romeo is buying granola. He can either buy it in bulk for $4.50 per pound, or he can buy a box that contains 1.25 pounds of granola for $6.

A. What is the cost per pound for each granola option?

_____

_____

B. How much does he save buying 2.5 pounds in bulk?

_____

C. How many pounds would he have to buy in order to save $3.00?

_____

Compare Proportional Relationships

1. **Financial Literacy** Hal's Hardware and Sal's Supermarket are both selling light bulbs.

A. (MP) **Use Structure** Complete the table.

Hal's Hardware	
Light bulbs	**Cost ($)**
1	
2	$2.08
3	
4	$4.16

SAL'S

Brilliant
Savings!

3
for
$4.26

3 Lightbulbs

3 Lightbulbs

B. Calculate the unit price of light bulbs at Sal's Supermarket.

_____

C. What is the cost of 6 light bulbs at each store?

_____

D. Compare the cost of 9 light bulbs from Sal's Supermarket to the cost of 9 light bulbs at Hal's Hardware. Which store is selling light bulbs at a lower unit price? How much less does it cost to purchase 9 light bulbs from that store?

_____

_____

_____

2. A coffee maker and a juice maker are making beverages. The rate at which the coffee is being made is given by $y = 6x$, where y represents the amount of coffee in mL and x represents the time passed in seconds. The amount of juice that has been made at different times is summarized in the table.

A. At what rate is the coffee maker making coffee?

_____

B. At what rate is the juice maker making juice?

_____

C. Is juice or coffee being made at a faster rate?

_____

Time (s)	Juice (mL)
0	0
1	8
2	16
3	24

Test Prep

3. A spider is crawling at a constant rate of 0.4 centimeters per second. The distance that a ladybug has walked over time is summarized in the table. The | spider / ladybug | is traveling at a faster rate.

Ladybug	
Time (s)	Distance traveled (cm)
2	1
3	1.5
4	2

4. The rate at which a mountain is eroding is given by $y = 0.5x$, where y represents the amount of erosion in millimeters and x represents the amount of time in years. A field is eroding at a rate of 2 millimeters per year. Is the field or the mountain eroding at a faster rate? By how much?

_____

5. A baker is baking muffins and a loaf of fruit bread. The bread is rising at a rate of 0.03 inch per minute. The amount that the muffins have risen from their initial size at different points of baking time is given on the graph.

The | loaf of bread / muffins | rise(s) at a faster rate.

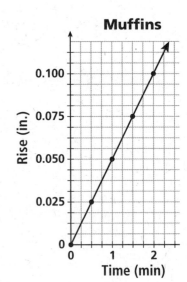

6. The unit rate of the proportional relationship

$y = 2x$ is _____.

(A) y

(B) $\frac{2}{1}$

(C) x

(D) $\frac{1}{2}$

7. A bumblebee visits 14 flowers in 38 minutes to collect pollen. A butterfly's progress in visiting flowers is shown in the table. Which insect is visiting flowers at a faster rate? _____

Butterfly	
Flowers visited	Time (minutes)
7	21
14	42
126	378

Spiral Review

8. Is the graph of the distance a person has driven over time an example of a continuous or discrete graph? _____

9. Solve $3x - 1 = 5$.

_____

10. Solve $4(2 + x) = 6 + 6x$.

_____

Vocabulary

Choose the correct term from the box to complete each sentence.

Vocabulary
continuous
discrete
rise
hypotenuse
leg
run

1. In a right triangle, the _____ is the side opposite the right angle, and a _____ is one of the sides that forms the right angle.

2. The slope of a non-vertical line is the ratio of the _____ to the _____ between any two points on the line.

3. The graph of the relationship between the time a train travels and the distance it travels at a constant speed would be a _____ graph.

Concepts and Skills

4. Which of these can be used to show that the slope of a non-vertical line is the same anywhere along the line?

   (A) acute triangles

   (B) obtuse triangles

   (C) right triangles

   (D) any triangles

5. (MP) **Use Tools** The table and the equation each show a proportional relationship between time x, in seconds, and distance y, in meters. Who would finish a 100-meter race faster? How much faster? State what strategy and tool you will use to answer the question, explain your choice, and then find the answer.

Lauren's Run: $y = 8x$

Amani's Run	
Time (s)	Distance (m)
3	18
5	30
8	48

6. The graph shows right triangles △ABC and △ADE. The hypotenuse of each triangle lies on the same line.

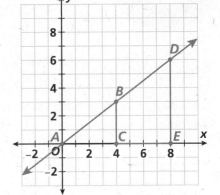

A. Explain how you know that the triangles are similar.

_____

_____

_____

B. How does knowing the triangles are similar help you show that the slope of the line through the hypotenuses is constant?

_____

_____

_____

_____

7. The graph of a proportional relationship is shown.

Kai's Earnings

A. What is the amount Kai earns per hour?

$ _____ per hour

B. Write an equation that relates Kai's earnings y, in dollars, to x, the number of hours he works.

_____

8. The coordinates of two points are given in the table. Complete the table by giving the coordinates of a third point collinear with the first two points.

x	y
0	0
5	4

9. A fire hose sprays 2 gallons of water every 1.5 seconds.

Water Sprayed by Hose

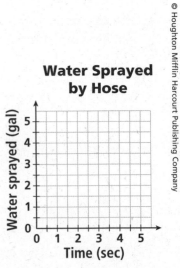

A. Model the relationship between the time in seconds and the amount of water sprayed in gallons with a graph.

B. At what rate is the hose spraying water, in gallons per second? Use numbers from the box to show the rate in simplest form. Write a number in each box.

Rate:

0 1 2 3 4 5 6 7 8 9

Name _____

Understand and Graph Functions

(**I Can**) graph a function given a table, and identify a function given a table or a graph.

Spark Your Learning

Gina is purchasing a mobile device. The graph represents Gina's total cost of owning a device for the first year. What can you interpret about her costs from the graph?

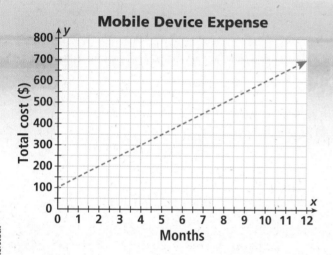

Mobile Device Expense

x	y

Turn and Talk The graph shows the cost for 12 months. How can you determine the cost for 13 or more months?

Build Understanding

A **function** is a rule that assigns exactly one output to each input. Multiple inputs may have the same output value, but one input value may not have multiple output values.

The set of all possible **input** values of a function is the **domain**. The set of all possible **output** values of a function is the **range**.

1 ▶ **A.** Gina's cost, rounded to the nearest dollar, to operate a mobile device is a function. Gina's cost accumulates over the number of months she has the account, so months are the input for the function. Since the function's domain is defined by its input, what is the domain of this function? Why?

_____

_____

_____

B. The total cost is the output of the function, which is the function's range. What is the range of the function? Why?

_____

_____

C. Gina's plan includes up to 50 free texts in the monthly fee. Does this table show a function? Explain.

Month	1	2	3	4	5	6
Texts used	41	26	32	35	37	43

_____

_____

D. The number of texts for month 5 is accidentally changed to be the same as for month 4. Does the table show a function? Explain.

Month	1	2	3	4	5	6
Texts used	41	26	32	35	35	43

_____

_____

E. If the 2 in the Month row is accidentally changed to a 1, does the table show a function? Explain.

Month	1	1	3	4	5	6
Texts used	41	26	32	35	33	43

_____

_____

 Turn and Talk Explain in your own words the difference between a function and a relation.

Step It Out

2 ▸ Erin is taking a taxi to a destination no more than 10 miles away. The cost of the taxi ride is $6.00 to be picked up and an additional $2.00 per mile (prorated for partial miles).

Miles	0	2	4	6	8	10
Cost ($)	6	10	14	18	22	26

A. Describe the domain.

The domain is the number of miles from

_____ to _____.

B. Describe the range.

The minimum charge is the charge for

0 miles, _____. The cost for 10 miles is _____.

The range is the numbers of dollars from

_____ to _____.

C. The *x*-axis scale is based on the ⬚domain / range⬚ and should include

values from _____ to _____. The *y*-axis scale is based on the

⬚domain / range⬚ and should include values from _____ to _____.

D. Plot the data in the table on the coordinate grid using the values in the table as ordered pairs, and draw a line through the plotted points. Miles are the input to the function and represented as *x*, and cost is the output of the function and represented by *y* in the ordered pair.

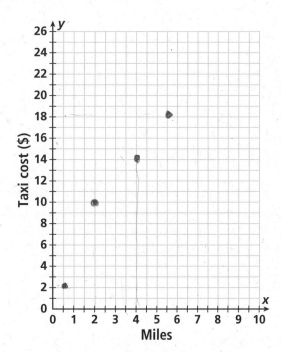

E. If Erin's taxi ride is 7 miles, how much will the taxi ride cost? Explain.

_____

_____

 Turn and Talk If Erin paid $24, how many miles was her taxi ride? Explain.

The **vertical line test** can help determine whether a graph is a function or not by visually identifying where a single domain value is associated with more than one range value. If any vertical line can be drawn that passes through the graph more than once, the graph is not a function.

3 For each plot, use the vertical line test to determine whether the plot shows a function. If the plot is not a function, draw a vertical line that intersects more than one point on the graph.

A.

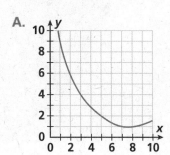

The graph ⏐ is / is not ⏐ a function.

B.

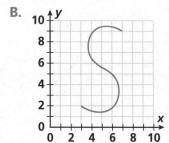

The graph ⏐ is / is not ⏐ a function.

C.

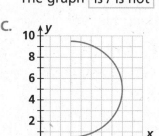

The graph ⏐ is / is not ⏐ a function.

D.

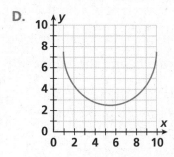

The graph ⏐ is / is not ⏐ a function.

Check Understanding

1. The function plotted represents the path of an object launched into the air. The object rises, then falls to the ground. From the graph, what are the domain, the range, and the coordinates of the points indicated on the graph?

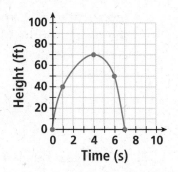

Domain: _____

Range: _____

Coordinates: _____

2. Does the oval graph represent a function? Why or why not?

_____

_____

_____

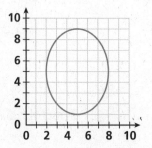

Name _____

LESSON 6.1
**More Practice/
Homework**

ONLINE

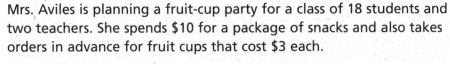

Video Tutorials and
Interactive Examples

Understand and Graph Functions

Use the information to answer Problems 1–3.

Mrs. Aviles is planning a fruit-cup party for a class of 18 students and two teachers. She spends $10 for a package of snacks and also takes orders in advance for fruit cups that cost $3 each.

1. Describe the domain of the function both in words and numbers.

_____

_____

2. What is the range of the function?

_____

3. Plot the data shown in the table on the coordinate plane. If the data are continuous, draw a solid line through the plotted points.

Fruit Cup Orders	0	5	10	15	20
Cost ($)	10	25	40	55	70

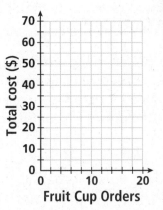

Use the graph to answer Problems 4–5.

4. (MP) **Construct Arguments** Does the graph represent a function? Explain.

_____

_____

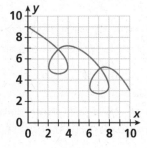

5. Name a section of the graph that, taken in isolation, is a function.

_____

_____

6. **Open Ended** Draw a graph that does not represent a function.

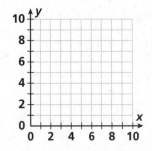

© Houghton Mifflin Harcourt Publishing Company • Image Credit: ©Oleksandra Naumenko/Shutterstock

Test Prep

7. Athar is buying hats for his baseball team. The shipping charge is $5, and each hat costs $8. There are ten people on his baseball team. The graph shows the total cost of the hats. Select all true statements.

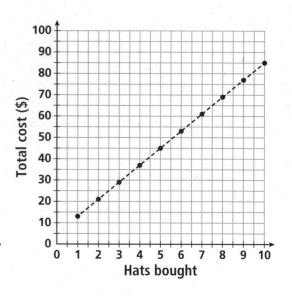

(A) The ordered pair for 1 hat bought is (1, 8).

(B) The domain is whole numbers of hats from 1 to 10.

(C) The range is numbers of dollars from 0 to 100 in increments of 5.

(D) The ordered pair for 5 hats bought is (5, 45).

(E) The cost of ordering 10 hats is double the cost of ordering 5 hats.

8. An engineer is launching a rocket and is measuring its speed when launched. The table shows the speed for the first five seconds. Plot the data in the provided coordinate plane.

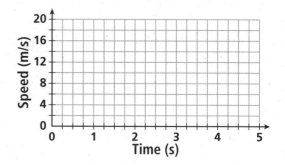

Time (s)	0	1	2	3	4	5
Speed (m/s)	0	4	8	12	16	20

Spiral Review

9. What is the unit rate for the proportional relationship represented in the graph?

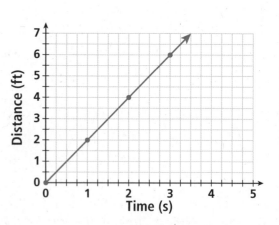

_____

10. If the slope of a proportional relationship is 3, what is the equation that represents that line?

_____

11. Gretchen is delivering boxes of cookies to her neighbors. Her wagon itself weighs 12 pounds when empty and will hold up to 9 boxes. If each box of cookies weighs 1 pound, what is the range of the total weight of her wagon while she is delivering cookies?

_____

_____

Name

Derive and Interpret $y = mx + b$

(I Can) derive the equation for a line in the form $y = mx + b$ given the slope of the line and a point.

Spark Your Learning

Based on data from a science experiment, Sierra graphs Lines *A*, *B*, and *C*. Compare the lines. How are the graphs the same? How are the graphs different?

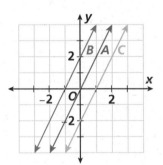

They have different equations

They have the same parralles.

x	y

 Turn and Talk What would be the equation of a line that passes through the origin and the point (1, −2)? Explain.

Build Understanding

1 ▶ The **y-intercept** of a graph is the *y*-coordinate of the point where the graph crosses the *y*-axis, or the value of *y* when *x* equals 0. A line that passes through the origin can be represented by an equation of the form $y = mx$.

A. Consider a line with slope *m* and *y*-intercept *b*. Write the ordered pair that represents the *y*-intercept.

_____

B. Recall that slope is rise over run, or the ratio of change in *y* to change in *x*. Complete the equation for the slope *m* of the line using the point from Part A and another point on the line (x, y).

$$m = \frac{y - \boxed{}}{\boxed{} - 0}$$

C. Solve the equation from Part B for *y*.

The $y = mx + b$ form of the equation of a line is called **slope-intercept form**.

D. Identify the slope and *y*-intercept of each graph.

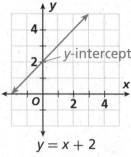

$y = x + 2$

slope: __0__

y-intercept: __2__

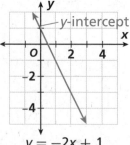

$y = -2x + 1$

slope: __-2__

y-intercept: __1__

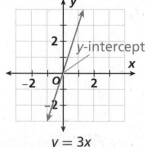

$y = 3x$

slope: __3__

y-intercept: __0__

E. How do the coefficient *m* of *x* and the constant *b* in each equation relate to the slope and *y*-intercept?

_____

_____

Step It Out

2   **A.** Is the slope of Line *A* positive or negative? Is the slope of Line *B* positive or negative?

A is postive and B is negatie.

B. Find the slope of each line.

Line *A*: $\boxed{1}$ Line *B*: $\boxed{-5}$

C. What are the *y*-intercepts of the lines?

2

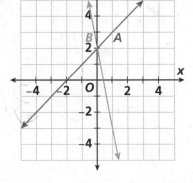

D. Write the equation of Line *A* in slope-intercept form.

$y = \boxed{1}\, x + \boxed{2}$

E. Write the equation of Line *B* in slope-intercept form.

$y = \boxed{-5}\, x + \boxed{2}$

3   A line has a slope $m = -1$. One point on the line is (2, 4). Substitute the *x*, *y*, and *m* values into the slope-intercept form of an equation to find the *y*-intercept. Then write the equation of the line in slope-intercept form.

$y = \boxed{4}\,, m = \boxed{-1}\,$, and $x = \boxed{2}$

$y = mx + b$

$\boxed{4} = -1\left(\boxed{2}\right) + b$

$\boxed{4} = \boxed{2} + b$

$\boxed{6} = b$

The *y*-intercept is ___b___.

The equation of the line is $y = \boxed{-1}\, x + \boxed{6}$.

 Turn and Talk Will the graph of $y = 3x - 3$ pass through the origin? If so, how do you know? If not, what is the *y*-intercept?

Linear functions contain only points that lie on a straight line. Some examples of nonlinear functions are:

$$yx = 5 \qquad y = \frac{2}{x} \qquad y = x^2 + 2$$

4 ▶ Solve each equation for y. Then determine whether the function is linear or nonlinear.

A. $5y = 13x - 9$

$y = \frac{13}{5}x - \frac{9}{5}$ linear

B. $\frac{y}{6} = 1$ (multiply)

$\frac{y}{6} = (1) 6 x + 0$ linear

C. $xy = 25$

$\frac{x}{x} \frac{25}{x}$ $y = \frac{25}{x}$ nonlinear

Nonlinear functions contain points that do not lie on a straight line with the other points. For example, the formula for the area of a square, $A = s^2$, is nonlinear because it contains the points (1, 1), (3, 9), and (4, 16), which do not all lie on a straight line.

○	$2y = 14x + 6$ divide both sides by 2 $y = 7x + 3$ **LINEAR**
○	$2xy = 36$ divide both sides by 2 $xy = 18$ divide both sides by x $y = \frac{18}{x}$ **NONLINEAR**

5 ▶ Graph three points for each equation on your own paper. Is the equation linear or nonlinear? List the 3 points you used.

A. $\frac{7}{2} = x - y$

B. $y = x^2 + x + 1$

C. $y - 3 = \frac{5x}{2}$

Check Understanding

$y = mx + b$
$m = $ slope -1
$b = y$-intercept
$\times 3$

1. The slope of a line is −3, and a point on the line is (4, −1). Can the equation of the line be expressed in slope-intercept form? If so, what is the equation? Does the line pass through the origin? How do you know?

$-1 = -3(4) + b \qquad -1 = -12 + b \qquad \boxed{y = -3x + 11}$
$\boxed{11 = b} \qquad +12 \qquad +12$

$y = -3x + 11$

2. Is the graph of $y = x^2 + 2$ a straight line? Explain.

Name _Vicky_

Derive and Interpret $y = mx + b$

1. (MP) **Reason** Tasha wants to graph a line that is parallel to the line with equation $y = 3x$. Give two examples of linear equations that represent lines she could draw: one that is above the original line and one that is below the original line.

    $y = 3x + 2$ $y = 3x - 2$

2. Shyann is trying to figure out if the line with equation $y = 5683x + 976$ will pass through the origin. Will the line pass through the origin? How do you know?

    No because y intercept is 976

ROBLa

3. Paulo identifies one point on a line as (6, 3), and he knows that the slope is 2. How can he derive the equation of the line?

    $y = 2x + 0$ slope is 2 $y =$
    intercept   15 because (6, 3)
    is   on the line.

    $y = mx + b$ $y = 2x + b$
    $x\ y$ to
    $(6, 3)$ $3 = 2x + b$
                    ↓
                 $3 = 2(6)$
                      b

4. **Math on the Spot** An arcade deducts 3.5 points from a 50-point game card for each game played. The linear equation $y = -3.5x + 50$ represents the number of points y on a card after x games played. Graph the equation using the slope and y-intercept.

    $y = 2x + b$ **Points on Game Card**

    $y = -3.5x + 50$

    $3 = 12 + b$
    $-12 \quad -12$
    $\boxed{-9 = b}$

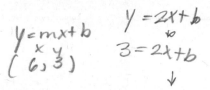

For Problems 5–6, write each equation in slope-intercept form and identify the y-intercept.

5. $5 = 10x - 5y$

6. $12x = -4y - 8$

For Problems 7–8, find the slope of the graph of the linear equation and indicate whether the graph rises or falls.

7. $y = 3x - 11$

8. $y = -\frac{1}{2}x + 2$

For Problems 9–10, identify the function as linear or nonlinear.

9. $y = \frac{3}{2}x + 9$

10. $y = \frac{3}{2x} + 9$

Test Prep

11. Find the equation of a line with slope -2 that contains the point $(-3, 3)$.

$y = \boxed{}\, x - \boxed{}$

For Problems 12–14, complete each statement for the equation $y = \frac{1}{2}x - \frac{1}{2}$.

12. Is the equation linear or nonlinear? _____

13. Is the equation a function? _____

14. The graph crosses the y-axis at $\left(0, \underline{} \right)$.

15. Roscoe has a pie baking business. His profit is given by the linear equation $y = 15x - 5$. Sheena has a cake baking business. Her profit is given by an equation with a graph that is parallel to the graph of the equation for Roscoe's profit. Which equation could be the equation for Sheena's business?

(A) $y = 15x + 10$ (C) $y = 5x - 5$

(B) $y = 3x - 1$ (D) $y = -15x - 3$

16. Identify whether each equation is linear or nonlinear.

	Linear	Nonlinear
$xy = 4$	☐	☐
$4 = x - y$	☐	☐
$y = \frac{5}{4}x + \frac{1}{2}$	☐	☐
$y = x^2 + 1$	☐	☐

Spiral Review

17. Mr. Chin asked his class to solve for y in the equation $8(3y - 5) = 9(y - 5) - 1$. Explain how to solve for y. Then solve.

_____

_____

18. Luna knows a line crosses the y-axis at $(0, -1)$. She also knows that the point $(3, 2)$ is on the line. What is the slope of this line?

_____

19. The slope of a line is 3. The point $(1, 4)$ is on the line. Is the point $(0, 1)$ on the line?

_____

Name _____

Interpret Rate of Change and Initial Value

(I Can) find and interpret initial value and rate of change.

Spark Your Learning

Bonnie has decided to join a gym for the next 3 months. Fabulous Fitness charges $45 per month. Greg's Gym charges $99 at the end of each quarter. How can she compare the two options to determine the better value?

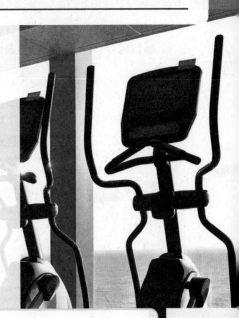

x	y

Turn and Talk What is the rate of change per month for each membership and how do you know?

Build Understanding

Many real-world functional relationships have only nonnegative inputs and rates of change that are constant. You can use initial value and the rate of change to analyze such functions. Initial value is the value of a function when the input is zero. A constant rate of change describes the slope or steepness of a graph, or how quickly two quantities change.

1 Bonnie continues to research gym options and finds out that Fabulous Fitness charges no sign-up fee, while Greg's Gym charges \$50 for the initial sign-up. She makes the following table to help her compare the two options.

Costs	FABULOUS FITNESS	GREG'S GYM
Sign-up fee	\$0	\$50
Month 1	\$45	\$0
Month 2	\$45	\$0
Month 3	\$45	\$99

A. How much would Bonnie need to pay just to join each gym?

FF is 0\$ and GG is 50\$
Just to Join each gym

B. How much would Bonnie need to pay per month at each gym?

Bonnie need to pay 45 at
FF and GG is 99\$ each.

C. Use an equation to calculate the total cost for three months of each gym option. Show your work.

3 months of each gym options.
5FF = 135 GG = 149

D. In the equation $y = mx + b$, the slope m represents the constant rate of change, or cost per month. What does the y-intercept b represent on the graph of the function?

y=mx+b , intercept
cost per month
m=45 x 3 b=0
Y=45x3+0

FF=45\$
x 3
=135
GG=
99
50=
99
x 1
99
+50
149

Turn and Talk Why is it important to consider both initial value and rate of change when modeling functions in the real world?

LESSON 6.3
**More Practice/
Homework**

ONLINE
Video Tutorials and
Interactive Examples
⊙Ed

Interpret Rate of Change and Initial Value

Use the information to answer Problems 1–2.

The following table shows the cost to order muffins to be delivered from a bakery.

Muffins	1	5	10	50	100
Cost ($)	17	25	35	115	215

$15 DELIVERY FEE

MUFFINS

1. (MP) **Use Structure** What is the rate of change, and what does it represent?

_____

_____

2. What is the initial value, and what does it represent?

_____

_____

Use the information to answer Problems 3–5.

The following linear function represents the cost of a home printer plus ink cartridges where *x* represents the number of ink cartridges purchased and *y* represents the total cost.

$$y = 25x + 115$$

3. What is the rate of change, and what does it represent?

_____

_____

4. How much does the printer itself cost?

_____

5. How much will the purchaser spend buying the printer and 6 ink cartridges?

_____

6. **Open Ended** Write a scenario that can be modeled by the linear function $y = 25x + 40$.

_____

_____

_____

Test Prep

7. Jose starts a savings account with $80. At the end of 6 months, the account has $350. Assuming there is a constant rate, how much did Jose save per month?

   (A) $270

   (B) $72

   (C) $60

   (D) $45

8. Camille wants to set up a hot chocolate stand to raise money. She spends $40 on hot chocolate and $0.25 for each paper cup. She uses the equation $y = 0.25x + 40$ to keep track of her spending. If Camille has $60 in donations to spend, what is the maximum number of paper cups she can buy?

   (A) 5 cups

   (B) 80 cups

   (C) 240 cups

   (D) 400 cups

9. Admission to a carnival costs $15. Each game costs $2 to play. Which statements about the function modeling the cost to attend the carnival are true? Select all that apply.

   (A) The slope is positive.

   (B) The initial value is $15.

   (C) The rate of change is $15.

   (D) The graph has a y-intercept of 2.

   (E) The graph passes through the origin.

Spiral Review

10. Solve $4x - 12 = -7x - 111$.

11. Calculate the slope of the line that passes through (3, 2) and (−7, 4).

12. The table shows a proportional relationship. Complete the table.

x	y
1	4
2	
3	12
5	20

Name _____

Construct Functions

5 feet per minute

(I Can) construct functions based on verbal descriptions, tables, and graphs.

Spark Your Learning

A scuba diver descends from the surface of the ocean at a constant rate of 5 feet per minute to a maximum depth of 130 feet. The diver's depth in feet y is a function of the number of minutes x since the diver began descending. What do you know about the function?

130 feet

x	y

 Turn and Talk Consider a function where x represents a number of people. Is this function discrete or continuous? What must be true of all x-values? Explain.

Build Understanding

1 ▸ The parking lot near the scuba company opens for the day at 6:00 a.m. Between 7:00 a.m. and 11:00 a.m., cars park at a constant rate of 50 per hour. At 10:00 a.m., 165 cars are parked in the lot. Write an equation that represents the situation in the form $y = mx + b$.

Parking Lot Hours
6 a.m.–10 p.m.

A. Write the ordered pair that represents 165 cars parked at 10:00 a.m. What does each coordinate of the point represent?

_____

_____

_____

B. What is the slope of the function? Use the slope and the point from Part A to find the y-intercept and write the equation of the line.

C. Can time be a fractional number? Why or why not?

_____

D. Can the number of cars be a fractional number? Explain.

_____

E. Is this function discrete or continuous? Why?

_____

_____

F. What are some restrictions for the possible values of y? Why?

_____

_____

_____

G. What are some restrictions for the possible values of x?

_____

H. What does the y-intercept of the function represent in this equation?

_____

Name _____

Step It Out

2 A factory produces mobile phones at a constant rate. The table shows four ordered pairs whose points exist on the graph of the function representing the factory's output. In the ordered pairs, x is the number of shifts worked and y is the number of mobile phones produced. Write the equation of the linear function that includes these points in the form $y = mx + b$.

(2, 240)
(5, 600)
(6, 720)
(8, 960)

A. Complete the sentence to describe how to find the slope of the graph of the function.

Find the change in ☐ -values divided by the change in ☐ -values.

B. Any two given points can be used to find the slope of the line. Use (2, 240) and (5, 600) to find the slope of the line.

$$m = \frac{600 - \boxed{}}{5 - \boxed{}}$$

$$= \frac{\boxed{}}{\boxed{}} = \boxed{}$$

C. Use the x- and y-values from (2, 240) and the slope from Part B to solve for the y-intercept b.

$$240 = \boxed{} (2) + b$$

$$\boxed{} = \boxed{} + b$$

$$b = \boxed{}$$

D. Write the equation of the line.

_____

E. Is this function discrete or continuous? Explain.

_____

_____

F. Are there any restrictions on the domain or range values? Explain.

_____

_____

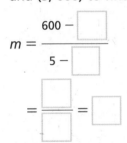

Turn and Talk Why does it make sense for the function to have a y-intercept of 0?

© Houghton Mifflin Harcourt Publishing Company • Image Credit: ©Wu Kailiang/Alamy

3 The following graph shows the weight of a newborn giant panda from birth to 16 months of age. Write the linear function in the form $y = mx + b$.

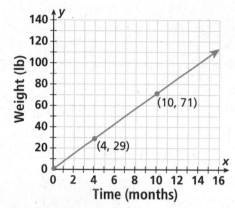

A. Use the points identified on the graph to find the slope of the line.

$$m = \frac{\boxed{} - \boxed{}}{\boxed{} - \boxed{}} = \frac{\boxed{}}{\boxed{}} = \boxed{}$$

B. Use the x- and y-values from any point to solve for the y-intercept b.

$$\boxed{} = 7\left(\boxed{}\right) + b$$

$$\boxed{} = \boxed{} + b$$

$$b = \boxed{}$$

C. Write the equation of the line.

_____

Check Understanding

1. Write a linear function with a slope of 4 that includes the point $(-1, 3)$.

_____

2. Write a function for the line that includes the points $(4, -5)$ and $(8, -7)$.

_____

3. Sullivan is filling a swimming pool and graphs the amount of water in the pool as a function over time. Explain whether the function is discrete or continuous.

_____

_____

On Your Own

Use the graph and information to answer Problems 4–9.

Bridget has 13 gallons of gasoline to use for her lawn-mowing business. She uses gasoline in the lawn mower at a constant rate. Let *x* represent the number of lawns mowed and *y* represent the amount of gasoline remaining. Look at the graph of this function. Construct the function for this scenario.

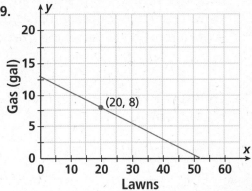

4. **(MP) Model with Mathematics** What is the equation of the line?

_____

5. What is the initial value of the function and what does it represent?

_____

_____

_____

6. What is the slope and what does it mean?

_____

_____

_____

7. **(MP) Reason** Is the function discrete or continuous? Why?

_____

_____

_____

_____

8. **(MP) Attend to Precision** What is the domain? Explain any restrictions.

_____

_____

_____

9. **(MP) Attend to Precision** What is the range? Explain any restrictions.

_____

_____

_____

10. (MP) **Model with Mathematics** Sabrina collects trading cards. She buys packages of 12 trading cards to add to her collection. After she adds 16 packages to her existing collection, she has a total of 274 cards. Write a function to model the size of Sabrina's collection.

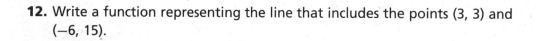

_____

11. Construct a linear function that represents the table of values shown.

x	y
4	−22
3	−17
−5	23

_____

12. Write a function representing the line that includes the points (3, 3) and (−6, 15).

_____

13. Write a linear function for the line with a slope of −5 that passes through the point (7, 3).

_____

14. (MP) **Reason** If you know one point on the graph of a line, what other piece of information do you need in order to construct the function representing that line in the form $y = mx + b$? Explain.

_____

_____

_____

_____

15. **Open Ended** The graph of a function passes through the point (2, 18). Choose another point on the graph and write the linear function representing those two points in the form $y = mx + b$.

_____

_____

© Houghton Mifflin Harcourt Publishing Company

 I'm in a Learning Mindset!

How can writing a linear function given points be a challenge? Is it still a challenge?

_____

_____

Construct Functions

ONLINE

Video Tutorials and
Interactive Examples

1. (MP) **Model with Mathematics** Cassidy is selling popcorn for a fundraiser sale at the price shown. He purchases a total of 150 containers of popcorn to sell. After he sells 15 containers, he will make a total profit, after his upfront costs, of $5.50. Cassidy's profit, after upfront costs, can be modeled by a linear function in the form $y = mx + b$.

   A. What is the slope of the line that models the function?

   _____

   B. How much were Cassidy's upfront costs?

   _____

   $1.50

   C. Will the function be discrete or continuous? Explain.

   _____

   _____

   D. Write the function that models Cassidy's profit.

   _____

   E. What is the domain of the function?

   _____

   F. What is Cassidy's profit or loss if he does not sell any popcorn?

   _____

   G. What is Cassidy's profit if he sells all of the popcorn?

   _____

   H. What is the range of the function?

   _____

For Problems 2–3, write a function for the line with the given slope that passes through the point.

2. passes through the point (4, 5); slope $= -\frac{1}{4}$

3. contains the point (2, 1); slope $= 5$

   _____

   _____

4. **Math on the Spot** Write the equation of the line that passes through (−3, 1) and (2, −1) in slope-intercept form.

   _____

Test Prep

5. Complete the equation of the line that passes through $(-2, 6)$ and $(-1, 18)$ in slope-intercept form.

$y = \boxed{}\, x + \boxed{}$

6. The cost c to rent a car for d days is shown in the table. Which equation represents this function?

Ⓐ $c = 75.3d$ Ⓒ $c = 67d$

Ⓑ $c = 72d - 40$ Ⓓ $c = 62d + 40$

Days, d	Cost, c
3	$226
4	$288
6	$412
8	$536

7. Choose the function that represents the graph on the coordinate plane.

Ⓐ $y = -4x$

Ⓑ $y = -4x - 4$

Ⓒ $y = -x - 4$

Ⓓ $y = -x + 4$

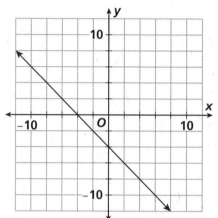

8. The graph of a function has a slope of -6, passes through the point $(-3, 4)$, and is a straight line. Choose all the statements that must be true.

Ⓐ The graph will pass through the point $(1, 20)$.

Ⓑ The graph will pass through the point $(-1, 8)$.

Ⓒ The graph represents a discrete function.

Ⓓ The function has a y-intercept at $(0, -14)$.

Ⓔ The constant rate of change is -6.

9. Is a function that can be graphed as a solid line discrete or continuous?

_____

Spiral Review

10. Solve for x: $7x - 14 = 14 - 7x$.

_____

11. Complete the table representing a linear function.

x	y
1	0
2	
5	40
	90

Name _____

Compare Functions

(I Can) compare functions presented in equations, tables, graphs, and verbal descriptions.

Step It Out

1 ▶ Four friends want to buy a drone for a science fair project. To afford the drone, they decide to buy a used lawn mower and start a lawn-care business. Each of the friends represents the profit of their business differently.

Peter's Representation	
Lawns mowed	**Profit ($)**
7	21
8	36
9	51
10	66
11	81

Marley's Representation

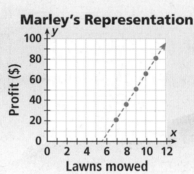

Robyn's Representation
We will raise the $441 to buy a drone by mowing lawns. Our initial cost will be the lawn mower. We will charge a flat fee to mow each lawn. Once we have mowed 6 lawns, we will pay off the lawn mower and have $6 towards our drone. We will need to mow 35 lawns in order to earn enough to buy the drone.

Claudia's Representation
$y = 15x - 84$

Describe their lawn-care business, including the meaning of the slope and y-intercept of the function modeling their business.

The unit rate is _____.

The initial cost of the lawn mower is _____.

The friends' profit is positive after they have mowed _____.

Turn and Talk Which representation do you prefer to interpret? Explain your preference. Which representation best illustrates the friends' process and their goal? Which contains the most information?

Choosing how to represent a linear function depends upon the situation and what you need to know. When linear functions are represented differently, finding the slope and y-intercept for each can help compare information.

2 The four friends researched companies to host a website with the results of their science fair project. They need to decide which company to use. Some of the companies charge a one-time fee for a domain name.

Peter found this table for Company A's costs.

Robyn found an ad for Company B.

Months	Cost ($)
5	20
6	22
7	24
8	26
9	28
10	30

Marley found this graph for Company C's costs.

Claudia found this equation for Company D's costs.

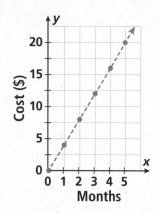

$$y = 3x + 5$$

A. What are the slope and y-intercept for each representation?

Company A: slope = ☐   y-intercept = ☐

Company B: slope = ☐   y-intercept = ☐

Company C: slope = ☐   y-intercept = ☐

Company D: slope = ☐   y-intercept = ☐

B. What does the slope represent for each company?

_____

C. What does the y-intercept represent for each company?

_____

D. Peter says that Company C will always be the least expensive option because the domain name is free. Is Peter correct? Peter is / is not correct. Company _____ is the least expensive option for the first _____ months, but then starts to become more expensive than the other plans because the _____ is greater.

E. Marley says that Company A charges $2 per month for their Web page. Is Marley correct? Marley is / is not correct. In the table, the cost increases by _____ for each additional month. This means the rate of change is / is not constant. The slope of the line is _____.

 Turn and Talk Which representation do you prefer to use to decide which company offers the best plan long term? Explain your choice.

Check Understanding

Use the given information to answer Problems 1–3.

SCIENCE BUDDIES

Science Club
Sign-up Fee $10.00
Monthly Fee $30.00

Lab Thinkers of Tomorrow has this table displayed on its website that shows its costs.

Months	Cost ($)
1	45
2	70
3	95
4	120
5	145

1. Peter wants to join a science club that sends him a new box of science experiments each month. Which club has the higher sign-up fee? Explain.

_____

_____

2. What is the slope of the graph of each function? What does the slope represent?

_____

_____

_____

3. If Peter wanted to join a club for only six months, which club would be the better deal? Why?

_____

_____

On Your Own

Use the given information to answer Problems 4–6.

Four aerial photographers will need 6 batteries to operate their drones. Each found a different website that sells rechargeable batteries.

Website A

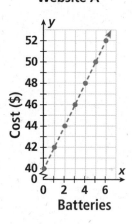

Website B

Rechargeable Batteries
$2.30 each

Battery Charger
$35.00

Website C

Batteries	Cost ($)
1	39.10
2	41.20
3	43.30
5	47.50
6	49.60

Website D

$$y = 3.5x + 28$$

4. (MP) **Attend to Precision** For each website, find the cost of 6 rechargeable batteries and a charger. Which website has the best price?

Website A charges _____ for 6 batteries and a charger.

Website B charges _____ for 6 batteries and a charger.

Website C charges _____ for 6 batteries and a charger.

Website D charges _____ for 6 batteries and a charger.

Website _____ has the best price.

5. The fixed value represents _____.
   The rate of change represents _____.

6. Determine the cost of the charger from Website A. _____

   Determine the cost of the charger from Website C. _____

   Determine the cost of the charger from Website D. _____

Name _____

Use the given information to answer Problems 7–11.

Leon and Jacey work for a florist. They each program a drone to deliver boxes of flowers to neighbors. With Leon's program, he must manually attach the box to the drone. With Jacey's program, the drone can pick up one box at a time from a pile.

Leon's Program

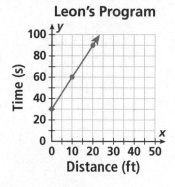

Jacey's Program	
Distance (ft)	Time (s)
10	80
20	100
30	120
40	140
50	160

7. How much time does it take Leon to attach a box?

_____

8. How much time does Jacey's drone take to pick up a box?

_____

9. (MP) **Reason** Which program has the drone traveling faster? How do you know?

_____

_____

_____

10. What does the *y*-intercept represent in this situation?

_____

_____

_____

11. Open Ended Why might the slower delivery program be a better choice?

_____

_____

_____

_____

For Problems 12–14, find the slope and *y*-intercept for each linear function.

12.

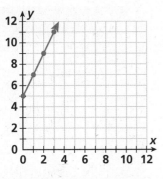

The slope is _____.

The *y*-intercept is _____.

13.

Days	Length of kudzu (ft)
1	6
2	7
3	8
4	9

The slope is _____.

The *y*-intercept is _____.

14. An online store sells music. Each download costs $0.99, and there is a one-time membership fee of $10.

_____

Kudzu

15. (MP) **Reason** The table and graph show the hourly charges for two parking garages. Compare the charges by finding slopes and *y*-intercepts and interpreting those values in the context of the situation.

Garage A	
Time (h)	Charge ($)
0	5
1	7
2	9
3	11
4	13

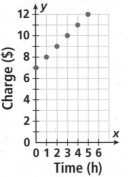

Garage B

_____

_____

_____

_____

_____

LESSON 6.5
**More Practice/
Homework**

ONLINE
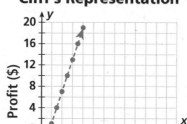
Video Tutorials and
Interactive Examples

Compare Functions

Use the given information to answer Problems 1–5.

To raise money to buy the microscope shown, four friends decide to start a dog-walking business.

Dylan's Representation	
Dogs walked	Profit ($)
8	19
9	22
10	25
11	28

Andre's Representation
$y = 3x - 5$

Cliff's Representation

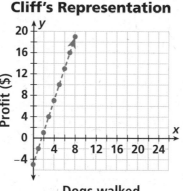

Profit ($) / Dogs walked

Tiana's Representation
In order to buy the microscope, we plan to walk dogs after school, charging $3 per dog. To reward the dogs, we will buy a box of treats for $5 as we start the business.

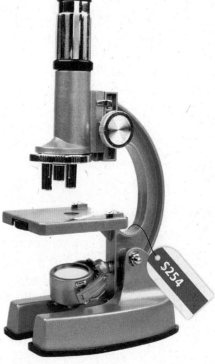

$254

1. **(MP) Reason** Do the table, graph, equation, and words represent the same situation? Explain.

_____

_____

2. What is the slope in this situation and what does it represent?

_____

_____

3. What is the *y*-intercept in this situation and what does it represent?

_____

_____

4. How many dogs do the friends need to walk in order to have enough money to buy the microscope? Which representation did you use to answer the question?

_____

5. How many dogs do they need to walk in order to pay for the box of treats?

_____

Test Prep

Martha earns $15 per hour for babysitting. The parents always give her a $5 tip. Use the information to answer Problems 6–8.

6. What is the slope in this situation?

   _____ dollars per hour

7. What is the *y*-intercept in this situation?

   _____ dollars

8. How many hours did Martha babysit if she made $65?

   _____ hours

9. Marlene started with a necklace that was 14 inches long. For every bead she adds, the necklace gets $\frac{1}{4}$ inch longer. What is the slope of the function that represents this situation?

   (A) $\frac{1}{4}$

   (B) 3.5

   (C) 4

   (D) 14

10. Two companies rent kayaks for up to 12 hours per day. Company A charges $10 per hour and $7 per day for safety equipment. Company B's daily charges for *x* hours of kayaking are represented by the equation $y = 7x + 10$. Which company has a greater fixed cost for a 12-hour day of kayaking?

    (A) Company A

    (B) Company B

    (C) They have the same fixed cost.

    (D) cannot be determined

11. Which has the greater rate of change, the function in the table or the function $y = 3x + 2$?

x	0	1	2	3
y	2	4	6	8

    (A) the function in the table

    (B) the function $y = 3x + 2$

    (C) The rate of change is the same.

    (D) cannot be determined

Spiral Review

12. What is the solution to the equation $2w - 3 = 11$?

    _____

13. Is the graph of the number of baskets a player shoots over time during a game discrete or continuous?

    _____

14. Brett spent $25 for a tennis racket and pays $5 each time she plays a game. What is the initial value? What is the slope?

    _____

Name _____

Describe and Sketch Nonlinear Functions

(I Can) convert between a verbal description of a function and its graph, and between a graph and a verbal description of a function.

Step It Out

1 ▶ Emanuel walks the North Trail at his local park. The graph shows his distance from the fountain at the center of the park as he walks along the trail. Use the graph to answer the questions.

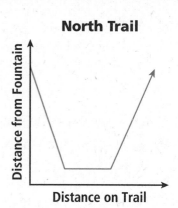

North Trail

A. Each section of the graph is | linear / nonlinear | .

B. The slope for the first part of his walk is

| positive / negative | , which means his distance from the

fountain is | increasing / decreasing | at a constant rate.

C. The slope for the second part of his walk is _____.

What does that mean about his distance from the fountain?

_____

D. The slope for the third part of his walk is | positive / negative | ,

which means his distance from the fountain is

| increasing / decreasing | at a constant rate.

E. Emanuel returns to the park the next day and walks the South Trail.

The South Trail graph is | linear / nonlinear | .

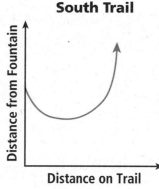

South Trail

F. Early on, does his distance from the fountain decrease at

a constant rate? _____

Near the end, does his distance from the fountain

increase at a constant rate? _____

How do you know? _____

Turn and Talk Describe potential scenarios for each path in relation to the fountain location.

2 When a state fair opened, the number of people attending the fair gradually increased at a constant rate in the morning. Then the number of people remained constant through the afternoon. In the evening, the attendance gradually decreased at a constant rate until near the end of the night, when the number of people decreased swiftly at a constant rate as they all left.

A. Where should the graph of the situation begin and why?

It starts at _____ because there were _____ people there until the fair opened.

B. Describe what happens to the graph as the number of people gradually increased at a constant rate in the morning. Will the slope of this part of the graph be positive or negative? Will it be steep or gradual?

It will be | positive / negative | and | steep / gradual |.

C. Describe what the graph looks like as the number of people remained constant through the afternoon.

This part of the graph will be _____ .

D. Describe what happens to the graph as the number of people gradually decreased at a constant rate. Will the slope of this part of the graph be positive or negative? Will it be steep or gradual?

It will be | positive / negative | and | steep / gradual |.

E. Describe what happens to the graph near the end of the night, when the number of people decreased swiftly as they all left. Will the slope of this part of the graph be positive or negative? Will it be steep or gradual?

It will be | positive / negative | and | steep / gradual |.

F. Use what you described to sketch the situation.

G. Suppose the number of people attending the fair continued to gradually increase at the same constant rate throughout the afternoon instead of remaining constant. Sketch a graph that represents this situation.

3 ▸ Kevin says that this graph describes an airplane that takes off, climbs to cruising altitude, stays at the cruising altitude for the flight, and then descends for landing. Kate says that the graph better describes a model rocket that launches, rises to a maximum altitude, and then falls faster and faster until it reaches the ground.

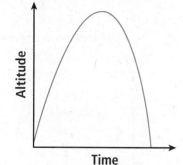

A. Is the graph linear, nonlinear, or a combination?

_____

B. Is the graph increasing at a constant rate? Is the graph decreasing at a constant rate?

_____

C. Is there a portion of the graph where the altitude is constant?

_____

D. Whose description does the graph better represent, Kevin's or Kate's? Why?

_____

_____

_____

 Turn and Talk Describe and sketch a graph to represent the airplane flight that Kevin suggested.

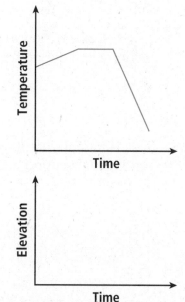

Check Understanding

1. Describe the temperature changes shown in the graph.

_____

_____

_____

2. Selena hikes a trail. Her elevation decreases at a constant rate until she reaches a stream. Her elevation stays the same walking by the stream until she climbs a hill at a constant rate to reach the campground. Sketch a graph to represent the situation.

On Your Own

3. The graph represents the speed of a swimmer during a race. Describe the swimmer's speed during the course of the race.

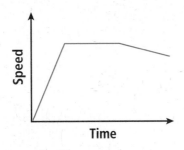

_____

_____

_____

4. The value of a stock increases gradually at a constant rate at the beginning of the day. The value quickly decreases at a constant rate to below the original value during the middle of the day. It then stays the same for the rest of the day.

A. (MP) **Model with Mathematics** Sketch a graph that represents the situation.

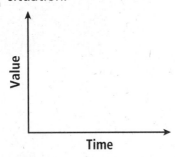

B. (MP) **Reason** How would the graph change if the stock gradually decreased during the middle of the day?

_____

_____

5. Sketch a graph that shows a value that starts increasing rapidly, then continues increasing but more gradually, then increases rapidly again.

For Problems 6–9, write a situation that the graph could represent.

6.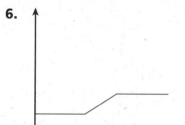

_____
_____
_____
_____
_____

7.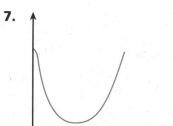

_____
_____
_____
_____
_____
_____
_____

8.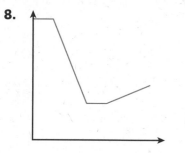

_____
_____
_____
_____
_____
_____

9.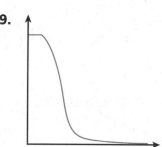

_____
_____
_____
_____
_____

10. Manny completes a video game level. The elevation of his video game character is constant and then increases rapidly at a constant rate to a new constant elevation. The elevation then decreases rapidly at a constant rate to a new constant elevation to complete the level. Sketch a graph that represents the situation.

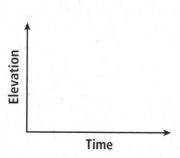

The graph represents the height of a ball over time as the ball rolls across a ledge, then falls off. Use the graph to answer Problems 11–14.

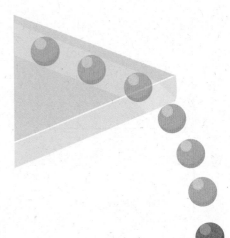

11. Starting at what time and ending at what time, when is the graph linear?

_____

12. Starting at what time and ending at what time, when is the graph nonlinear?

_____

13. What does the linear part of the graph describe?

_____

_____

14. STEM What does the nonlinear part of the graph describe? Why is it nonlinear?

_____

_____

_____

_____

_____

_____

_____

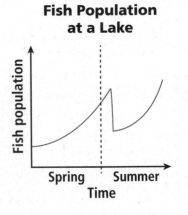

Fish Population at a Lake

Use the graph to answer Problems 15–16.

15. Social Studies What happens to the fish population in the spring? Use either the term *linear* or *nonlinear* in your response.

_____

16. A fishing competition is held on the lake once a year.

A. Which part of the graph shows the result of the competition? In what season is the competition held?

_____

B. Describe what happens to the fish population after the competition. Use either the term *linear* or *nonlinear* in your response.

_____

Describe and Sketch Nonlinear Functions

LESSON 6.6
**More Practice/
Homework**

ONLINE
Video Tutorials and
Interactive Examples

Ed

1. **Open Ended** Write a situation that this graph could represent.

_____

_____

_____

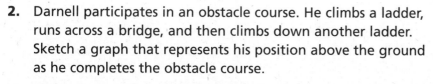

2. Darnell participates in an obstacle course. He climbs a ladder, runs across a bridge, and then climbs down another ladder. Sketch a graph that represents his position above the ground as he completes the obstacle course.

3. (MP) **Reason** The two graphs show the speeds of bicycles as they are coming to a stop. Describe how each of the bicycles comes to a stop.

Bicycle A

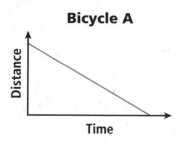

Bicycle B

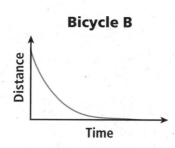

_____

_____

For Problems 4–5, sketch a graph that represents the given situation.

4. The number of points Sally earns in a video game increases at a constant rate, then stays constant, and then increases at a constant rate.

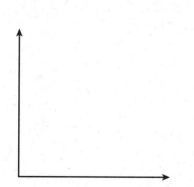

5. Rebecca drove at a constant speed on a street. She slowed at a constant rate to turn onto the highway and then accelerated at a constant rate to drive at the speed limit.

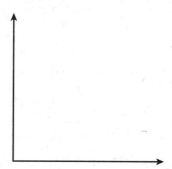

Test Prep

6. Which graph is a linear function decreasing at a constant rate?

(A)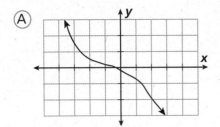

(C)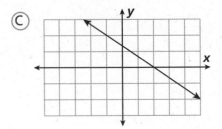

(B)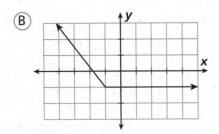

(D)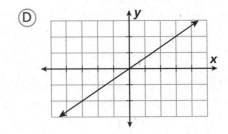

7. Select all statements that are true of the graph shown.

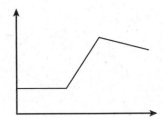

(A) The rate of the increase is greater than the rate of the decrease.

(B) The first segment of the graph is constant.

(C) The second segment of the graph increases at a constant rate.

(D) The rate of the decrease is greater than the rate of the increase.

(E) The third segment of the graph is decreasing at a constant rate.

Spiral Review

8. Jamie starts a savings account with $75. She deposits $30 in her account monthly. Her friend Carmen's savings account balance is described by the equation $b = 25m + 100$, where b is the account balance and m is the number of months. Which account has a greater balance after 6 months?

_____

9. Store A sells two sweatshirts for $25 and seven sweatshirts for $87.50. Store B sells three sweatshirts for $39 and six sweatshirts for $78. Which store has a lower price for one sweatshirt?

_____

Review

Vocabulary

For Problems 1–6, choose the correct term from the box to complete each sentence.

<table>
<tr><td>Vocabulary</td></tr>
<tr><td>domain
function
linear
nonlinear
range
relation</td></tr>
</table>

1. A _____ is any set of ordered pairs.

2. The _____ of a function is the set of all possible input values.

3. A function whose graph is not a straight line is _____.

4. The _____ of a function is the set of all possible output values.

5. A _____ is a relation with exactly one output for each input.

6. A function whose graph is a straight line is _____.

7. What is $y = mx + b$, and what do m and b represent?

_____

_____

Concepts and Skills

8. (MP) **Use Tools** The graph shows the temperature in a refrigerator over time, where x is the time in hours and y is the temperature in degrees Celsius. Write the equation of the line shown in the graph. State what strategy and tool you will use to answer the question, explain your choice, and then find the answer.

_____

_____

Refrigerator Temperature

9. Which of these functions are linear? Select all that apply.

   (A) $y = \frac{4}{x}$ (D) $y = 2^x + 8$

   (B) $y = -4x + 1$ (E) $y = 4 - \frac{2}{3}x$

   (C) $y = 2x^3 + 3$ (F) $y = 5(x - 0.6)$

10. On the coordinate plane, draw a linear function that increases at a constant rate.

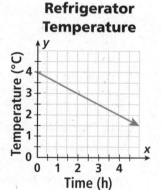

11. Is the relation shown in the graph a function? Explain.

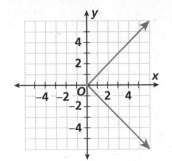

_____

_____

_____

12. The table shows the total cost *t* of owning a smartphone for *m* months. Write an equation that represents this function.

Months, *m*	2	3	4	8
Total cost ($), *t*	268	322	376	592

_____

13. Which function has the greatest rate of change?

(A)

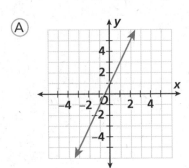

(C)

x	1	2	4	5
y	7	12	22	27

(B) $y = 3x + 7$

(D) You pay an initial fee of $10 and then $1.00 per week for *x* weeks.

14. The equation $y = 5x - 30$ models a scuba diver's elevation in feet *y* after *x* minutes. Based on the equation, which statement is true?

(A) The diver starts at sea level and reaches a depth of 30 feet after 5 minutes.

(B) The diver starts at the ocean floor and reaches a depth of 5 feet after 30 minutes.

(C) The diver starts 30 feet below sea level and ascends 5 feet per minute.

(D) The diver starts 5 feet above sea level and descends 30 feet per minute.

15. It takes Zeke 45 minutes to walk 1.5 miles from his house to the library. He starts out walking fast and then stops for 10 minutes to talk to a friend. Then he continues on at a slower rate. Draw segments to complete a possible graph of Zeke's walk.

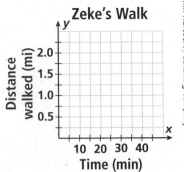

16. Complete the table to show a relation that is **not** a function.

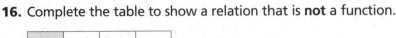

x	−2		
y		5	

© Houghton Mifflin Harcourt Publishing Company

Systems of Linear Equations

Wags Per Mile

Nikki's Dog Care
I take care of your pup while you're away!

Vacation Package:
★ $10 flat fee plus $15 per day
★ Each day includes two 30-minute visits.

Jaden's Dog Sitting
Your dog won't even miss you!

Travel package:
• $20 flat fee plus $13 per day
• Each day includes 2 half-hour visits.

Write expressions showing the cost of using each service for d days.

A. Nikki's: _____   B. Jaden's: _____

Find when the dog services will cost the same.

C. The dog services cost the same on day _____.

 Turn and Talk

Describe the steps you used to solve Part C.

Are You Ready?

Complete these problems to review prior concepts and skills you will need for this module.

Identify Solutions of Equations

Use substitution to determine whether the given value of the variable is a solution of the equation.

1. $6x - 2x = 10$; $x = 2$

2. $4n + 4 = 14$; $n = 2.5$

3. $\frac{1}{3}a - 1 = \frac{1}{4}a$; $a = 12$

4. $\frac{3}{4}(t - 6) = 9$; $t = 20$

Solve Multi-Step Equations

Solve each equation.

5. $3b + 4 = 5b - 8$

6. $-2(x + 6) = 4x$

7. $\frac{1}{4}(s + 6) = -3$

8. $2m + 1.5 = 3m - 11.7$

Special Cases of Equations

Complete each equation by writing a number in the box so that the equation has the given number of solutions.

9. $\boxed{}\, x + 5 = 3(2x + 1)$; no solution

10. $-4n + 8 = 4n - 8n + \boxed{}$; infinitely many solutions

11. Saskia is solving an equation in one variable and gets the equivalent equation $3 = 3$. Assuming her work is correct, what can she conclude about the original equation? Explain.

Name

Represent Systems by Graphing

(I Can) graph a pair of linear equations and draw a
conclusion from the graph.

Spark Your Learning
PAIRS

Natasha is comparing two
rock climbing gyms in her
town. Each gym charges
a fixed fee for gear rental
(shoes, harness, etc.) and
an hourly fee for climbing.
The graph shows the total
cost at each gym based on
the time spent climbing.

Natasha wants to
choose the gym with
the better deal. What
recommendations can
you make?

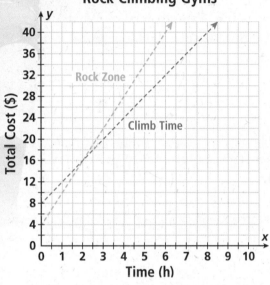

Rock Climbing Gyms

Rock Zone

Climb Time

Total Cost ($) vs Time (h)

x	y

Turn and Talk What information do you get by comparing the y-intercepts
of the lines? What information do you get by comparing the slopes of the lines?

Build Understanding

1 ▷ Cody is comparing the total costs of two climbing gyms. Each gym charges a fixed fee for gear rental and an hourly fee for climbing. Cody graphs a pair of equations, as shown, to help him compare the costs.

A. What does the slope represent in this context?

_____

B. How do the slopes of the graphs compare? What does this tell you about the rock climbing gyms?

_____

_____

_____

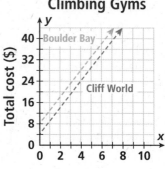

Climbing Gyms

C. What does the *y*-intercept represent in this context?

_____

D. What do the *y*-intercepts of the graphs tell you about the rock climbing gyms?

_____

_____

_____

_____

E. What does the difference in the *y*-intercepts mean in this context?

_____

_____

F. Which gym is a better deal if Cody plans to climb for 2 hours? if Cody plans to climb for 5 hours? How do you know?

_____

_____

G. Is there ever a situation in which Boulder Bay will cost less than Cliff World? Why or why not?

_____

_____

 Turn and Talk Suppose Cliff World increases their gear rental fee to $6 but keeps their hourly rate the same. Does this change the answer to any of the Task 1 questions? Explain.

Name _____

2 ▸ A mobile hotspot is a portable device that provides Wi-Fi. Both Cool Connect and Mobile Me offer mobile hotspots for have a total monthly cost of y, which includes a fixed fee plus a charge for the gigabytes (GB) of data you use, x.

A. Graph and label each equation on the coordinate plane.

Mobile Hotspot Rates

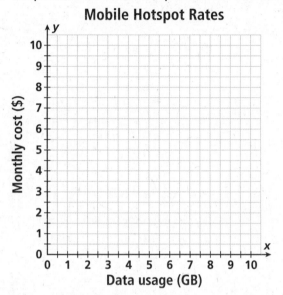

Mobile Hotspot Rates	
Cool Connect	$y - 0.5x + 7$
Mobile Me	$y = 2x + 1$

B. What is the slope of each line? What do the slopes tell you?

_____

_____

_____

_____

C. What is the y-intercept of each line? What do the y-intercepts tell you?

_____

_____

_____

D. What does the point of intersection of the lines represent?

_____

_____

E. When does one mobile hotspot cost less than the other? Explain your thinking.

_____

_____

_____

_____

_____

3 Two shops that rent snorkeling equipment have their pricing information shown. Each store charges a fixed fee for gear rental (snorkel, mask, fins) and an hourly rate. The total cost y for renting equipment for x hours at The Sea Shack is given by the equation $y = 2x + 3$. The total cost for Water Town is given in the table.

Water Town			
Time, h (x)	1	2	3
Total cost, $ (y)	5	7	9

A. Graph and label each equation on the coordinate plane.

B. What do you notice about the graphs?

_____

C. What do the y-intercepts and the slopes tell you?

_____

_____

_____

D. Which shop is the better deal? Explain.

_____

_____

Equipment Rental

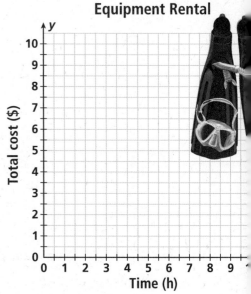

Check Understanding

Use the information to solve Problems 1–4.

Jovan is considering two job offers. Each company pays a fixed monthly salary plus a commission based on the amount of sales. The graph shows the income potential for each job.

1. Which company pays a greater monthly salary? Explain.

_____

_____

2. Which company pays a greater commission? Explain.

_____

3. If Jovan plans to have monthly sales of $5000, which job pays more?

_____

4. For what value of monthly sales do the two companies pay the same total income?

_____

Monthly Salary

Company A
$y = 500x + 4000$

Company B
$y = 250x + 5000$

On Your Own

Use the graph comparing the cost of two ice skating rinks to answer Problems 5–7. Each rink charges a fixed fee for skate rentals and an hourly fee for skating.

Ice Skating Rinks

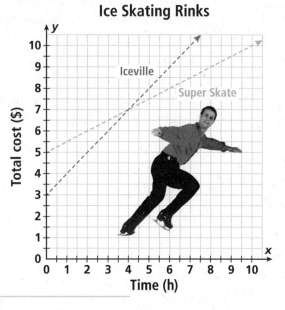

5. Compare the slopes of the lines. What do they tell you in this context?

_____

_____

_____

_____

6. Compare the *y*-intercepts of the graphs. What does this tell you in this context?

_____

_____

_____

7. **Financial Literacy** Under what circumstances does Super Skate charge less? Explain.

_____

_____

_____

Use the graph comparing two phone plans to answer Problems 8–10. Each plan includes a fixed monthly fee, plus a fee based on the number of hours used.

Phone Plans

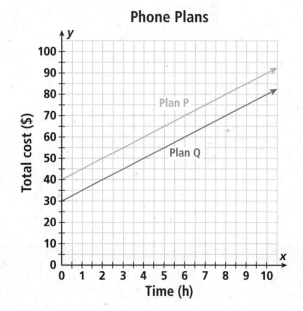

8. Compare the slopes of the lines. What do they tell you in this context?

_____

_____

9. Compare the *y*-intercepts of the lines. What do they tell you in this context?

_____

_____

_____

10. **Financial Literacy** Which plan offers a better deal? Does it depend on how long Suki expects to talk on the phone?

_____

11. There are two taxi companies in Kara's town. The total cost y for a ride based on distance driven x (in miles) for XYZ Taxi is given by the equation $y = 0.5x + 4$. The total cost for Quick Ride is given in the table.

Quick Ride			
Distance, mi (x)	1	2	3
Total cost, $ (y)	5.50	6.00	6.50

A. Graph and label the equation representing XYZ Taxi. Graph the data from the table for Quick Ride onto the coordinate plane and connect the points with a line.

B. Calculate, compare, and interpret the slopes and the y-intercepts.

_____

_____

_____

_____

C. (MP) **Reason** What can you conclude from your graph?

_____

_____

_____

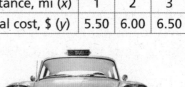
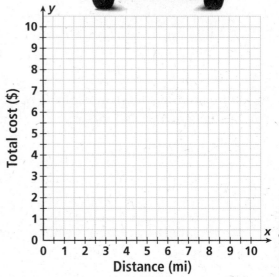

12. (MP) **Use Structure** The total cost in dollars y of a bus pass for x months in City A is given by $y = 30x + 5$. The total cost in City B is given by $y = 30x + 4.5$. After graphing both equations on your own paper, which city offers a better deal? How do you know?

_____

_____

_____

_____

13. Mitchell is comparing the cost of frozen yogurt at two different shops. He makes a graph relating the number of ounces of yogurt on the x-axis to the cost of the yogurt on the y-axis. The graph for each shop is a straight line and the lines intersect at (4, 3.25). What can you conclude from this?

_____

_____

 I'm in a Learning Mindset!

How do I know if representing multiple equations is an appropriate challenge for me?

_____

_____

Represent Systems by Graphing

Use the graph comparing the cost of two laundry services to answer Problems 1–3. Each service charges a fixed fee and a price per pound of laundry.

1. Compare the slopes. What does this tell you?

_____

_____

2. Compare the *y*-intercepts. What does this tell you?

_____

_____

_____

3. **Financial Literacy** Which service offers a lower total price? Explain.

_____

_____

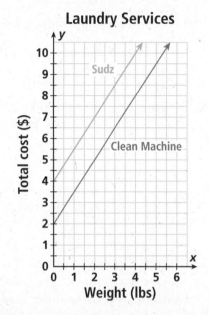

Laundry Services

4. Compare the costs of two tablet computers. In addition to the cost of the tablet, there is a monthly data fee.

A. Graph and label the equations on the coordinate plane shown.

B. **Financial Literacy** Which tablet has a lower monthly data fee? Explain.

_____

_____

_____

_____

C. (MP) **Construct Arguments** If the plan is to use the tablet for eight months, which tablet costs less overall? Explain.

_____

_____

_____

_____

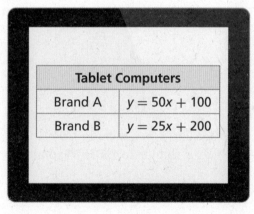

Tablet Computers	
Brand A	$y = 50x + 100$
Brand B	$y = 25x + 200$

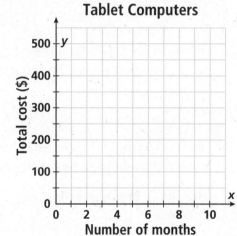

Tablet Computers

Test Prep

Bike Rentals

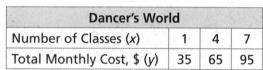

Use the graph to answer Problems 5–6.

5. Based on the graph, which of the following is true?

    (A) For a 1-hour rental, Shop X is a better deal.

    (B) For a 6-hour rental, both shops have the same cost.

    (C) Shop Y is a better deal for any number of hours.

    (D) It costs $6 to rent a bike for 3 hours at either shop.

6. If you plan to rent a bike for 5 hours, how much do you save by choosing Shop X rather than Shop Y?

    (A) $0.50   (C) $2.00

    (B) $1.00   (D) $2.50

7. There are two dance studios. The tables show the total monthly cost y for each studio based on the number of classes taken that month x. Graph the data from each table on your own paper and connect the points with a line. What can you conclude from your graph?

    _____

    _____

    _____

Dancer's World			
Number of Classes (x)	1	4	7
Total Monthly Cost, $ (y)	35	65	95

Ultimate Dance			
Number of Classes (x)	2	3	8
Total Monthly Cost, $ (y)	45	55	105

Spiral Review

8. Can you conclude from the figure that $\triangle ABC$ is similar to $\triangle DEF$? Explain.

    _____

    _____

    _____

    _____

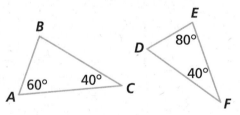

9. In the figure, $\angle Q$ is congruent to $\angle T$, and $\angle R$ is congruent to $\angle U$. What are the measures of $\angle P$ and $\angle S$?

    _____

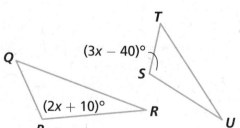

For Problems 10–11, tell whether each equation has no solution or infinitely many solutions.

10. $3(x + 2) = x + 2x + 2$

11. $1.5y + y + 10 = 2.5(y + 4)$

    _____   _____

232

© Houghton Mifflin Harcourt Publishing Company

Name _____

Solve Systems by Graphing

(I Can) solve a system of linear equations by graphing and check that my solution is correct.

Spark Your Learning

Wes is laying out model train tracks along equations on a coordinate grid and wants to know if there is a place where the two trains might collide. Determine whether there is any such place, and explain your reasoning.

Model Train Tracks	
Section A	$y = 3x + 3$
Section B	$y = -\frac{1}{2}x - 4$

x	y

  Turn and Talk How can you check that you correctly determined any possible places where the trains might collide?

Build Understanding

1   Gabriela is using a coordinate plane to design a race course for remote-controlled cars. She wants to use straight sections laid out according to the equations in the table. She needs to know where the cars might collide, if anywhere.

Model Train Tracks	
Section P	$y = -x + 2$
Section Q	$y = -2x - 4$

A. Graph the equations on the coordinate plane.

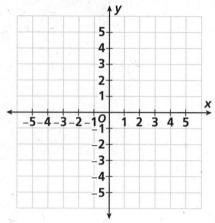

B. What method did you use to graph the lines?

_____

_____

_____

C. Did you draw a point of intersection on the graph? Does that mean that the cars will or will not collide? Explain.

_____

_____

_____

_____

D. Are the lines you graphed parallel? How do you know?

_____

_____

E. What does this tell you about the two lines?

_____

_____

F. What can you do to graph the lines differently so that you can see the point of intersection?

_____

_____

_____

_____

G. Graph and label Gabriella's equations, $y = -x + 2$ and $y = -2x - 4$, on the grid so that the point of intersection of the lines is shown. Draw the x- and y-axis, and indicate the scale of your graph.

H. At what point do the cars have the potential to collide? Why?

_____

_____

I. Compare your graph with those of other students. Did everyone make the same choices to see the point of intersection? Explain.

_____

_____

_____

_____

J. Is it possible that there is more than one point of intersection? Explain.

_____

_____

K. Show how you can use the coordinates of the intersection point and the given equations to check that you found the correct point.

 Turn and Talk How can you tell just by looking at two given equations whether they must have a point of intersection?

Step It Out

2 When you graph a system of linear equations, the point of intersection of the lines, if any, is the **solution of the system**.

A. Graph and label each equation on the coordinate plane. $\begin{cases} y = \frac{1}{3}x + 3 \\ y = -2x + 4 \end{cases}$

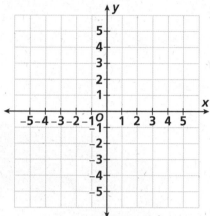

> **Connect to Vocabulary**
>
> A **system of equations** is two or more equations that contain two or more variables.

B. Estimate the solution to the system of equations.

_____

C. Why is it difficult to determine the point of intersection from your graph directly?

_____

_____

D. A student claimed that the point of intersection of the lines is $\left(\frac{1}{4}, 3\frac{1}{2}\right)$. Is the student correct? How do you know?

_____

_____

Check Understanding

1. A city planner uses the equations $y = -3x - 2$ and $y = x - 10$ to represent two streets.

   A. Graph the system. What is the point of intersection of the lines? What does it represent?

   _____

   B. Describe how can you check your solution.

   _____

   _____

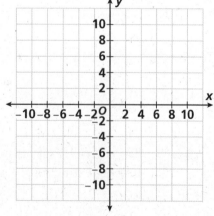

On Your Own

2. **STEM** A laboratory incubator grows biological samples at various temperatures. A scientist uses two incubators to heat samples. In the equations, x represents the number of hours since the experiment started and y represents degrees Celsius.

Laboratory Incubators	
Incubator J	$y = x + 8$
Incubator K	$y = 0.5x + 8$

A. Graph and label the equations on the coordinate plane.

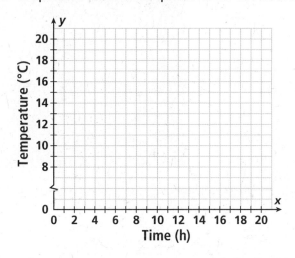

B. What is the intersection point of the lines? Explain what it represents.

_____

_____

C. Explain how to check that you found the correct intersection point.

_____

_____

3. The graph shows a system of equations.

A. **Open Ended** Write a real-world problem, including a system of equations, that could be solved by drawing the graph shown.

_____

_____

_____

_____

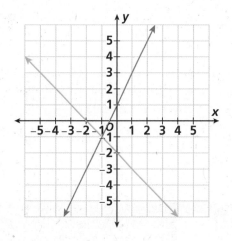

B. Show how you can check that the point of intersection is a solution of the system you wrote.

_____

_____

4. Dustin is drawing a map of Elmwood on a coordinate plane. There are two bike paths in the town.

A. Graph and label each equation on the coordinate plane.

Elmwood Bike Paths	
Riverside Path	$y = -3x - 2$
Hilltop Path	$y = -\frac{1}{2}x + 1$

B. Estimate the solution of the system and explain what it represents.

_____

_____

5. (MP) **Critique Reasoning** Brianna was asked to use graphing to solve the system of equations $y = 2x + 3.5$ and $y = 2.5x - 1$.

A. Brianna said the lines are parallel and do not intersect, so the system has no solution. Do you agree or disagree? Explain.

_____

_____

_____

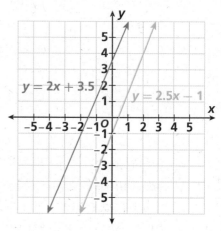

B. Another student said the solution is (9, 21.5). Is he correct? Explain.

_____

_____

I'm in a Learning Mindset!

How was solving systems by graphing an appropriate challenge for me?

_____

_____

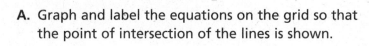
Solve Systems by Graphing

1. Deshawn is using a coordinate plane to design a mural. Two of the straight lines on the mural are represented by the equations $y = 2x + 8$ and $y = \frac{1}{2}x - 4$.

A. Graph and label the equations on the grid so that the point of intersection of the lines is shown.

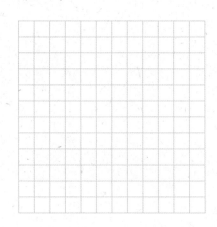

B. At what point do the lines intersect? _____

C. (MP) **Reason** Show how you can check that the point of intersection is a solution.

_____

_____

_____

2. (MP) **Model with Mathematics** The total cost y of renting a paddleboat for x hours is given by $y = 2x + 3$ at Lake Mitchell and by $y = \frac{1}{3}x + 7$ at Lake Sutro.

A. Graph and label each equation on the coordinate plane.

B. Estimate the solution of the system. What does the solution represent?

_____

_____

_____

Paddleboat Rental

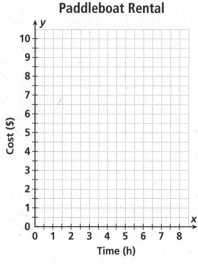

3. Math on the Spot Use a separate sheet of graph paper to solve each system by graphing. Check your answer.

A. $\begin{cases} y = x + 2 \\ y = -2x + 5 \end{cases}$ _____

B. $\begin{cases} x - y = 2 \\ y = \frac{1}{2}x \end{cases}$ _____

Test Prep

4. Which system of linear equations has a solution that is represented by a point in Quadrant II?

(A) $\begin{cases} y = x \\ y = -x + 3 \end{cases}$

(C) $\begin{cases} y = -x \\ y = x + 3 \end{cases}$

(B) $\begin{cases} y = x \\ y = x + 3 \end{cases}$

(D) $\begin{cases} y = -x \\ y = -x - 3 \end{cases}$

5. Alicia is using a coordinate plane to help her write a program for a video game. In the game, a rabbit moves along the line $y = -4x + 8$ and a fox moves along the line $y = -0.5x - 6$. Graph the two lines on the coordinate plane provided. Where do the lines intersect?

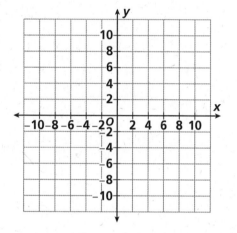

_____

6. Which of the following is the solution to this system of equations?

$\begin{cases} y = -3x - 5 \\ y = 5x \end{cases}$

(A) $(-1, -3)$

(B) $\left(-\frac{5}{8}, -\frac{25}{8}\right)$

(C) $\left(-\frac{5}{2}, -\frac{25}{2}\right)$

(D) $(-3, -5)$

Spiral Review

7. The table gives the altitude, y, of a weather balloon, in meters, at various times, x, in minutes, since the balloon was released from a platform. Construct a function of the form $y = mx + b$ that describes the data.

Time (x)	Altitude (y)
3	170
4	220
5	270

_____

8. Construct a linear function that has a slope of -3 and passes through the point $(-2, 3)$.

_____

9. Solve the equation $3(x - 1) = 27 - 2x$. Check your solution.

_____

Name _____

Solve Systems by Substitution

(I Can) solve systems of equations by substitution.

Spark Your Learning

A state fair offers two pricing plans. Each includes a flat fee for admission and a price per ride. The equations in the table show the total cost y, in dollars, to attend the fair and go on x rides. For how many rides do the two pricing plans cost the same? Solve this problem without graphing and explain your reasoning.

State Fair Pricing	
Super Saver	$y = 4x + 7$
Fun Pack	$y = 2x + 17$

 Turn and Talk How can you check that you correctly found a solution to a system of linear equations?

Build Understanding

1 ▸ Solve the system. $\begin{cases} y = -2x - 4 \\ y = 2x + 8 \end{cases}$

A. Graph the system to estimate a solution.

_____

_____

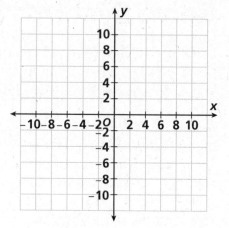

B. Since $y = -2x - 4$ and $y = 2x + 8$, what do you know about $-2x - 4$ and $2x + 8$ at the intersection point of the two lines?

_____

C. Solve the equation $-2x - 4 = 2x + 8$.

D. What does the solution in Part C represent?

_____

_____

E. How can you find the value of the other variable? What is the value?

_____

_____

F. What does the y-value tell you?

_____

_____

G. Check your solution by substituting x and y back into both original equations. Show your work.

H. What is the solution to the system of equations? _____

Step It Out

2 ▶ Solve this system using substitution. $\begin{cases} x = 2y + 7 \\ 2x + 5y = 5 \end{cases}$

A. How can you use $x = 2y + 7$ to substitute for x in the second equation?

Since the equation is solved for _____ ,

you can substitute _____ for x in the second equation.

B. Complete the following solution.

$$2x + 5y = 5$$

$$2\Big(\underline{\qquad}\Big) + 5y = 5$$

$$\underline{\qquad} + 5y = 5$$

$$\underline{\qquad} + 14 = 5$$

$$9y = \underline{\quad}$$

$$y = \underline{\quad}$$

C. Since $y = $ _____ , $x = 2\Big(\underline{\quad}\Big) + 7$,

so $x = $ _____ $+ 7$ or _____ .

The solution is _____ .

3 ▶ For admission to a concert at the state fair, child tickets cost x dollars and adult tickets cost y dollars. Solve the system shown to find the price of each type of ticket. $\begin{cases} x + y = 10 \\ 4x + 8y = 64 \end{cases}$

A. Solve the system by first solving for x in the first equation. Then substitute the resulting expression in the second equation and solve for one of the variables.

Since $x + y = 10$, $x = $ _____ .

Substitute into the other equation:

$$4x + 8y = 64$$

$$4\Big(\underline{\qquad}\Big) + 8y = 64$$

$$\underline{\qquad} + 8y = 64$$

$$\underline{\qquad} + 4y = 64$$

$$4y = \underline{\quad}$$

$$y = \underline{\quad}$$

1 Adult + 1 Child = $10

B. Since $y = $ _____ , $x = 10 - $ _____ , and $x = $ _____ . The cost of each child ticket is _____ , and the cost of each adult ticket is _____ .

Turn and Talk In Part B, what would change if you substituted $y = 6$ into $4x + 8y = 64$ instead? What would remain the same?

4 Solve this system of equations.

$$\begin{cases} 4x - 3y = -5 \\ -8x + 2y = 2 \end{cases}$$

A. Solve for one of the variables in one of the equations.

$4x - 3y = -5$

$4x = \underline{\hspace{1cm}} - 5$

$x = \underline{\hspace{2cm}}$

B. Make a substitution in the other equation and then solve for the variable that remains after the substitution.

Substitute $x = \underline{\hspace{3cm}}$ into $-8x + 2y = 2$. Then solve for y.

$-8\left(\underline{\hspace{3cm}} \right) + 2y = 2$

$\underline{\hspace{3cm}} + 2y = 2$

$\underline{\hspace{1cm}} + 10 = 2$

$-4y = \underline{\hspace{1cm}}$

$y = \underline{\hspace{1cm}}$

C. Solve for x.

Substitute $y = \underline{\hspace{1cm}}$ in $4x - 3y = -5$. Then solve for x.

$4x - 3(\underline{\hspace{1cm}}) = -5$

$4x - \underline{\hspace{1cm}} = -5$

$4x = \underline{\hspace{1cm}}$

$x = \underline{\hspace{1cm}}$

The solution is $\underline{\hspace{1.5cm}}$.

Check Understanding

1. Describe the steps for solving a system of two equations in two variables by substitution. Explain how to check the solution.

   _____

   _____

   _____

   _____

2. What is the solution to the system shown? $\begin{cases} x - y = 3 \\ 2x - 0.5y = 0 \end{cases}$

   _____

On Your Own

3. **STEM** Scientists use drones with digital cameras to help them identify plants, predict flooding, and construct 3-D maps of different landscapes. A team of scientists is using two drones to map a region. The heights of the drones are represented by the equations given, where x is the number of minutes since the drones were released by the scientists and y is the height in meters.

$y = 8x + 5$

$y = 6x + 25$

A. Solve the system of equations.

_____

B. What does your solution tell you about the drones?

_____

_____

4. Tickets for a school play have one price for students, x, and a different price for non-students, y. The system of equations shown is based on two different ticket orders in which the prices x and y are in dollars.

$$\begin{cases} 2x + 3y = 49 \\ x + 2y = 30 \end{cases}$$

A. What is the first step in solving the system by substitution? Justify your answer.

_____

_____

_____

B. Solve the system and explain what your solution represents.

_____

_____

5. Consider the system of equations $\begin{cases} 2x + 5y = 18 \\ 3x + 1.5y = 9 \end{cases}$.

A. Graph to estimate the solution of the system.

Estimated solution: _____

B. Solve the system by substitution.

_____

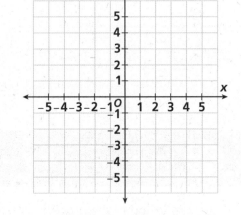

6. Complete the system of two linear equations so it has the solution $(-1, 7)$. Check by using substitution to solve the system.

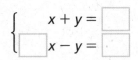

$$\begin{cases} x + y = \boxed{} \\ \boxed{}\,x - y = \boxed{} \end{cases}$$

7. The map of a small city is placed on a coordinate plane. Two of the town's straight roads can be represented by the equations in the system shown here.

$$\begin{cases} -4x - 2y = -6 \\ 2x + 2y = 7 \end{cases}$$

   A. Without graphing, in what quadrant of the coordinate plane do the roads intersect? How do you know?

   _____

   _____

   B. (MP) **Attend to Precision** Check your answer by graphing and labeling the equations.

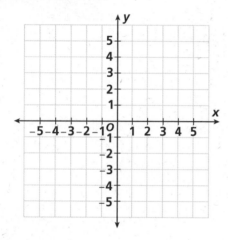

For Problems 8–13, solve the system of equations.

8. $\begin{cases} 3x - y = 15 \\ x + y = 1 \end{cases}$

9. $\begin{cases} -2x + y = 8 \\ y = 6 \end{cases}$

10. $\begin{cases} 4y = 20 \\ x - y = 7 \end{cases}$

11. $\begin{cases} 3x - 6y = 5 \\ 2x + y = 0 \end{cases}$

12. $\begin{cases} -5x + 2y = -8 \\ 2x - 3y = 12 \end{cases}$

13. $\begin{cases} 4x + 2y = 18 \\ -2x + 3y = 23 \end{cases}$

➖✖️➕➗ **I'm in a Learning Mindset!**

How can I modify my process for solving systems by substitution to maintain an appropriate level of challenge?

_____

_____

Solve Systems by Substitution

1. There are x trumpet players and y saxophone players in a school's jazz band. The equations in the system shown here relate x and y. Solve the system by substitution. What does the solution mean?

$$\begin{cases} 2x + 3y = 23 \\ y = 3x - 7 \end{cases}$$

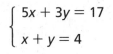

_____

_____

2. Students in Ms. Chu's science class are building model rockets. Jars of baking soda cost x dollars each, and bottles of vinegar cost y dollars each. The system shown relates the prices of these items.

$$\begin{cases} 5x + 3y = 17 \\ x + y = 4 \end{cases}$$

A. Graph to estimate the solution of the system.

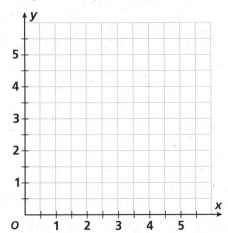

Estimated solution: _____

B. (MP) **Attend to Precision** Solve the system. What does the solution represent?

_____

_____

3. Use the system of equations shown for Parts A and B.

$$\begin{cases} 3x - 2y = -10 \\ -4x + 3y = 13 \end{cases}$$

A. Solve one of the equations for either variable.

_____

B. Use substitution to find the solution of the system.

_____

4. **Math on the Spot** Solve each system by substitution.

A. $\begin{cases} y = 3x \\ y = x + 4 \end{cases}$ B. $\begin{cases} x - y = 4 \\ x + 2y = 4 \end{cases}$

_____ _____

Test Prep

5. Which is a correct step in solving this system of equations by substitution? $\begin{cases} x + y = 3 \\ 3x - 4y = -5 \end{cases}$

- (A) Substitute $x + 3$ for x in the equation $3x - 4y = -5$.
- (B) Substitute $x + 3$ for y in the equation $3x - 4y = -5$.
- (C) Substitute $-x + 3$ for x in the equation $3x - 4y = -5$.
- (D) Substitute $-x + 3$ for y in the equation $3x - 4y = -5$.

6. Brodie is using a coordinate plane to design two straight paths in a community garden. The paths are represented by the lines $2x + 3y = 6$ and $-3x - 2y = 1$. At what point, if any, do the two paths intersect?

_____

7. Celia used substitution correctly to solve one of the systems of equations shown here. As part of her solution process, she solved the equation $-2x + 3(-2x + 4) = -3$. Which system did Celia solve?

- (A) $\begin{cases} -2x + y = 4 \\ -2x + 3y = -3 \end{cases}$
- (C) $\begin{cases} 2x + y = 4 \\ -2x + 3y = -3 \end{cases}$
- (B) $\begin{cases} 2x - y = 4 \\ -2x + 3y = -3 \end{cases}$
- (D) $\begin{cases} -2x - y = 4 \\ -2x + 3y = -3 \end{cases}$

8. Which is a true statement about the solution of this system of equations? $\begin{cases} 6x - 2y = -3 \\ 4x + 6y = 9 \end{cases}$

- (A) The values of both x and y are integers.
- (B) The values of x and y are equal.
- (C) The solution lies in Quadrant III of the coordinate plane.
- (D) The solution lies on one of the axes of the coordinate plane.

9. Solve the system $\begin{cases} 2x + 3y = -9 \\ -x + 4y = 10 \end{cases}$.

_____

Spiral Review

In the figure, Line m is parallel to Line n. Use the figure to solve Problems 10–12.

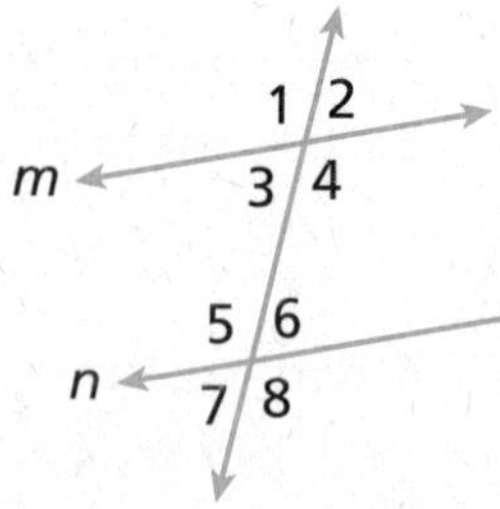

10. Name all of the pairs of corresponding angles in the figure.

_____

11. The measure of $\angle 3$ is $(4x + 1)°$ and the measure of $\angle 6$ is $(6x - 29)°$. Find the value of x and the measures of $\angle 3$ and $\angle 6$.

_____

12. Solve the equation $4(x + 3) + 3 = 5(x + 4)$.

_____

Name

Solve Systems by Elimination

(I Can) solve a system of linear equations by elimination and check my solution.

Spark Your Learning

A football team is selling pennants and shirts. One fan bought 6 shirts and 2 pennants for $114.00. Later the fan returned 4 shirts and 2 pennants for $84.00.

How could you use an operation with equations to determine the price for each shirt and each pennant?

© Houghton Mifflin Harcourt Publishing Company

Turn and Talk If the fan only returned 1 shirt and 1 pennant, would you still be able to determine the price for each shirt and each pennant using the same method? Explain.

Build Understanding

You previously learned how to solve a system of equations by replacing a variable through substitution with an equivalent expression. **Elimination** is the algebraic process of eliminating a variable in a system of equations by adding the equations together to eliminate one of the variables.

1 ▶ Solve the system of equations using elimination.

$$\begin{cases} 3x + 2y = 24 \\ 7x - 2y = 36 \end{cases}$$

A. Which variable has coefficients that sum to zero? _____

B. If you add the x terms together, what is the result? _____

C. If you add the constant terms together, what is the result? _____

D. Add the two equations, then solve the resulting equation.

$x =$ _____

$$\begin{array}{llll} 3x & + 2y & = 24 \\ 7x & - 2y & = 36 \\ \hline \end{array}$$

$\boxed{}\, x + \boxed{}\, y = \boxed{}$

E. Substitute the value of x into either original equation to solve for y.

F. Write the solution as an ordered pair. _____

G. Check your solution by substituting the values into both original equations.

> **Turn and Talk** In Task 1, Part E, would you get a different solution if you had substituted the value of x into the other original equation? Explain.

Step It Out

2 Solve the system of equations.

$$\begin{cases} x + y = 7 \\ 2x + 4y = 18 \end{cases}$$

A. Graph the system and estimate the solution.

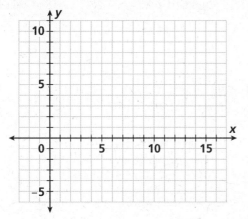

I estimate the solution is $\left(\boxed{}, \boxed{} \right)$.

B. Multiply the first equation by a number so that the coefficient of the *x*-term is the opposite of the coefficient of the *x*-term in the second equation.

$$\boxed{}\, x + \boxed{}\, y = \boxed{}$$

$$2x + 4y \quad = 18$$

C. Add the equations. Solve for *y*.

$$\boxed{}\, y = \boxed{}$$

$$y = \boxed{}$$

D. Use the value of *y* to solve for *x* in either original equation.

$$x + \boxed{} = 7 \qquad \text{or} \qquad 2x + 4\left(\boxed{} \right) = 18$$

$$x = \boxed{} \qquad\qquad\qquad\qquad 2x + \boxed{} = 18$$

$$2x = \boxed{}$$

$$x = \boxed{}$$

E. Check that the values of *x* and *y* make both equations true:

$$\boxed{} + \boxed{} \overset{?}{=} 7 \qquad 2\left(\boxed{} \right) + 4\left(\boxed{} \right) \overset{?}{=} 18$$

$$\boxed{} = 7 \qquad\qquad\qquad \boxed{} + \boxed{} \overset{?}{=} 18$$

$$\boxed{} = 18$$

F. The solution is $\left(\boxed{}, \boxed{} \right)$.

3 A store sells two blends of snack mix. The situation is represented by the system of equations shown.

$$\begin{cases} 2c + 3p = 34 \\ 3c + 5p = 55 \end{cases}$$

	Packs of cranberries	Packs of pecans	Cost of mix ($)
Blend 1	2	3	34
Blend 2	3	5	55

A. Is one coefficient of c a multiple of the other? _____
   Is one coefficient of p a multiple of the other? _____

B. Eliminate c by multiplying the first equation by −3 and the second equation by 2, so that the new coefficients of c are opposites:

$-3(2c) + -3(3p) = -3(34) \rightarrow$ ☐ $c +$ ☐ $p =$ ☐

$2(3c) + 2(5p) = 2(55) \rightarrow$ ☐ $c +$ ☐ $p =$ ☐

C. Add the equations and solve.

☐ $p =$ ☐

$p =$ ☐

D. Use the value of p to solve for c in either equation.

$2c + 3$ ☐ $= 34$

$2c +$ ☐ $= 34$

$2c =$ ☐

$c =$ ☐

The pecans cost _____ per pack and the cranberries

cost _____ per pack.

Check Understanding

1. The system of equations shown represents the length and width in centimeters of a rectangle. What are the length and width?

   $$\begin{cases} 2L + 2W = 52 \\ L - W = 2 \end{cases}$$

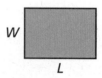

W

L

_____

2. What is the solution to the given system of equations?

   $$\begin{cases} 3x - y = 2 \\ 3x - 2y = 10 \end{cases}$$

On Your Own

3. Gareth has 15 total quarters and dimes with a total value of
$2.10. The system of equations shown can be used to solve
for the number of each Gareth has.

$$\begin{cases} Q + D = 15 \\ 25Q + 10D = 210 \end{cases}$$

Complete the table to show the
quantities and values of the coins
Gareth has.

	Quarters	Dimes
Quantity		
Total value		

4. Liliana spends $4.00 on 2 boxes of popcorn and 2 drinks. Nadette spends
$5.25 on 2 boxes of popcorn and 3 drinks. The prices of the popcorn and
drinks can be determined by solving the system of equations shown.

$$\begin{cases} 2p + 2d = 4.00 \\ 2p + 3d = 5.25 \end{cases}$$

A. What variable will you eliminate first? How?

B. What is the solution to the system?

C. What is the price of a box of popcorn? a drink?

5. (MP) **Construct Arguments** Consider the system of equations. $\begin{cases} x + y = 6 \\ x - y = 12 \end{cases}$

A. To solve by elimination, which variable would you eliminate and why?

B. Will the solution be different if substitution is used instead of
elimination? Explain.

6. What is the solution to the system? $\begin{cases} 3x + 2y = 37 \\ 7x - 6y = 1 \end{cases}$

For Problems 7–10, solve the system of equations using elimination.

7. $\begin{cases} 3x - 2y = 5 \\ x + 2y = 3 \end{cases}$

8. $\begin{cases} 4x + 3y = 3 \\ 4x - 2y = 18 \end{cases}$

_____

_____

9. $\begin{cases} x - y = 3 \\ 2x + 2y = 50 \end{cases}$

10. $\begin{cases} 3x + 5y = 22.5 \\ 5x + 3y = 17.5 \end{cases}$

_____

_____

11. **STEM** A chemist uses the system of equations shown to find the amounts of pure water and salt water needed to make a new solution.

$\begin{cases} x + y = 80 \\ x + 0.25y = 32 \end{cases}$

A. Graph the system and estimate the solution.

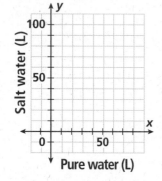

_____

B. Solve the system for the precise answer. How many liters of pure water did the chemist use? How many liters of salt water?

_____

12. **Open Ended** Complete the system of equations so that it has a solution of (4, 7).

$\begin{cases} 5x + \boxed{}\,y = 34 \\ 2x - \boxed{}\,y = \boxed{} \end{cases}$

 I'm in a Learning Mindset!

How was solving systems by elimination a challenge for me? Is it still a challenge?

_____

_____

Solve Systems by Elimination

1. A rectangular box has a perimeter of 76 inches. If two of the boxes are placed next to each other on the long side, the new box is a rectangular shape with a perimeter of 112 inches.

   The system represents the perimeters of the boxes:

   $$\begin{cases} 2L + 2W = 76 \\ 2L + 4W = 112 \end{cases}$$

   What are the dimensions of the original box?

   _____

L   L

W   2W

2. **Math on the Spot** Solve the system by eliminiation.

   $$\begin{cases} 2x + 5y = 4 \\ 2x - y = -8 \end{cases}$$

   A. Which variable would you eliminate to solve the system using elimination? Explain.

   _____

   _____

   B. What is the solution to the system?

   _____

3. (MP) **Critique Reasoning** Carsen incorrectly solved a system of equations. His first step is shown.

   $6x + 5y = 36 \quad \rightarrow \quad 6x + 5y = 36$
   $3x - 2y = -9 \rightarrow -6x - 4y = 18$

   What was Carsen's error? What is the correct solution to the system?

   _____

   _____

For Problems 4-7, solve the system of equations by elimination.

4. $\begin{cases} 2x - 3y = 2 \\ -2x - y = -26 \end{cases}$

5. $\begin{cases} 4x + y = -16 \\ 2x - 3y = -8 \end{cases}$

6. $\begin{cases} 7x + 2y = 28 \\ 3x + 2y = 20 \end{cases}$

7. $\begin{cases} 3x + 4y = 1 \\ 5x + 3y = -2 \end{cases}$

Test Prep

8. Bailey and Miranda sell ads for the school yearbook. Their first month's sales totals are represented by the system shown, where x is the price of a small ad and y is the price of a full-page ad. What are the prices of small ads and of full-page ads?

$$\begin{cases} 14x + 5y = 975 \\ 10x + 4y = 750 \end{cases}$$

small ad: \$ ▭

full-page ad: \$ ▭

9. What is the y-coordinate of the solution to the system of equations shown?

$$\begin{cases} 2x + 3y = 5 \\ 3x - 2y = -12 \end{cases}$$

- (A) −3
- (B) −2
- (C) 2
- (D) 3

10. A triangle has two congruent angles and one unique angle. The system of equations shown represents the relationship between the angle measures. What are the measures of the angles in the triangle?

$$\begin{cases} 2x + y = 180 \\ x - y = 30 \end{cases}$$

Spiral Review

11. Explain how similar triangles can be used to prove the slope of the line is the same through Points $A(0, 3)$ and $B(2, 8)$ as through $B(2, 8)$ and $C(6, 18)$.

12. What is the equation of the line through the points (4, 6), (8, 12), and (10, 15)?

13. What is the domain of the function with points (−2, 4), (−1, 1), (0, 0), (1, 1), and (2, 4)?

Name _____

Examine Special Systems

I Can identify the number of solutions to a system of linear equations in any form.

Spark Your Learning

What values would give you no solutions to the system of equations. How do you know?

$$\begin{cases} y = 2x + 5 \\ y = \boxed{}\, x + \boxed{} \end{cases}$$

 Turn and Talk What values would make the system of equations have an infinite number of solutions?

Build Understanding

Just as when solving a linear equation, the solution set for a system of two linear equations can have one solution, no solution, or infinitely many solutions.

A system of two linear equations has **no solution** if the graphs of the two lines never intersect because the lines are parallel.

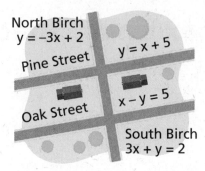

North Birch
$y = -3x + 2$

Pine Street

$y = x + 5$

Oak Street

$x - y = 5$

South Birch
$3x + y = 2$

1 On a map, a street that runs in a straight line can be represented by a linear equation.

A. Solve the system of equations represented by Oak Street and Pine Street.

B. What was the result? What does it tell you about the number of solutions to the system?

C. What are the slopes of the two streets? the *y*-intercepts?

A system of two linear equations has **infinitely many solutions** if the graphs of the two lines are concurrent and therefore intersect at infinitely many points.

D. Solve the system of equations represented by South Birch and North Birch.

E. What was the result? What does this tell you about the number of solutions to the system?

F. What are the slopes of the two streets? the *y*-intercepts?

Turn and Talk Compare the answers for Part C and F. Explain the similarities and differences between a system with no solutions and infinitely many solutions.

Step It Out

2 The system $\begin{cases} x + 2y = 6 \\ 2x + 4y = 12 \end{cases}$ has infinitely many solutions.

A. Graph the system on your own paper. What do you notice?

_____

B. What do you notice about the pair of equations?

_____

C. Fill in the blanks to use elimination to solve the system:

$\boxed{}\ (x + 2y = 6) \rightarrow \boxed{}\ x + \left(\boxed{}\ y\right) = \boxed{}$

$2x + 4y = 12 \rightarrow \underline{\quad 2x + \qquad 4y = 12 \quad}$

$\boxed{} = \boxed{}$

D. How does the final equation relate to the system having infinitely many solutions?

_____

_____

_____

3 The system $\begin{cases} 2x + y = 3 \\ 4x + 2y = 8 \end{cases}$ has no solution.

A. Graph the system on your own paper. What do you notice?

_____

B. What do you notice about the pair of equations?

_____

_____

C. Fill in the blanks to solve the system by substitution:

$2x + y = 3 \rightarrow y = \boxed{}\ x + \boxed{}$ $\qquad$ $4x + \boxed{}\ x + \boxed{} = 8$

$4x + 2\left(\boxed{}\right) = 8$ $\qquad\qquad$ $\boxed{} = 8$

D. How does the final equation relate to the system having no solutions?

_____

_____

 Turn and Talk If you solve the equations in Task 3 for y, what equations do you get? How is that related to the graph of the two lines?

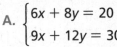 How many solutions does each system of equations have?

A. $\begin{cases} 6x + 8y = 20 \\ 9x + 12y = 30 \end{cases}$

$6x + 8y = 20$ can be simplified by a factor of _____, resulting in the equation _____.

$9x + 12y = 30$ can be simplified by a factor of _____, resulting in the equation _____.

The given equations are equivalent / unique . Therefore the system has _____ solution(s).

B. $\begin{cases} 5x + 2y = 7 \\ 15x + 6y = 24 \end{cases}$

All terms in $15x + 6y = 24$ can be divided by _____, resulting in the equation _____.

The expression $5x + 2y$ can / cannot equal both 7 and _____.
Therefore the system has _____ solution(s).

Check Understanding

1. Rory bought a pencil and a folder for $0.35.
   Emily bought 3 pencils and 3 folders for $1.05.
   The system of equations shown represents this.

   $\begin{cases} x + y = 35 \\ 3x + 3y = 105 \end{cases}$

   Could each of them have paid the same price for pencils and for folders?

   _____

   _____

Use the information to answer Problems 2–4.

Consider the system of equations $\begin{cases} 6x + 4y = 14 \\ 9x + 6y = C \end{cases}$.

2. Which value(s) of C represent a system with infinitely many solutions?

   _____

3. Which value(s) of C represent a system with no solution?

   _____

4. Is there any value of C that would result in the system having one solution? Why or why not?

   _____

   _____

On Your Own

Stacy
36 minutes

Bridget
12 minutes

5. Stacy and Bridget are wrapping presents. Their times are represented by the system shown, where x is the wrapping rate in minutes per box and y is the packing rate in minutes per bag.

$$\begin{cases} 6x + 3y = 36 \\ 2x + y = 12 \end{cases}$$

How many solutions does the system have? Explain.

_____

_____

Use the information to answer Problems 6–7.

A system of two equations includes the equation $2x + 6y = 8$. The other equation in the system was smudged but shows $3x + $ ▮ $ = 12$.

6. (MP) **Reason** Is it possible for the system to have infinitely many solutions? If so, what could be the smudged term? If not, explain your reasoning.

_____

7. (MP) **Reason** Is it possible for the system to have no solutions? If so, what could be the smudged term? If not, explain your reasoning.

_____

_____

_____

8. **Open Ended** Provide an equation that, when combined with the equation $7x - y = 5$, could form a system with the given number of solutions.

A. infinitely many solutions _____

B. no solutions _____

For Problems 9–12, state the number of solutions to the system: one, none, or infinitely many.

9. $\begin{cases} 3x + 4y = 7 \\ 3x + 4y = 9 \end{cases}$

10. $\begin{cases} x + y = 2 \\ y - x = 12 \end{cases}$

11. $\begin{cases} y = 3x - 5 \\ y = -3x - 5 \end{cases}$

12. $\begin{cases} y = 5 + 2x \\ y = 2x + 5 \end{cases}$

13. Rosie spends 2 hours building each model plane x and 6 hours building each model boat y. She has a total of 40 hours to spend each week. Yuri spends 1 hour building each model plane and 3 hours building each model boat, but has only 20 hours to spend each week. The system represents their total work times.

$$\begin{cases} 2x + 6y = 40 \\ x + 3y = 20 \end{cases}$$

How many solutions does the system have? Explain.

14. (MP) **Reason** Devante and Jim each draw a rectangle. The perimeter of Devante's rectangle is 60 centimeters. The sum of the length and width of Jim's rectangle is 15 centimeters. The system shown represents the dimensions of their rectangles.

$$\begin{cases} 2L + 2W = 60 \\ L + W = 15 \end{cases}$$

Do the rectangles have the same dimensions? Explain.

For Problems 15–20, solve each system of equations.

15. $\begin{cases} x + 2y = 7 \\ 4x + 8y = 28 \end{cases}$

16. $\begin{cases} 5x - 2y = 19 \\ 5x + 2y = 11 \end{cases}$

17. $\begin{cases} 6x - 4y = 2 \\ -9x + 6y = 3 \end{cases}$

18. $\begin{cases} -4x + 2y = 12 \\ y = 2x + 6 \end{cases}$

19. $\begin{cases} 12x - 18y = 9 \\ 2x - 3y = 1 \end{cases}$

20. $\begin{cases} x = 2y - 10 \\ 4y = x + 12 \end{cases}$

I'm in a Learning Mindset!

Which special systems were the most challenging for me? Why?

© Houghton Mifflin Harcourt Publishing Company • Image Credit: ©akihiro1963/iStock/Getty Images Plus/Getty Images

Examine Special Systems

1. Gabe bought 6 singles and 9 albums from an online music store. Jenny bought 4 singles and 6 albums at a different online music store. The system shown represents their totals for singles that cost x dollars each and albums that cost y dollars each.

$$\begin{cases} 6x + 9y = 96 \\ 4x + 6y = 38 \end{cases}$$

   A. Solve the system. What does the solution mean?

   _____

   B. Is it possible to know if Gabe and Jenny purchased the singles and albums for the same prices? Explain.

   _____

For Problems 2–4, use the system of equations shown.

$$\begin{cases} 3x + 5y = 4 \\ 6x + 10y = 4 \end{cases}$$

2. Does the system have a solution? Explain.

   _____

   _____

3. (MP) **Critique Reasoning** Manuel says that he can change the 4 in the second equation to any number and the system will have no solution. Is Manuel correct? Explain.

   _____

   _____

4. How can one number in the second equation be changed so the system has only one solution? Explain.

   _____

   _____

For Problems 5–10, solve the system of equations.

5. $\begin{cases} x + y = 3 \\ x - y = -3 \end{cases}$

6. $\begin{cases} 5x + y = 7 \\ 10x + 2y = 16 \end{cases}$

7. $\begin{cases} 3x + 4y = 9 \\ 12x + 16y = 36 \end{cases}$

8. $\begin{cases} 4x + 3y = 11 \\ 3x + 4y = 17 \end{cases}$

9. $\begin{cases} 3x + 12y = 9 \\ 5x + 20y = 15 \end{cases}$

10. $\begin{cases} 4x - 2y = 16 \\ -14x + 7y = -49 \end{cases}$

Test Prep

11. The system of equations $\begin{cases} ax + 4y = 10 \\ -9x - 6y = -15 \end{cases}$ has infinitely many solutions.

What is the value of a?

(A) 5   (C) 7

(B) 6   (D) 8

12. Consider the system of equations $\begin{cases} y = -\frac{3}{2}x + 4 \\ y = -\frac{3}{2}x - 4 \end{cases}$.

The system has [no / one / infinitely many] solution(s).

13. Mark whether each system has infinitely many solutions, no solution, or one solution.

	Infinitely many solutions	No solution	One solution
$\begin{cases} x + 3y = 6 \\ 6x + 18y = 36 \end{cases}$	☐	☐	☐
$\begin{cases} 2x - 3y = -3 \\ 4x + 6y = 18 \end{cases}$	☐	☐	☐
$\begin{cases} 3x + 2y = 6 \\ 6x - 4y = 24 \end{cases}$	☐	☐	☐
$\begin{cases} 8x - 10y = 6 \\ -4x + 5y = 3 \end{cases}$	☐	☐	☐
$\begin{cases} 4x + 10y = 16 \\ 10x + 25y = 40 \end{cases}$	☐	☐	☐

Spiral Review

Use the information to answer Problems 14–15.

The height in inches of a candle that has been burning for x hours is represented by the equation $h = 16 - 2x$.

14. What is the meaning of the slope in the context of the burning candle?

_____

15. What is the meaning of the y-intercept in the context of the burning candle?

_____

16. What is the solution of the system of equations? $\begin{cases} x = 2y - 5 \\ 2x + y = 20 \end{cases}$

_____

Name _____

Apply Systems of Equations

(**I Can**) write and solve a system of equations to solve a real-world problem.

Step It Out

1 ▶ There are 12 people in an adventure club going to an adventure park. An adult's pass is $55, a child's pass is $42, and they spend a total of $569. How many adults and how many children go together to the park?

A. What equation can you write to represent the number of adults a and children c that are in the group?

$$\boxed{} + \boxed{} = 12$$

B. How much is an adult's pass? How much is a child's pass? What was the total spent on day passes?

_____

What equation can you write to represent the total amount spent by the group?

$$\boxed{}\, a + \boxed{}\, c = \boxed{}$$

C. You can use the two equations from Parts A and B to write a system of equations to solve the problem. Write the system of equations.

$$\boxed{} + \boxed{} = 12$$

$$\boxed{}\, a + \boxed{}\, c = \boxed{}$$

D. Solve the system of equations using elimination.

$$a = \boxed{} \qquad\qquad c = \boxed{}$$

E. How many adults and how many children go together to the park?

_____ adults

_____ children

 Turn and Talk Is there another way to solve the system of equations? Explain.

© Houghton Mifflin Harcourt Publishing Company • **Image Credit:** ©Francesco Gustincich/Alamy

2 Kailee is holding an event at a ballroom with tables that seat 6 people and tables that seat 4 people. Kailee orders a total of 12 tables for the 57 people coming to the event. How many tables of each kind should she order?

Round: seats 6

Square: seats 4

A. Let x represent the number of tables that seat 6 people and y represent the number of tables that seat 4 people. Complete the equation to represent the total number of tables.

$$\boxed{} + \boxed{} = \boxed{}$$

B. Complete the equation that represents the seating capacity of the tables Kailee orders, relative to her seating needs.

$$\boxed{}\,x + \boxed{}\,y = 57$$

C. These two equations comprise the system of equations that represent the problem. Begin solving the system of equations by first solving one equation for y.

$$x + y = 12 \rightarrow y = \boxed{}$$

Substitute the resulting expression for y into the second equation and solve for x.

$$6x + 4y = 57 \qquad\qquad \boxed{} + \boxed{} = 57$$

$$6x + 4\left(\boxed{}\right) = 57 \qquad\qquad \boxed{} = \boxed{}$$

$$6x + \boxed{} - \boxed{} = 57 \qquad\qquad x = \boxed{}$$

D. Does the value for x make sense for this problem? Why or why not?

_____

E. Round the value for x up to the nearest whole number, and use that value to solve for y.

$$\boxed{} + y = 12 \rightarrow y = \boxed{}$$

She should order _____ tables that seat 6 people and _____ tables that seat 4 people.

F. Substitute x and y into the second equation. If Kailee orders these tables, will she have enough seats for all attendees? Explain.

$$7\left(\boxed{}\right) + 5\left(\boxed{}\right) = \boxed{}$$

_____

 Turn and Talk If a value doesn't make sense for the solution to a problem, do you always round the value up? Explain.

3 ▸ Line *A* passes through points (0, 1) and (2, 5). Line *B* passes through points (1, 1) and (4, 10).

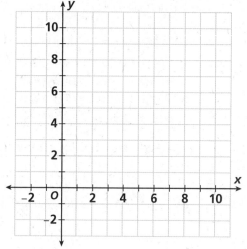

A. Plot the points for Line *A* and draw a line through them.

B. Plot the points for Line *B* and draw a line through them.

C. Do the lines intersect? _____

D. Use the graph to estimate the point of intersection.

_____

E. How could you find the exact point of intersection?

_____

Check Understanding

Write and solve a system of equations to solve Problems 1–3.

1. The Spartan basketball team scored 108 points in last night's game. They scored 48 baskets in all, making a combination of two-point and three-point baskets. There were no points due to free throws. How many three-point baskets did the Spartans make?

_____

_____

2. Mr. Chen buys 5 tomato plants and 3 cucumber plants for $33.00. His neighbor buys 4 tomato plants and 2 cucumber plants of the same varieties for $24.90 at the same nursery. What is the cost of each type of plant?

_____

_____

_____

3. One line passes through (0, 1) and (4, −7). A second line passes through (−1, −1) and (1, −5). Do the two lines intersect? If so, where? Show your work.

_____

_____

_____

Tomato plant

Cucumber plant

On Your Own

4. (MP) **Model with Mathematics** A museum charges different rates for adults and students. Mrs. Lopez's class went to the museum last week and spent $232.50 on 25 tickets. How many students and how many adults went to the museum?

Museum Prices	
Adults	Students
$14.50	$8.00

A. Write a system of equations to model the problem.

B. Find the solution using any method.

C. What is the meaning of the solution in the context of the problem?

5. Tony is hiking on a trail when he sees his friend Nathan 30 feet in front of him.

A. Graph a system of equations modeling the situation.

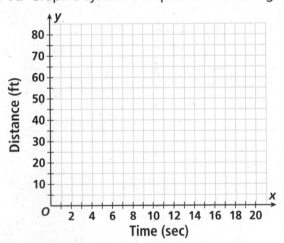

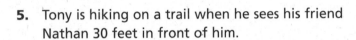

2 feet per second

4 feet per second

B. Will Tony catch up to Nathan? Explain.

6. (MP) **Model with Mathematics** The sum of two numbers is 18. The sum of the greater number and twice the lesser number is 25.

A. Let x represent the greater number and y represent the lesser number. Write a system of equations to find the numbers.

B. Solve the system. What are the two numbers? _____

7. Two angles are complementary if the sum of their measures is equal to 90°. Georgia draws two complementary angles. One of the angles measures 15° more than 2 times the other angle's measure.

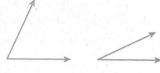

  A. (MP) **Model with Mathematics** Write a system of equations to represent the situation. _____

  B. What are the measures of the two angles? _____

8. **Open Ended** Write a problem that could be solved using the graph shown. Explain what happens and how it relates to the solution.

_____

_____

_____

_____

_____

_____

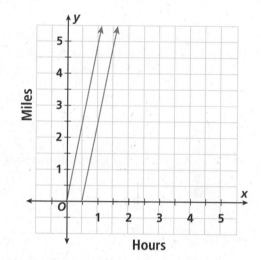

9. (MP) **Reason** Mrs. Bennett gives her math class a test worth 145 points. Some of the questions are worth two points and some are worth five points. Is there enough information to determine how many five-point questions are on the test? If so, how many? If not, what additional information is needed?

_____

_____

10. The Fairplay sporting goods store sells two different models of a popular fitness tracker. In one month the store sold 42 trackers for a total of $6574.

Fitness Trackers	
Model A	Model B
$127	$189

  A. (MP) **Model with Mathematics** Write a system of equations that represents the situation.

_____

  B. How many of each type of tracker were sold?

_____

11. Bowling costs $6 per game and virtual golf costs $0.50 per hole. Bowling takes 30 minutes per game and virtual golf takes 7.5 minutes per hole. Toni spends 1 hour and $8 between the two activities.

    A. (MP) **Model with Mathematics** Write a system of equations relating b, the number of games of bowling played, to g, the number of holes of virtual golf played.

    _____

    B. Solve the system you wrote and interpret your solution.

    _____

    _____

12. The table shows two options provided by an internet service provider.

	Setup fee	Monthly fee
Option 1	$100	$55
Option 2	$30	$75

    A. (MP) **Model with Mathematics** Write a system of equations modeling this situation, where c represents the total cost for m months of service.

    _____

    B. After how many monthly payments will the cost of the two options be the same? Explain.

    _____

    _____

    C. (MP) **Construct Arguments** Which option would you recommend for someone who is only going to stay in town for 5 months? Why?

    _____

    _____

    _____

13. (MP) **Model with Mathematics** Alicia bought 4 sandwiches and 5 bowls of soup, spending $38.50. Adam spent $47.25 to buy three sandwiches and nine bowls of soup. Write and solve a system of equations to find out the cost of each sandwich and each bowl of soup.

_____

_____

_____

Apply Systems of Equations

1. A builder is developing a neighborhood of one-bedroom and two-bedroom houses. The builder wants to build 12 houses and has 88 windows. The one-bedroom houses need 6 windows and the two-bedroom houses need 9 windows.

   A. (MP) **Model with Mathematics** Write and solve a system of equations to represent the situation.

   _____

   B. How many of each type of house should the builder build?

   _____

2. **Math on the Spot** Doug has 45 coins worth $9.00. The coins are all quarters or dimes. How many of each type of coin does Doug have?

   _____

3. A young horse, Alex, is chasing an older horse, Champ. Alex is 60 meters behind Champ. Graph a system of equations to solve the problem. Will Alex catch up to Champ? If so, when? If not, why not?

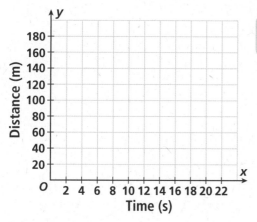

Alex:
15 meters per second

Champ:
5 meters per second

4. (MP) **Reason** A family owns two cars. One car gets 35 miles per gallon and the other car gets 27 miles per gallon. In one week the family drove a total of 480 miles and used 16 gallons of gas. Can you determine the number of miles the family drove each car? Explain.

   _____

   _____

   _____

Test Prep

5. The Greenery landscaping company puts in an order for 2 pine trees and 5 hydrangea bushes for a neighborhood project. The order costs $150. They put in a second order for 3 pine trees and 4 hydrangea bushes that cost $144.50. What is the cost for one pine tree?

$ _____

6. Sonia is older than her brother Eddie. The sum of their ages is 38. The difference is 14. How many years old are Sonia and Eddie?

Sonia: ☐ years old

Eddie: ☐ years old

7. The Chenery School sold a total of 78 tickets for the spring concert. Advance tickets sold for $5.00 and tickets purchased the night of the concert cost $10.50. If the total revenue for the night was $533, how many advance tickets were sold?

_____ tickets

8. Two angles are supplementary. This means that the sum of the two angles is equal to 180°. One of the angles measures 20 degrees more than three times the other angle. What is the measure of the larger angle?

Ⓐ 40°   Ⓒ 140°

Ⓑ 120°   Ⓓ 200°

Spiral Review

9. Which two triangles are similar? How do you know?

A.

B.

C.

_____

_____

10. A line passes through the origin and (4, 6). What are two other points on this line?

_____

11. What is an equation of the line with slope −3 through the point (3, 5)?

_____

Review

Vocabulary

Choose the correct term from the Vocabulary box.

1. A _____ is two or more equations that contain two or more variables.

2. A method of solving a system of equations that involves adding equations to remove a variable is called _____.

3. A method of solving a system of equations that involves replacing a variable with a number or another expression is called _____.

Concepts and Skills

4. North Shore Kayak and South Shore Kayak each charge a flat fee plus an hourly rate. The graph shows y, the cost in dollars, for renting a kayak from each company for x hours. Which statement about the companies is true?

   Ⓐ The companies have the same hourly rate.

   Ⓑ South Shore costs more when renting a kayak for 2 hours.

   Ⓒ The flat fee is higher for North Shore than for South Shore.

   Ⓓ The companies cost the same when renting a kayak for 1 hour.

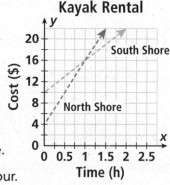

Kayak Rental

5. A graph of a system of two equations is shown. What is the solution of the system? Write the ordered pair.

   (_____ , _____)

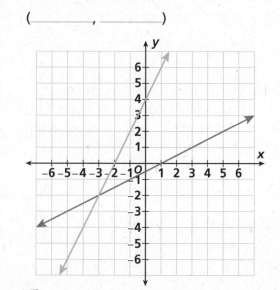

6. (MP) **Use Tools** Determine the solution of the system of equations shown. State what strategy and tool you will use to answer the question, explain your choice, and then find the answer.

$$\begin{cases} y = x + 1 \\ y = -2x + 4 \end{cases}$$

_____

_____

_____

Determine the solution of each system of equations.

7. $\begin{cases} y = -6x + 4 \\ y = 2x + 12 \end{cases}$ (_____ , _____)

8. $\begin{cases} 3x + 2y = 9 \\ 4x - y = 34 \end{cases}$ (_____ , _____)

9. A system of equations is shown. Which method could be used to eliminate a variable from the system?

$$\begin{cases} 5x + 6y = 28 \\ 4x + 2y = 14 \end{cases}$$

  Ⓐ Multiply the first equation by −4, and then add the equations.

  Ⓑ Multiply the first equation by −2, and then add the equations.

  Ⓒ Multiply the second equation by −3, and then add the equations.

  Ⓓ Multiply the second equation by −2, and then add the equations.

10. Select the number of solutions for each system of two linear equations.

	No solution	One solution	Infinitely many solutions
$\begin{cases} 3x + 5y = 10 \\ 2x + 5y = 10 \end{cases}$	☐	☐	☐
$\begin{cases} x - 3y = 4 \\ 2x - 6y = 8 \end{cases}$	☐	☐	☐
$\begin{cases} 4x - 2y = 6 \\ 4x - 2y = 8 \end{cases}$	☐	☐	☐

11. Tickets for a high school basketball game cost $4 for adults and $3 for students. The school sells 120 tickets and makes $412 in ticket sales. The system of equations shown can be used to determine the number of adult tickets a and the number of student tickets s the school sold. How many adult tickets and how many student tickets did the school sell?

$$\begin{cases} a + s = 120 \\ 4a + 3s = 412 \end{cases}$$

_____ adult tickets   _____ student tickets

12. Corinne's pumpkin weighs 28 ounces and is growing at a rate of 5 ounces per week. Ron's pumpkin weighs 10 ounces and is growing at a rate of 13 ounces per week. Let t represent time in weeks and w represent weight in ounces. Which system of equations can be used to determine when the weights of the two pumpkins will be equal?

  Ⓐ $\begin{cases} w = 5 + 28t \\ w = 13 + 10t \end{cases}$

  Ⓒ $\begin{cases} w = 5t - 28 \\ w = 13t - 10 \end{cases}$

  Ⓑ $\begin{cases} w = 5(t + 28) \\ w = 13(t + 10) \end{cases}$

  Ⓓ $\begin{cases} w = 5t + 28 \\ w = 13t + 10 \end{cases}$

Statistics and Probability

Meteorologist

STEM
POWERING INGENUITY

Meteorologists use scientific processes to study the atmosphere and forecast the weather. They use complex math to model and interpret weather data. You're probably most familiar with meteorologists who work for television or radio stations. However, meteorologists may also be employed by government agencies, airlines, utility companies, and universities. Modern meteorology relies heavily on computers to produce accurate weather forecasts.

STEM Task:

Weather forecasts in the United States usually give temperatures in degrees Fahrenheit (°F), rather than in degrees Celsius (°C). The equation $F = 1.8C + 32$ relates the two temperature scales. Graph this equation. An air temperature of 129 °F was recorded in Death Valley, California, in 2013. Use your graph to estimate the equivalent temperature in degrees Celsius. Explain your method.

Learning Mindset

Challenge-Seeking Makes Decisions

Learning something new can be exciting. When you first discover a new interest, the possibilities seem endless. But then you have to make some decisions. For example, how much money can you afford to spend on your new interest? How much time? Is it just a hobby, or do you think you might want to pursue it more seriously, perhaps even as a career? Here are some tips for making important decisions.

- Talk to teachers, parents, and others that you trust. Ultimately you will have to make the final decision yourself, but that doesn't mean you can't ask for others' input.

- Don't rush. There's plenty of time ahead of you. Think carefully before you make a decision, especially if you are feeling uncertain or unhappy.

- Don't be afraid to make a mistake. Very few decisions are irreversible. If you make a decision that doesn't work out, you can almost always go back and make a different decision.

Reflect

Q What decisions did you make as you worked on the STEM Task? How did those decisions help you complete the task?

Q Think about a decision you made that led to a mistake. What did you learn from it?

© Houghton Mifflin Harcourt Publishing Company • Image Credit: ©FrameStockFootages/Shutterstock

Scatter Plots

TAKEN for a RIDE

Use the graphs to answer the questions.

A. The graph shows the cost *y* of using Company A's ride-sharing service for a trip of *x* miles. Find the rate of change in the graph. What does it represent?

Cost for Company A

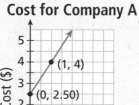

B. Company B wants to compete with Company A. It will have the same initial fee as Company A, but a lower price per mile.

Write the equation of a function that could represent the total cost *y* of using Company B's ride-sharing service for a trip of *x* miles. Then graph your equation.

Cost for Company B

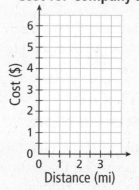

 Turn and Talk

How does the equation you wrote for Company B indicate the initial fee and the rate of change?

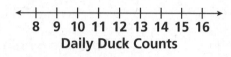
Are You Ready?

Complete these problems to review prior concepts and skills you will need for this module.

Dot Plots

1. Marie recorded the number of ducks seen at a pond each day for 12 days. The data set is listed.

   8, 10, 12, 14, 13, 15, 13, 15, 14, 15, 16, 16

   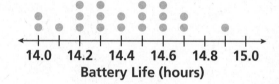

   Daily Duck Counts

   A. Display Marie's data in the dot plot.

   B. Describe the center, spread, and overall shape.

   _____

   _____

Draw Inferences from Random Samples

A phone company tested the battery life of a random sample of 20 of its newest model phones. The dot plot shows the company's results. Use the dot plot to answer Problems 2–3.

2. Calculate the mean battery life of the phones in the sample.

   _____

3. Based on the sample, how many of the newest phone models in a shipment of 2000 phones can be expected to have a battery life of less than 14.2 hours?

   _____

Interpret Linear Functions

The graph shows the linear relationship between the number of hours a candle burns and the weight in ounces of the candle. Use the graph to answer Problems 4–6.

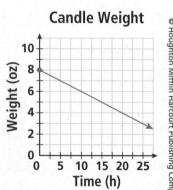

4. What is the initial value in this situation, and what does it represent?

   _____

5. What is the rate of change in this situation, and what does it represent?

   _____

6. Write the equation of the function.

   _____

Name _____

Construct Scatter Plots and Examine Association

(I Can) construct a scatter plot, determining whether an association is positive or negative, strong or weak, and nonlinear or linear. I can recognize outliers and clusters.

Spark Your Learning

Mrs. Tenney gave her students a test. The students had 3 weeks to study for the test, and Mrs. Tenney tracked the number of hours that each student studied and the scores they got on the test. Graph the data in the table. Describe the graph.

Study time (h)	Test score
19	97
12	81
16	89
20	98
10	75
12	99
15	90
15	88
19	100
16	91
8	72
10	78
15	72
18	95
21	98

16 hours   20 hours   15 hours
19 hours
12 hours   10 hours

Turn and Talk Why do you think there is not a constant rate of change for the number of hours studied and the test scores?

Build Understanding

An **association** is the description of the relationship between two data sets. Two data sets have a **positive association** when their data values increase together or decrease together.

Connect to Vocabulary

A **scatter plot** is a graph with points plotted to show a possible relationship between two sets of data.

1 ➤ The graph of the data from Mrs. Tenney's class is shown in a scatter plot.

A. Describe the change that you see in the graph.

As the _____ increases,

the _____ increases.

B. When data points lie roughly along a line, the data set displays a **linear association**. When the data seem to follow a pattern resembling anything other than a line, the data set either displays a **nonlinear association** or no association at all. Do you think the relation between test scores and study time appears linear? Explain.

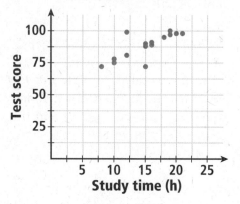

_____

_____

Two data sets have a **negative association** if one set of data values increases while the other decreases.

Mrs. Tenney also tracked the number of hours students spent on social media sites and the scores they got on the test. The data are shown in the scatter plot.

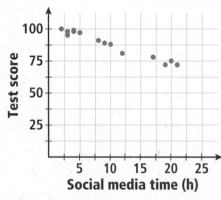

C. Describe the change that you see in the graph.

As the _____ increases, the _____ decreases.

D. Do you think the relation between test scores and social media time appears linear? Explain.

_____

_____

© Houghton Mifflin Harcourt Publishing Company • Image Credit: (br) ©Monkey Business Images/Shutterstock

Two data sets have **no association** when there is no relationship between their data values.

Mrs. Tenney wanted to see if there was any relationship between the number of siblings that a student has and their score on the test. The data are shown in the scatter plot.

E. Describe the change in test scores that you see in the graph.

_____

_____

_____

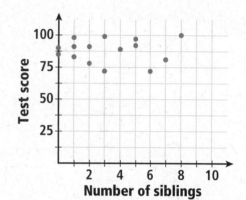

F. Do you think the relation between test scores and number of siblings appears linear? Explain.

_____

_____

Step It Out

Connect to Vocabulary

An **outlier** for a data set of ordered pairs is a point that does not follow the overall pattern on a graph of the data set.

2 ▷ If a scatter plot has an association, that association can also be strong or weak. For linear data, the association is stronger the closer the points are to making a line.

A
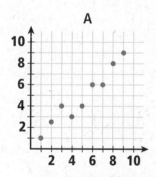

B
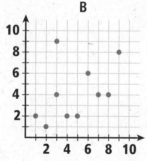

C
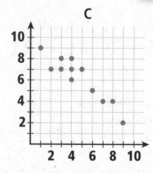

D
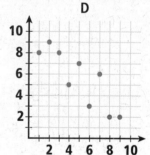

A. Which scatter plot(s) have a positive association? Is the association of each strong positive or weak positive?

_____

B. Which graph or graphs appear to have outliers? _____

C. A **cluster** is a set of closely grouped data.
   Which graph or graphs appear to have a cluster? _____

 Turn and Talk Which scatter plot(s) have a negative association? Is the association of each scatter plot strong negative or weak negative? How do you know?

3 ▸ Jack earned $60 doing odd jobs for his neighbor. Each week he spends some of the money and records the amount of money left.

Week	1	2	3	4	5	6	7
Money remaining	$57.00	$53.00	$49.00	$48.00	$47.00	$44.00	$19.00

A. Graph the data.

B. Does the scatter plot have a negative or positive association?

_____

_____

C. Describe and interpret the shape of the graph.

_____

_____

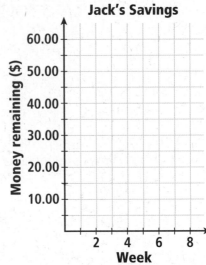

Jack's Savings

D. Are there any clusters or outliers? If so, what might explain the cluster or outliers?

_____

_____

E. Is the association strong or weak? _____

Check Understanding

1. The table shows the amount of money Anna spends at the thrift store each week.

Items	1	2	3	4	5	5	6	6
Spent	$1.90	$3.50	$4.25	$6.00	$6.25	$6.50	$6.20	$5.90

A. Graph the relationship in the scatter plot.

B. Describe the relationship in the scatter plot, including any outliers or clusters.

_____

_____

_____

Thrift Store Purchases

© Houghton Mifflin Harcourt Publishing Company • Image Credit: ©plastique/Shutterstock

On Your Own

2. **(MP) Use Structure** The Pep Club is selling bracelets to raise money for a pet shelter. The club members staff the booth for a total of 12 hours selling bracelets. The table records the amount of money they earned each hour.

A. Graph the data in the table.

Hour	Money earned ($)
1	$17
2	$22
4	$16
5	$40
6	$28
7	$25
9	$31
10	$27
11	$21

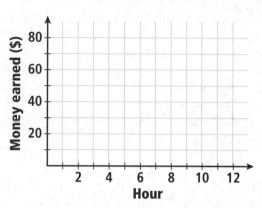

B. Describe in detail the association of the graph. Include whether it is linear or nonlinear, whether it is positive or negative, whether it is strong or weak, and whether it has any clusters or outliers.

_____

_____

_____

_____

3. Bob works at a movie theater collecting tickets. He tracked how many people came to each showing one day. Which showtime is an outlier?

Showtime	Attendance
11:00 a.m.	16
2:00 p.m.	17
4:00 p.m.	15
6:30 p.m.	115
9:00 p.m.	20

Module 8 • Lesson 1

283

4. **(MP) Critique Reasoning** Chantelle says that the scatter plot has a strong positive association because the numbers at the bottom of the graph are increasing and the shape of the graph is linear. Is she correct? Explain.

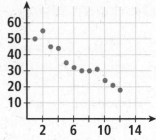

_____

_____

_____

5. **Open Ended** Ellianna made a scatter plot that showed a positive association and had one outlier. Write a possible scenario for Ellianna's scatter plot.

_____

_____

_____

_____

_____

Use the graph to answer Problems 6–8.

6. Is there any association to the data? If so, which type?

_____

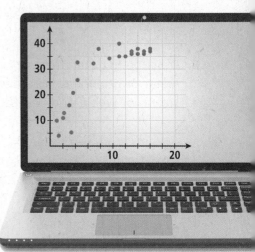

7. Is the scatter plot linear or nonlinear?

_____

8. Are there any outliers or clusters in the graph?

_____

9. **Open Ended** Give an example of a scenario for a scatter plot that would show no association.

_____

_____

_____

 I'm in a Learning Mindset!

What types of decisions did I make when I analyzed scatter plots?

_____

_____

LESSON 8.1
**More Practice/
Homework**

ONLINE
Ⓔ**d** Video Tutorials and
Interactive Examples

Construct Scatter Plots and Examine Association

1. The table shows the number of fundraiser items each person in the band sold and how much money each raised.

Items sold	Money raised
6	$34
2	$12
7	$52
8	$66
6	$32
6	$30
21	$98
5	$28

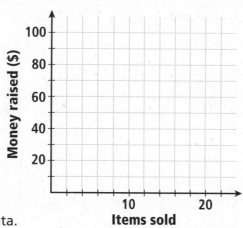

A. Construct a scatter plot for the data.

B. Describe the association and any features of the scatter plot.

_____

_____

Use the graph to answer Problems 2–4.

2. Describe the association, if there is one.

_____

3. (MP) **Use Structure** Does the scatter plot appear linear or nonlinear?

_____

4. (MP) **Use Structure** Are there any outliers or clusters in the scatter plot?

_____

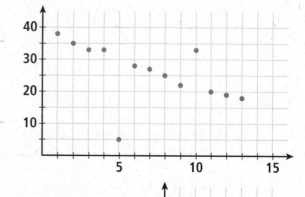

5. **Math on the Spot** The table shows the number of runs scored by a softball team in their first 7 games of the year. Use the given data to make a scatter plot. Describe the association.

Game	1	2	3	4	5	6	7
Runs scored	3	1	5	9	12	10	12

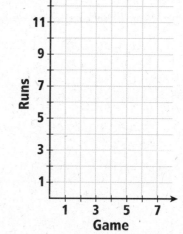

_____

_____

Test Prep

6. Choose all the sentences that describe this scatter plot.

   (A) It shows a positive association.

   (B) It shows a negative association.

   (C) It has at least one outlier.

   (D) It shows no association.

   (E) It shows a cluster.

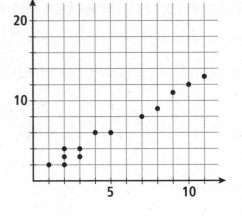

7. Describe each scatter plot as having positive linear, negative linear, positive nonlinear, negative nonlinear, or no association.

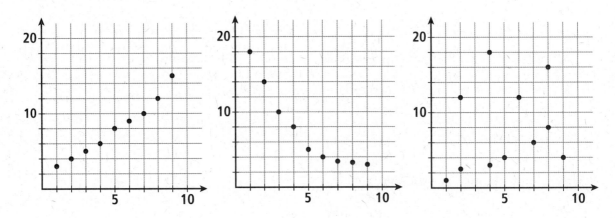

_____   _____   _____

Spiral Review

8. Breck has 22 dimes and nickels. The total value of the coins is $1.45. How many dimes and how many nickels does Breck have?

_____

9. Solve this system of linear equations.

$$\begin{cases} 4x + 4y = 12 \\ 6x - 4y = -32 \end{cases}$$

_____

10. Find an equation of the line with a slope of –7 that passes through the point (–3, 12).

_____

Name _____

Draw and Analyze Trend Lines

(I Can) draw a trend line and informally assess a trend line by judging the closeness of the data points to the line.

Spark Your Learning

Skyler collected data from several different types of cars. The scatter plot displays the relationship between the weight of each car and the average number of miles it can travel in the city on a single gallon of gas. What conclusions can you draw from the data?

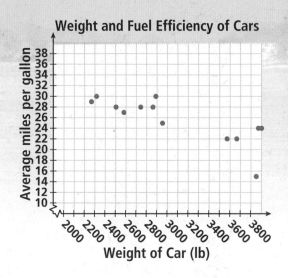

Weight and Fuel Efficiency of Cars

Average miles per gallon / Weight of Car (lb)

Turn and Talk Estimate the average miles per gallon for a car weighing 3400 pounds. How did you determine your estimate?

Build Understanding

1 A class draws four different models, or trend lines, for the same data set. To evaluate each trend line, consider the following questions.

How many points lie above the trend line? How many points lie below? How many points does the trend line touch or pass through? What is the greatest vertical distance between any point and the trend line?

Connect to Vocabulary

A **trend line** models the behavior of data displayed in a scatter plot. When a scatter plot shows a positive association, the trend line will have a positive slope. The trend line for data with a negative association will have a negative slope.

Model A

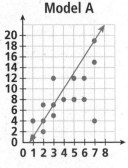

Model B

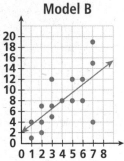

Model C

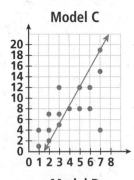

Model D

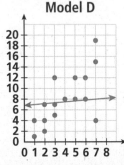

 Turn and Talk Which trend line is the best model of the relationship? Explain.

Step It Out

2 ▶ The scatter plot shows a negative linear association.

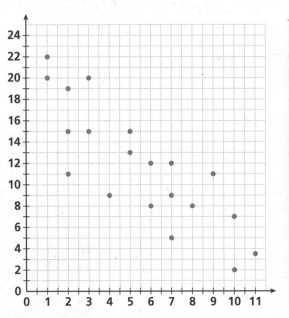

A. How many points are there in the data set? About how many points would an ideal trend line have above and below it?

_____

B. Use a ruler to sketch a trend line to model the association shown.

_____

C. How many points does your trend line touch or pass through?

_____

D. How many points lie above your trend line? How many lie below your trend line?

_____

E. How many points have a vertical distance from the trend line of more than 3 units?

_____

F. What is the greatest vertical distance between any point and the trend line?

_____

 Turn and Talk Describe a real-world situation that could be modeled by this data.

3 **A.** Analyze the scatter plots, and sketch a trend line for each.

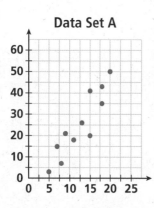
Data Set A

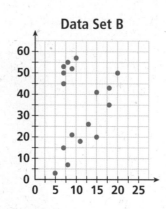
Data Set B

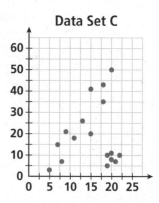
Data Set C

B. Compare the trend lines for data sets A, B, and C. How do the outliers influence the trend lines?

_____

_____

_____

_____

_____

_____

_____

_____

_____

_____

Check Understanding

1. What are key characteristics of a reasonable trend line for a scatter plot?

_____

_____

2. Harold and Chloe each drew a trend line for the given data set.

A. Whose trend line is a closer fit? Why?

_____

_____

_____

B. For the other line, analyze what mistake might have been made.

_____

_____

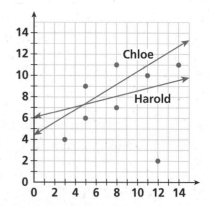

On Your Own

3. (MP) **Reason** The Flan family enjoys making cat videos and posting them on social media sites. They construct the scatter plot shown.

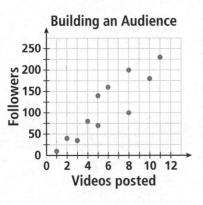

Building an Audience

103 views

A. Is a trend line an appropriate way to model these data? Explain.

_____

_____

B. Sketch a reasonable trend line for this data and justify your choice.

_____

_____

_____

C. Estimate the number of followers that the Flan family might expect when they have posted 20 videos.

_____

D. How did you make your estimate? What might cause your estimate to be incorrect?

_____

_____

_____

4. When is it *not* appropriate to model the relationship in a scatter plot with a trend line?

_____

_____

5. **Open Ended** The trend line of a data set is shown. Plot a data set with at least 5 points on the graph that could result in the trend line shown.

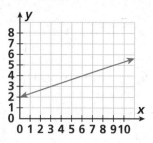

6. **STEM** The average length of an animal's life is related to the average length of pregnancy for that type of animal. The scatter plot shows data for several different animals.

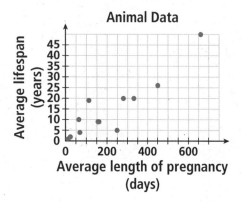

Animal Data

A. Sketch a trend line to model the data. Circle the outlier and explain how it influences your choice for the trend line.

_____

_____

_____

B. How would the trend line change if the outlier were removed?

_____

_____

C. The average length of pregnancy for a polar bear is 240 days. Use the trend line to estimate the average length of a polar bear's life.

_____

 I'm in a Learning Mindset!

What types of decisions did I make when drawing and analyzing trend lines?

_____

_____

Draw and Analyze Trend Lines

1. A. (MP) **Construct Arguments** Is the trend line shown on the scatter plot a good fit for the data? Explain. If the line is not a good fit, sketch a more appropriate trend line.

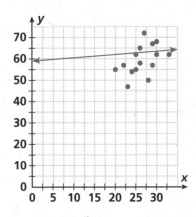

_____

_____

_____

B. The point (25, 20) is added to the data set. How will its addition influence the trend line?

_____

_____

_____

_____

2. **Open Ended** Plot at least 5 points to display a data set that has the trend line $y = \frac{1}{2}x$. Include the graph of the trend line in your sketch.

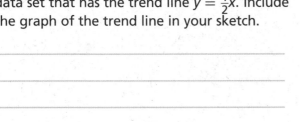

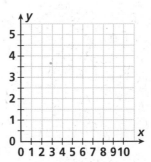

3. (MP) **Critique Reasoning** Mateo sketches a trend line to model a data set. Eight points lie above the trend line and three points lie below. Did Mateo make a mistake? Explain your reasoning.

_____

_____

_____

Test Prep

4. Select all true statements about the scatter plot shown.

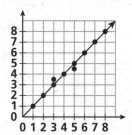

(A) There are equal numbers of points above the trend line and below it.

(B) The data set shows nonlinear association.

(C) The greatest vertical distance of any data point from the trend line is less than 1.

(D) The trend line touches most of the points in the data set.

(E) The data set shows negative linear association.

5. Explain how adding outliers to a data set might not influence the data set.

_____

_____

6. Calhoun sketched a scatter plot comparing the numbers of hours studied to test scores for the latest test his class took. He found a trend line that was a good fit for the data. Which would you expect to be true? Select all that apply.

(A) There are data points above and below the trend line.

(B) The data have a linear association.

(C) The data points on the graph line up in a perfectly straight line.

(D) The slope of the trend line is positive.

(E) There are more data points that are outliers than data points that are not outliers.

Spiral Review

7. Solve the equation $3(x - 7) = 2(x - 5)$. _____

8. What is the solution to the system of equations?

$$\begin{cases} 2x - 6y = 10 \\ -5x + 15y = 30 \end{cases}$$

_____

9. Write an equation of a linear function with slope -2 that passes through the point $(4, -5)$. _____

Name _____

Interpret Linear Data in Context

(I Can) use the equation of a line to solve problems in the context of bivariate measurement data, interpreting the slope and intercept.

Step It Out

1 ▸ Janelle is making a graph that compares the salaries and ages of the members of the planning department. She lists the salaries by tens of thousands of dollars and the ages by years.

Age (years)	Salary ($10,000's)
25	4.5
31	2.9
31	6.0
35	5.5
35	6.2
37	7.2
38	6.8
43	8.3
46	12.1
50	11.9

A. Use the graph provided to make a scatter plot using the data in the table.

B. The line $y = 0.36x - 6.1$ is a trend line for the scatter plot. Add the trend line to the graph.

C. Complete the interpretation of the slope of the trend line.

The slope is _____. This means that for every 1 year increase in age, there is a salary increase of _____ of $10,000. For every one year increase in age, there is a salary increase of $_____.

 Turn and Talk Does every older worker make more money than any particular younger worker? Explain.

2 Hampton wanted to see whether there was an association between the average time people in his class spent exercising per day and the average time they spent sleeping each night. His scatter plot and the equation of his trend line are shown.

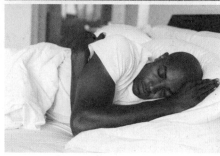

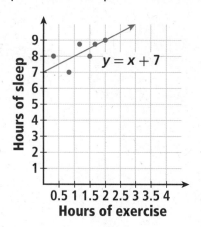

$y = x + 7$

Hours of sleep (y-axis)
Hours of exercise (x-axis)

A. How much does the person who exercises 2 hours per day sleep? What does the trend line suggest as the amount of sleeping time for a typical person who exercises 2 hours per day?

B. According to the trend line, about how many hours of sleep would someone who exercises about 1 hour per day get?

C. According to the trend line, what change in sleep time is associated with each increase of 1 hour of exercise?

D. According to the trend line, about how long might you sleep if you exercised 3 hours per day?

E. What would the data point (1.3, 7.8) mean on this graph? Is it on the trend line?

F. The coordinates of the initial value are _____.

A person who doesn't exercise at all sleeps about _____ hours per night.

3 An educator decided to investigate the relationship between the amount of time a group of students spent reading and the amount of time they spent watching television in one week. She graphed her results as shown.

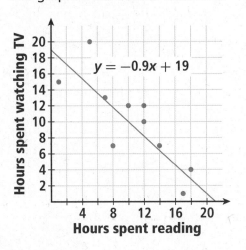

$$y = -0.9x + 19$$

Hours spent watching TV

Hours spent reading

A person reads about 4 hours per week. If he or she also watched television about 4 hours per week, would you consider that data point to be an outlier? Explain.

Turn and Talk Why might predictions made from a trend line not always be accurate?

Check Understanding

1. For the graph in Task 3, what does the trend line show?

2. For the data set given in the table, estimate the rate of change of a trend line with good fit.

Time (minutes)	4.3	5.8	24.0	2.3	1.7	105.0	19.0
Boxes assembled	2	3	15	1	1	50	11

On Your Own

3. **Health and Fitness** The coach of a basketball team compared the heights of the players and their average numbers of rebounds per game.

A. Graph the data and the trend line, $y = 4.4x - 22$.

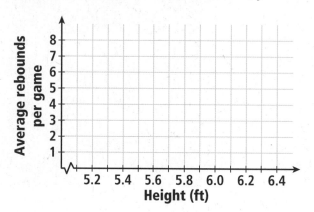

Height (ft)	Average rebounds per game
5.3	2.5
5.6	1.2
5.8	2
5.9	3.7
5.9	2.9
6.0	4
6.0	3.4
6.2	6.3
6.3	4
6.4	7.1

B. What is the *y*-intercept of the trend line?

_____

C. What does the *y*-intercept mean in this situation? Is it useful? Explain.

_____

_____

D. The scatter plot shows that as players get taller they tend to get more rebounds. Does that mean that the tallest player would get the most rebounds?

_____

_____

_____

_____

E. The coach also made this scatter plot of the average number of points made by the five top-scoring players, compared to their heights. Compare the general trends from each scatter plot.

_____

_____

_____

_____

_____

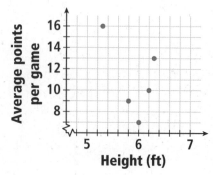

Use the information to answer Problems 4–6.

The scatter plot shows how many trees different people who volunteer at the park can plant in a day, as compared with their years of experience planting trees. The equation for the trend line is also included.

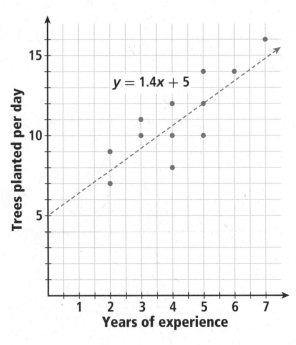

$y = 1.4x + 5$

Trees planted per day

Years of experience

4. A. What does the *y*-intercept of the trend line show?

_____

_____

B. How might a person who is planning a tree-planting event use the *y*-intercept?

_____

_____

_____

5. What does the trend line suggest about the association between experience and tree-planting ability?

_____

_____

_____

6. (MP) **Reason** Would an outlier change the trend line? Explain.

_____

_____

Use the information to answer Problems 7–8.

Mr. Peabody asked his class to keep track of how many hours they spent studying for the midterm math exam. Then he made the scatter plot shown. A 10 was the best a person could do on the test.

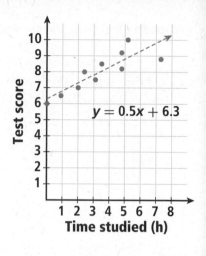

$y = 0.5x + 6.3$

Test score / Time studied (h)

7. (MP) **Critique Reasoning** Mr. Peabody said the scatter plot and trend line show that people who studied more got higher scores on the test. Would you agree? Explain.

_____

_____

_____

_____

8. According to the equation of the trend line, each additional hour spent studying raises test scores by how much? How do you know?

_____

_____

9. (MP) **Model with Mathematics** Mr. Peabody wanted to see if there was a relationship between students' grades in math and in music. Nine of his students who studied both math and music agreed to share their grades in each subject.

A. Make a scatter plot of the data. Draw a trend line.

Math grade, x	Music grade, y
75	80
80	70
80	85
87	97
90	100
92	75
95	90
97	85
100	95

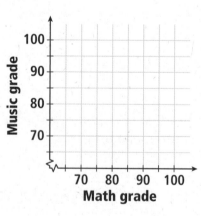

Music grade / Math grade

B. How would you describe the association, if any? Explain.

_____

_____

_____

© Houghton Mifflin Harcourt Publishing Company • Image Credit: ©GaudiLab/Shutterstock

Name _____

Interpret Linear Data in Context

ONLINE

Video Tutorials and Interactive Examples

1. **(MP)** **Construct Arguments** A group of people aged 15 to 30 were asked to rate a movie they had just seen from 1 to 5 stars. The managers of the theater looked at the scatter plot of the data to see what they could learn about the movie. The provided trend line is $y = -\frac{x}{8} + 6\frac{1}{8}$.

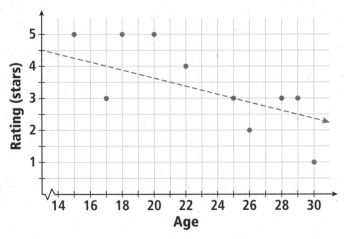

What does the direction of the trend line tell you about the popularity of the movie with older audiences? Explain.

_____

_____

2. A sports watch company conducted a trial of its new watch with eight people. The watches tracked the distance each person walked per day.

Age (x)	Miles walked (y)
20	3.2
21	8.7
23	6.3
25	4.2
26	9.4
27	5.2
27	8.4
28	7.4

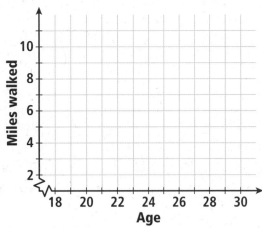

A. Make a scatter plot of the data.

B. **Open Ended** What type of association between the variables does the scatter plot show? Can you draw a good trend line? If so, give its equation.

_____

_____

Test Prep

3. Diners were surveyed after eating at a restaurant. Their ages were associated with their rating of the food. A good trend line for the scatter plot was $y = 0.002x + 4$. What does the slope tell you about the scatter plot?

Ⓐ No one liked the food.

Ⓑ The rating changed quickly depending on age.

Ⓒ Both young and old diners liked the food about the same.

Ⓓ The younger the diner, the better chance they liked the food.

4. A scatter plot is made comparing x, the number of hours since midnight, with y, the number of lights turned on in a house. What would a point at (7, 8) on the scatter plot mean?

When the time was _____, there were _____ lights on.

Use the graph to answer Problems 5–7. The slope of the trend line (not shown) is about 12.5.

5. According to the trend, if Jesse finds a 26-inch television for $75, is that a good deal? Explain.

_____

_____

_____

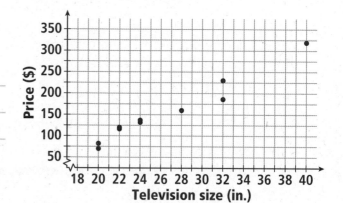

6. A 38-inch television is on sale for $250. Raphaela considers this an outlier to the trend shown in the graph because it is not near any of the other data points. Correct her mistake.

_____

_____

7. An increase of 5 inches in television size is associated with an increase of _____.

Ⓐ $5.00   Ⓑ $12.50   Ⓒ $25.00   Ⓓ $62.50

Spiral Review

8. Solve the system of equations: $\begin{cases} y = 8x + 14 \\ y = 4x + 14 \end{cases}$

9. A sprinter runs 100 yards in 10 seconds. A long-distance runner runs a mile in 4 minutes. Find the times it takes each of them to run 10 yards. How much faster is the sprinter over the 10-yard distance?

_____

_____

Review

Vocabulary

Choose the correct term from the Vocabulary box.

Vocabulary
outlier
cluster
trend line
association
scatter plot
domain

1. A(n) _____ is a set of closely grouped data points.

2. A(n) _____ is a data point that is far from the other points on the graph of a set of paired data.

3. A(n) _____ is a description of the relationship between two data sets.

4. A(n) _____ is a line on a scatter plot that helps show a linear association.

5. A(n) _____ is a graph that uses points to show how two data sets are related.

Concepts and Skills

6. (MP) **Use Tools** The scatter plot shows the relationship between the numbers of hours players spent playing a video game and their high scores. Draw a trend line for the scatter plot. State what strategy and tool you will use to answer the question, explain your choice, and then find the answer.

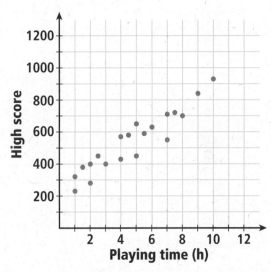

_____

_____

_____

7. The scatter plot shows the ages of the used cars at a car dealership and the numbers of miles the cars have been driven. Select all statements that correctly interpret the scatter plot.

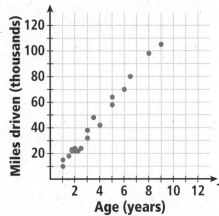

Ⓐ The data show a positive association.

Ⓑ The data point at (9, 105) is an outlier.

Ⓒ The data show a negative association.

Ⓓ The data show a nonlinear association.

Ⓔ There is a cluster of data points near (2, 23).

8. The scatter plot shows data for students in Brenna's class. A trend line for the data is $y = 0.054x - 0.099$.

Use the trend line to predict how long, to the nearest minute, it would take a student in Brenna's class to walk 5 miles.

_____ minutes

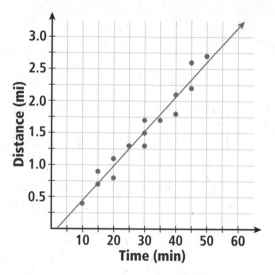

9. Calista surveyed eight classmates about the numbers of texts they sent and received in the past 3 hours. The table shows her results. Use the data set from the table to complete the scatter plot.

Name	Texts sent	Texts received
Daniel	5	10
Ahmed	6	7
Rosa	10	10
Lea	7	8
Malory	3	8
Nico	7	6
Cameron	3	9
Keri	1	4

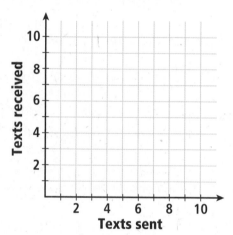

A good trend line for the data in the table is $y = -0.0036x + 70.64$. Use this trend line for Problems 10 and 11.

10. What does the number -0.0036 in the trend line represent in this situation?

_____

_____

_____

11. What does the number 70.64 in the trend line represent?

_____

_____

_____

Elevation (ft), x	Average annual temperature (°F), y
4852	53.7
4856	52.6
5285	50.2
6178	49.0
7233	45.5
7530	44.0
8054	42.1
8645	37.8

Two-Way Tables

Build a Deck

A new card game will have a deck of 100 cards. Each card will have a number and a color. The deck needs to follow these rules: When selecting a card from the deck at random, drawing ...

- a pink card is as likely as unlikely.

- a purple card is unlikely.

- a blue card is impossible.

- a number less than 10 is likely.

- a number less than or equal to 20 is certain.

Design a deck of cards that follows the rules. Tell how many cards of each color will be in the deck and how the cards of each color will be numbered.

_____

_____

_____

_____

 Turn and Talk

Explain how you know that the deck needs to include at least 3 colors of cards.

Are You Ready?

Complete these problems to review prior concepts and skills you will need for this module.

More Likely, Less Likely, Equally Likely

For Problems 1–2, state whether each event is certain, likely, as likely as unlikely, unlikely, or impossible.

1. getting a number less than 2 when rolling a number cube with faces numbered from 1 to 6

2. having rain on a day when the weather forecast states that the probability of rain is 80%

3. Give an example of an event that has a probability of 50%.

Experimental Probability

The crackers in a box come in three shapes. Max randomly chose one cracker at a time 40 times, returning the cracker to the box each time. Use the table to answer Problems 4–6.

Shape	Frequency
Oval	18
Rectangle	14
Star	8

4. **A.** Find the experimental probability of choosing an oval cracker.

B. Predict how many times Max will choose an oval cracker if he carries out this process 200 times.

5. **A.** Find the experimental probability of choosing a rectangular cracker.

B. Predict how many times Max will choose a rectangular cracker if he carries out this process 400 times.

6. **A.** Find the experimental probability of choosing a cracker that is not star-shaped

B. Predict how many times Max will choose a star-shaped cracker if he carries out this process 500 times.

Name _____

Construct and Interpret Two-Way Frequency Tables

(I Can) construct a two-way table summarizing data, complete a table given partial data, and interpret data to determine whether there is an association between two variables.

Spark Your Learning PAIRS

A technology company conducts a survey to find out how many people have a selfie stick and how many have a photo-editing app on their phone. The table shows the results of the survey.

What can you determine from the data in the table?

	Has selfie stick	No selfie stick
Has app	51	26
No app	31	42

 Turn and Talk Does there seem to be any relationship between owning a selfie stick and having a photo editing app? Explain.

Build Understanding

1 A software company gives its employees the choice of using a treadmill desk or a regular desk. Employees can also choose a laptop computer or a tablet computer. The two-way table shows the results from a survey of 200 company employees.

	Treadmill desk	Regular desk	TOTAL
Laptop		79	
Tablet	20		
TOTAL	34		200

A. Explain how you can fill in the missing value in the bottom row of the table. Then fill in the value.

_____

_____

_____

B. Explain how you can fill in the missing values in the "Treadmill desk" column and "Regular desk" column. Then fill in the values.

_____

_____

_____

_____

_____

_____

Treadmill Desk

C. Explain how you can fill in the missing values in the "TOTAL" column on the right side of the table. Then fill in the values.

_____

_____

_____

D. Explain how you can check that the values you wrote in the "TOTAL" column are correct.

_____

_____

 Turn and Talk Is there a different sequence of steps you can use to fill in the two-way table? Explain.

Name _____

Step It Out

2 A survey asked 80 adults about gym memberships and exercise apps. Of those without a gym membership, 16 had an exercise app on their phone. Construct a two-way frequency table to display the data.

36 adults have a gym membership and an exercise app.

48 adults have a gym membership.

A. Fill in the given information: the TOTAL number of adults in the bottom right cell, the 48 TOTAL adults with a membership, the 16 adults without a membership and with an exercise app, and the 36 adults with both a membership and an exercise app.

	Has app	No app	TOTAL
Has membership			
No membership			
TOTAL			

B. Complete the TOTAL column: you know that 48 of the 80 adults surveyed have a gym members.

$\boxed{} - \boxed{} =$ _____ adults do not have a membership

C. Now fill in the top row. Use the fact that 36 of those with a gym membership have an exercise app on their phone.

$\boxed{} - \boxed{} =$ _____ adults with a membership have no app

D. Next, fill in the second row.

$\boxed{} - \boxed{} =$ _____ adults without a membership have no app on their phone

E. Finally, in each column, add the values in the top two rows to get the value for the TOTAL cell in the bottom row.

F. What percentage of the adults surveyed have an exercise app?

$$\frac{\text{Total number of adults with app}}{\text{Total number of adults surveyed}} = \frac{\boxed{}}{80} = \boxed{} = \boxed{}\%$$

G. What percentage of the adults surveyed who have a gym membership have an exercise app?

$$\frac{\text{Number of adults with gym membership and app}}{\text{Total number with gym membership}} = \frac{\boxed{}}{48} = \boxed{} = \boxed{}\%$$

H. Is there an association between having a gym membership and having an exercise app? Explain.

_____

_____

> ### Connect to Vocabulary
>
> To determine if there is an *association* between two categories, divide the number of people who fit into both categories by the total for one of those categories. If that percentage is greater than the percentage of all people surveyed who are in that one category, then the categories have an association.

© Houghton Mifflin Harcourt Publishing Company • Image Credit: ©Peter Muller/age fotostock

3 At a school, 120 students were asked whether they take the subway to school. They were also asked whether they arrived late to school in the past week. The two-way table shows the results. Is there an association between taking the subway and arriving late to school?

	Takes subway	Does not take subway	TOTAL
Late	12	6	18
Not late	18	84	102
TOTAL	30	90	120

A. Find the percentage of all students who arrived late at school.

$$\frac{\text{Total number of students who arrived late}}{\text{Total number of students surveyed}} = \frac{\boxed{}}{120} = \boxed{} = \boxed{}\%$$

B. Find the percentage of students who arrived late among those who took the subway.

$$\frac{\text{Number of students who took subway and arrived late}}{\text{Total number of students who took subway}} = \frac{\boxed{}}{\boxed{}} = \boxed{} = \boxed{}\%$$

C. Students who took the subway to school were $\boxed{\text{more / less}}$ likely to arrive late than the general population of students. There $\boxed{\text{is / is not}}$ an association between taking the subway and arriving late.

Check Understanding

1. Customers at a sporting goods store were surveyed.

   A. Complete the table.

   B. How many customers were surveyed?

	Plays soccer	Does not play soccer	TOTAL
Watches soccer		216	
Does not watch soccer		84	140
TOTAL	200		

   C. Is there an association between watching and playing soccer? Explain.

_____

_____

_____

On Your Own

2. In a survey of 160 people who have reptiles as pets, 40% have a pet snake. Of those with a pet snake, 25% also have a pet lizard. Of those who do not have a pet snake, 75% have a pet lizard.

A. Construct a two-way frequency table to display the data.

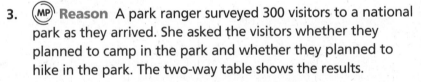

	Has lizard	No lizard	TOTAL
Has snake			
No snake			
TOTAL			

B. What percentage of those surveyed have a pet lizard?

_____

C. What percentage of those surveyed have both a snake and a lizard?

_____

3. (MP) **Reason** A park ranger surveyed 300 visitors to a national park as they arrived. She asked the visitors whether they planned to camp in the park and whether they planned to hike in the park. The two-way table shows the results.

	Camping	No camping	TOTAL
Hiking	135	30	165
No hiking	45	90	135
TOTAL	180	120	300

Is there an association between camping in the park and hiking in the park? Explain.

_____

_____

_____

_____

_____

4. **STEM** Scientists often use two-way frequency tables to determine the effectiveness of a treatment. Suppose scientists want to know whether a new herbal tea helps reduce headaches. They may ask a group of people to drink the tea for a week and record whether or not they get a headache.

	Headache	No headache	TOTAL
Tea	156	84	240
No tea	234	126	360
TOTAL	390	210	600

Based on the results in the two-way frequency table, can the scientists conclude that the herbal tea helps reduce headaches? Explain.

_____

_____

_____

_____

5. **Open Ended** Conduct a survey of students in your class. Each student that you survey should be asked whether or not the student has a curfew on school nights and whether or not the student has assigned chores at home. Record your survey data in the table.

	Curfew	No curfew	TOTAL
Chores			
No chores			
TOTAL			

Is there evidence of an association between having a curfew on school nights and having chores? Explain.

_____

_____

_____

_____

 I'm in a Learning Mindset!

How did the decisions I made constructing two-way frequency tables support my learning and that of others in my class?

_____

_____

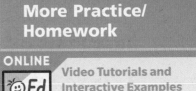
Construct and Interpret Two-Way Frequency Tables

1. (MP) **Attend to Precision** In a survey of 200 people who visited China, 85% visited the Great Wall. Of those who visited the Great Wall, 30% also visited the Chengdu Panda Center. Of those who did not visit the Great Wall, 80% visited the Panda Center. Complete the two-way frequency table.

	Visited Great Wall	Did not visit Great Wall	TOTAL
Visited Chengdu Panda Center			
Did not visit Chengdu Panda Center			
TOTAL			

2. **Math on the Spot** Determine whether there is an association between the events.

A. Thirty-two students were polled about whether they have a phone plan with texting and whether they have had an accident. Find the percentages of those having an accident for both the general population of students and for students who have a phone with texting. Is there an association between having a phone with texting and having an accident?

	Accident	No accident	TOTAL
Phone plan with texting	12	8	20
Phone plan without texting	4	8	12
TOTAL	16	16	32

B. Middle school and high school students were polled about whether they had visited an amusement park. Find the percentages of those having visited an amusement park for both the general population of students and for high school students. Is there an association between being a high school student and visiting an amusement park?

	Visited	Did not visit	TOTAL
Middle school student	20	5	25
High school student	60	15	75
TOTAL	80	20	100

Test Prep

3. Keysha surveyed adults in her city. The results are shown in the table. Which of the following is a true statement?

	Bike	No bike	TOTAL
Car	27	41	68
No car	38	4	42
TOTAL	65	45	110

(A) More people own a bike than own a car.

(B) A total of 68 people surveyed own a bike.

(C) Of the people with a bike, 27 also have a car.

(D) There are 42 bike owners who do not own a car.

4. A gardener tried a new spray on some plants to see if the spray prevents aphids. The table shows the results. What is the value of x?

	Spray	No spray	TOTAL
Aphids	6		13
No aphids		x	
TOTAL	24		41

(A) 7　　　　　　　(C) 18

(B) 10　　　　　　(D) 28

5. Students at a local community college can study Spanish or French. They also have a choice of band or chorus for their music classes. The table shows the results of surveying 100 students. Which is a correct statement about students who study Spanish and students who choose band?

	Spanish	French	TOTAL
Band	16	9	25
Chorus	48	27	75
TOTAL	64	36	100

(A) There is no association because students who study Spanish are no more or less likely than other students to choose band.

(B) There is no association because students who study Spanish are less likely than other students to choose band.

(C) There is an association because students who study Spanish are more likely than other students to choose band.

(D) There is an association because students who study Spanish are less likely than other students to choose band.

Spiral Review

6. A chili cook-off has adult tickets a and child tickets c. A group of visitors buys 3 adult tickets and 2 child tickets and pays a total of $26. Another group buys 5 adult tickets and 3 child tickets and pays $42. Write and solve a system of equations to find the price of each type of ticket.

_____

7. Without graphing, find the point of intersection of the lines $-x + 2y = -4$ and $2x + y = 3$. _____

8. The graph of a proportional relationship passes through the point (6, 21). What is the equation for the relationship? _____

Name _____

Construct Two-Way Relative Frequency Tables

(I Can) construct a two-way relative frequency table, complete a relative frequency table given partial data, and interpret joint and marginal relative frequencies.

Spark Your Learning

Lamar surveyed 200 people who visited Everglades National Park in Florida. He asked them to name their favorite activity in the park and he made this frequency table to show the results.

	Airboat tour	Gator farm	Other	TOTAL
Frequency	94	60	46	200

Using what you know about proportions and percents, what information can you determine from the table?

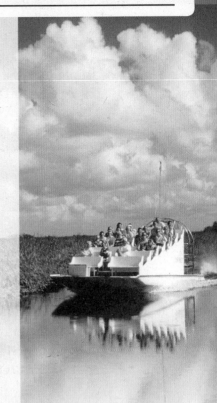

 Turn and Talk How can you check that you calculated correctly?

Build Understanding

1 Lamar makes a two-way frequency table by breaking down the Everglades data for children and adults.

	Airboat tour	Gator farm	Other	TOTAL
Children	44	12	16	72
Adults	50	48	30	128
TOTAL	94	60	46	200

Connect to Vocabulary

A frequency is the number of times a data value occurs. A **relative frequency** is the frequency of a specific data value divided by the total number of data values in the set. It shows how common a data value is, relative to its data set.

A **two-way relative frequency table** is a two-way table that displays relative frequencies.

A. Divide each value in the frequency table by the total number of data values. Write each quotient as a decimal, rounding to the nearest hundedth.

	Airboat tour	Gator farm	Other	TOTAL
Children				
Adults				
TOTAL				

B. What do you notice about the value in the lowest right cell of the relative frequency table? Why does this number make sense?

C. Why might it be useful to fill the two-way table with relative frequencies rather than absolute frequencies?

© Houghton Mifflin Harcourt Publishing Company

Step It Out

2 The table you constructed in the previous task is useful for determining various relative frequencies.

A **joint relative frequency** is the frequency in a particular category divided by the total number of data values.

A. Identify the joint relative frequency of children whose favorite activity was the airboat tour in the table you constructed in the previous task.

_____

A **marginal relative frequency** is the sum of the joint relative frequencies in a row or column of a two-way table.

B. The marginal relative frequency of children in the table is

_____.

C. Add the joint relative frequencies in each row and in each column. What do you notice?

"Children" row: _____ + _____ + _____ = _____

"Adult" row: _____ + _____ + _____ = _____

"Airboat tour" column: _____ + _____ = _____

"Gator farm" column: _____ + _____ = _____

"Other" column: _____ + _____ = _____

The sum of the _____ frequencies in a row or column

equals the _____ frequency.

D. What percentage of visitors were children?

_____

E. What percentage of visitors were children whose favorite activity was the airboat tour?

_____

Turn and Talk What do the marginal relative frequencies for the columns represent? Explain your reasoning.

3 ▸ A factory produces bottles of orange juice and bottles of cranberry juice. A quality control manager selects a random sample of bottles and checks that they contain the correct amount of juice.

	Orange juice	Cranberry juice	TOTAL
Correct amount	0.61		
Incorrect amount		0.08	
TOTAL	0.68		

A. Use an equation to find the missing value in the first column.

$0.61 + x = 0.68$ $x =$ _____

B. What value goes in the bottom right cell of the table? _____

C. Use an equation to find the missing value in the TOTAL row.

$0.68 + y =$ _____ $y =$ _____

D. Use an equation to find the missing value in the middle column.

$z + 0.08 =$ _____ $z =$ _____

E. Add to find the missing values in the TOTAL column.

$0.61 +$ _____ $=$ _____

_____ $+ 0.08 =$ _____

F. Fill in the missing values in the table.

G. Is it possible to know how many bottles of juice the quality control manager checked? Explain.

_____

_____

Check Understanding

1. The table shows the results of a survey of student bike-riding habits.

   A. Complete the two-way relative frequency table.

   B. List the joint relative frequencies.

   _____

   C. List the marginal relative frequencies.

   _____

	Bikes	Does not bike	TOTAL
7th grader		0.21	
8th grader	0.16		0.51
TOTAL		0.56	

On Your Own

2. A company that organizes whale watching tours keeps track of the time of day the boats leave and whether or not any whales were spotted. A frequency table is made to show the results.

	Morning	Afternoon	TOTAL
Whales	35	3	38
No whales	4	8	12
Total	39	11	50

A. (MP) **Attend to Precision** Convert the table to show the relative frequencies.

	Morning	Afternoon	TOTAL
Whales			
No whales			
TOTAL			

B. What is the joint relative frequency of morning trips that saw whales? What percentage of morning trips spotted whales?

_____

C. What is the marginal relative frequency of not seeing whales? What percentage of trips did not see whales?

_____

3. Carolina checks CDs and DVDs when they are returned to the public library. She keeps track of whether or not the items are damaged. The two-way relative frequency table shows her findings.

	CD	DVD	TOTAL
Damaged			
Not damaged		0.7	0.91
TOTAL	0.24		

A. Complete the two-way relative frequency table.

B. What is the marginal relative frequency of CDs returned? _____

C. What is the marginal relative frequency of DVDs returned? _____

D. (MP) **Reason** What is the relationship between these two numbers? Why?

_____

_____

Use the information for Problems 4–5.

(MP) **Use Structure** Boba tea is a drink made from tea and tapioca "pearls" (or "bubbles"). A boba tea shop offers two flavors and two sizes. The owner of the shop keeps track of sales and makes a relative frequency table.

	Strawberry	Mango	TOTAL
Small	a	b	c
Large	d	e	f
TOTAL	g	h	1

Strawberry   Mango

4. Write an equation that relates the quantities a, b, and c.

_____

5. Write an equation solved for c in terms of f.

_____

6. **STEM** A doctor participated in a study of a new allergy treatment. The doctor kept track of whether or not her patients got a rash or a headache as a side effect of the treatment. The two-way relative frequency table shows the results.

Did you get a rash or a headache?

	Rash	No rash	TOTAL
Headache	0.03	0.04	0.07
No headache	0.02	0.91	0.93
TOTAL	0.05	0.95	1

What percentage of patients got a headache but not a rash? If the doctor tried the treatment on 300 patients, how many got a headache but not a rash?

_____

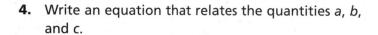

I'm in a Learning Mindset!

What was challenging about determining how many patients got a headache but not a rash in Problem 6?

_____

_____

© Houghton Mifflin Harcourt Publishing Company • **Image Credits:** (t) ©stockcreations/Shutterstock; (b) ©Stuart Jenner/Shutterstock

Construct Two-Way Relative Frequency Tables

1. **(MP) Reason** A nursery sells bulbs for purple tulips and red tulips. The tulips are available as parrot tulips, with a feathery edge, or lily-flowered tulips, with pointed petals. The table shows the numbers of bulbs sold during one week.

	Purple	Red	TOTAL
Parrot	33	63	96
Lily-flowered	24	30	54
TOTAL	57	93	150

Parrot Tulip

Lily-flowered Tulip

A. Construct a two-way relative frequency table for the data.

	Purple	Red	TOTAL
Parrot			
Lily-flowered			
TOTAL			

B. What percentage of the bulbs were purple? What value tells you this?

_____

_____

C. What percentage of the bulbs were red with feathery edges? What value in the table gives you this information?

_____

_____

2. **STEM** An optometrist surveys some patients to find out whether they mostly wear glasses or contacts and whether or not they sometimes need eye drops during the day to help with dry eyes. The optometrist records the data in a table. Complete the table.

	Eye drops	No eye drops	TOTAL
Glasses		0.07	0.37
Contacts	0.51		
TOTAL			

Test Prep

Use the information and table to solve Problems 3–4.

The students at Harriet Tubman Middle School are choosing a new school mascot and new school color. This relative frequency table shows the results.

	Eagles	Jaguars	TOTAL
Green	0.24	0.08	0.32
Yellow	0.46	0.22	0.68
TOTAL	0.7	0.3	1

3. What percentage of students surveyed prefer Eagles as the school mascot?

  (A) 7%   (C) 46%

  (B) 24%   (D) 70%

4. What is the marginal relative frequency of students who prefer Jaguars as the school mascot?

  (A) 0.22   (C) 0.32

  (B) 0.3   (D) 0.7

5. The relative frequency table shows preferences of customers at a breakfast buffet, but some values are missing. Complete the table.

	Juice	Milk	TOTAL
Pancakes	0.4		0.58
Omelet			
TOTAL		0.31	

Spiral Review

Use the system of equations to solve Problems 6–7. $\begin{cases} 2x + y = -2 \\ x - y = -4 \end{cases}$

6. Describe the main steps for solving the system by substitution.

_____

_____

7. Solve the system and explain how to check your answer.

_____

_____

8. Does the scatter plot show any association? If so, describe the association. If not, explain why not.

_____

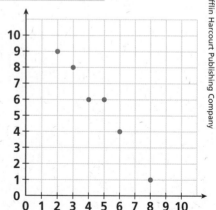

Name _____

Interpret Two-Way Relative Frequency Tables

(I Can) calculate conditional relative frequencies to determine whether there is an association between two variables and compare likelihoods from a table.

Spark Your Learning

Previously, you constructed this relative frequency table about two favorite activities of 200 visitors to Everglades National Park.

	Airboat tour	Gator farm	Other	TOTAL
Children	0.22	0.06	0.08	0.36
Adults	0.25	0.24	0.15	0.64
TOTAL	0.47	0.30	0.23	1

What information can you determine about visitors to the park from the table?

© Houghton Mifflin Harcourt Publishing Company • Image Credits: (t) ©Nick Fox/Alamy; (b) ©Pola Damonte/Moment/Getty Images

 Turn and Talk How is determining relationships from a relative frequency table similar to and how is it different from determining relationships from a frequency table?

Build Understanding

1 A travel company had 150 London visitors surveyed to find out whether they rode the London Eye, a Ferris wheel in England, during their visit. The company made this table to show the data.

You can use a two-way relative frequency table to find conditional relative frequencies. A **conditional relative frequency** is the ratio of a joint relative frequency to a related marginal relative frequency. It is used to find the likelihood of an event assuming another event also occurred.

Connect to Vocabulary

	Rode	Did not ride	TOTAL
Children	0.32	0.08	0.4
Adults	0.2	0.4	0.6
TOTAL	0.52	0.48	1

The manager of the travel company wants to know if there is an association between age and whether a visitor rode the London Eye.

A. To determine if there is an association between age and riding the London Eye, first find the overall percentage of visitors who rode the London Eye. Where can you find this information in the table?

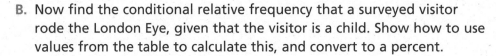

B. Now find the conditional relative frequency that a surveyed visitor rode the London Eye, given that the visitor is a child. Show how to use values from the table to calculate this, and convert to a percent.

C. Compare the percentages you calculated in Parts A and B. Is there an association between age and riding the London Eye? Explain.

The London Eye

D. Calculate the conditional relative frequency that a surveyed visitor rode the London Eye, given that the visitor is an adult, and convert it to a percent. Do you see the same association between age and riding the London Eye? Explain.

E. Is it more likely that a surveyed visitor rode the London Eye given that the visitor is an adult, or that a surveyed visitor is an adult given that the visitor rode the London Eye? Explain.

Step It Out

2 A landscaper uses a new fertilizer on some orchid plants, and he keeps track of whether or not the orchid plants produce flowers. The relative frequency table shows the data. The landscaper wants to know if there is an association between an orchid plant receiving the fertilizer and producing flowers.

	Fertilizer	No fertilizer	TOTAL
Flowers	0.27	0.18	0.45
No flowers	0.33	0.22	0.55
TOTAL	0.6	0.4	1

A. What is the marginal relative frequency that an orchid plant produced flowers? What is the marginal relative frequency that an orchid plant received fertilizer?

_____

B. What is the conditional relative frequency that an orchid plant produced flowers given that the orchid plant was fertilized?

$$\frac{\boxed{}}{0.6} = \boxed{}$$

C. Were the orchid plants that received the fertilizer more, less, or equally likely to produce flowers than the overall population?

_____

D. Is there an association between an orchid plant receiving the fertilizer and producing flowers? _____

E. What is the marginal relative frequency that an orchid plant did not produce flowers? What is the marginal relative frequency that an orchid plant did not receive fertilizer?

_____

F. What is the conditional relative frequency that an orchid plant did not produce flowers given that the orchid plant did not receive fertilizer?

$$\frac{\boxed{}}{0.4} = \boxed{}$$

G. Is there an association between an orchid plant not receiving fertilizer and not producing flowers? _____

Turn and Talk Based on the information in the task, should the landscaper continue to spend the money to fertilize the orchid plants? Why or why not?

3 The table shows the results of a survey of people who went bird watching. Is there an association between using binoculars and seeing finches?

	Binoculars	No binoculars	TOTAL
Saw finches	0.21	0.04	0.25
No finches	0.49	0.26	0.75
TOTAL	0.7	0.3	1

Zebra Finches

A. What is the marginal relative frequency that a person who was surveyed saw finches?

_____

B. What is the conditional relative frequency that a surveyed person saw finches, given the person used binoculars?

$$\frac{\boxed{}}{\boxed{}} = \boxed{}$$

C. Is there an association between using binoculars and seeing finches?

_____

D. What is the marginal relative frequency that a person who was surveyed did not see finches? _____

E. What is the conditional relative frequency that a surveyed person did not see finches given the person did not use binoculars? Round to the nearest hundredth.

$$\frac{\boxed{}}{\boxed{}} \approx \boxed{}$$

F. Is there an association between not using binoculars and not seeing finches? _____

Check Understanding

1. The relative frequency table shows the results of a survey of hikers as they enter a trail in a state park.

   A. Find the conditional relative frequency that a hiker who was surveyed has a backpack, given that the hiker has a water bottle, and convert it to a percent.

	Water bottle	No water bottle	TOTAL
Backpack	0.59	0.05	0.64
No backpack	0.21	0.15	0.36
TOTAL	0.8	0.2	1

   _____

   B. Is there an association between having a backpack and having a water bottle? Explain.

   _____

   _____

Name _____

On Your Own

Use the information to solve Problems 2–4.

Moira grows pumpkins to sell at a farmer's market. She sorts the pumpkins by color and size and then makes this frequency table to display the data.

	Small	Medium	Large	TOTAL
Green	3	15	12	30
Orange	22	17	21	60
TOTAL	25	32	33	90

2. Find the conditional relative frequency that a pumpkin is orange, given that it is a small pumpkin. Express your answer as a fraction, decimal, and percent. _____

3. Find the conditional relative frequency that a pumpkin is a medium pumpkin, given that it is green. Express your answer as a fraction, decimal, and percent. _____

4. Is it likely that a pumpkin is a small pumpkin, given that it is green? Use a conditional relative frequency to justify your answer.

_____

5. A restaurant offers a choice of two soups and two sandwiches. The manager keeps track of the orders and makes this relative frequency table.

	Chicken soup	Tomato soup	TOTAL
Ham sandwich	0.06	0.34	0.4
Turkey sandwich	0.09	0.51	0.6
TOTAL	0.15	0.85	1

A. What is the conditional relative frequency that a customer orders tomato soup, given that he or she orders a turkey sandwich?

_____

B. (MP) **Construct Arguments** Is there an association between the type of sandwich a customer orders and the type of soup he or she orders? Why or why not?

_____

_____

_____

© Houghton Mifflin Harcourt Publishing Company • Image Credit: ©Ramon Espelt Gorgozo/Alamy

Module 9 • Lesson 3

6. **(MP) Critique Reasoning** The two-way relative frequency table shows data from a mayoral election. Chris said there is no association between the candidate a person voted for and whether or not a person supports the new ballpark because 55% voted for Chan but 80% support the new ballpark. Do you agree or disagree? Why?

	Supports new ballpark	Does not support new ballpark	TOTAL
Voted for Chan	0.5	0.05	0.55
Voted for Moya	0.3	0.15	0.45
TOTAL	0.8	0.2	1

7. **Open Ended** The two-way relative frequency table shows data about the sea stars at an aquarium.

	Orange	Purple	TOTAL
Has 5 legs	0.59	0.2	0.79
Has more than 5 legs	0.09	0.12	0.21
TOTAL	0.68	0.32	1

Write a question about the data that can be answered using a conditional relative frequency. Provide the answer to the question.

I'm in a Learning Mindset!

How did I collaborate with classmates when solving problems involving conditional relative frequencies?

Interpret Two-Way Relative Frequency Tables

1. **Math on the Spot** Ross has been teaching music lessons for three years. The table shows the types of instruments played by his 40 students.

   A. Make a table of the joint and marginal relative frequencies.

		Guitar	
		Yes	No
Drums	Yes	10	12
	No	15	3

   B. What is the conditional relative frequency that a student plays drums, given that the student also plays guitar? Express your answer as a decimal and percent.

2. **STEM** Rock pocket mice live in the deserts of the southwestern United States. The mice have dark fur or light fur depending on the color of the rocks or sand where they live. The relative frequency table shows data about a biologist's sample of rock pocket mice.

	Male	Female	TOTAL
Dark fur	0.42	0.33	0.75
Light fur	0.14	0.11	0.25
TOTAL	0.56	0.44	1

Light fur; lives in sand

Dark fur; lives in rocks

Is there an association between the mouse being male or female and the color of the fur for the sample? Explain.

Test Prep

Use the information and table to solve Problems 3–4.

A manager at a gas company collects data on a sample of 200 customers to find out whether they paid their last bill by mail or online and whether they paid late or on time. This two-way table shows the results.

	Paid by mail	Paid online	TOTAL
Paid on time	66	101	167
Paid late	20	13	33
TOTAL	86	114	200

3. To the nearest hundredth, what is the conditional relative frequency that a customer paid his or her bill on time, given that he or she paid online?

   Ⓐ 0.57   Ⓒ 0.84

   Ⓑ 0.60   Ⓓ 0.89

4. To the nearest hundredth, what is the conditional relative frequency that a customer paid by mail, given that the customer paid late?

   Ⓐ 0.23   Ⓒ 0.61

   Ⓑ 0.33   Ⓓ 0.86

5. The two-way relative frequency table displays data from a survey of customers at a health food store. Is there an association between taking vitamins and drinking green tea? _____

	Green tea	No green tea	TOTAL
Vitamins	0.18	0.36	0.54
No vitamins	0.02	0.44	0.46
TOTAL	0.2	0.8	1

Spiral Review

6. The graph represents the price of a stock during the course of one day. Describe how the price of the stock changes during the day.

   _____

   _____

   _____

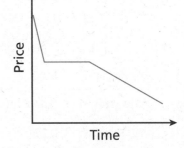

7. Bucket A is filled with water according to the equation $y = 2.5x$, where x is the time in minutes and y is the volume in fluid ounces. Bucket B is filled with water according to the data in the table. Which bucket is filled at a faster rate? How do you know?

Time (min)	Volume (fl oz)
3	12.6
4	16.8
5	21.0
6	25.2

   _____

   _____

8. Solve for x: $4(x + 1.5) = 3x + 9.2$.

   _____

Name _____

Review

Vocabulary

For Problems 1–3, tell whether each description represents a *joint*, *marginal*, or *conditional relative frequency* for the two-way table.

	Preferred Frozen Yogurt Flavor		
	Strawberry	Mango	TOTAL
Adults	20	32	52
Children	36	28	64
TOTAL	56	60	116

1. the ratio of the number of people who chose mango to the total number of people surveyed

2. the ratio of the number of children who chose strawberry to the total number of people who chose strawberry

3. the ratio of the number of adults who chose strawberry to the total number of people surveyed

4. What does it mean when a two-way table shows an association between two data sets?

Concepts and Skills

5. Two hundred twenty students were surveyed about whether a mural should be painted on a wall of the cafeteria. Complete the two-way table showing the results of the survey.

	Agree	Disagree	TOTAL
7th graders		20	
8th graders	94		
TOTAL		38	220

6. (MP) **Use Tools** Three hundred people at a movie theater were asked whether they bought popcorn or a drink at the theater. How many more people surveyed did NOT buy popcorn than did buy popcorn? State what strategy and tool you will use to answer the question, explain your choice, and then find the answer.

	Drink	No drink	TOTAL
Popcorn	76	5	
No popcorn	58	161	
TOTAL			

7. Three hundred students were surveyed about whether they are right- or left-handed. Complete the two-way relative frequency table.

	Right-handed	Left-handed	TOTAL
7th graders		0.05	
8th graders			0.49
TOTAL	0.89		1.00

8. Five hundred randomly-selected voters were surveyed about whether they support a new park. The two-way table shows the results of the survey. Which statement is **best** supported by the survey results?

	For park	Against park	TOTAL
Under 40	144	48	192
40 or older	182	126	308
TOTAL	326	174	500

(A) A voter's age appears to be unrelated to his or her opinion about the park.

(B) Voters aged 40 or older are more likely to be for the park than voters under age 40.

(C) Voters against the park are more likely to be under age 40 than voters for the park.

(D) Voters under age 40 are more likely to be for the park than voters aged 40 or older.

9. A random sample of 200 students at a school were surveyed about whether they prefer red or blue as a new school color. Complete the relative frequency table. Based on the table, select all the true statements.

	Red	Blue	TOTAL
7th graders	0.25	0.20	
8th graders	0.27	0.28	
TOTAL			

(A) More 8th graders were surveyed than 7th graders.

(B) More of the surveyed students prefer red than prefer blue.

(C) 8th graders at the school are more likely to prefer red than 7th graders are.

(D) A randomly selected 7th grader at the school is more likely to prefer red than blue.

(E) Students at the school who prefer blue are more likely to be in 7th grade than 8th grade.

10. The table shows data for a random sample of flights for a particular airline. Complete the table. Based on the table, what is the conditional relative frequency that a flight will be on time given that it is a morning flight?

	On time	Delayed	TOTAL
Morning	528	132	
Afternoon	251	89	
TOTAL			

Real Numbers and the Pythagorean Theorem

Historian

We know that the pyramids of Egypt were built about 5000 years ago and that the people who built them used math to do so. But *how* do we know? Our knowledge is largely due to historians, who study the people, events, and ideas of the past and their influence on today's world. Historians use the information they gather to develop theories and draw conclusions about their subjects.

STEM Task:

An ancient Egyptian multiplication method based on doubling is used below to find 11×19. Use the method to find 13×24.

$11 \times 19 = 209$

①	19	19
②	38	38
4	76	
⑧	152	+152
16	304	
		209

Learning Mindset

Resilience Manages the Learning Process

Resilience is the ability to "bounce back" after experiencing a disappointment or a defeat. When you encounter difficulty or setbacks, watch out for a fixed-mindset voice in your head telling you to give up. Here are some statements you can tell yourself to activate your growth–mindset voice and strengthen your resilience. Can you think of others?

- Mistakes and challenges are opportunities to learn.

- If this were easy, I would not learn anything from it.

- I have overcome challenges in the past, so I know I can do it again.

- When I solve this problem, I can be proud because it is not easy.

- I may be struggling, but I am still making progress.

Reflect

Q As you worked on the STEM Task, did anything trigger a fixed-mindset voice in your head? If so, what?

Q In the past, what situations have caused a fixed-mindset response in your head? What is your plan for activating your growth mindset when you encounter similar situations in the future?

10 Real Numbers

Track the Distance

$\frac{6}{10}$ mile $\frac{3}{5}$ mile $\frac{1}{3}$ mile

$\frac{5}{8}$ mile $\frac{3}{4}$ mile

A group of five friends went running at the school track. They ran the distances shown.

Use the clues to determine which friend ran each distance.

- Ara and Tyrone ran the same distance.

- Morgan's distance written as a decimal has 3 nonzero digits.

- Shane's distance in miles is equal to a repeating decimal.

- Julius ran the greatest distance.

- Tyrone's distance in miles is given as a fraction in simplest form.

Ara ran _____ mile.   Morgan ran _____ mile.

Shane ran _____ mile.   Julius ran _____ mile.

Tyrone ran _____ mile.

 Turn and Talk

Another friend, Knox, ran farther than Shane but not as far as Tyrone. What possible distance could Knox have run? Explain.

Are You Ready?

Complete these problems to review prior concepts and skills you will need for this module.

Solve One-Step Equations

Solve each equation.

1. $x + 5 = 25$ _____ **2.** $x + 4 = 7$ _____

3. $x - 3 = 7$ _____ **4.** $x - 2 = 6$ _____

5. $19x = 76$ _____ **6.** $5x = 70$ _____

7. $\frac{x}{4} = 12$ _____ **8.** $\frac{x}{3} = 8$ _____

Rational Numbers on a Number Line

Plot each rational number on the number line.

9. 0.75 **10.** $-\frac{5}{8}$

11. -1.5 **12.** $1\frac{1}{8}$

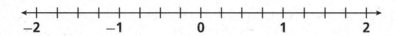

Convert Fractions to Decimals

13. How can you convert a fraction to a decimal?

_____

_____

Write each fraction as a decimal.

14. $\frac{4}{5}$ **15.** $\frac{3}{8}$

_____ _____

16. $\frac{11}{20}$ **17.** $\frac{3}{4}$

_____ _____

18. $\frac{1}{16}$ **19.** $\frac{13}{25}$

_____ _____

Name _____

Understand Rational and Irrational Numbers

(I Can) determine whether a number is rational and write a given rational number as a fraction.

Spark Your Learning

In softball, a player's batting average is the number of hits divided by the number of at-bats. Write each player's batting average as a decimal.

What do you notice?

Player	Hits	At-bats
Jamilla	2	5
Callie	1	8
Mayumi	4	9
Elena	37	99
Kaycee	7	36

Turn and Talk Do you think all fractions have decimal representations that either end or have digits that repeat? Try some additional fractions and discuss your conjecture.

Build Understanding

A **rational number** is any number that can be written as a ratio in the form $\frac{a}{b}$, where a and b are integers and b is not 0. Every rational number can be written as a **terminating decimal** or a **repeating decimal**. Examples of rational numbers are:

$\frac{3}{8} = 0.375$ $7 = \frac{7}{1}$

$0.2 = \frac{1}{5}$ $0.11111... = \frac{1}{9}$

1 ▶ Is every number rational?

A. Consider the decimal 1.345345634567... .

Does the decimal appear to have a repeating pattern? Explain.

_____

Do you think 1.345345634567... is a rational number? Why or why not?

_____

B. You have learned that **pi (π)** is the ratio of the **circumference** of any circle to its **diameter**. The decimal value of pi is shown below.

$\pi = 3.1415926535897932...$

Pi is an irrational number, but it can be written as a ratio. How can this be?

_____

_____

_____

_____

There are two ways to write a repeating decimal. You can use an ellipsis (three dots) to show that the repeating pattern continues:

0.111... , 0.235235235... , and 0.244444444...

Or, you can write an overbar over the part of the decimal that repeats:

$0.\overline{1}$, $0.\overline{235}$, and $0.2\overline{4}$

Turn and Talk Convert $\frac{1}{36}$ to a decimal. Write the decimal using an ellipsis and using an overbar. Explain the process you used.

Step It Out

2 ▸ A basketball player's free throw percentage is 82.5%, or 0.825. Write this as a fraction.

A. Identify the place value of the last digit in the terminating decimal. Use this to determine the denominator of the fraction. The digits to the right of the decimal point are the **numerator** of the fraction.

$$0.825 = \frac{825}{\boxed{}}$$

B. Write the fraction in lowest terms. Identify the **greatest common factor** (GCF) of the numerator and denominator. Divide the numerator and denominator by the GCF.

$$0.825 = \frac{825}{\boxed{}} = \frac{825 \div \boxed{}}{\boxed{} \div \boxed{}} = \frac{\boxed{}}{\boxed{}}$$

3 ▸ You can also convert a repeating decimal to a fraction.

A. Write $0.\overline{5}$ as a fraction.   Let x be the given decimal.

Write the first few repeating digits. $x = 0.555...$

Multiply both sides of the equation by 10 so that the repeating digit appears just to the *left* of the decimal point. $10x = 5.555...$

$$10x = 5.555...$$

Subtract an expression equal to x from both sides. $\underline{-x \quad -0.555...}$

$$9x = 5$$

Solve for x. $x = \dfrac{\boxed{}}{\boxed{}}$

B. Write $0.\overline{18}$ as a fraction.   Let x be the given decimal.

Write the first few repeating digits. $x = 0.1818...$

Multiply both sides of the equation by 100 so that the repeating digits appear just to the *left* of the decimal point. $100x = \underline{}$

Subtract an expression equal to x from both sides. $100x = \underline{}$

$$\underline{-x \quad -0.1818...}$$

$$99x = \underline{}$$

Solve for x. Then simplify the fraction. $x = \dfrac{\boxed{}}{\boxed{}} = \dfrac{\boxed{}}{\boxed{}}$

4 ▸ The average number of goals scored per game for a soccer team is shown. Write this rational number as a fraction or mixed number.

> The average number of goals scored per game for a soccer team is 1.62333... .

Identify the repeating digit(s) of the decimal. _____

Let x be the given decimal.

Write an equation with the decimal. $x = 1.62333...$

Multiply by a **power** of 10 so that the first repeating digit appears just to the *right* of the decimal point.

   Multiply both sides of the equation by 100. $100x = 162.333...$

Multiply by a power of 10 so that the first repeating digit appears just to the *left* of the decimal point.

   Multiply both sides of the equation by 1000.

$$1000x = \underline{\hspace{3cm}}$$

Subtract the expression equal to $100x$ from both sides.

$$\begin{array}{r} -100x \quad -162.333... \\ \hline 900x = \underline{\hspace{2cm}} \end{array}$$

Solve for x. Write the fraction as a mixed number and simplify.

$$x = \frac{\boxed{}}{\boxed{}} = \boxed{}\,\frac{\boxed{}}{\boxed{}}$$

Check Understanding

1. Convert $\frac{1}{18}$ to a decimal.

   A. Write the decimal using an ellipsis.

   _____

   B. Write the decimal using an overbar.

   _____

2. Use your calculator to find the decimal equivalent of $\sqrt{17}$. Do you think this is a rational number? Why or why not?

_____

_____

For Problems 3–5, write the rational number as a simplified fraction or as a mixed number in simplest form.

3. 1.905

4. 0.828282...

5. $0.4\overline{3}$

_____

On Your Own

6. The diagram shows the number of instruments in the string section of an orchestra. There are 7 cellos, 4 double basses, and 11 each of first violins, second violins, and violas.

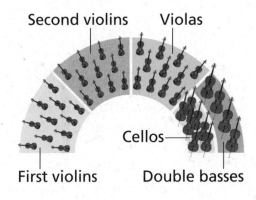

Second violins   Violas

Cellos—

First violins   Double basses

  A. Use ratio notation and decimal notation to describe the relationship between the number of double basses and the total number of instruments in the string section.

  _____

  B. Is the relationship in Part A rational or irrational? Give two different justifications for your answer.

  _____

  _____

7. The ratio of 8th graders in a chess club to the total number of members is $0.\overline{45}$. Write the decimal as a fraction. Show your work.

8. (MP) **Critique Reasoning** A student claimed that the number −4 is not rational because it is not a ratio of two integers. Do you agree or disagree? Explain.

_____

_____

_____

9. (MP) **Use Repeated Reasoning** Pi (π) is an irrational number. What can you say about the numbers $\frac{\pi}{2}$, $\frac{\pi}{3}$, $\frac{\pi}{4}$, and so on? Are these rational or irrational?

_____

_____

10. **STEM** The atomic weight of an element is the total mass of the protons, neutrons, and electrons. The ratio of the mass of the protons in radon to the atomic mass of radon is 0.387387387... . Write the decimal as a fraction.

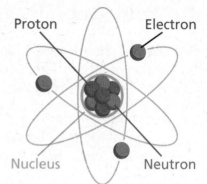

Proton   Electron

Nucleus   Neutron

_____

11. Convert $\frac{1}{15}$ to a decimal. Write the decimal using an ellipsis, then write the decimal using an overbar.

_____

12. (MP) **Critique Reasoning** Mitchell was asked to write 0.616161... as a fraction. His work is shown. Do you agree with his answer? If not, explain Mitchell's error and correct it.

Let $x = 0.616161...$
Then $10x = 6.16161...$
Subtract: $10x = 6.16161...$
$\underline{\quad -x \qquad -0.616161...}$
$9x = 6$
$x = \frac{6}{9} = \frac{2}{3}$

_____
_____
_____
_____
_____

For Problems 13–18, write the number as a fraction or mixed number in simplest form.

13. 4.024

14. −1.111...

15. $-0.\overline{39}$

16. $0.61\overline{4}$

17. 2.484848...

18. 0.7222...

- × +• ÷ **I'm in a Learning Mindset!**

How am I using formative feedback to solve problems about rational numbers?

_____
_____

Understand Rational and Irrational Numbers

1. Kara and Nathan participated in a 60-minute maze race.

   A. Use ratio notation and decimal notation to describe the relationship between Kara's time and the total time of the race.

   _____

   B. Is the relationship in Part A rational or irrational? Justify your answer.

   _____

   _____

Kara: 32 minutes

Nathan: 40 minutes

2. **Math on the Spot** Write the decimal $0.\overline{63}$ as a fraction in simplest form.

   _____

3. The average number of hourly visitors to an art exhibit is $45.1\overline{3}$. Write the average number of hourly visitors as a mixed number in simplest form.

   _____

4. (MP) **Critique Reasoning** Katrina said the number 0.101100111000... is a rational number because it consists only of the digits 0 and 1, and these digits repeat. Do you agree or disagree? Explain.

   _____

   _____

   _____

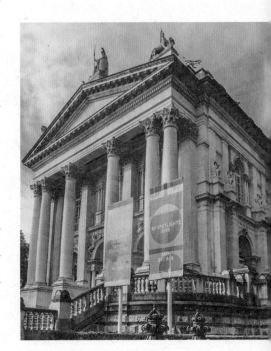

5. Convert $\frac{1}{27}$ to a decimal. Write the decimal using an ellipsis, then write the decimal using an overbar.

   _____

Write the rational number as a fraction or mixed number in simplest form.

6. 0.0606060...

7. −8.725

8. 0.424242...

9. 1.52888...

10. $-10.\overline{7}$

11. $0.\overline{57}$

Test Prep

12. Midori wrote a ratio of two integers. Which of the following must be true about the number Midori wrote?

- (A) The decimal form of the number is a terminating decimal.
- (B) The decimal form of the number is a repeating decimal.
- (C) The number is rational.
- (D) The number is irrational.

13. Which of the following is $0.\overline{15}$ written as a fraction in simplest form?

- (A) $\frac{1}{15}$
- (B) $\frac{1}{9}$
- (C) $\frac{3}{20}$
- (D) $\frac{5}{33}$

14. Paolo keeps track of his favorite baseball player's batting average, and notices the average is 0.4727272... . If his player has 55 at bats, what is the number of hits?

_____ hits

Spiral Review

In a survey of 120 people who visited a lake, 20% went fishing. Of those who went fishing, 75% also went swimming. Of those who did not go fishing, 50% went swimming. Use this information to solve Problems 15–16.

15. Construct a two-way frequency table to display the data.

	Fishing	No fishing	TOTAL
Swimming			
No swimming			
TOTAL			

16. What percent of those surveyed did not go swimming?

_____

17. In the figure, line p is parallel to line q. Write an equation you can use to find the value of y, and explain why you can use it. Then solve the equation and use your result to help you find the measure of $\angle 1$.

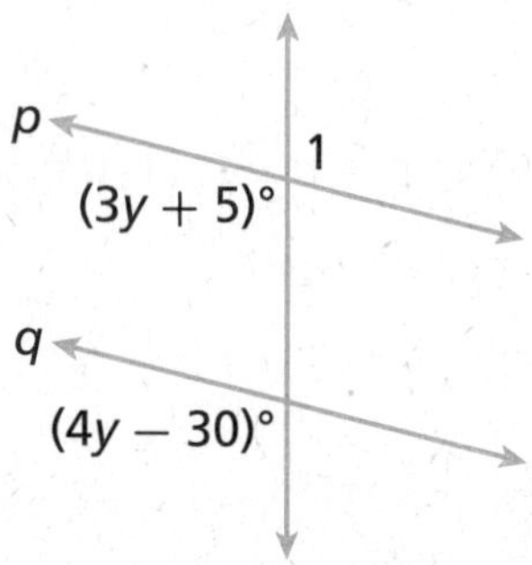

p 1

$(3y + 5)°$

q

$(4y - 30)°$

_____

_____

_____

Name _____

Investigate Roots

 I Can evaluate square roots and cube roots.

Spark Your Learning SMALL GROUPS

Aaron plans to make origami cranes, which can be folded from a square piece of paper. He starts by drawing small squares with side lengths 1 inch, 2 inches, 3 inches, and 4 inches.

Find the area of each square. What do you notice about the relationship between the side lengths and the area of each square?

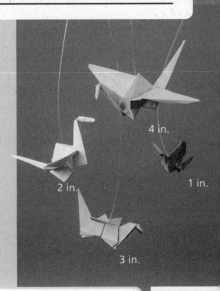

4 in.

2 in.

1 in.

3 in.

 Turn and Talk Consider a square with an area of 23 square inches. Explain how you would determine the length of each side for such a square.

Build Understanding

1 ▶ Aaron is also planning to make origami **cubes** of different sizes. The edge lengths of the cubes are 1 inch, 2 inches, 3 inches, and 4 inches.

A. Talk to a partner, then write down a formula to determine the volume of a cube.

_____

B. Find the volume of each of the cubes. Complete the table and look for patterns.

Edge length (in.)	Volume (in³)
1	
2	
3	
4	

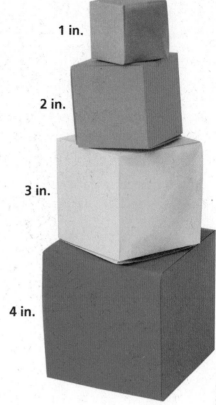

1 in.

2 in.

3 in.

4 in.

C. What do you notice about how the volumes change as the edge length increases?

_____

_____

_____

D. If you are given the volume of a cube, how can you find the edge length?

_____

_____

E. What is the edge length of a cube with a volume of 125 cubic inches? Why is it difficult to express the edge length of a cube with a volume of 10 cubic inches?

_____

_____

_____

 Turn and Talk A student completed the above table and claimed it is impossible for a cube to have a volume of exactly 50 cubic centimeters since this number will not appear in the "Volume" column. Do you agree? Why or why not?

Step It Out

The **square root** of a positive number p is x when $x^2 = p$. Note that every positive number has two square roots. For example, $3^2 = 9$ and $(-3)^2 = 9$, so the two square roots of 9 are 3 and -3. These are sometimes written together as ±3, and read as "plus or minus three."

A **perfect square** is a whole number whose square roots are integers. For example, 16 is a perfect square since its square roots are the integers 4 and -4. The square root of any number that isn't a perfect square is another example of an irrational number.

The symbol $\sqrt{}$ (**radical symbol**) is used to indicate the positive square root, or **principal square root**, of a number. So, $\sqrt{16} = 4$.

2   Use the information about roots to evaluate each expression.

A. Find the square roots of 81.

$\boxed{}^2 = 81$ and $\boxed{}^2 = 81$.

So, the square roots of 81 are _____ and _____.

B. Find $\sqrt{\dfrac{4}{9}}$.

Both $\left(\dfrac{\boxed{}}{\boxed{}}\right)^2 = \dfrac{4}{9}$ and $\left(-\dfrac{\boxed{}}{\boxed{}}\right)^2 = \dfrac{4}{9}$.

The square root symbol indicates the principal square root.

So, $\sqrt{\dfrac{4}{9}} = \dfrac{\boxed{}}{\boxed{}}$.

Suppose Aaron wants a square piece of origami paper with an area of 2 square centimeters.

C. What is the length of one side of the piece of paper? Use a square root symbol in your answer.

_____ centimeters

D. Is 2 a perfect square? Why or why not?

$\boxed{\text{yes / no}}$; There $\boxed{\text{is / is not}}$ an integer whose square is 2.

E. Is the square root of 2 rational or irrational?

$\boxed{\text{rational / irrational}}$; $\sqrt{2}$ $\boxed{\text{can / cannot}}$ be written as a ratio of two integers.

The **cube root** of a positive number p is x when $x^3 = p$. Every positive number has one cube root. For example, $4^3 = 64$, so the cube root of 64 is 4. The symbol for a cube root is similar to the symbol for square root, and written as $\sqrt[3]{\ }$. $\sqrt[3]{64} = 4$ is read out loud as, "The cube root of 64 equals 4."

A **perfect cube** is a whole number whose cube root is an integer. For example, 64 is a perfect cube since its cube root is an integer, 4.

3   Find the cube root of $\frac{8}{27}$.

$\boxed{}^3 = 8$ and $\boxed{}^3 = 27$, so $\left(\dfrac{\boxed{}}{\boxed{}}\right)^3 = \dfrac{8}{27}$.

So, the cube root of $\frac{8}{27}$ is $\left(\dfrac{\boxed{}}{\boxed{}}\right)$. You also can write $\sqrt[3]{\dfrac{8}{27}} = \dfrac{\boxed{}}{\boxed{}}$.

4   Solve each problem.

A. What is the side length of the square picture frame shown?

$x^2 = 100$ Write the equation.

$x = \pm\sqrt{100}$ Apply the definition of square root.

$x = \pm$ _____   Find integers that when squared equal 100.

The side length of the picture frame is _____ inches.

Note that the square root -10 is not used since it is not a possible length for a real-world object.

100 in²

B. Solve for y: $y^3 = \frac{1}{14}$.

$y = \sqrt[3]{\dfrac{1}{14}}$ Apply the definition of cube root.

Since no rational number when cubed equals $\frac{1}{14}$, _____ represents the solution to $y^3 = \frac{1}{14}$.

Check Understanding

1. Solve each equation.

    A. $x^2 = 7$ $x =$ _____

    B. $x^3 = \frac{1}{64}$ $x =$ _____

For Problems 2–4, find the indicated root.

2. $\sqrt{121}$ **3.** $\sqrt{\dfrac{16}{25}}$ **4.** $\sqrt[3]{125}$

On Your Own

5. A band stores its equipment in a large cube. The cube has sound-dampening foam designed to allow the drummer to play inside the cube when the band is practicing.

125 cubic feet

A. Is 125 a perfect cube? Why or why not?

_____

_____

B. What is the edge length of the band's cube? Explain.

_____

6. Find the square roots of 400.

_____

7. Find the cube root of $\frac{8}{125}$. Show how you can check that you found the cube root correctly.

_____

8. (MP) **Reason** A student claimed 7 and −7 are the two cube roots of 343. Do you agree or disagree? Explain.

_____

_____

9. Solve the equation $x^2 = 196$. Show your work and explain your steps.

10. Solve the equation $z^3 = \frac{125}{216}$. Show your work and explain your steps.

11. **Open Ended** A square tile has an area of less than 1 square foot. The area and length are rational numbers. What is a possible area for the tile in square feet? What is the corresponding edge length?

_____

12. (MP) **Use Repeated Reasoning** What do perfect squares have in common?

   A. Complete the table of squares.

x	1	2	3	4	5	6	7	8	9	10	11	12
x^2												

   B. What do you notice about the ones digit in each of the perfect squares in your table?

   _____

   C. Suppose you extend the table and continue to find perfect squares. Do you think the number 10,402 will eventually appear in the x^2 row? Explain.

   _____

   _____

   _____

13. Does the square root of 0 exist? What about the cube root of 0? Explain your answers.

_____

For Problems 14–16, find each root.

14. $\sqrt{225}$ 15. $\sqrt[3]{729}$ 16. $\sqrt[3]{\frac{64}{343}}$

_____

For Problems 17–19, solve each equation.

17. $x^2 = \frac{1}{49}$ 18. $n^3 = 19$ 19. $y^3 = \frac{27}{125}$

_____

 I'm in a Learning Mindset!

How did I provide constructive feedback when solving Problem 12?

_____

_____

LESSON 10.2
**More Practice/
Homework**

ONLINE

**Video Tutorials and
Interactive Examples**

Investigate Roots

1. A puzzle maker built the cube puzzle shown.

    A. What is the edge length of the cube puzzle? Explain.

    _____

    B. Suppose the puzzle maker wants to build a larger cube puzzle and wants the volume to be a perfect cube when measured in cubic inches. If the volume must be less than 1000 cubic inches, what are some volumes the puzzle maker could use? Explain.

    _____

    _____

    _____

216 cubic inches

2. Find the square roots of 169. Then find $\sqrt{169}$. Explain why the answers are not exactly the same.

_____

3. Solve the equation $y^3 = \frac{64}{729}$. Show your work and explain your steps.

4. **Math on the Spot** Solve each equation for x.

    A. $x^2 = 81$ **B.** $x^2 = \frac{25}{144}$

    _____   _____

For Problems 5–10, find each root.

5. $\sqrt{289}$ **6.** $\sqrt[3]{512}$ **7.** $\sqrt[3]{\frac{1}{1000}}$

_____   _____   _____

8. $z^2 = \frac{81}{121}$ **9.** $x^3 = 343$ **10.** $y^3 = \frac{8}{729}$

_____   _____   _____

Test Prep

11. Which of the following is NOT a perfect cube?

  (A) 1   (B) 8   (C) 9   (D) 27

12. Iris wrote a square root of 144 on a piece of paper. Which one of the following must be true about the number she wrote?

  (A) The number is 12.

  (B) The number is −12.

  (C) The number multiplied by itself equals 144.

  (D) None of the above is true.

13. Which of the following is an irrational number?

  (A) $\sqrt[3]{1}$ (B) $\sqrt{2}$ (C) $\sqrt[3]{27}$ (D) $\sqrt{25}$

14. Which number when squared makes 26?

  (A) 52   (B) 13   (C) 5.5   (D) $\sqrt{26}$

15. A square flower bed has an area of $\frac{169}{36}$ square yards. What is the perimeter of the flower bed?

 yards

Spiral Review

Use the information and graph to solve Problems 16–17.

Ava is comparing the pricing at two different parking lots in the downtown area of her city. Both lots charge a fixed fee as well as an hourly rate. Ava makes the graph shown to compare the lots.

16. Which parking lot charges a greater hourly rate? Explain.

_____

_____

17. Which parking lot charges a greater fixed fee? Explain.

_____

_____

18. Is the number 0.575757... rational or irrational? If it is rational, express it as a fraction in simplest form. If it is irrational, explain why.

_____

_____

Name _____

Order Real Numbers

(I Can) accurately order a list of real numbers containing
fractions, decimals, and irrational numbers.

Step It Out

All **real numbers** correspond to a position on a **number line**. Real
numbers include rational and irrational numbers.

1 ▶ Estimate $\sqrt{50}$ to the nearest tenth.

A. Find the two perfect squares closest to 50, one greater than
50 and one less than 50.

_____ and _____

B. What are the square roots of the two perfect squares?

_____ and _____

C. The whole number that most closely estimates $\sqrt{50}$ is _____.

D. Refine your estimate of $\sqrt{50}$. Circle the true statement. Then
underline the value closer to 50.

$7.0^2 < 50 < 7.1^2$ $7.2^2 < 50 < 7.3^2$ $7.4^2 < 50 < 7.5^2$

$7.1^2 < 50 < 7.2^2$ $7.3^2 < 50 < 7.4^2$ $7.5^2 < 50 < 7.6^2$

2 ▶ Estimate $\sqrt[3]{100}$ to the nearest hundredth.

A. Find the two perfect cubes closest to 100, one greater than
100 and one less than 100.

_____ and _____

B. What are the cube roots of the two perfect cubes?

_____ and _____

C. Circle the pair of cubes $\sqrt[3]{100}$ lies between.

4.5^3 4.6^3 4.7^3 4.8^3 4.9^3 5.0^3

D. Within your interval, test cubes of values expressed in
hundredths. Which cube is closest to 100? "Approximately
equal to" is represented by the $\approx$ symbol.

_____ is closest to 100, so $\sqrt[3]{100} \approx$ _____.

 Turn and Talk What is your strategy for estimating a square root or a cube
root to the nearest hundredth?

3 You can use estimates of square roots to help you estimate and compare numerical expressions involving square roots.

A. Compare the values below. Write < or > to complete each statement.

2 ◯ 6, so $\sqrt{3} + 2$ ◯ $\sqrt{3} + 6$.

−1 ◯ −3, so $\sqrt{7} - 1$ ◯ $\sqrt{7} - 3$.

6 ◯ 7, so $2\sqrt{6}$ ◯ $2\sqrt{7}$.

−5 ◯ −7, so $-5\sqrt{3}$ ◯ $-7\sqrt{3}$.

B. Complete the statement with consecutive integers.

8 is between the perfect squares _____ and _____,

so the value of $\sqrt{8}$ is between the integers _____ and _____.

Use this information to complete the inequality with integer values.

_____ < $\sqrt{8} + 3$ < _____

C. Compare the values below. Write < or > to complete each statement.

$\sqrt{7}$ ◯ $\sqrt{3}$, so $2\sqrt{7}$ ◯ $2\sqrt{3}$.

$\sqrt{11}$ ◯ $\sqrt{21}$, so $5\sqrt{11}$ ◯ $5\sqrt{21}$.

Complete the statement with consecutive integers.

5 is between the perfect squares _____ and _____,

so the value of $\sqrt{5}$ is between the consecutive integers _____ and _____.

Use this information to complete the inequality with integer values.

_____ < $3\sqrt{5}$ < _____

D. Complete the inequalities using consecutive integers.

_____ < $\sqrt{13} - 1$ < _____

_____ < $\sqrt[3]{40} + 1$ < _____

_____ < $\sqrt[3]{25} + 2$ < _____

_____ < $\sqrt{111} - 4$ < _____

_____ < $\sqrt{109} - 1$ < _____

_____ < $\sqrt{30} + 5$ < _____

 Turn and Talk Explain the strategy you used to complete Part D.

4 ▶ **A.** Identify the integers between which each number is located.

_____ $< \frac{3}{2} <$ _____

_____ $< \pi <$ _____

_____ $< \sqrt{5} <$ _____

_____ $< 0.\overline{3} <$ _____

Use the comparisons to plot and label the points on the number line.

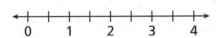

B. Identify the consecutive integers between which each number is located.

_____ $< -\sqrt{12} <$ _____

_____ $< -4.75 <$ _____

_____ $< \sqrt{3} - 8 <$ _____

_____ $< -\frac{17}{3} <$ _____

Use the comparisons to plot and label the points on the number line.

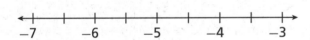

Check Understanding

For Problems 1–3, use $<$ or $>$ to compare the expressions.

1. $\sqrt{6}$ ◯ $\sqrt{7}$ **2.** $\sqrt{10}$ ◯ $\sqrt[3]{25}$ **3.** $\sqrt{5} + 4$ ◯ $\sqrt{50} + 1$

Use the information to solve Problems 4–5.

Marc and Amber are producing a design for a side table. They want the top of the table to have a length of $\sqrt{7}$ feet and the side of the table to have a length of $\sqrt{3}$ feet. Estimate each length to the nearest tenth, then label the points on the number line.

4. $\sqrt{3}$ feet

_____

5. $\sqrt{7}$ feet

_____

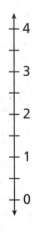

On Your Own

For Problems 6–8, answer the question and complete the statement.

6. Is $\sqrt{14}$ between 3.0 and 3.5 or 3.5 and 4.0? _____

   To the nearest integer, $\sqrt{14} \approx$ _____ .

7. Is $\sqrt{35}$ between 5.75 and 5.85 or 5.85 and 5.95? _____

   To the nearest tenth, $\sqrt{35} \approx$ _____ .

8. Is $\sqrt{75}$ between 8.655 and 8.665 or 8.665 and 8.675? _____

   To the nearest hundredth, $\sqrt{75} \approx$ _____ .

9. (MP) **Reason** How do the intervals selected in Problem 7 help you estimate the value of the square root?

   _____

   _____

   _____

10. Estimate $\sqrt{84}$

    A. to the nearest integer. $\sqrt{84} \approx$ _____

    B. to the nearest tenth. $\sqrt{84} \approx$ _____

11. Estimate $\sqrt[3]{60}$

    A. to the nearest integer. $\sqrt[3]{60} \approx$ _____

    B. to the nearest tenth. $\sqrt[3]{60} \approx$ _____

12. **History** The Spiral of Theodorus was used to prove the irrationality of several square roots. Estimate $\sqrt{2}$ to the nearest hundredth. Show your work.

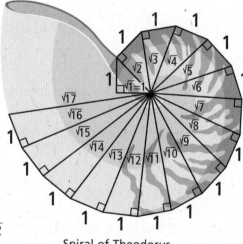

Spiral of Theodorus

For Problems 13–16, write $<$ or $>$ to complete each statement.

13. $\sqrt{15} - 4$ $\bigcirc$ $\sqrt{15} - 7$

14. $2\sqrt{18}$ $\bigcirc$ $2\sqrt{21}$

15. $-\sqrt[3]{30}$ $\bigcirc$ -3

16. $\sqrt{8} + 1$ $\bigcirc$ $\sqrt{17} - 2$

For Problems 17–20, complete each inequality using the greatest possible integer for comparison.

17. $\sqrt{42}$ $>$ _____

18. $\sqrt{150}$ $>$ _____

19. $\sqrt{245}$ $>$ _____

20. $\sqrt{398}$ $>$ _____

For Problems 21–24, circle the lesser of the two numbers.

21. $\sqrt{30} + 4$ $\qquad$ 8

22. $\sqrt{11}$ $\qquad$ $\sqrt{20} - 2$

23. $\sqrt{7}$ $\qquad$ $\sqrt[3]{40}$

24. $15 - \sqrt{2}$ $\qquad$ $\sqrt{125}$

For Problems 25–31, complete each inequality using a pair of consecutive integers.

25. _____ $< \sqrt{10} + 4 <$ _____

26. _____ $< \sqrt{19} + 8 <$ _____

27. _____ $< \sqrt{61} - 5 <$ _____

28. _____ $< \sqrt{92} - 11 <$ _____

29. _____ $< \sqrt[3]{50} - 1 <$ _____

30. _____ $< \sqrt[3]{100} + 2 <$ _____

31. _____ $< \sqrt[3]{17} + 5 <$ _____

32. (MP) **Reason** Is there a limit to the number of decimal places you can use to approximate an irrational number? Explain.

_____

_____

_____

For Problems 33–35, plot the expressions on the number line.

33. $\sqrt{10}$, $\frac{7}{4}$, $2.\overline{2}$, $(\sqrt{13} - 1)$

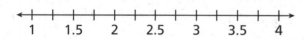

34. $-\sqrt{15}$, $-\frac{5}{3}$, $-\sqrt[3]{27}$, $(\sqrt{12} - 6)$

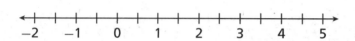

35. $(\sqrt{24} - 5)$, $(\sqrt{48} - 8)$, $(\sqrt{60} - 5)$, $\sqrt{17}$

For Problems 36–37, order the expressions from greatest to least.

36. $\sqrt{27}$, $\frac{17}{6}$, $\sqrt[3]{70}$, π, 1.8

37. $\frac{2}{3}$, $\sqrt{2}$, $\frac{2}{9}$, $(\sqrt{3} - 1)$, $\frac{10}{9}$

For Problems 38–39, order the expressions from least to greatest.

38. $0.\overline{7}$, $2\sqrt{3}$, $(\sqrt{32} - 8)$, $(-2 + \sqrt{19})$, $\left(4 - \frac{21}{4}\right)$

39. $-\frac{12}{5}$, $(-6 + \sqrt{30})$, $(\sqrt{15} - 7)$, $\left(3 - \frac{30}{7}\right)$, $-3\sqrt{2}$

40. Which number is the best approximation for π^2: 9, 9.3, 9.6, or 9.9?

41. Which number is the best approximation for $\frac{\pi}{3}$: 1, 1.03, 1.05, or 1.07?

Order Real Numbers

1. **(MP) Attend to Precision** Through calculations, Jack and Kelsey estimated the diameter of the fountain in the park. If the actual length is 15 feet, which student's estimate is more accurate? Explain your reasoning.

   _____

   _____

2. Complete the inequality with consecutive integers.

   _____ $< \sqrt{357} <$ _____

3. **Math on the Spot** Compare the expressions. Write $<$, $>$, or $=$.

   $\sqrt{6} + 3$ ⬭ $6 + \sqrt{3}$

4. Estimate $\sqrt{74}$ and $\sqrt[3]{74}$ to the nearest tenth.

   _____

5. **Open Ended** Identify two rational numbers and one irrational number between $\sqrt{2}$ and $\sqrt{3}$. Show how you know they are in this range.

   _____

   _____

For Problems 6–7, plot the expressions on a number line.

6. $\sqrt{17}, \frac{\pi}{2}, \pi, \frac{11}{4}$

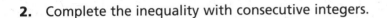

7. $\sqrt{15}, (\sqrt{22} - 6), \frac{16}{5}, (-5 + \sqrt{25})$

8. Order the expressions from least to greatest.

   $\sqrt{31}, \frac{29}{9}, (\sqrt{24} + 2), \sqrt[3]{90}$ _____

9. Order the expressions from greatest to least.

   $(\sqrt[3]{99} - 5), (-\sqrt{45} + 9), (\sqrt{71} - 8), \frac{12}{7}, -\frac{8}{5}$

   _____

Test Prep

10. Which numbers make the inequality true? Select all that apply.

$$7 < \boxed{} < 8$$

(A) $\sqrt{56}$

(B) $\sqrt{99} - 1$

(C) $\sqrt{38} + 1$

(D) $3\sqrt{3} + 2$

(E) $2\sqrt{2} + 3$

11. Which is the best estimate of $\sqrt{200}$?

(A) 14.0

(B) 14.1

(C) 14.2

(D) 14.3

12. Which is the best estimate of $\sqrt[3]{84}$?

(A) 4.38

(B) 4.39

(C) 4.40

(D) 4.41

13. Order the numerical expressions from least to greatest.

$$-\frac{52}{5} \qquad -\sqrt{130} \qquad -3 - \sqrt{47}$$

Spiral Review

14. Would the number of hours traveled and the remaining distance to a destination likely have a strong negative or a strong positive association? Why?

15. Does your music preference influence your choices for pet ownership? Keisha conducted a study of 41 students at her middle school. The results are displayed in the table to the right. Compare relative frequencies to determine whether there is a strong association between music choices and owning pets.

	Favorite Type of Music		
	Country	Hip-hop	Pop
Pet	4	5	6
No pet	7	8	11

16. Solve the equation $5x - 7 = 2(x + 8)$.

Vocabulary

For Problems 1–4, give two examples of each type of number.

1. rational number

2. irrational number

3. terminating decimal

4. repeating decimal

5. Explain how the terms *perfect square* and *square root* are related.

Concepts and Skills

6. Select all numbers that are irrational.

(A) $-\frac{5}{12}$ (C) $0.\overline{15}$ (E) $\frac{1}{6}$

(B) $\frac{\pi}{2}$ (D) $\sqrt{5}$ (F) $\sqrt{25}$

7. Determine whether each number is rational or irrational.

	Rational	Irrational
$\sqrt{49}$	☐	☐
$\sqrt{90}$	☐	☐
$\sqrt{125}$	☐	☐
$\sqrt{169}$	☐	☐

8. (MP) **Use Tools** Write a fraction equivalent to $0.\overline{24}$? State what strategy and tool you will use to answer the question, explain your choice, and then find the answer.

For Problems 9–10, write each repeating decimal as a fraction.

9. $0.\overline{18}$ _____

10. $0.3\overline{6}$ _____

11. Do you see a pattern in the number 0.31311311131111...? Is it rational or irrational? Explain your reasoning.

_____

_____

_____

_____

For Problems 12–13, find all solutions of the equation.

12. $x^3 = 11$

$x =$ _____

13. $n^2 = 0.16$

$n =$ _____

14. A cube has a volume of 216 cubic inches. What is the edge length of the cube?

  (A) 6 inches

  (B) 15 inches

  (C) 18 inches

  (D) 36 inches

15. Explain why the equation $x^2 = 64$ has two solutions, but the equation $x^3 = 64$ has only one solution.

_____

_____

_____

_____

For Problems 16–17, estimate the value of the root to the nearest whole number.

16. $\sqrt{53}$ _____

17. $\sqrt[3]{118}$ _____

18. Select all values that are greater than 4.

  (A) $\sqrt[3]{8}$

  (B) $\sqrt{9}$

  (C) $\sqrt{10}$

  (D) $\sqrt[3]{12} + 2$

  (E) $\sqrt{27}$

  (F) 2π

For Problems 19–20, plot the set of numbers at their approximate locations on the number line.

19. $\sqrt[3]{6}$, $\sqrt[3]{39}$, and $\sqrt[3]{150}$

20. $\sqrt{2}$ and $\sqrt{8}$

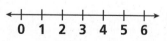

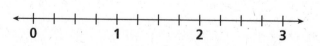

The Pythagorean Theorem

Try Your Angle

A worker is making wooden triangles to use as obstacles for minigolf. The sides of the triangles can have any of the lengths shown. A triangle can be isosceles, but none of the triangles can be equilateral.

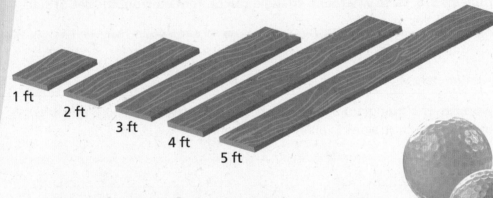

1 ft
2 ft
3 ft
4 ft
5 ft

Name the side lengths of four different triangles to be used as obstacles. No two triangles should have the same set of lengths.

Triangle 1: _____, _____, and _____

Triangle 2: _____, _____, and _____

Triangle 3: _____, _____, and _____

Triangle 4: _____, _____, and _____

 Turn and Talk

How do you know that each set of lengths can form a triangle?

Are You Ready?

Complete these problems to review prior concepts and skills you will need for this module.

Order of Operations

Determine the value of each expression.

1. $18 + 7^2 - 24$ _____

2. $2(10 - 4)^2 + 8$ _____

3. $8^2 + 5^2$ _____

4. $20^2 - 12^2$ _____

Draw Shapes with Given Conditions

For Problems 5–6, state whether a triangle can be formed from the set of side lengths. Write *yes* or *no*.

5. 1 centimeter, 2 centimeters, and 4 centimeters _____

6. 2 centimeters, 2 centimeters, and 3 centimeters _____

7. Two sides of a triangle measure 6 inches and 8 inches. What is a possible length of the third side? Explain your reasoning.

_____

_____

_____

Use Roots to Solve Equations

For Problems 8–11, solve the equation.

8. $a^2 = 100$

9. $c^2 = 35$

_____   _____

10. $b^2 = 144$

11. $x^2 = 225$

_____   _____

12. A square park has an area of 8100 square meters.

A. Write an equation that can be used to determine the side length s, in meters, of the park.

_____

B. Solve your equation, and interpret the solution.

_____

_____

Name _____

Prove the Pythagorean Theorem

(I Can) prove the Pythagorean Theorem, use the Pythagorean Theorem to find unknown side lengths of right triangles, and identify a Pythagorean triple.

Spark Your Learning

PAIRS

The given squares form a right triangle. Find the side lengths and areas of each. What patterns do you notice about the squares and side lengths?

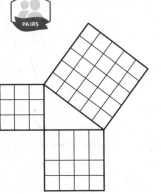

 Turn and Talk What types of objects in the real-world are in the shape of a right triangle? Can you find some right triangles in the classroom?

Build Understanding

The **Pythagorean Theorem** states that in a right triangle, the square of the length of the hypotenuse is equal to the sum of the squares of the lengths of the legs.

If a and b are the lengths of the legs and c is the length of the hypotenuse, then $a^2 + b^2 = c^2$.

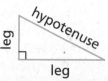

1 ▶ Pythagoras was a Greek philosopher and mathematician whose name is given to the Pythagorean Theorem. You can use what you know about similar triangles to prove the Pythagorean Theorem.

A. Using $\triangle ABC$, draw a line from Point C perpendicular to the hypotenuse. Label the point where this line intersects the hypotenuse as Point D. This breaks the length c into two parts and forms two smaller triangles. Label AD as length e, and label DB as length f. Repeat the labels in the two smaller triangles.

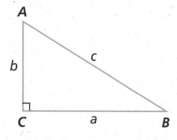

B. Because of Angle-Angle Similarity, $\triangle ABC$ is similar to $\triangle CBD$ and $\triangle ACD$. What do you know about the corresponding sides of similar triangles?

_____

C. Use similar triangles to compare corresponding hypotenuses and corresponding longer legs in $\triangle CBD$ and $\triangle ABC$.

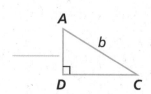

$$\frac{a}{c} = \frac{f}{\boxed{}}$$

Use similar triangles to compare corresponding hypotenuses and corresponding shorter legs in $\triangle ABC$ and $\triangle ACD$.

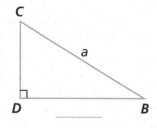

$$\frac{c}{b} = \frac{b}{\boxed{}}$$

D. Use the Multiplication Property of Equality to rewrite the equations. $cf =$ _____ and $b^2 =$ _____

E. Use addition to write $a^2 + b^2$ in terms of c, e, and f. Then simplify to complete the proof.

Step It Out

2 ▶ Use the Pythagorean Theorem to find the length of
the set of stairs.

A. Use the equation $a^2 + b^2 = c^2$. Substitute the leg
lengths into the equation and simplify.

$$a^2 + b^2 = c^2$$

$$\boxed{}^2 + \boxed{}^2 = c^2$$

$$\boxed{} + \boxed{} = c^2$$

$$\boxed{} = c^2$$

B. Take the square root of both sides to solve for c, the
hypotenuse.

$$\sqrt{\boxed{}} = \sqrt{c^2}$$

$$\boxed{} = c$$

The length of the set of stairs is _____ feet.

3 ▶ Only certain right triangles have side lengths that are all
integers. The set of integers 5, 12, and 13 is one example
of a Pythagorean triple, a set of integers that can form
a right triangle. To find another common triple, find the
length of the hypotenuse in the triangle shown.

Connect to Vocabulary

A **Pythagorean triple** is a
set of positive integers a,
b and c that fits the rule
$a^2 + b^2 = c^2$.

$$a^2 + b^2 = c^2$$

$$\boxed{}^2 + \boxed{}^2 = c^2$$

$$\boxed{} + \boxed{} = c^2$$

$$\boxed{} = c^2$$

$$\boxed{} = c$$

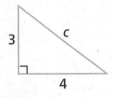

The set of integers 3, 4, and _____ is a common Pythagorean triple.

 Turn and Talk Multiply 3, 4, and 5 each by 2. Is the new set of numbers a
Pythagorean triple? Does this hold true for any multiple of 3, 4, and 5?

4 Use the Pythagorean Theorem to find the unknown leg length.

Use the equation $a^2 + b^2 = c^2$. Substitute the given lengths for one leg and the hypotenuse, and then simplify.

17   8
?

$$a^2 + b^2 = c^2$$

$$\boxed{}^2 + b^2 = \boxed{}^2$$

$$\boxed{} + b^2 = \boxed{}$$

$$b^2 = \boxed{}$$

$$b = \boxed{}$$

 Turn and Talk One leg of a right triangle is 9 inches and the hypotenuse is 21 inches. Find the length of the second leg. Do the lengths of the sides form a Pythagorean triple? Explain your reasoning.

Check Understanding

1. Complete the statement about this triangle.

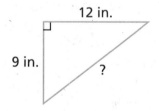

12 in.

9 in.

?

Since the triangle is _____ and

the _____ lengths are 9 and

12 inches, by the Pythagorean Theorem, the hypotenuse length is

_____ inches.

2. **A.** Find the unknown side length of the right-triangle sail.

_____

B. Do these lengths form a Pythagorean triple? _____

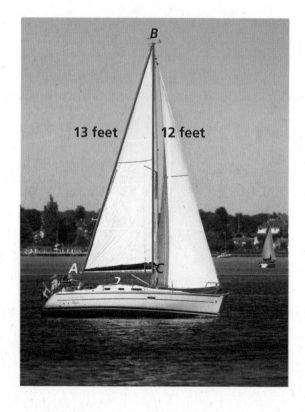

B

13 feet   12 feet

A   C
?

On Your Own

3. **Open Ended** In your own words, describe the Pythagorean Theorem and how you can use it.

   _____

   _____

   _____

4. Find the unknown length.

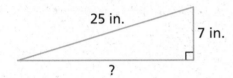

5. A right triangle has leg lengths of 12 centimeters and 16 centimeters. What is the length of the hypotenuse?

   _____

6. (MP) **Critique Reasoning** Rafael found the unknown side length of the given triangle using the Pythagorean Theorem. Is he correct? Explain.

   $5^2 + 13^2 = c^2$

   $25 + 169 = c^2$

   $194 = c^2$

   $14 \approx c$

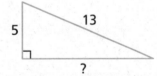

   _____

   _____

   _____

   _____

7. A right triangle has a leg length of 10 meters and a hypotenuse that is 26 meters. What is the length of the other leg?

   _____

8. **Open Ended** What is a Pythagorean triple? Give one example.

   _____

   _____

   _____

9. **Geography** A land surveyor wants to measure the distance across a portion of a lake. The surveyor forms the right triangle shown by forming two legs of a right triangle measured on land. What is the distance across the lake? Show your work.

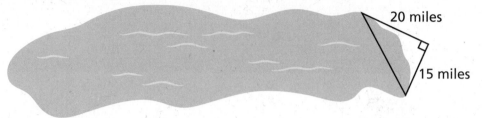

20 miles

15 miles

10. A sculpture shaped like a pair of right triangles has leg lengths of 8 feet and 15 feet. What is the length of the hypotenuse of the sculpture?

_____

11. (MP) **Critique Reasoning** Ashley claims she found the unknown side length of the triangle. Is she correct? Explain.

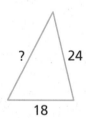

?   24

18

$$18^2 + 24^2 = c^2$$
$$324 + 576 = c^2$$
$$900 = c^2$$
$$30 = c$$

_____

_____

I'm in a Learning Mindset!

What constructive feedback would you give Ashley to correct her misconception about the unknown side length of the triangle in Problem 11?

_____

_____

Name _____

Prove the Pythagorean Theorem

1. **Open Ended** Draw a right triangle on graph paper. Measure the length of each leg and the hypotenuse. Write an equation using your triangle's side lengths to show the Pythagorean Theorem holds true for your triangle.

2. A window shaped like a right triangle has the measurements shown. What is the length of the other leg?

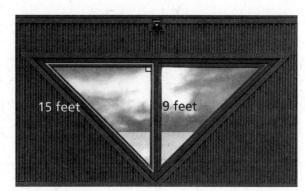

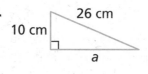

3. A right triangle has leg lengths of 7 inches and 24 inches. What is the length of the hypotenuse?

4. **Math on the Spot** Find each unknown side length.

    A.

    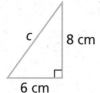

    c   8 cm

    6 cm

    B.

    10 cm   26 cm

    a

5. A. Find the unknown side length of a triangle with leg length 5 yards and hypotenuse length 13 yards.

    B. Find the unknown side length of a triangle with leg length 30 yards and hypotenuse length 78 yards.

    C. ⓂⓅ **Use Structure** How are the lengths of the leg and hypotenuse in Part B related to the lengths of the leg and hypotenuse in Part A?

    D. ⓂⓅ **Use Structure** How is the length of the unknown side in Part B related to the length of the unknown side in Part A?

Test Prep

6. What is the unknown side length?

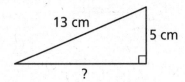

_____ centimeters

7. Which are examples of Pythagorean triples?
Select all that apply.

   Ⓐ 6, 8, 10   Ⓓ 12, 16, 20

   Ⓑ 8, 10, 12   Ⓔ 14, 18, 20

   Ⓒ 10, 16, 15

8. A right triangle has leg lengths of 12 inches and 9 inches. What is the length of the hypotenuse?

_____ inches

9. A right triangle has leg lengths of 7 feet and 8 feet. What is the length of the hypotenuse? Round to the nearest tenth.

_____ feet

Spiral Review

10. Solve the system of equations by graphing. Check your solution.

$$\begin{cases} y = 1 - x \\ y = 5 - 2x \end{cases}$$

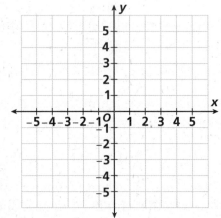

11. Order the numbers from least to greatest.

$\frac{10}{4}$, -3, $\sqrt{8}$, 2.7

Name _____

Prove the Converse of the Pythagorean Theorem

 I Can prove the converse of the Pythagorean Theorem and use it to determine if a triangle is a right triangle, and I can determine whether three side lengths form a Pythagorean triple.

Spark Your Learning

Previously, you used the Pythagorean Theorem equation with right triangles. Does the equation hold true for other types of triangles? Draw a non-right triangle and investigate.

 Turn and Talk Which type of triangle did you draw? Did the Pythagorean Theorem equation hold true?

© Houghton Mifflin Harcourt Publishing Company • **Image Credit:** ©Jordi De Rueda Roige/Alamy

Build Understanding

Consider this statement: *If I am in this class, then I am in the 8th grade.* The converse of this statement is: *If I am in the 8th grade, then I am in this class.* The **converse** of a theorem reverses the hypothesis and the conclusion.

The Pythagorean Theorem states:
If a triangle is a right triangle, then the sum of the squares of the shorter sides is equal to the square of the longest side.

The converse of that statement is:
If the sum of the squares of the two shorter sides of a triangle is equal to the square of the longest side, then the triangle is a right triangle.

1 Show that, given a triangle *ABC* with side lengths *a*, *b*, and *c*, if $a^2 + b^2 = c^2$, then the triangle is a right triangle with a right angle at *C*.

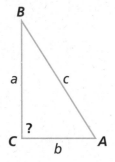 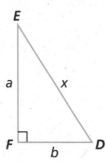

A. Let Triangle *DEF* be a triangle such that $EF = a$, $DF = b$, $DE = x$, and *F* is a right angle. We need to show that Triangles *ABC* and *DEF* are congruent.

B. Can we apply the Pythagorean Theorem to Triangle *DEF*? Why or why not? If so, what can we conclude?

_____

C. How can we relate *x* to *c*?

_____

_____

D. What can you conclude about the measure of Angle *C*? Explain, and include the classification for Triangle *ABC*.

_____

_____

_____

_____

Step It Out

2 Given each set of side lengths, determine whether each triangle is a right triangle.

A. Side *a* measures 4 inches.

Side *b* measures 6 inches.

Side *c* measures 8 inches.

$$a^2 + b^2 \overset{?}{=} c^2$$

$$\boxed{}^2 + \boxed{}^2 \overset{?}{=} \boxed{}^2$$

$$\boxed{} + \boxed{} \overset{?}{=} \boxed{}$$

Circle the correct answers to complete the sentence.

The square of *a* plus the square of *b* | does / does not | equal the square of *c*, so the triangle | is / is not | a right triangle.

B. Side *a* measures 5 inches.

Side *b* measures 12 inches.

Side *c* measures 13 inches.

$$a^2 + b^2 \overset{?}{=} c^2$$

$$\boxed{}^2 + \boxed{}^2 \overset{?}{=} \boxed{}^2$$

$$\boxed{} + \boxed{} \overset{?}{=} \boxed{}$$

Circle the correct answers to complete the sentence.

The square of *a* plus the square of *b* | does / does not | equal the square of *c*, so the triangle | is / is not | a right triangle.

C. Side *a* measures 9 miles.

Side *b* measures 9 miles.

Side *c* measures 9 miles.

$$a^2 + b^2 \overset{?}{=} c^2$$

$$\boxed{}^2 + \boxed{}^2 \overset{?}{=} \boxed{}^2$$

$$\boxed{} + \boxed{} \overset{?}{=} \boxed{}$$

Circle the correct answers to complete the sentence.

The square of *a* plus the square of *b* | does / does not | equal the square of *c*, so the triangle | is / is not | a right triangle.

Turn and Talk Given the side lengths of a triangle, how can you determine whether it is a right triangle or not?

3 Determine whether each set of measurements is a Pythagorean triple. Remember, a Pythagorean triple is a set of three integers that can be the lengths of the sides of a right triangle.

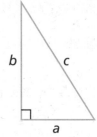

A. Side *a* measures 5 inches.

Side *b* measures 16 inches.

Side *c* measures 20 inches.

Are the side lengths integers? _____

Does $a^2 + b^2 = c^2$? _____

Is the triangle a right triangle? _____

This ⌐ is / is not ⌐ a Pythagorean triple.

B. Side *a* measures $\sqrt{3}$ inches.

Side *b* measures $\sqrt{4}$ inches.

Side *c* measures $\sqrt{7}$ inches.

Are the side lengths integers? _____

Does $a^2 + b^2 = c^2$? _____

Is the triangle a right triangle? _____

This ⌐ is / is not ⌐ a Pythagorean triple.

Check Understanding

For Problems 1–2, determine whether each set of measurements is a Pythagorean triple.

1. Side *a* measures 7 inches.

Side *b* measures 24 inches.

Side *c* measures 25 inches.

Are the side lengths integers? _____

Does $a^2 + b^2 = c^2$? _____

Is the triangle a right triangle? _____

Is the triple a Pythagorean triple? _____

2. Side *a* measures $\sqrt{3}$ inches.

Side *b* measures 2 inches.

Side *c* measures $\sqrt{7}$ inches.

Are the side lengths integers? _____

Does $a^2 + b^2 = c^2$? _____

Is the triangle a right triangle? _____

Is the triple a Pythagorean triple? _____

On Your Own

3. **STEM** A high school is converting an entry staircase into a ramp to increase accessibility. The entrance door is 7 feet off the ground. By law, a ramp this height needs to start 24 feet away from the building. If the length of the ramp is 25 feet, will the ramp form a right triangle with the building?

   A. Fill in the measurements on the illustration shown.

   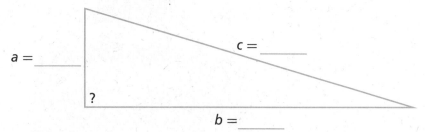

   $a =$ _____ $c =$ _____

   ?

   $b =$ _____

   B. Determine whether the ramp forms a right triangle.

   Does ☐² + ☐² = ☐² ?

   Does ☐ + ☐ = ☐ ?

   By the _____, since the sum of the squares of the leg lengths equals the square of the hypotenuse length, the ramp _____ form a right triangle.

For Problems 4–9, determine whether each set of side lengths form a right triangle.

4. 4, 5, and 6 _____

5. 5, 12, and 13 _____

6. 8, 15, and 17 _____

7. 5, 8, and 12 _____

8. 6, 8, and 10 _____

9. 9, 40, and 41 _____

10. **Open Ended** List one set of three side lengths not used in Problems 4–9 that form a right triangle, and one set that form a triangle but not a right triangle.

_____

_____

_____

_____

11. Use each number from the box exactly once to complete each Pythagorean triple.

4	5	6	9
10	24	25	40

A. $3^2 + \boxed{}^2 = \boxed{}^2$

B. $\boxed{}^2 + 8^2 = \boxed{}^2$

C. $7^2 + \boxed{}^2 = \boxed{}^2$

D. $\boxed{}^2 + \boxed{}^2 = 41^2$

12. Determine whether each set of three side lengths forms a right triangle.

A. 9, 12, and 15

B. 1.5, 2, and 2.5

C. 12, 35, and 37

D. 8, 11, and 13

E. 7, 10, and 12

F. 0.3, 0.4, and 0.5

G. (MP) **Construct Arguments** Consider which of these sets of side lengths forms a right triangle. Which set(s) of lengths do not form a Pythagorean triple? Explain your reasoning.

_____

_____

_____

_____

I'm in a Learning Mindset!

How did I apply the feedback I was given about the Pythagorean Theorem to my understanding of the converse of the Pythagorean Theorem?

_____

_____

Prove the Converse of the Pythagorean Theorem

1. Given the side lengths, determine whether or not they form a right triangle.

Side *a* measures 36 inches.

Side *b* measures 77 inches.

Side *c* measures 85 inches.

This triangle _____ a right triangle because

_____

2. Determine whether the set of measurements is a Pythagorean triple.

Side *a* measures 5 feet.

Side *b* measures 16 feet.

Side *c* measures 20 feet.

Is this a Pythagorean triple? _____

3. (MP) **Critique Reasoning** Winston says that a triangle with side lengths measuring 25, 36, and 64 must be a right triangle because all of the sides are perfect squares. Is he correct? Why or why not?

_____

_____

_____

_____

4. **Math on the Spot** Lynnette is buying a triangular parcel of land. If the lengths of the three sides are 300 yards, 400 yards, and 500 yards, will the parcel of land have a right angle? Explain.

_____

_____

_____

For Problems 5–8, determine whether each set of three side lengths could form a right triangle.

5. 10, 24, and 26

6. 8, 16, and 24

7. 5, 5, and 5

8. 20, 21, and 29

Test Prep

9. Identify in the table whether the measurements could be the side lengths of a right triangle or not.

	Right triangle	Not a right triangle
6, 8, and 14	☐	☐
3, 4, and 5	☐	☐
9, 12, and 15	☐	☐
5, 6, and 7	☐	☐
6, 8, and 10	☐	☐
5, 7, and 12	☐	☐

10. Which of the following are Pythagorean triples? Select all that apply.

Ⓐ 12, 16, 20   Ⓔ 5, 10, 15

Ⓑ 10, 12, $\sqrt{19}$ Ⓕ 4, 14, 25

Ⓒ 21, 28, 35   Ⓖ 1, 2, $\sqrt{5}$

Ⓓ 7, 14, 21

11. Amber claims a triangle with sides measuring 3 inches, 6 inches, and 9 inches is a right triangle because $3 + 6 = 9$. Explain her error.

_____

_____

_____

12. The square of the hypotenuse of a right triangle is 625. Which could be the side lengths?

Ⓐ 4 and 27   Ⓒ 100 and 525

Ⓑ 49 and 576   Ⓓ 7 and 24

Spiral Review

13. Which of $\left\{10, 3.\overline{31}, 4.2123417..., \frac{16}{3}\right\}$ are rational, and which are irrational?

_____

14. Charles placed a number of identical blocks on a table in a square shape with no gaps or holes. What is a possible number of blocks that could have been used? Explain how you know.

_____

Name _____

Apply the Pythagorean Theorem

(I Can) apply the Pythagorean Theorem to solve real-life problems
involving the legs and hypotenuse of a right triangle, including
problems in three dimensions.

Step It Out

1▶ The red team and blue team are
playing Capture the Flag. Each team
places their flag at opposite corners
of the field. The red team sends two
players, Alfredo and Angelina, from
the red flag to capture the blue flag.

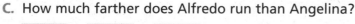

A. Alfredo must follow the white arrows
to the flag. How far does he run?

☐ + ☐ = ☐

Alfredo runs _____ meters.

B. Angelina must follow the black arrow
to the flag. Use the Pythagorean
Theorem to determine how far she
runs. Round to the nearest tenth.

$$a^2 + b^2 = c^2$$

$$\boxed{}^2 + \boxed{}^2 = c^2$$

$$\boxed{} = c^2$$

$$\sqrt{\boxed{}} = c$$

$$\boxed{} \approx c$$

Angelina runs _____ meters.

150 m

85 m

C. How much farther does Alfredo run than Angelina?

☐ − ☐ = ☐

Alfredo runs _____ meters farther than Angelina.

Turn and Talk Will the direct route always be shorter than a route between
two points with a right angle? Why or why not?

The Pythagorean Theorem can be used to find lengths inside a three-dimensional object by finding right triangle relationships inside the object.

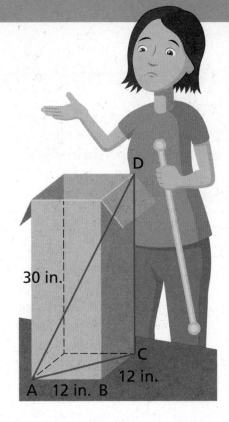

2 Jada wants to ship a 3-foot curtain rod to a customer. The biggest box at the post office is shown. Jada wants to know if the box is large enough to ship the curtain rod.

A. The longest distance in the box is the diagonal *AD* between opposite corners.

It forms the hypotenuse of △*ACD*.

What is the length of $\overline{DC}$? _____ inches

B. To find the length of $\overline{AD}$ we must know the length of $\overline{AC}$. Look at the bottom of the box. $\overline{AC}$ is the hypotenuse of another right triangle, △*ABC*. Use the Pythagorean Theorem to find the length of $\overline{AC}$. Round to the nearest tenth if necessary.

$$a^2 + b^2 = c^2$$

$$\boxed{}^2 + \boxed{}^2 = c^2$$

$$\boxed{} = c^2$$

$$c = \sqrt{\boxed{}} \approx \boxed{}$$

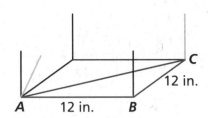

The length of $\overline{AC}$ is about _____ inches.

C. Use the length of $\overline{AC}$ to find the length of $\overline{AD}$. Round to the nearest tenth of an inch.

$$AC^2 + CD^2 = AD^2$$

$$\boxed{}^2 + \boxed{}^2 = c^2$$

$$\boxed{} = c^2$$

$$c = \sqrt{\boxed{}} \approx \boxed{}$$

The length of $\overline{AD}$ is about _____ inches.

D. About how long is the longest rod that could fit in the box?

_____ inches

E. Can the curtain rod fit in the box? Why or why not?

_____

_____

3 Cara measured the **radius** and outside length of an ice cream cone. Identify the right triangle in the cone, then use Cara's measurements to find the **height** of the cone. Round your final answer to the nearest hundredth.

$\boxed{}^2 + b^2 = \boxed{}^2$

$\boxed{} + b^2 = \boxed{}$

$b^2 = \boxed{} - \boxed{}$

$b = \sqrt{\boxed{}}$

$b \approx \boxed{}$

The height of the cone is about _____ centimeters.

2.5 cm

11.7 cm

 Turn and Talk Cara has another ice cream cone. The radius and the height of the second cone is known. Explain how to use these dimensions to find the outside length of the cone.

Check Understanding

1. Computer monitors are measured diagonally, from corner to corner. If the rectangular screen of a 40-inch monitor is 35 inches wide, what is the height of the monitor? Round to the nearest tenth.

_____

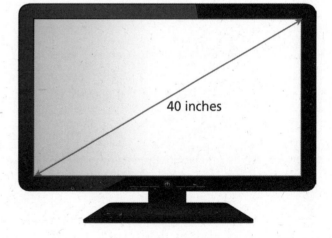
40 inches

2. A 20-inch rod fits perfectly in a box 15 inches tall. What is the measurement of x in the diagram? Round to the nearest tenth.

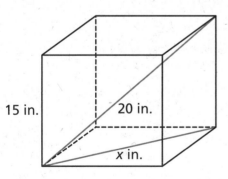
15 in.   20 in.

x in.

On Your Own

3. Alexa can follow the sidewalk from the library to the school or she can travel across the grass directly.

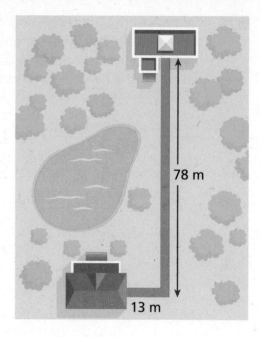

    A. Which route is longer?

_____

    B. What is the difference between the lengths of the two routes?

_____

4. Adam's closet measures 36 inches by 24 inches by 96 inches. What is the longest distance between corners inside his closet? Round to the nearest tenth.

_____

5. The top of a building is a cone 10 meters tall with a radius of 4 meters at the base. What is the measurement of x in the diagram? Round to the nearest hundredth.

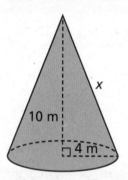

_____

6. **Open Ended** Brianne purchased a box with a base diagonal length that is 45 centimeters long. What are two possible pairs of dimensions for the length and width of the box? Round to the nearest tenth.

_____

_____

_____

For Problems 7–9, find the value for the unknown measurement in each rectangular prism or right cone. Round to the nearest tenth.

7.

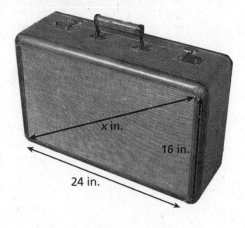

x in.

16 in.

24 in.

_____

8.

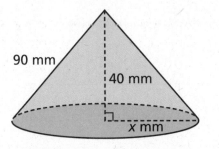

90 mm

40 mm

x mm

_____

9.

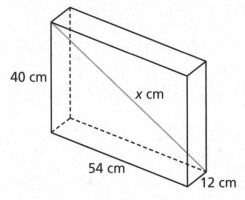

40 cm

x cm

54 cm

12 cm

_____

10. (MP) **Use Structure** The Maron Luggage Company claims they have a suitcase large enough to fit a 34-inch baseball bat inside. If the suitcase has height and depth 17 inches by 11 inches, what must its whole-number length be, at minimum?

_____

© Houghton Mifflin Harcourt Publishing Company • Image Credit: ©Corbis

11. A. Which is taller, Cone A or Cone B?

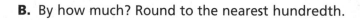

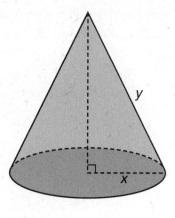

	x	y
Cone A	10 cm	17 cm
Cone B	12 cm	18 cm

_____

B. By how much? Round to the nearest hundredth.

_____

12. Find the value of x in the diagram to the nearest tenth.

13. (MP) **Reason** What is the length of the longest rod that can fit inside this cube? Round to the nearest tenth, and show your work.

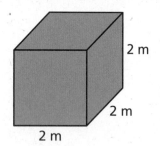

© Houghton Mifflin Harcourt Publishing Company • **Image Credit:** ©Julie Diebolt-Price/Alamy

Apply the Pythagorean Theorem

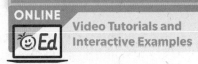
1. **Geography** The distances between Centerville, Springfield, and Capital City form a right triangle. The distance between Centerville and Springfield is 913 kilometers and the distance between Springfield and Capital City is 976 kilometers.

   A. What is the direct distance between Centerville and Capital City? Round to the nearest kilometer.

   _____

   B. Anwell travels from Centerville to Springfield, then on to Capital City. Yue travels directly from Centerville to Capital City. How much farther does Anwell travel than Yue? Round to the nearest kilometer.

   _____

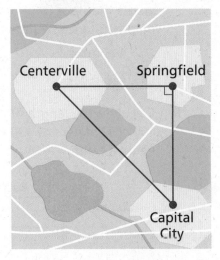

2. (MP) **Attend to Precision** Find the radius of this ice cup. Round to the nearest tenth.

   _____

3. **Math on the Spot** A child has an empty box that measures 4 inches by 6 inches by 3 inches. What is the length of the longest pencil that will fit into the box, given that the length of the pencil must be a whole number of inches? Do not round until your final answer.

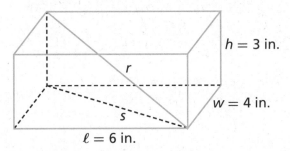

$h = 3$ in.

r

$w = 4$ in.

s

$\ell = 6$ in.

   _____

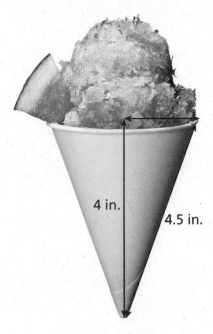

4 in.

4.5 in.

4. Mr. Johnston supports a young tree by using a stake and a string forming a right angle with the ground. What is the length of the string? Round to the nearest tenth.

   _____

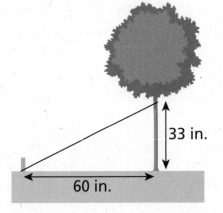

33 in.

60 in.

Test Prep

5. The state of Wyoming is almost rectangular, with an approximate width of 365 miles and an approximate height of 276 miles. If you fly across the state from opposite corners, what is the best approximation of the distance you travel?

   Ⓐ 448 miles   Ⓒ 458 miles

   Ⓑ 450 miles   Ⓓ 462 miles

6. Calculate the length of the longest rod that can fit in a box measuring 100 centimeters by 130 centimeters by 400 centimeters. Round to the nearest tenth.

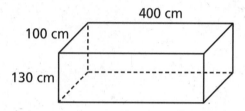

   _____ centimeters

7. Which set of measurements could possibly fit the given cone diagram?

   Ⓐ $x = 3, y = 4, z = 5$ Ⓒ $x = 3, y = 8, z = 5$

   Ⓑ $x = 9, y = 6, z = 10$ Ⓓ $x = 6, y = 10, z = 8$

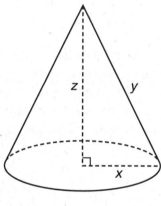

Spiral Review

8. A fun park charges $10 for admission and then $2 for every ride. Write a function that determines the amount of money spent, y, based on the number of rides ridden, x.

   _____

9. Reflect the triangle across the y-axis and draw the image.

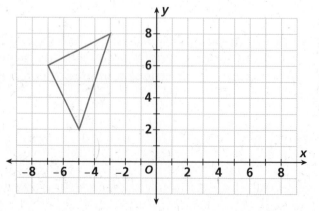

Name

Apply the Pythagorean Theorem in the Coordinate Plane

(I Can) apply the Pythagorean Theorem to find the lengths of line segments on the coordinate plane, including line segments that are part of a composite figure.

Step It Out

1 To find the distance between two points in the coordinate system (on a coordinate plane), draw a right triangle using the horizontal and vertical lines of the grid, with the given points as endpoints of the hypotenuse. Use the Pythagorean Theorem to find the distance between the points.

A. Plot the Points $P(9, 8)$ and $Q(2, 4)$, then use a straight edge to draw a line between the points.

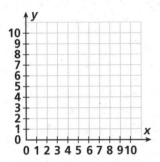   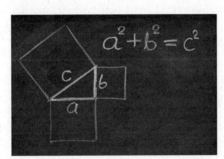

B. Use the horizontal and vertical lines of the coordinate system to draw the legs of a right triangle with Point P and Point Q as vertices.

C. Determine the length of the horizontal and vertical legs, then use the Pythagorean Theorem to determine the length of $\overline{PQ}$. Round to the nearest tenth.

$$a^2 + b^2 = c^2$$

$$\boxed{}^2 + \boxed{}^2 = c^2$$

$$\boxed{} + \boxed{} = c^2$$

$$\boxed{} = c^2$$

$$c = \sqrt{\boxed{}} \approx \boxed{}$$

The distance between Points P and Q is approximately _____ units.

Turn and Talk How many right triangles can you draw using a given pair of points as the endpoints of the hypotenuse? Justify your reasoning.

2 Use the Pythagorean Theorem to find the distance between two points on the coordinate plane.

A. In the coordinate plane, graph Points $G(-4, -1)$ and $H(5, -8)$. Draw a line segment connecting the points.

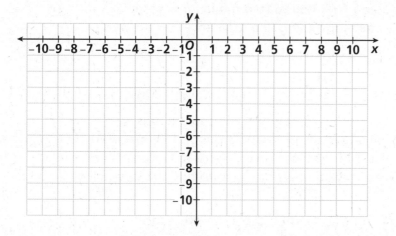

B. Use the horizontal and vertical grid lines to draw the legs of a right triangle with $\overline{GH}$ as the hypotenuse. Label the point where the legs meet as Point J. Give the coordinates of Point J.

_____

C. Determine the length of the horizontal and vertical legs, then use the Pythagorean Theorem to determine the length of $\overline{GH}$. Round to the nearest tenth.

$$a^2 + b^2 = c^2$$

$$\boxed{}^2 + \boxed{}^2 = c^2$$

$$\boxed{} + \boxed{} = c^2$$

$$\boxed{} = c^2$$

$$\sqrt{\boxed{}} = c$$

$$\boxed{} \approx c$$

The distance between $(-4, -1)$ and $(5, -8)$ is approximately

_____ units.

Turn and Talk Can a right triangle be formed using any two points on the coordinate plane? Explain.

3 The Purple Movers drew their logo on graph paper. They want to know the perimeter of the design.

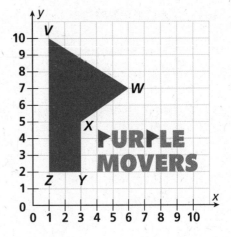

A. Complete the table with the coordinates.

Point	Coordinates
V	(1, 10)
W	
X	
Y	
Z	

B. Use the Pythagorean Theorem to calculate the length of $\overline{VW}$. Round to the nearest tenth.

_____ units

C. Use the same method to determine the length of $\overline{WX}$. Round to the nearest tenth.

_____ units

D. What is the perimeter of the Purple Movers logo? Round to the nearest tenth.

_____ units

Check Understanding

1. On the graph provided, draw a right triangle with Points *G* and *H* as endpoints of the hypotenuse. Find the distance between Points *G* and *H*. Round to the nearest tenth.

_____

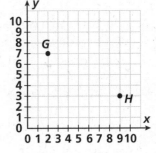

2. A. On your own paper, plot the points (−2, 6) and (5, −5). Find the distance between these two points. Round to the nearest tenth.

_____

B. What is the perimeter of a triangle that has (−2, 6) and (5, −5) as the end points of its hypotenuse? Round to the nearest tenth.

_____

3. On your own paper, plot the points (3, 60) and (−5, 45). Find the distance between these two points. Round to the nearest tenth if necessary.

_____

On Your Own

4. **(MP) Use Structure** The town halls of Havertville and Northtown are shown on the map. If the distance between grid lines represents 1 mile, what is the distance between the two town halls? Round your answer to the nearest tenth.

_____

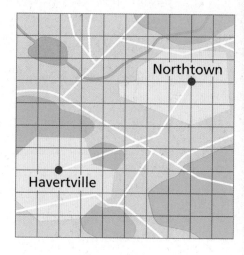

Northtown

Havertville

Use the graph to answer Problems 5–6.

5. **(MP) Attend to Precision** Which point is exactly 10 units from (0, 0)?

_____

6. What is the distance between Points *E* and *H*? Round to the nearest tenth.

_____ units

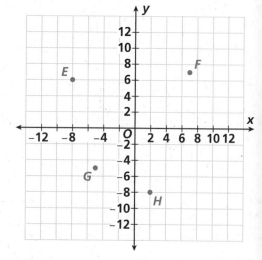

7. On your own paper, graph the points (−5, 4) and (4, 2). Use the grid lines to draw a right triangle with the given points as endpoints of the hypotenuse.

A. Give the two possible coordinates of the third vertex.

_____

B. Find the distance between the given points. Round to the nearest tenth of a unit.

_____

C. Find the perimeter of the triangle to the nearest tenth of a unit.

_____

8. A fencing company is putting fences around the properties shown on the map. Each unit on the map is 1 yard. They need to decide which property has the longest perimeter so they know which will require the most fencing.

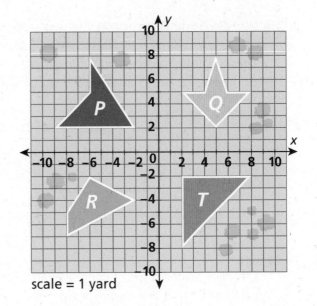

scale = 1 yard

A. Complete the table with the perimeters of each of the properties. Round to the nearest tenth.

Property	Perimeter (yd)
P	
Q	
R	
T	

B. The property with the shortest perimeter is _____.

C. The property with the longest perimeter is _____.

9. (MP) **Use Tools** On your own paper, graph the points $(-8, 7)$ and $(-5, -4)$. Use the grid lines to draw a right triangle with the given points as endpoints of the hypotenuse.

A. Give two possible coordinate pairs for the third vertex.

_____

B. Find the distance between the given points. Round to the nearest tenth.

_____

C. What is the perimeter of the triangle you drew?

_____

D. (MP) **Reason** Does your answer change depending on which of the two possible third vertices you chose? Explain.

_____

_____

_____

10. (MP) **Critique Reasoning** Elena plots the points (1, −1), (1, 2), and (5, 2). She claims the length of the hypotenuse of the triangle formed by these points, rounded to the nearest tenth, is equal to 2.6 units, and the perimeter of the triangle is 9.6 units. Is Elena correct? How do you know?

_____

_____

_____

_____

_____

11. Georgia placed a grid over the map of the post office and the local library.

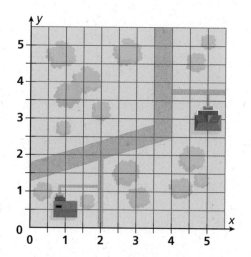

  A. Give the coordinates of the post office and the library.

  _____

  B. If each grid mark represents 0.5 mile, find the distance between the two buildings. Round to the nearest hundredth.

  _____

12. Ali drew the 3-pointed star shown on the graph.

  A. What is the perimeter of this 3-pointed star? Round to the nearest tenth.

  _____

  B. Explain how you used right triangles to find the perimeter.

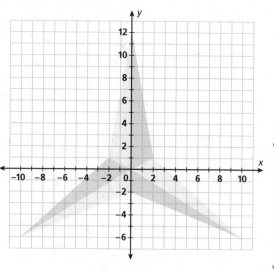

  _____

  _____

  _____

  _____

  _____

  _____

  _____

Apply the Pythagorean Theorem in the Coordinate Plane

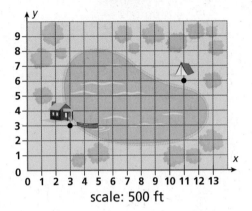
1. Renee takes a boat directly from the lodge to the campsite. If the distance between grid lines represents 500 feet, how far does Renee travel? Round to the nearest 10 feet.

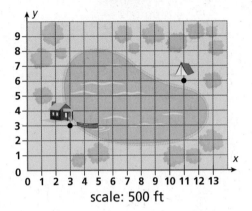
scale: 500 ft

2. (MP) **Use Tools** On your own paper, plot the Points $E(-2, 2)$ and $F(8, 10)$. Use the vertical and horizontal grid lines to draw a right triangle with these two points as vertices.

   A. Label the third vertex of your right triangle Point G. Identify the two possible coordinates of Point G.

   _____

   B. What is the distance between Points E and F? Round to the nearest tenth of a unit.

   _____

   C. What it the perimeter of $\triangle EFG$? Round to the nearest tenth of a unit.

   _____

3. (MP) **Use Tools** On your own paper, graph the points $(-2, -4)$ and $(4, -1)$. Use the grid lines to draw a right triangle with the given points as endpoints of the hypotenuse.

   A. Give a possible coordinate pair of the third vertex.

   _____

   B. What is the vertical distance between the points? What is the horizontal distance between the points?

   _____

   C. Find the distance between the given points. Round to the nearest tenth of a unit.

   _____

   D. What is the perimeter of the triangle you drew? Round to the nearest tenth of a unit.

   _____

Test Prep

4. What is the direct distance between Point *A* and Point *C* on Parallelogram *ABCD*?

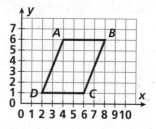

- (A) 4.8 units
- (C) 5.2 units
- (B) 5 units
- (D) 5.4 units

Use the graph for Problems 5–7.

5. Which pair of points is exactly 5 units apart?

- (A) *J* and *K*
- (C) *N* and *P*
- (B) *L* and *M*
- (D) *Q* and *R*

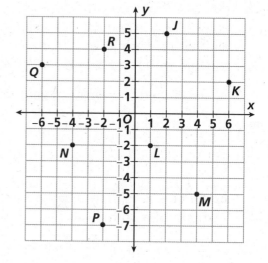

6. How far apart are *L* and *M*?

- (A) 6 units
- (C) $\sqrt{12}$ units
- (B) $\sqrt{9}$ units
- (D) $\sqrt{18}$ units

7. Which pair of points is $\sqrt{29}$ units apart?

- (A) *J* and *L*
- (C) *N* and *P*
- (B) *P* and *M*
- (D) *Q* and *R*

8. What is the perimeter of Trapezoid *EFGH*?

- (A) 24 units
- (C) 25 units
- (B) 24.3 units
- (D) 25.3 units

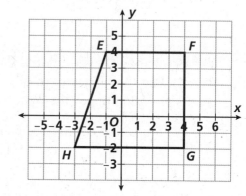

Spiral Review

9. Find the value of *x* that makes the equation true.

$12x = 4(x + 2) + 20$

_____

10. A line has a slope of 8 and crosses the *y*-axis at (0, 12). Express this line in slope-intercept form.

_____

Review

Vocabulary

For Problems 1–3, choose the correct term from the Vocabulary box to complete each sentence.

> **Vocabulary**
>
> hypotenuse
> leg
> Pythagorean Theorem
> Pythagorean triple

1. The _____ describes the relationship among the lengths of the sides of any right triangle.

2. A _____ of a right triangle is one of the sides that forms the right angle.

3. A _____ is a set of three positive integers that could be the side lengths of a right triangle.

4. Write the converse of this statement: *If a triangle has a right angle, then it is a right triangle.*

_____

Concepts and Skills

5. Which set of side lengths could form a right triangle?

   Ⓐ 5 cm, 5 cm, and 10 cm   Ⓒ 8 cm, 15 cm, and 17 cm

   Ⓑ 6 cm, 7 cm, and 8 cm   Ⓓ 9 cm, 12 cm, and 16 cm

6. (MP) **Use Tools** The diagram represents a set of beams that form part of a bridge support. Label $\overline{AB}$ and $\overline{BD}$ with their lengths, rounded to the nearest foot. State what strategy and tool you will use to answer the question, explain your choice, and then find the answer.

   _____

   _____

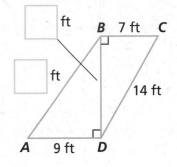

For Problems 7 and 8, determine the unknown side length of each right triangle to the nearest hundredth.

7. What is the length of $\overline{JL}$?

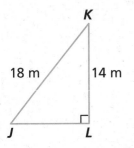

_____ meters

8. What is the length of $\overline{ST}$?

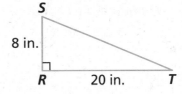

_____ inches

9. The steps shown can be used to prove the Pythagorean Theorem.

Step 1: Draw a figure using two squares. 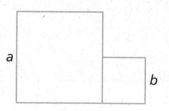	Step 2: Draw two congruent right triangles inside the figure. 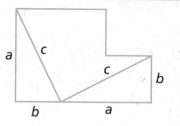
Step 3: Rotate the two triangles. 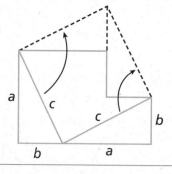	Step 4: The resulting figure is a square of side length *c*. 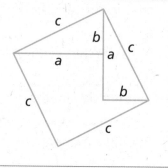

Explain how the steps prove the Pythagorean Theorem. *Hint:* Write expressions for the total area of the figures in Step 1 and in Step 4.

_____

_____

_____

_____

10. Which set of side lengths could form a right triangle?

Ⓐ 3 ft, 5 ft, 12 ft   Ⓒ 12 ft, 13 ft, 16 ft

Ⓑ 5 ft, 12 ft, 13 ft   Ⓓ 13 ft, 16 ft, 24 ft

11. Meg is making a scale model of an Egyptian pyramid. The model is a right square pyramid as shown. To the nearest centimeter, what is the base length *b* of the model?

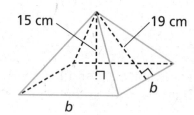

Ⓐ 12 cm   Ⓒ 23 cm

Ⓑ 16 cm   Ⓓ 48 cm

For Problems 12–14, determine the distance between the pair of points, to the nearest hundredth of a unit.

12. $A(-2, 1)$ and $B(3, 5)$ _____ units

13. $C(-5, -2)$ and $D(0, -4)$ _____ units

14. $E(7, 3)$ and $F(-2, 6)$ _____ units

Exponents, Scientific Notation, and Volume

Cosmologist

People who lived 600 years ago believed the sun, the planets, and the stars revolved around Earth, which was thought to be at the center of the universe. Today, we know this is not true thanks to discoveries by cosmologists, scientists who study the origin and evolution of the universe. Cosmologists are curious about the universe and sometimes work for decades to solve problems related to it.

STEM Task:

Light travels at a speed of about 186,000 miles per second in a vacuum. About how many miles does light travel in one hour? Write your answer in standard form and as a number multiplied by a power of 10.

Learning Mindset

Strategic Help-Seeking Identifies Need for Help

It is impossible to know the exact number of people who worked to develop all of the technology required to send spacecraft to the moon. But it is reasonable to estimate that hundreds of thousands of people from universities, government, and industry contributed, and continue to contribute to the task.

No one could have done such a complex task alone. People had to collaborate with and help each other. Remember that when you need to ask for help. Here are some tips on when, where, and how to seek help strategically.

- Try to solve a problem three ways before you ask another person for help. Identify resources such as books or videos you could use to solve the problem.

- When you seek help from others, describe exactly what you understand about the problem and what you do not understand. Be as clear and specific as you can.

Reflect

Q Were you able to work through the challenges of the STEM Task on your own, or did you need help from another person? How did you know you needed help?

Q What resources did you use to complete the STEM Task?

Exponents and Scientific Notation

A-Mazing Expressions

Find a path through the maze by evaluating each of the expressions shown. You can move from one space to the next only if the value of the expression in the space you are in is less than the value of the expression in the space you are moving to. You can move left, right, up, or down, but not diagonally.

START

$(4 + 2) \div 5^2$	$(8 \div 10^2) + 2.3$	$1.5 \times 6 - 4 \times 2$
_____	_____	_____
$1.8 \div 10^2$	$12 - 3.8 + 4.7$	$15 + (7 - 5)^3$
_____	_____	_____
$5 \times 71 - 340$	$0.8^2 + 4^3$	$(1.4 \times 10^2) \div 5$
_____	_____	_____
$(10 + 2)^2 - 1$	2.46×10^2	6.74×10^3
_____	_____	_____

FINISH

 Turn and Talk

Explain how to determine whether you can move from 2.46×10^2 to 6.74×10^3 without performing any operations.

Are You Ready?

Complete these problems to review prior concepts and skills you will need for this module.

Order of Operations

For Problems 1–8, determine the value of each expression.

1. 36×10^5 _____

2. 1.24×10^4 _____

3. $179 \div 10^3$ _____

4. $1.5 \div 10^2$ _____

5. $(3.5 \times 10^3) + (4.27 \times 10^3)$ _____

6. $(6.7 \times 10^4) - (5.82 \times 10^2)$ _____

7. $(8.3 \times 10^3) \times (9.71 \times 10^2)$ _____

8. $(5.52 \times 10^2) \div (4.6 \times 10^3)$ _____

Solve Multi-Step Problems

9. At a grocery store, sliced turkey from the deli counter costs $7.92 per pound. A customer purchases 0.625 pound of sliced turkey. Excluding tax, how much change will she receive if she pays with a $20 bill?

    $ _____

10. It takes Steven 12.25 minutes to run 1.4 miles. At this rate, how long will it take him to run 2.6 miles?

    _____ minutes

11. An account with $600 earns 4% simple interest per year. The next year all the money is put into a new account that earns 4.5% simple interest per year. How much money does the account have at the end of the second year? Explain.

    _____

    _____

    _____

    _____

12. Anthony has two cube-shaped pots with an interior edge length of 8 inches and two cube-shaped pots with an interior edge length of 6.5 inches. He wants to fill each pot full of potting soil. His bag of potting soil is one cubic foot. How much soil will he have left after he fills each pot full of soil?

Name _____

Know and Apply Properties of Exponents

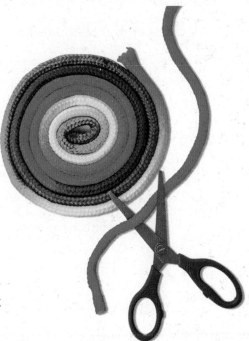

(I Can) use properties of integer exponents to simplify expressions.

Spark Your Learning

Alex has a rope that is 2^4, or 16 feet long. He folds the rope in half and cuts it, so he now has two pieces of rope that are each 2^3, or 8 feet long. Alex then folds each of the new pieces in half and cuts them, so he now has four pieces of rope that are each 2^2, or 4 feet long. Alex repeats this process until his pieces of rope are each 1 foot long. What would happen if Alex took each 1-foot section of rope and continued this process? What pattern do you notice?

x	y

Turn and Talk Look for patterns in how these pairs are related: 2^{-3} and 2^3, 2^{-2} and 2^2, 2^{-1} and 2^1. What generalization can you make about a^{-b}, where a and b are natural numbers (1, 2, 3,...)?

Build Understanding

Connect to Vocabulary

The **properties of exponents** are rules for operations with exponents. In the power 2^4, 2 is the **base** and 4 is the **exponent**.

1 ▸ The patterns in the Spark Your Learning lead to the following two properties of exponents.

If $a \neq 0$ and b is an integer, then $a^{-b} = \frac{1}{a^b}$.

If $a \neq 0$, then $a^0 = 1$.

A. You can look for patterns to develop the product of powers property for multiplying powers with the same base. Complete the table.

Product of powers	Factors	Single power
$3^2 \cdot 3^4$	$(3 \cdot 3) \cdot (3 \cdot 3 \cdot 3 \cdot 3)$	3^6
$7^3 \cdot 7^2$		
$2^4 \cdot 2^3$		

$2^1 = 2$

$2^2 = 4$

B. How are the exponents in the left column and the exponent in the right column related?

_____

_____

_____

$2^3 = 8$

C. You also can look for patterns to develop the quotient of powers property for dividing powers with the same base. Complete the table.

$2^4 = 16$

Quotient of powers	Factors	Single power
$\frac{2^7}{2^4}$	$\dfrac{2 \cdot 2 \cdot 2 \cdot 2 \cdot 2 \cdot 2 \cdot 2}{2 \cdot 2 \cdot 2 \cdot 2}$	2^3
$\frac{6^5}{6^3}$		
$\frac{5^8}{5^2}$		

D. How are the exponents in the left column and the exponent in the right column related?

_____

_____

E. Make a conjecture about two additional properties of exponents based on your findings.

_____

_____

Turn and Talk Can you use the properties of exponents you discovered to simplify $5^2 \cdot 2^5$? If so, how? If not, why not?

Step It Out

2 ▸ In 2002, a high school student broke the record for folding a sheet of paper in half multiple times. When the paper was opened, the number of regions formed was $(2^4)^3$. How many times did the student fold the paper? To answer, you can develop the power of a power property.

A. First look for patterns using specific examples of a power of a power. Complete the table.

Power of powers	Expanded form	Factors	Single power
$(5^2)^3$	$5^2 \cdot 5^2 \cdot 5^2$	$(5 \cdot 5) \cdot (5 \cdot 5) \cdot (5 \cdot 5)$	5^6
$(7^4)^2$			
$(8^3)^2$			
$(4^3)^3$			

B. How are the exponents in the far-left column and the exponent in the far-right column related?

The _____ of the exponents in the far-left column equals the

_____ in the far-right column.

C. Complete the conjecture about a property of exponents based on your findings:

If $a \neq 0$, then $\left(a^{\boxed{}}\right)^{\boxed{}} = a^{\boxed{}}$.

D. The number of regions formed by the high school student's folded paper was $(2^4)^3$. Use a single exponent to write this expression.

$(2^4)^3 = 2^{\boxed{}}$

E. How many times did the student fold the paper in half?

The student folded the paper _____ times. This is because 1 fold results

in $2^{\boxed{}}$ regions, 2 folds results in $2^{\boxed{}}$ regions, and so on.

Continuing the pattern shows that _____ folds results in $\boxed{}^{12}$ regions.

 Turn and Talk Does the property of exponents you discovered apply to negative powers? For example, can you use it to simplify $(7^{-2})^2$? Explain.

3 ▷ Simplify each expression.

A. $2^4 \cdot 2^9$

$= 2^{\boxed{} + \boxed{}}$ Apply the product of powers property.

$= 2^{\boxed{}}$ Add the exponents.

$= \underline{\hspace{2cm}}$ Simplify.

B. $3^3 \cdot 3^{-5}$

$= 3^{\boxed{} + \boxed{}}$ Apply the product of powers property.

$= 3^{\boxed{}}$ Add the exponents.

$= \dfrac{\boxed{}}{\boxed{}}$ Write the power without a negative exponent.

$= \underline{\hspace{2cm}}$ Simplify.

$3^0 = 1,\ \ 3^1 = 3,\ \ 3^2 = 9$

C. $(4 + 8)^0$

$= \boxed{}^{\,0}$ Simplify within parentheses.

$= \underline{\hspace{2cm}}$ Simplify.

D. $\dfrac{(5^2)^5}{5^6}$

$= \dfrac{\boxed{}}{\boxed{}}$ Apply the power of powers property in the numerator.

$= \boxed{}^{\boxed{}}$ Apply the quotient of powers property.

$= \underline{\hspace{2cm}}$ Simplify.

Powers of 5

Check Understanding

1. If $a \neq 0$, what is the value of $a^m \cdot a^{-m}$? How do you know?

2. Simplify $3^0 - 3^4 \cdot 3^{-5}$. Show your work and write the result as a fraction.

On Your Own

3. **STEM** According to one estimate, the number of stars in the Milky Way Galaxy is about $10^2 \cdot 10^3 \cdot 10^6$.

   A. Write the number of stars in the Milky Way Galaxy as a single power. Which property of exponents did you use?

   _____

   B. Write the estimated number of stars in the Milky Way Galaxy without using exponents.

   _____

4. The formula for the volume V of a cube with edge length s is $V = s^3$. The formula for the surface area A of the cube is $A = 6s^2$.

   A. A cube has edges of length 2 centimeters. Write expressions using exponents for the volume of the cube (in cubic centimeters) and for the surface area of the cube (in square centimeters).

   _____

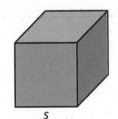

s

   B. (MP) **Reason** What is the ratio of the cube's volume to its surface area? Use the expressions you wrote in Part A and show how to simplify the ratio. Show your work and name any properties of exponents you use.

For Problems 5–7, use the table shown.

Description	Distance (m)
Distance from the Sun to Saturn	$(10^2)^6$
Diameter of the Solar System	$10^5 \cdot 10^8$
Diameter of Saturn	$((10^2)^2)^2$
Diameter of the disc of the Milky Way	$\dfrac{10^{23}}{10^2}$

5. What is the greatest distance shown? Write it as a power of 10 with a single exponent.

   _____

6. What is the least distance shown? Write it as a power of 10 with a single exponent.

   _____

7. The distance from Earth to the star Vega is approximately 10^{17} meters. Which of the distances in the table, if any, are less than this?

   _____

   _____

8. **Open Ended** Write an expression involving two or more operations and three or more powers of 5 that can be simplified to $\frac{1}{5}$.

9. 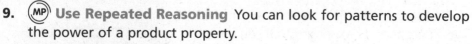 **Use Repeated Reasoning** You can look for patterns to develop the power of a product property.

   A. Complete the table.

Power of product	Factors	Product of powers
$(4 \cdot 3)^2$	$(4 \cdot 3) \cdot (4 \cdot 3) = (4 \cdot 4) \cdot (3 \cdot 3)$	$4^2 \cdot 3^2$
$(2 \cdot 9)^2$		
$(5 \cdot 8)^3$		

   B. Look for patterns in the table. State a property of exponents based on what you observe.

   C. Show two different ways to simplify the expression $(3 \cdot 2)^5$.

For Problems 10–13, simplify each expression. Write your answer without using exponents.

10. $3^2 \cdot 3^0 \cdot 3^4$

11. $\frac{4^6 \cdot 4^{-2}}{4^5}$

12. $\frac{2^5}{(2^2)^5}$

13. $8^0 + 8^6 \cdot 8^{-4}$

 I'm in a Learning Mindset!

What is challenging about solving a problem involving exponents? Can I work through it on my own, or do I need help?

Name _____

Know and Apply Properties of Exponents

Problems 1–2 involve crayon production.

1. According to one crayon manufacturer, the average number of crayons produced in their factories each day is greater than $\frac{10^4 \cdot 10^6}{10^3}$.

    A. Write the number of crayons as a single power of 10. Which property or properties of exponents did you use?

    _____

    _____

    B. Write the number of crayons without using exponents.

    _____

2. One of the boxes produced by the crayon manufacturer contains $2^2 \cdot 2^0 \cdot 2^4$ crayons. How many crayons are in the box?

    _____

3. Katie and Lawrence collect guitar picks. Katie has $(2^2)^4$ guitar picks in her collection. Lawrence has $(3^2)^2$ guitar picks in his collection. Who has more guitar picks? How many more?

    _____

4. (MP) **Reason** Simplify $3^0 + 3^4 \cdot 3^{-6}$. Show your work and explain your steps.

For Problems 5–8, simplify each expression.

5. $8^{-1} \cdot 8^{-5} \cdot 8^3$

6. $4^3 \cdot 4^{-4} \cdot 4^2$

7. $\frac{9^{-2} \cdot 9^7}{9^3}$

8. $\frac{[6^3]^5}{6^{18}}$

© Houghton Mifflin Harcourt Publishing Company • Image Credit: ©William Thomas Cain/Stringer/Getty Images

Test Prep

9. Which expression is equivalent to $3^2 \cdot 3^{-8} \cdot 3^0$?

    (A) $\frac{1}{3^6}$
                    (C) 3^6

    (B) $\frac{1}{3^{-6}}$
                  (D) 3^0

10. Draw a line to match each expression to its value.

$\dfrac{4^2 \cdot 4^{-4}}{4^3}$	$\dfrac{1}{1024}$
$4^2 \cdot 4^8 \cdot 4^{-7}$	$\dfrac{1}{256}$
$\dfrac{4^6}{4 \cdot 4^3}$	1
$4^{-2} \cdot 4^2 \cdot 4^{-4}$	16
$\dfrac{4^3 \cdot 4^0}{4^2 \cdot 4}$	64

11. What is the value of the expression $(-2 + 9)^5 \cdot (4 + 3)^{-3} + 7^0$?

    (A) $\frac{1}{343}$
                  (C) 49

    (B) $1\frac{1}{49}$
                  (D) 50

Spiral Review

12. Miguel keeps track of whether or not he brought an umbrella with him to work and whether or not it actually rained that day. He collects the data and makes the two-way relative frequency table shown.

	Rain	No rain	TOTAL
Umbrella	0.2		
No umbrella		0.47	
TOTAL	0.35		

    A. Complete the two-way relative frequency table.

    B. On what percent of the days did Miguel bring an umbrella? Which value in the table gives you this information?

13. Solve the equation $y^3 = \frac{27}{1000}$.

Name _____

Understand Scientific Notation

(I Can) use scientific notation to describe very large or very small quantities and to compare quantities.

Step It Out

1 What does one trillion dollars look like? If you could stack one trillion one-dollar bills, the stack would be about 68,000 miles tall. This is more than one-fourth the distance from the Earth to the moon!

The **standard, or decimal, form** of a number is one way to write numbers. It uses the base-ten system to show all of a number's digits. For example, the way to write one trillion in standard form is 1,000,000,000,000.

There is a shorthand way, called **scientific notation**, to write large numbers without so many zeros. 1,000,000,000,000 in scientific notation is 1×10^{12}.

A. To write 68,000 miles in scientific notation, first move the decimal point to the left to get a number that is greater than or equal to 1 but less than 10.

$$68,000.$$
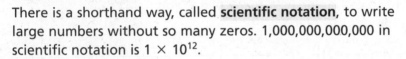

The decimal point moves _____ places to the left.

Remove the extra zeros to get the first factor for

scientific notation: _____.

B. Use this factor and a power of 10 to write the number in scientific notation.

$$68,000 = \underline{\hspace{1.5cm}} \times 10^{\square}$$

When you write a number in scientific notation, its value does not change.

C. Write one billion, 1,000,000,000, in scientific notation.

$$1,000,000,000 = \underline{\hspace{1.5cm}} \times 10^{\square}$$

> **Connect to Vocabulary**
>
> **Scientific notation** is a method of writing very large or very small numbers by using powers of 10. In scientific notation, a number is written as the product of two factors. The first factor is greater than or equal to 1 but less than 10, and the second factor is a power of 10.

 Turn and Talk Is the number 16×10^7 written in scientific notation? Why or why not?

2 You can also use scientific notation for very small numbers. The thickness of a dollar bill is about 0.0043 inches. Write this quantity in scientific notation.

A. First move the decimal point to the right to get a number that is greater than or equal to 1 but less than 10.

0.0043   The decimal point moves _____ places to the right.

Remove the extra zeros to get the first factor: _____.

B. Since 0.0043 is less than 1, you moved the decimal point to the right, so the exponent in the power of 10 will be negative.

$0.0043 = $ _____ $\times 10^{\boxed{}}$

3 In 2016, the United States Mint produced about 9.1×10^9 pennies. Write this quantity in standard form.

A. Use the power of 10 to determine how many places you will need to move the decimal point.

Move the decimal point _____ places.

B. Write the number with placeholder zeros. Then move the decimal point to the right the appropriate number of places.

9.100000000   So, $9.1 \times 10^9 = $ _____.

4 Scientific notation makes it easy to compare quantities.

2016 Half-Dollar Production	
Denver Mint	2.1×10^6
All U.S. mints	4.2×10^6

A. The table shows the number of half-dollar coins produced in 2016. Use a ratio to compare these quantities.

$$\frac{4.2 \times 10^6}{2.1 \times 10^6}$$

The powers of 10 are the same: $\frac{10^6}{10^6} = 10^0$ or _____.

Compare the first factors: $\dfrac{\boxed{}}{2.1} = $ _____.

So, the total number of half-dollar coins minted

is about $\boxed{} \cdot \boxed{} = $ _____ times the number of half-dollar coins minted in Denver.

 Turn and Talk Why is scientific notation a good way to express very large or very small numbers that you are estimating?

B. Use the ratio $\dfrac{3.45 \times 10^{-8}}{3.45 \times 10^{-11}}$ to compare 3.45×10^{-8} and 3.45×10^{-11}.

First compare the powers of 10.

$\dfrac{\boxed{}}{10^{-11}} = 10^{\boxed{}} = $ _____

Compare the first factors: $\dfrac{\boxed{}}{3.45} = $ _____.

So, 3.45×10^{-8} is $\boxed{} \cdot \boxed{} = $ _____ times as great as 3.45×10^{-11}.

C. Use a ratio to compare 4.8×10^9 and 12,000,000.

Write 12,000,000 in scientific notation. 12,000,000 = _____

Compare the powers of 10. Compare the greater power to the lesser power.

$\dfrac{10^9}{\boxed{}} = 10^{\boxed{}} = $ _____

Compare the first factors: $\dfrac{4.8}{\boxed{}} = $ _____.

So, 4.8×10^9 is _____ $\times$ _____ = _____ times as great as 12,000,000.

D. Use a ratio to compare 0.00222 and 66,600.

In scientific notation, 0.00222 = _____.

In scientific notation, 66,600 = _____.

66,600 is _____ $\times$ _____ = _____ times as great as 0.00222.

Check Understanding

1. Which number is greater: 8.9×10^5 or 2.1×10^7? How can you tell without writing the numbers in standard notation?

_____

2. Write 0.000501 in scientific notation.

_____

3. Write 5.31×10^3 in standard form.

_____

On Your Own

4. The photo shows a road sign in western Australia.

   A. Write the distance to Rome in scientific notation.

   _____

   B. Write the distance to Sydney in scientific notation.

   _____

   C. (MP) **Reason** Explain how you can use the scientific notation version of the distances to determine whether it is farther to Rome or to Sydney.

   _____

   _____

5. **STEM** The diameter of a carbon atom is approximately 0.000000017 centimeter.

   A. When the diameter is expressed in scientific notation, will the exponent be positive or negative? How do you know?

   _____

   B. Write the diameter in scientific notation. Show your work and explain your steps.

For Problems 6–7, use the table which shows the number of miles on the odometers of several cars.

Car	Miles
A	7.51×10^4
B	6.03×10^3
C	1.1×10^5
D	4×10^4
E	8.9×10^3

6. Write the number of miles on Car A's odometer in standard form.

   _____

7. (MP) **Attend to Precision** Nicole wants to buy a used car with fewer than 50,000 miles on the odometer. Which of the cars shown should Nicole consider? Explain.

   _____

   _____

For Problems 8–9, use the table of bridge lengths shown.

Bridge	Length (ft)
Atchafalaya Basin	9.6×10^4
General W.K. Wilson Jr.	3.2×10^4
Manchac Swamp	1.2×10^5
Frank Davins Memorial	2.9×10^4

8. Which of the bridges shown is the longest? How do you know?

_____

_____

9. How many times as long as General W.K. Wilson Jr. Bridge is Atchafalaya Basin Bridge? Explain.

_____

_____

_____

10. **STEM** A geologist is comparing two rock samples. Sample A has a mass of 0.0015 gram. Sample B has the mass shown on the scale.

   A. Write the masses in scientific notation.

   _____

   B. How many times as great as the mass of Sample A is the mass of Sample B? Show your work.

11. (MP) **Use Tools** Most calculators display scientific notation when a result is longer than the number of digits the screen can display.

   A. To find out how your calculator displays scientific notation, enter 2^{40} and press the ENTER key. What does the calculator display? What number in scientific notation does it represent?

   _____

   B. Write the value of 2^{40} rounded to the nearest trillion.

   _____

12. (MP) **Reason** What must be true about the exponent when you write a whole number between 1 and 10 in scientific notation? Why? Give an example.

_____

_____

For Problems 13–16, write each number in scientific notation.

13. 47,100,000

14. 6004

15. 0.0000000009

16. 0.00053

For Problems 17–20, write each number in standard form.

17. 3.2×10^8

18. 5.111×10^2

19. 1.06×10^{-3}

20. 7.7×10^{-9}

For Problems 21–24, determine which number is greater and tell how many times as great.

21. 2×10^5 and 8×10^9

22. 3.9×10^4 and 1.3×10^{-1}

23. 24,000,000 and 2.4×10^{10}

24. 1.5×10^{-6} and 0.0063

25. Social Studies The Smithsonian Institution in Washington, D.C., is the world's largest museum, with approximately 15.4×10^7 artifacts. Explain why this number is not written in scientific notation and show how to write it correctly.

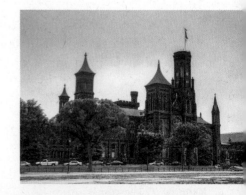

_____

_____

Understand Scientific Notation

1. A group of researchers in Hawaii estimated that the number of grains of sand on Earth is 7,500,000,000,000,000,000. Write this number using scientific notation.

_____

2. A snail moves across a table at a rate of 0.00093 mile per hour. Write this rate in scientific notation.

_____

3. **Math on the Spot** The approximate population of Brazil in 2008 is shown. Write this number in standard form.

Population: 1.86×10^8

_____

For Problems 4–7, write each number in scientific notation.

4. 239,000,000,000

5. 405

6. 0.0000101

7. 0.00000000000006

For Problems 8–11, write each number in standard form.

8. 5.5×10^5

9. 6.07×10^7

10. 2.04×10^{-4}

11. 4×10^{-6}

For Problems 12–14, determine which number is greater and tell how many times as great.

12. 7×10^{12} and 3.5×10^9

_____

13. 1.4×10^{-5} and 2.8×10^{-4}

_____

14. 16,000 and 1.6×10^8

_____

15. **Open Ended** Write two numbers in scientific notation so that the second number is 10 times as great as the first number.

_____

Test Prep

16. Kendrick wants to write the number 0.000065 in scientific notation. What exponent should he use for the power of 10?

(A) −5

(B) −4

(C) 4

(D) 5

17. Jenna collected data about the number of annual visitors to two sports blogs. The table shows the data. The number of visitors to Sports Space is _____ times the number of visitors to Team Zone.

(A) 4

(B) 40

(C) 400

(D) 4000

Blog	Annual visitors
Sports Space	4.8×10^5
Team Zone	12,000

18. What is 5.003×10^3 written in standard form?

(A) 0.0005003

(B) 0.005003

(C) 5003

(D) 5,003,000

19. Which of the following numbers is greatest?

(A) 6.1×10^7

(B) 8.9×10^6

(C) 55,000,000

(D) 9,070,000

Spiral Review

20. The figure shows the dimensions of a rectangular city park. A member of the parks commission is considering a new diagonal path that would cut through the park from A to C. If the path is built, how much shorter would it be to walk along the path from A to C rather than walking along the edge of the park from A to C? Explain.

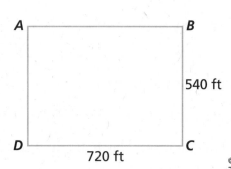

_____

_____

_____

21. What is the height of the cone shown? Round to the nearest tenth of a centimeter.

_____

22. Simplify the expression $7^0 + \dfrac{7^2}{(7^3)^2}$.

_____

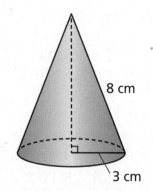

Vocabulary

In Problems 1–3, complete each sentence with the correct operation to explain the properties of exponents.

1. To raise a power to a power, keep the base the same and _____ the exponents.

2. To divide two powers with the same base, keep the base the same and _____ the exponents.

3. To multiply two powers with the same base, keep the base the same and _____ the exponents.

4. What is the difference between the standard form of a number and the number written in scientific notation?

_____

_____

_____

_____

Concepts and Skills

5. (MP) **Use Tools** Write an expression with a single exponent that is equivalent to $8^{-4} \cdot (8^2)^4$. State what strategy and tool you will use to answer the question, explain your choice, and then find the answer.

_____

_____

6. Compare each expression to 6^6.

	Less than 6^6	Greater than 6^6	Equal to 6^6
$(6^{-1} \cdot 6^4)^2$	☐	☐	☐
$\dfrac{6^8}{(6^2)^2}$	☐	☐	☐
$\left(\dfrac{6^2}{6^0}\right)^4$	☐	☐	☐

7. Select all the expressions equivalent to $\dfrac{9^3 \cdot 9^5}{9^2}$.

(A) 3^8 (C) 9^6 (E) 27^2

(B) 3^{12} (D) 9^4 (F) 27^4

8. What are possible values for a and b in the equation $\frac{4^a}{4^b} = 4^{-1}$? What must be true about the values of a and b?

$a =$ _____ $b =$ _____

_____

9. The diameter of Earth is about 1×10^4 kilometers, and the diameter of a basketball is about 2×10^{-4} kilometer. About how many times as great is the diameter of Earth as the diameter of a basketball?

(A) 5000 times as great

(B) 50,000 times as great

(C) 50,000,000 times as great

(D) 500,000,000 times as great

10. A bee hummingbird has a mass of 0.0023 kilogram. What is the mass of a bee hummingbird written in scientific notation?

_____ kilogram

11. Naomi says that 9.8×10^5 is greater than 3.2×10^6. Is Naomi correct? Explain your reasoning.

_____

_____

_____

12. Which expression is equivalent to $\dfrac{(8 \times 10^3) + (4 \times 10^3)}{(3 \times 10^{-2})}$?

(A) 4×10^1

(B) 4×10^4

(C) 4×10^5

(D) 4×10^8

13. What is the difference between 8.5×10^{-4} and 2.8×10^{-4}, written in standard form?

_____

14. Mount Everest is growing at a rate of about 1.1×10^{-5} meter per day. Express this rate using units of a more appropriate size, and explain why the units you chose are more appropriate.

_____

_____

_____

_____

15. An elephant has a mass of 4500 kilograms. How many mice, with a mass of 2×10^{-2} kilogram each, would it take to equal the mass of the elephant?

Write your answer in standard form. _____ mice

Reduce the Juice

A company wants to reduce the volume of its juice box by 20%. The diagram shows the dimensions of the company's current juice box.

A. The new juice box's volume will be

_____ cubic centimeters.

B. Produce two designs for new juice boxes with the reduced volume. Give the dimensions for each design.

10 cm

6.5 cm   4 cm

Design 1	
Length: _____ cm	
Width: _____ cm	
Height: _____ cm	

Design 2	
Length: _____ cm	
Width: _____ cm	
Height: _____ cm	

 Turn and Talk

- Explain how you determined the volume of a new juice box.

- Which of your designs for new juice boxes would require more materials to make? Explain your reasoning.

Are You Ready?

Complete these problems to review prior concepts and skills you will need for this module.

Volume of Rectangular Prisms

For Problems 1–3, determine the volume of each rectangular prism.

1.
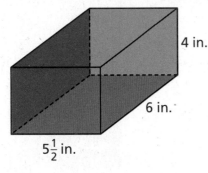
4 in.

6 in.

$5\frac{1}{2}$ in.

_____ in³

2.
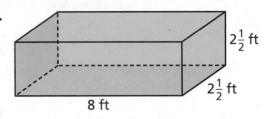
$2\frac{1}{2}$ ft

$2\frac{1}{2}$ ft

8 ft

_____ ft³

3. a rectangular prism that is 7.3 centimeters by 8.5 centimeters by 4.2 centimeters _____

4. A packing box is 3.5 feet by 1.4 feet by 1.8 feet. A box that is 3.1 feet by 1.1 feet by 1.4 feet is placed inside the first box. The rest of the box is filled with packing foam. How many cubic feet does the packing foam take up? _____

Area of Circles

For Problems 5–7, determine the area of each circle. Use 3.14 for π. Round each answer to the nearest hundredth.

5.
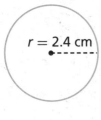
$r = 2.4$ cm

_____ cm²

6.
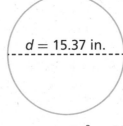
$d = 15.37$ in.

_____ in²

7. a circle with a radius of 9.4 ft _____

8. On the ice of a hockey rink, there is one circle with a 12-inch diameter, and one with a 24-inch diameter. How much more area does the larger circle have than the smaller? Explain how you know. Use 3.14 for π.

_____

_____

Name _____

Find Volume of Cylinders

(I Can) find the volume of a cylinder or the dimensions of a cylinder given the volume.

Spark Your Learning SMALL GROUPS

You have seen that the volume of a rectangular prism is the area of the base times the height. This may be written as $V = Bh$. Since the area of the rectangular base is the length times the width, the formula can also be written as $V = \ell wh$.

Rectangular Prism

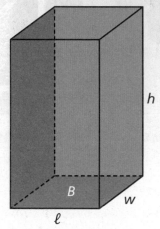

Cylinder

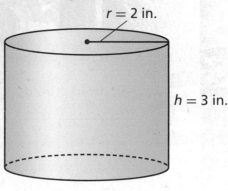

The base of a cylinder is a circle. What is the volume of the cylinder shown? (*Hint*: Recall that the formula for the area A of a circle is $A = \pi r^2$.) Show your steps.

 Turn and Talk How is finding the volume of a cylinder similar to finding the volume of a rectangular prism? How is it different?

Build Understanding

The formula for the volume of a cylinder is similar to the formula for the volume of a rectangular prism. The formula states that the volume V is the product of the area of the base B and the height h. The only difference is in how to calculate B. You can use the fact that the base of a cylinder is a circle to write the formula in terms of the radius r.

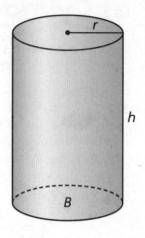

$$V = Bh$$
or
$$V = \pi r^2 h$$

1 ▶ Find the volume of the cylindrical can of tomato soup shown. Leave your answer in terms of π.

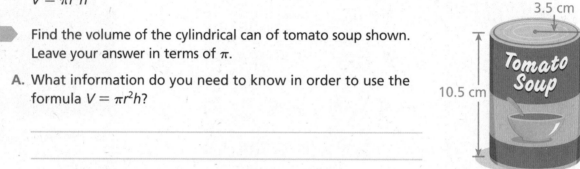

A. What information do you need to know in order to use the formula $V = \pi r^2 h$?

_____

_____

B. What are the radius and the height of the cylinder?

_____

_____

C. Show how to substitute for r and h in the formula. Then simplify and leave your answer in terms of π. Be sure to include an appropriate unit for the volume.

_____

_____

_____

D. Now show how to use 3.14 as an approximation for π. Round the volume to the nearest tenth.

_____

_____

_____

 Turn and Talk How can you use estimation to show that the volume you found is reasonable?

Step It Out

2 ▶ You can find the volume of a cylinder when you know the radius (or diameter) of the cylinder and its height.

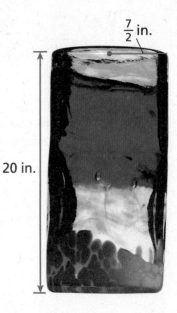

$\frac{7}{2}$ in.

20 in.

A. Find the volume of the cylindrical vase shown. Use $\frac{22}{7}$ for π.

The radius is 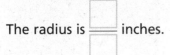 inches.

The height is _____ inches.

Substitute values for the radius r and the height h. Substitute $\frac{22}{7}$ for π.

$V = \pi r^2 h$

$\approx \left(\frac{22}{7}\right)\left(\dfrac{\boxed{}}{\boxed{}}\right)^2 \left(\boxed{}\right)$

$\approx \left(\frac{22}{7}\right)\left(\dfrac{\boxed{}}{\boxed{}}\right) \left(\boxed{}\right)$

$\approx$ _____

The volume of the cylinder is approximately _____ cubic inches.

B. Find the volume of the cylinder shown. Leave the answer in terms of π and then use 3.14 for π. Express the volume in scientific notation and round the first factor to the nearest tenth.

4.1×10^{-2} cm

2.4×10^{-2} cm

The diameter is 2.4×10^{-2} centimeter, so the radius is

_____ $\times 10^{\boxed{}}$ centimeter.

Now use the formula for the volume of a cylinder. Substitute values for the radius r and the height h.

$V = \pi r^2 h$

$= \pi(\underline{} \times 10^{-2})^2 (\underline{} \times 10^{-2})$

$= \pi(\underline{} \times 10^{-4}) (\underline{} \times 10^{-2})$

$= \pi(\underline{} \times 10^{\boxed{}})$

$\approx (3.14) (\underline{} \times 10^{\boxed{}})$

$\approx \underline{} \times 10^{-6}$

$\approx \underline{} \times 10^{-5}$

The volume of the cylinder is (_____ $\times 10^{-6})\pi$, or approximately

_____ $\times 10^{-5}$ cubic centimeter.

3 The volume of the cylinder shown is 602.88 ft³. Find the height of the cylinder. Use 3.14 for π. (Note that the height of a cylinder is not always a vertical distance.)

4 ft

A. Use the formula for the volume of a cylinder. Substitute the known values for the volume V and for the radius r. Use 3.14 for π. Then solve for h.

$$V = \pi r^2 h$$

_____ $\approx (3.14)\ (_____)^2 h$

_____ $\approx (3.14)\ (_____)h$

_____ $\approx (_____)h$

$h \approx \dfrac{\boxed{}}{\boxed{}} \approx$ _____

The height of the cylinder is approximately _____ feet.

B. How can you check that your answer is reasonable?

The height is _____ feet, the radius is _____ feet, and π

rounded to the nearest whole number is _____.

The volume is approximately $\boxed{} \cdot \boxed{}^2 \cdot \boxed{} = \boxed{}$ cubic feet.

This is close to the given volume, so the answer is reasonable.

Check Understanding

1. What information do you need to know in order to find the volume of a cylinder?

_____

_____

2. The volume of this cylinder is 32π yd³. Find the height.

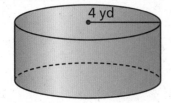

4 yd

3. Find the volume. Use 3.14 for π. Round the volume to the nearest tenth.

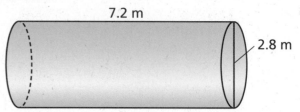

7.2 m

2.8 m

_____ _____

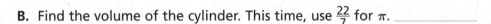

On Your Own

4. (MP) **Attend to Precision** The height of the cylindrical container shown is 7 inches.

2 in.

  A. Find the volume of the cylinder. Leave your answer in terms of π.

  _____

  B. Find the volume of the cylinder. This time, use $\frac{22}{7}$ for π. _____

  C. Find the volume of the cylinder. Use 3.14 for π. Round the volume to the nearest tenth. _____

  D. Which of the volumes that you calculated, if any, are the exact volume? Which are approximations? Explain.

  _____

  _____

  _____

For Problems 5–6, find the volume of each cylinder. Use 3.14 for π. Round the volume to the nearest tenth.

5.

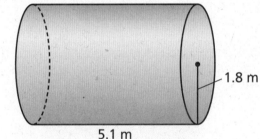

1.8 m

5.1 m

6.

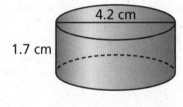

4.2 cm

1.7 cm

For Problems 7–8, the table shows the radius and height for three different cylinders.

7. (MP) **Construct Arguments** Without calculating, which cylinder has the greatest volume? Explain.

Cylinder	Radius (ft)	Height (ft)
A	2	4
B	4	6
C	4	4

_____

_____

_____

8. What is the ratio of the volume of Cylinder C to the volume of Cylinder A? _____

For Problems 9–12, find the approximate height of each cylinder. Use 3.14 for π.

9. Volume = 37.68 in³

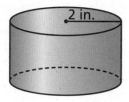
2 in.

_____

10. Volume = 146.952 cm³

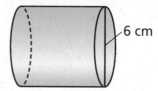
6 cm

_____

11. Volume = 196.25 mm³

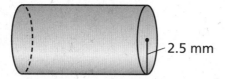
2.5 mm

_____

12. Volume = 48.2304 m³

6.4 m

_____

13. Find the approximate volume of the cylinder shown. Use 3.14 for π. Express the volume in scientific notation and round the first factor to the nearest tenth. _____

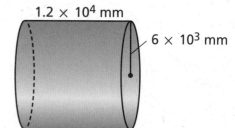
1.2×10^4 mm
6×10^3 mm

14. Open Ended Give the radius and height of a cylinder whose volume is greater than 1000 cubic feet but less than 2000 cubic feet.

15. (MP) **Attend to Precision** Consider a cylinder with the radius and height shown in the image.

3.55 cm
3.55 cm

  A. Find the approximate volume of the cylinder using the π key on your calculator. Round your answer in a way that seems most appropriate. _____

  B. Explain how you decided how many digits to include in your answer.

_____

_____

I'm in a Learning Mindset!

What is challenging about using the formula for the volume of a cylinder? Where can I go to get help if needed?

_____

_____

Find Volume of Cylinders

1. The radius of a cylinder is 49 feet, and the height is 180 feet. Find the volume of the cylinder. Leave your answer in terms of π.

2. **Math on the Spot** Find the approximate volume of each cylinder. Use 3.14 for π. Round the volume to the nearest cubic unit if necessary.

A.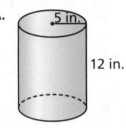
5 in.

12 in.

B.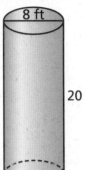
8 ft

20 ft

C.
$\left(\frac{h}{3} + 1\right)$cm

$h = 18$ cm

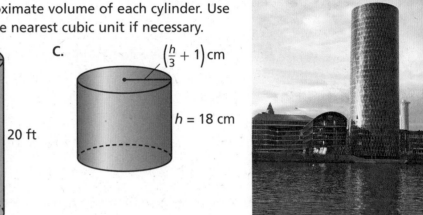

For Problems 3–4, approximate the volume of each cylinder. Use 3.14 for π. Round the volume to the nearest cubic unit if necessary.

3.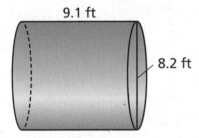
9.1 ft

8.2 ft

4.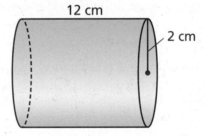
12 cm

2 cm

5. A cylinder has diameter d and height h. Write a formula for the volume V of the cylinder in terms of d and h.

For Problems 6–7, find the approximate height of each cylinder. Use 3.14 for π.

6. Volume = 7.85 ft³

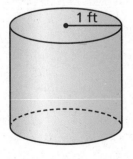
1 ft

7. Volume = 668.6944 m³

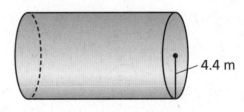
4.4 m

Test Prep

8. Which of the following values for the radius and height of a cylinder result in a cylinder with the greatest volume?

(A) radius = 1 ft; height = 4 ft   (C) radius = 3 ft; height = 2 ft

(B) radius = 2 ft; height = 3 ft   (D) radius = 4 ft; height = 1 ft

9. Which value or values for the radius of the cylinder shown results in a cylinder with a volume that is greater than 100 cubic centimeters but less than 600 cubic centimeters? Select all that apply.

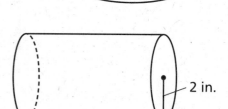

(A) 1 cm   (D) 6 cm

(B) 3 cm   (E) 8 cm

(C) 5 cm   (F) 10 cm

5 cm

10. The cylinder shown has a volume of 62.8 cubic inches. Which of the following is closest to the height of the cylinder?

(A) 5 in.   (C) 20 in.

(B) 10 in.   (D) 30 in.

2 in.

11. The radius of Cylinder P is 6 millimeters, and the radius of Cylinder Q is 3 millimeters. The cylinders have the same height. Which is a true statement about the cylinders?

(A) The volume of Cylinder P is 2 times the volume of Cylinder Q.

(B) The volume of Cylinder P is 4 times the volume of Cylinder Q.

(C) The volume of Cylinder P is 18 times the volume of Cylinder Q.

(D) The volume of Cylinder P is 36 times the volume of Cylinder Q.

Spiral Review

12. Find the height of the cone. Round your answer to the nearest tenth of a centimeter.

_____

13. Write the number 0.0000000058 in scientific notation.

_____

14. Find the difference and express your answer in scientific notation.

$(3.4 \times 10^6) - (4.9 \times 10^5)$

_____

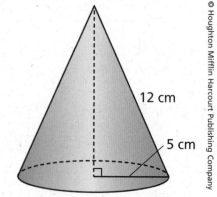

12 cm

5 cm

Name _____

Find Volume of Cones

(I Can) find the volume of a cone and the dimensions of
a cone given its volume.

Step It Out

1 In a right cone, a line drawn from
the vertex (tip) perpendicular to
the base passes through the center
of the base. The distance from the
vertex to the center of the base is
the height of the right cone.

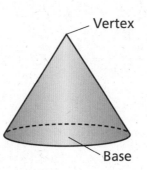

Vertex

Base

You can use the following reasoning to develop a
formula for the volume of a cone.

A. Consider a cone with radius r and height h. Imagine that the cone is
made of cardboard and has an open top, as shown. Also, consider a
cylinder with the same radius and the same height.

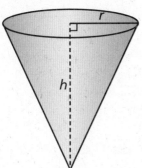

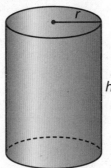

You can fill the cone with sand and pour the sand into the cylinder. It
takes 3 cones full of sand to fill the cylinder completely.

This means the volume of the _____ is $\frac{1}{3}$ the volume of the _____.

B. Complete the following to write a formula for the volume of a cone.

volume of cone = ____ (volume of cylinder)

$$= \_\_\_ B\;\square = \frac{\square}{\square}\;\square\;\square^2\;\square$$

🗨 **Turn and Talk** How is the formula for the volume of a cone similar to the
formula for the volume of a cylinder? How is it different?

2 You can use this formula to find the volume of a cone when you know, or can calculate, its radius and height.

A. The cone-shaped party hat shown here has a radius of 3 inches. Find the volume of the cone. Use $\frac{22}{7}$ for π.

7 in.

$V = \frac{1}{3}\pi r^2 h$

$\approx \frac{1}{3}\left(\frac{22}{7}\right)($ _____ $)^2 ($ _____ $)$

$\approx \frac{1}{3}\left(\frac{22}{7}\right)($ _____ $) ($ _____ $)$

$\approx$ _____

The volume of the cone is approximately _____ cubic inches.

B. Find the volume of the cone. Leave your answer in terms of π. Then approximate the volume by substituting 3.14 for π and rounding the volume to the nearest tenth.

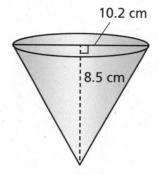

10.2 cm

8.5 cm

The diameter of the cone is _____ centimeters.

So, the radius of the cone is _____ centimeters.

$V = \frac{1}{3}Bh$

$= \frac{1}{3}\pi r^2 h$

$= \frac{1}{3}\pi($ _____ $)^2 ($ _____ $)$

$=$ _____ π

$\approx$ _____

The exact volume of the cone (in terms of π) is

_____ cubic centimeters.

The volume is approximately _____ cubic centimeters.

Turn and Talk Why might you want to express the volume of a cone in terms of π? Why might you use 3.14 or $\frac{22}{7}$ as an approximation for π?

3 The **slant height** of a right cone is the distance from the vertex of the cone to a point on the edge of the base.

You can find the volume of a cone if you know the radius and the slant height by using properties of right triangles.

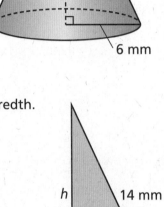

Slant height
14 mm

6 mm

Find the approximate volume of the cone shown. Use 3.14 for π and round the volume to the nearest tenth.

A. First find the height h of the cone.

The line segments representing the height, radius, and slant height form a right triangle.

Use the Pythagorean Theorem to find h to the nearest hundredth.

$$a^2 + b^2 = c^2$$

$$h^2 + (\underline{})^2 = (\underline{})^2$$

$$h^2 + \underline{} = \underline{}$$

$$h^2 = \underline{}$$

$$h \approx \underline{}$$

h 14 mm

6 mm

B. Next, find the approximate volume. Round to the nearest tenth.

$$V = \tfrac{1}{3}\pi r^2 h$$

$$\approx \tfrac{1}{3}(3.14)\,(\underline{})^2\,(\underline{})$$

$$\approx \tfrac{1}{3}(3.14)\,(\underline{})\,(\underline{})$$

$$\approx \underline{}$$

The volume of the cone is approximately _____ cubic millimeters.

Check Understanding

1. How do the volumes of a cone and cylinder that share a radius and height compare?

_____

_____

2. A. A cone has a radius of 6 inches and a slant height of 10 inches. What is the height of the cone?

_____

B. What is the volume of the cone in Part A? Leave your answer in terms of π.

_____

On Your Own

3. The cone-shaped candle to the right has a radius of 6 centimeters and height as shown.

21 cm

   A. Find the volume of the cone. Leave your answer in terms of π.

   _____

   B. (MP) **Construct Arguments** A cylinder has the same radius and height as the cone. What is the volume of the cylinder in terms of π? Explain how you know.

   _____

   _____

   _____

4. The cylinder and cone shown have the same radius and the same height. What is the volume of the cone? Give the answer in scientific notation.

   _____

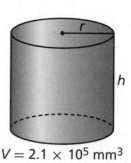

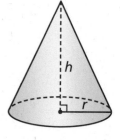

$V = 2.1 \times 10^5 \text{ mm}^3$

For Problems 5–8, find the approximate volume of the cone. Use 3.14 for π and round the volume to the nearest tenth.

5.

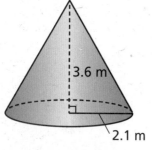

3.6 m

2.1 m

6.

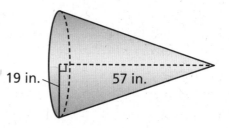

19 in.   57 in.

7.

8.8 cm

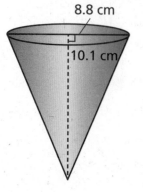

10.1 cm

8.

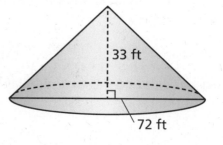

33 ft

72 ft

Name _____

Use the cone-shaped hedge shown to answer Problems 9–10.

9. What is the volume of the hedge? Leave the answer in terms of π.

   _____

11 ft

6 ft

10. Find the approximate volume of the hedge using $\frac{22}{7}$ for π.
    Round the volume to the nearest tenth. _____

11. The cone shown has a radius of 3 inches.

   A. (MP) **Reason** Explain how to find the height of the cone.
      What is the height?

      _____

      _____

      _____

      _____

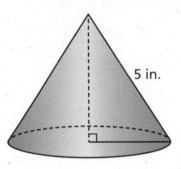

5 in.

   B. Find the volume of the cone. Leave your answer in terms
      of π. Then use 3.14 for π and round the volume to the
      nearest tenth.

      _____

For Problems 12–15, find the approximate volume of each cone. Use 3.14 for π.

12.

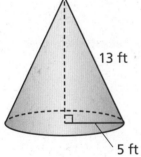

13 ft

5 ft

13.

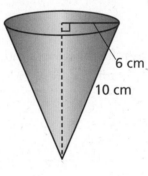

6 cm

10 cm

14.

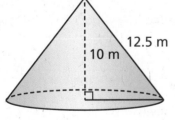

12.5 m

10 m

15.

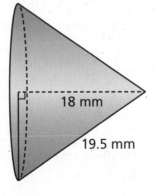

18 mm

19.5 mm

16. **Open Ended** Determine a possible radius and height for the cone shown in the photo. Justify your answer.

Volume = 9π in³

_____

_____

17. (MP) **Critique Reasoning** The cone and cylinder in the figure below have the same radius. The height of the cylinder is 3 times the height of the cone. Jared looked at the figure and concluded that the volume of the cylinder must be 3 times the volume of the cone. Therefore, he said the volume of the cylinder is 3 × 40, or 120 cubic centimeters.

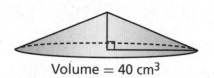

Volume = 40 cm³

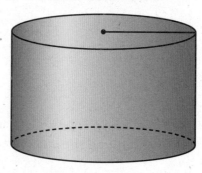

Do you agree with Jared's reasoning? Explain.

_____

_____

_____

18. Consider a set of cones that all have a radius of 1 centimeter. The heights of the cones are 1 centimeter, 2 centimeters, 3 centimeters, 4 centimeters, and 5 centimeters.

    A. Complete the table. Leave the volumes in terms of π.

Height (cm)	1	2	3	4	5
Volume (cm³)					

    B. Is the relationship in the table a proportional relationship? Why or why not?

    _____

    _____

    C. (MP) **Model with Mathematics** Write an equation that gives the volume y of a cone with radius 1 centimeter if you know the height x of the cone. Describe the graph of the equation.

    _____

    _____

Find Volume of Cones

1. (MP) **Construct Arguments** What is the volume of a cylinder
   that has the same radius and same height as the cone fountain
   shown? Explain.

   _____

   _____

   _____

2. A cone has a height of 6×10^3 millimeters and a radius of
   2×10^3 millimeters. Find the volume of the cone. Leave your
   answer in scientific notation and in terms of π.

   _____

$V = 2.6 \text{ m}^3$

**For Problems 3–6, approximate the volume of each cone. Use 3.14
for π and round the volume to the nearest tenth.**

3.

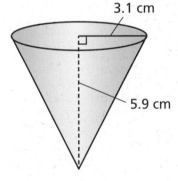

3.1 cm

5.9 cm

4.

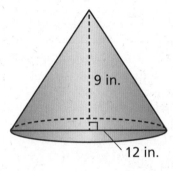

9 in.

12 in.

5.

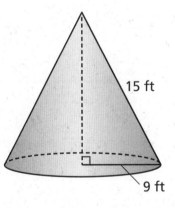

15 ft

9 ft

6.

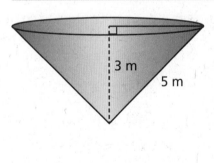

3 m

5 m

7. (MP) **Model with Mathematics** A cone has diameter d and height h.
   Write a formula for the volume V of the cone in terms of d and h.

   _____

Test Prep

8. Fill in the formula for the volume of the cone shown here by writing a numerical value in each box.

$$V = \frac{\boxed{}}{\boxed{}} \, \pi \left(\boxed{} \right)^2 \left(\boxed{} \right) \text{ cm}^3$$

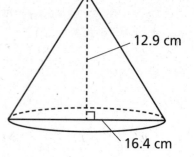

12.9 cm

16.4 cm

9. A cone has a radius of 3 feet and a height of 5 feet. A cylinder has the same radius and height as the cone. Which of the following statements are true? Select all that apply.

- (A) The volume of the cone is 15π ft^3.
- (B) The volume of the cylinder is 45π ft^3.
- (C) The volume of the cone is 3 times the volume of the cylinder.
- (D) The volume of the cylinder is 3 times the volume of the cone.
- (E) The ratio of the volume of the cone to the volume of the cylinder is $\frac{1}{3}$.
- (F) The ratio of the volume of the cylinder to the volume of the cone is $\frac{1}{3}$.

10. Which radius and height result in a cone with the least volume?
- (A) radius = 7 m; height = 1 m
- (C) radius = 3 m; height = 10 m
- (B) radius = 5 m; height = 5 m
- (D) radius = 1 m; height = 15 m

Spiral Review

11. Latreesha collected data on the daily high temperature and the number of quarts of iced coffee sold at a cafe. She made a scatter plot of the data and then drew a trend line, as shown. The line passes through the points (10, 50) and (30, 100). What is the slope of the line? What does it represent in this context?

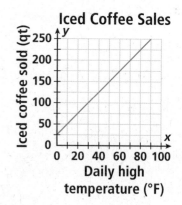

_____

_____

_____

12. Solve the system of equations $\begin{cases} -3x + 5y = 21 \\ 2x - 3y = -13 \end{cases}$.

_____

13. Approximate the volume of a cylinder with a radius of 3.4 meters and a height of 1.2 meters. Use 3.14 for π and round the volume to the nearest tenth.

_____

Name _____

Find Volume of Spheres

(I Can) find the volume of a sphere and the dimensions of a sphere
given its volume.

Step It Out

1 A **sphere** is a three-dimensional figure with all points the same distance
from the center. The radius of a sphere is the distance from the center to
any point on the sphere.

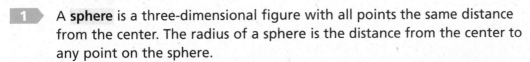

You can use the following reasoning to develop
a formula for the volume of a sphere.

A. Start with a sphere of radius r. How is the height
of the sphere related to the radius?

$h =$ _____ r

B. Consider a cylinder with the same radius and the
same height as the sphere.

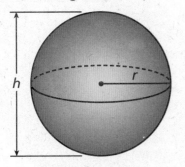

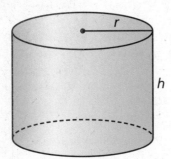

Imagine filling the sphere with sand and pouring the sand into the
cylinder. The sand will fill $\frac{2}{3}$ of the cylinder.

volume of sphere $= \dfrac{\square}{\square}$ volume of cylinder

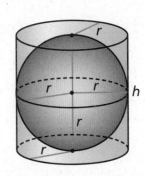

$= \dfrac{\square}{\square} \pi r^2 h = \dfrac{\square}{\square} \pi r^2 (\underline{\quad})$

$= \dfrac{\square}{\square} \pi r^3$

Turn and Talk How is the formula for the volume of a sphere similar to the
formula for the volume of a cone? How is it different?

You can use this formula to find the volume of a sphere when you are given or can calculate its radius.

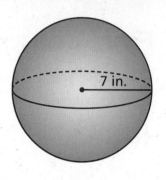

7 in.

A. Approximate the volume of the sphere. Use $\frac{22}{7}$ for π and leave your answer as an improper fraction.

To find the volume, use the volume formula with

$r =$ _____.

$V = \frac{4}{3}\pi r^3$

$\approx \frac{4}{3}\left(\frac{22}{7}\right)(\underline{\hspace{1.5cm}})^3$

$\approx \frac{4}{3}\left(\frac{22}{7}\right)(\underline{\hspace{1.5cm}})$

$\approx \underline{\hspace{1.5cm}}$

The volume of the sphere is

approximately _____ cubic inches.

B. Approximate the volume of Earth. Use 3.14 for π. Express your answer in scientific notation, rounding the first factor to the nearest tenth.

To find the volume, use the volume formula with

$r =$ _____

$V = \frac{4}{3}\pi r^3$

$= \frac{4}{3}\pi(\underline{\hspace{1cm}} \times \underline{\hspace{1cm}})^3$

$= \frac{4}{3}\pi(\underline{\hspace{1cm}})^3 \times (\underline{\hspace{1cm}})^3$

$\approx \frac{4}{3}(3.14)(\underline{\hspace{1cm}}) \times 10^{\square}$

$\approx \underline{\hspace{1cm}} \times 10^{\square}$

$\approx \underline{\hspace{1cm}} \times 10^{\square}$

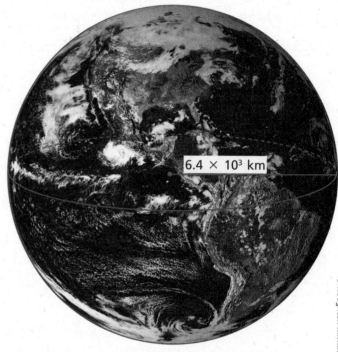

6.4 × 10³ km

The volume of Earth is approximately _____ cubic kilometers.

Turn and Talk At what points did you use a property of exponents in simplifying the expression for the volume in Part B? What property or properties did you use?

Name _____

3 ▸ You can find the volume of a sphere if you know its diameter.

A. Find the exact volume of the spherical rubber-band ball. Leave your answer in terms of π.

The diameter of the sphere is _____ centimeters.

So, the radius of the sphere is _____ centimeters.

$V = \frac{4}{3}\pi r^3$

$\quad = \frac{4}{3}\pi ($ _____ $)^3$

$\quad = \frac{4}{3}\pi ($ _____ $)$

$\quad = $ _____

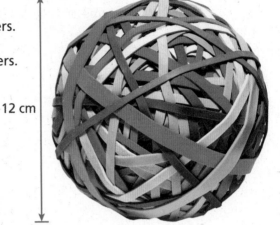

12 cm

The volume of the sphere is _____ cubic centimeters.

B. Approximate the volume of a sphere with a diameter of 7.4 millimeters. Use 3.14 for π. Round the volume to the nearest tenth.

The radius of the sphere is _____ millimeters.

$V = \frac{4}{3}\pi r^3$

$\quad = \frac{4}{3}\pi ($ _____ $)^3$

$\quad \approx \frac{4}{3}($ _____ $)($ _____ $)$

$\quad \approx$ _____

The volume of the sphere is approximately _____ cubic millimeters.

Check Understanding

1. In the figure, the sphere fits perfectly inside the cylinder, with the top and bottom of the sphere just touching the bases of the cylinder. How does the volume of the sphere compare to the volume of the cylinder?

_____

_____

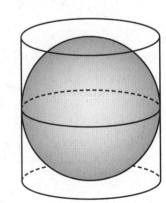

2. Approximate the volume of a sphere with a diameter of 20 meters. Leave your answer in terms of π. Then use 3.14 for π and round the volume to the nearest tenth.

_____

On Your Own

3. A sphere has a radius of 5 feet.

   A. Find the volume of the sphere. Leave your answer in terms of π. Then use 3.14 for π and round the volume to the nearest tenth.

   _____

   B. (MP) **Construct Arguments** Explain how you can use estimation to justify that the volume you found is reasonable.

   _____

   _____

   _____

   _____

$r = 12$ cm

4. Approximate the volume of the basketball. Use $\frac{22}{7}$ for π and round the volume to the nearest tenth. _____

For Problems 5–10, approximate the volume of each sphere. Use 3.14 for π and round the volume to the nearest tenth.

5.

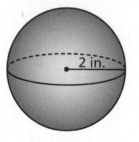

2 in.

_____

6.

4.8 mm

_____

7.

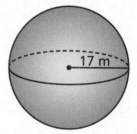

17 m

_____

8.

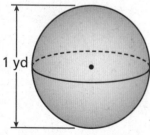

1 yd

_____

9.

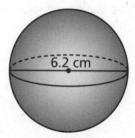

6.2 cm

_____

10.

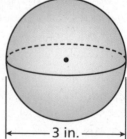

3 in.

_____

For Problems 11–12, use the spherical marble shown.

Radius 5×10^{-3} m

11. (MP) **Attend to Precision** What is the exact volume? Leave your answer in terms of π. Round the first factor in scientific notation to the nearest tenth.

_____

12. Find the volume of the marble to the nearest cubic millimeter using $\frac{22}{7}$ for π. Explain your method.

_____

_____

_____

For Problems 13–18, approximate the volume of each sphere. Use 3.14 for π and round the first factor in scientific notation to the nearest tenth.

13.

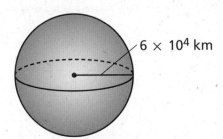

6×10^4 km

14.

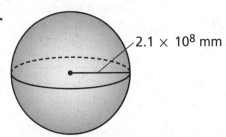

2.1×10^8 mm

15.

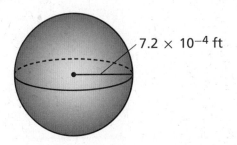

7.2×10^{-4} ft

16.

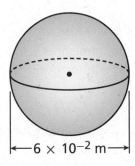

$\leftarrow 6 \times 10^{-2}$ m $\rightarrow$

17.

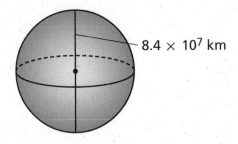

8.4×10^7 km

18.

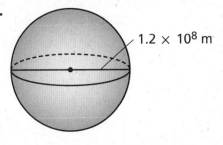

1.2×10^8 m

19. Open Ended In the photo, *V* represents the volume of the spherical plant shown. Determine a possible radius for the sphere. Justify your answer.

1000 in³ < V < 4000 in³

_____

_____

_____

20.  **Use Tools** You can measure the diameter of a spherical object by putting the object on a flat surface and placing blocks or books on either side of the object, as shown. Then use a ruler to measure the distance between the blocks or books. Find a spherical object, measure its diameter, and find its volume. Describe the object, and give its diameter and volume.

_____

_____

_____

21. When you cut a sphere in half by passing a plane through its center, the result is a hemisphere.

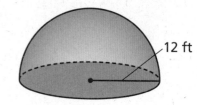

12 ft

A. Write a formula for the volume *V* of a hemisphere. Explain how you found it.

_____

_____

B. Find the volume of the hemisphere shown. Leave your answer in terms of π. Then use 3.14 for π and round the volume to the nearest tenth.

_____

C. Approximate the volume of a hemisphere with a diameter of 6.2 meters. Use 3.14 for π and round the volume to the nearest tenth.

_____

22. **Critique Reasoning** A student said that when you double the radius of a sphere, you double the volume of the sphere. Do you agree or disagree? Give one or more specific examples to justify your answer.

Find Volume of Spheres

1. (MP) **Construct Arguments** The spherical and the cylindrical candles shown have the same radius and the same height. The volume of the cylindrical candle is 6 cubic centimeters. What is the volume of the spherical candle? Explain.

_____

_____

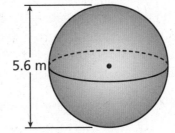

2. **Math on the Spot** Approximate the volume of a sphere with a radius of 7 feet, both in terms of π and to the nearest tenth. Use 3.14 for π.

_____

For Problems 3–6, approximate the volume of the sphere. Use 3.14 for π and round the volume to the nearest tenth.

3.

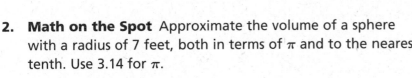

7.5 in.

4.

20 mm

5.

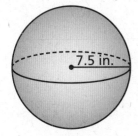

7.8 cm

6.

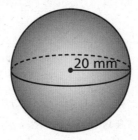

5.6 m

7. (MP) **Critique Reasoning** A student was asked to find the exact volume of the sphere shown, leaving the answer in terms of π. The student's work is shown. Explain the student's error.

$$V = \tfrac{4}{3}\pi r^3 = \tfrac{4}{3}\pi(6)^3 = \tfrac{4}{3}\pi(216) = 288\pi \text{ ft}^3$$

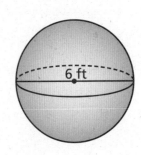

6 ft

_____

_____

Test Prep

8. A sphere has a diameter of 14.6 feet. Fill in the formula for the volume of the sphere by writing a numerical value in each box.

$$V = \frac{\boxed{}}{\boxed{}}\, \pi \left(\boxed{}\right)^3$$

9. A student has a set of six spheres with radii 1, 2, 3, 4, 5, and 6 centimeters. Which of the following is the volume of a sphere in the set? Select all that apply.

Ⓐ $\frac{4}{3}\pi$ cm³

Ⓑ $\frac{8}{3}\pi$ cm³

Ⓒ $\frac{32}{3}\pi$ cm³

Ⓓ 36π cm³

Ⓔ 125π cm³

Ⓕ 288π cm³

10. Sphere A has a radius of 9 feet. Sphere B has a diameter of 36 feet. Which of the following is a correct description of how the volumes of the spheres are related?

Ⓐ The volumes are equal.

Ⓑ The volume of Sphere B is 2 times the volume of Sphere A.

Ⓒ The volume of Sphere B is 4 times the volume of Sphere A.

Ⓓ The volume of Sphere B is 8 times the volume of Sphere A.

Spiral Review

11. Edwin collects data on the ages of several used phones and the current value of the phones. He plots the data to make a scatter plot, with age along the x-axis and value along the y-axis. What can you predict about the slope of the trend line for Edwin's scatter plot? Explain.

_____

_____

_____

12. Approximate the volume of the cone shown here. Use 3.14 for π and round the volume to the nearest tenth.

_____

13. A triangle has sides of length 3 inches, 5 inches, and 6 inches. Is the triangle a right triangle? Explain how you know.

_____

_____

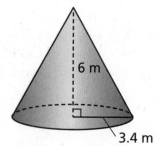

6 m

3.4 m

Name _____

Apply Volume

(I Can) use the formulas for the volumes of cones, cylinders, and spheres to solve real-world problems.

Step It Out

1 A youth sports club is holding its yearly tri-county tournament. The club is selling fruit cups in two different sizes. Fill in the missing information in the table after completing Parts A and B.

	Radius (in.)	Volume (in³)
Regular, $3.00	1.4	
Large, $3.50		

7 in.

3 in.

A. Find the volume of the large fruit cup to the nearest hundredth. Use the given diameter to find the radius. Use 3.14 for π.

$V = \pi r^2 h$ $\qquad$ $r = \dfrac{d}{2} = \dfrac{(\ \ )}{2} = ($_____$)$

$\quad = \pi \,($_____$)^2\,($_____$)$

$\quad \approx ($_____$)\,($_____$)\,($_____$)$

$\quad \approx$ _____

B. Find the volume of the regular fruit cup to the nearest hundredth. Substitute in the given values and simplify. Use 3.14 for π.

$V = \pi r^2 h$

$\quad = \pi \,($_____$)^2\,($_____$)$

$\quad \approx ($_____$)\,($_____$)\,($_____$)$

$\quad \approx$ _____

6 in.

2.8 in.

Turn and Talk Which is the better buy? Why?

© Houghton Mifflin Harcourt Publishing Company • Image Credits: (t) ©Houghton Mifflin Harcourt; (b) ©Houghton Mifflin Harcourt

2 A paper cone cup has a height of 3.6 inches and a volume of 2.028π cubic inches.

A. What is the radius of the cone?

Use the formula for the volume of a cone. Substitute values for the volume V and the height h.

$$V = \frac{1}{3}\pi r^2 h$$

$$(\underline{\hspace{1.5cm}})\pi = \frac{1}{3}\pi r^2(\underline{\hspace{1.5cm}})$$

$$(\underline{\hspace{1.5cm}})\pi = (\underline{\hspace{1.5cm}})\pi r^2$$

$$\frac{\boxed{}\pi}{\boxed{}\pi} = r^2$$

$$\underline{\hspace{2cm}} = r^2$$

$$\underline{\hspace{2cm}} = r$$

The radius of the cone is _____ inches.

B. The diameter of the cone is _____ inches.

C. Estimate the volume of the cup in cubic inches. Use 3.14 for π and round to four decimal places.

_____ cubic inches

D. One fluid ounce of water has a volume of 1.8 cubic inches. About how many fluid ounces will the cup hold? Round your answer to the nearest tenth.

_____ fluid ounces

Turn and Talk Why did you need to find a square root in Part A? What tools did you use to find the square root?

3 Holly has an empty cylindrical container. She places four tennis balls, each with a diameter of 2.6 inches, inside the container. What is the approximate volume of air remaining inside the container?

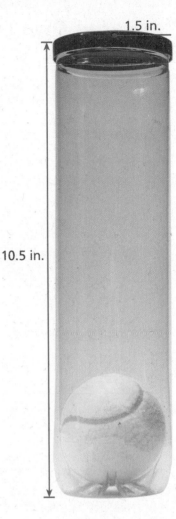

1.5 in.

A. Find the volume of the cylindrical container to the nearest hundredth. Use 3.14 for π.

$V = \pi r^2 h$

$= \pi(\underline{\hspace{1.5cm}})^2 (\underline{\hspace{1.5cm}})$

$\approx (\underline{\hspace{1cm}})(\underline{\hspace{1cm}})(\underline{\hspace{1cm}})$

$\approx \underline{\hspace{1.5cm}}$ in^3

10.5 in.

B. Find the volume taken up by the four tennis balls to the nearest hundredth. Use 3.14 for π.

$V = \frac{4}{3}\pi r^3 \cdot 4$

$= \frac{4}{3}\pi(\underline{\hspace{1.5cm}})^3 \cdot 4$

$\approx \frac{4}{3}(\underline{\hspace{1cm}})(\underline{\hspace{1cm}}) 4$

$\approx (\underline{\hspace{1.5cm}}) 4$

$\approx \underline{\hspace{1.5cm}}$ in^3

C. Subtract to find the difference.

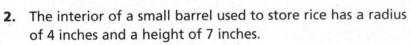

Check Understanding

1. Keisha is making cone-shaped snack holders for a party. The cones are 11 centimeters tall and have a radius of 6 centimeters. What is the volume of each cone? Use 3.14 for π.

2. The interior of a small barrel used to store rice has a radius of 4 inches and a height of 7 inches.

A. What is the interior volume of the barrel in cubic inches? Give your answer in terms of π.

B. How many scoops of rice can the barrel hold if each scoop is a hemisphere with radius 1 inch?

On Your Own

3. The Westhafen tower in Germany is in the shape of a cylinder. It has a height of 109 meters and a diameter of 38 meters. What is the volume of the building? Express your answer in terms of π.

_____

4. (MP) **Reason** The conical cup, cylindrical cup, and hemispherical bowl shown have the same unknown radius, r. If the height of each container is the same as that radius, which of the containers holds the most liquid? Explain.

_____

_____

_____

5. (MP) **Attend to Precision** Brady has a beach ball with a diameter of 16 inches when it is inflated. What is the volume of the beach ball, to the nearest hundredth of a cubic inch? Use 3.14 for π.

_____

6. (MP) **Attend to Precision** A conical container can hold up to 654 cubic centimeters of sand. If the radius of the cone is 5 centimeters, what is the height of the cone? Round your answer to the nearest whole centimeter. Use 3.14 for π.

_____

7. (MP) **Attend to Precision** A cylindrical water tank is 7 feet tall and has a diameter of 12 feet. If the tank is currently half full, how much more water can be poured into the tank? Use $\frac{22}{7}$ for π and round your answer to the nearest cubic foot.

_____

8. (MP) **Attend to Precision** Brittany makes dough and packages it in cylindrical containers that each have a height of 4 inches. What is the radius of each container if a pack of 6 containers contains 169.56 cubic inches of dough? Use 3.14 for π and round the radius to the nearest tenth of an inch.

_____

9. (MP) **Attend to Precision** A large spherical helium balloon has a diameter of 20 feet. What is the volume of the balloon? Use 3.14 for π and express your answer in scientific notation, with the first factor rounded to the nearest hundredth.

10. Mr. Jonas has a set of cylindrical containers. Fill in the missing information to complete the table. Round each volume to the nearest hundredth of a cubic inch. Use 3.14 for π.

	Diameter (in.)	Radius (in.)	Height (in.)	Volume (in³)
Small		2.5	6.5	
Medium	6		8	
Large	7		9.5	

11. **STEM** One of the most common types of volcanoes is called a cinder cone volcano. These types of volcanoes are the smallest type of volcano, ranging between 300 feet and 1200 feet tall, and are in the shape of a cone. Find the volume of a cinder cone volcano with a height of 350 feet and a diameter of 1100 feet. Use 3.14 for π and round your answer to the nearest cubic foot.

12. (MP) **Construct Arguments** Corrie wants to buy cylindrical containers to package leftover soup. The containers need to each have a volume of 66 cubic inches. To fit on a shelf, they can be no more than 6 inches tall. Would containers with a volume of 66 cubic inches and a radius of 2 inches fit? Explain.

13. (MP) **Critique Reasoning** A cylindrical container is three times as tall as a cone with the same diameter. Jeff says the volume of the cylinder will be three times the volume of the cone. Is Jeff correct? Explain.

Diameter = 8.15 in.

14. What is the volume of the volleyball rounded to the nearest cubic inch? Use 3.14 for π. _____

15. What is the volume of the snow globe to the nearest hundredth of a cubic centimeter? Use 3.14 for π.

_____

16. A small cylinder-shaped jar has a volume of 3.768×10^5 mm³ and a height of 75 millimeters. What is the radius of the jar? Use 3.14 for π.

_____

7 cm

17. Bethany is installing some new water pipes. One pipe has a diameter of 1.5 inches and is 23 inches long. The other pipe has the same diameter but a length of 30 inches. How much more water can the larger pipe hold? Use 3.14 for π and round your answer to the nearest cubic inch.

_____

18. Lu Chen makes a large paper hat in the shape of a cone. Approximate the volume of the hat to the nearest cubic inch. Use $\frac{22}{7}$ for π.

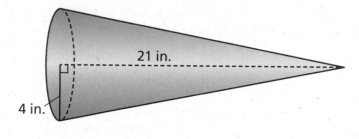

21 in.

4 in.

_____

19. (MP) **Attend to Precision** Sonia fills half of the spherical bowl shown with sand using the cylindrical scoop shown. How many scoops of sand will it take to fill half of the bowl?

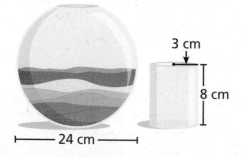

3 cm

8 cm

24 cm

_____

20. A swimming pool has a radius of 8 feet and a height of 5 feet. The swimming pool is shaped like a cylinder. What is the volume of the swimming pool, to the nearest cubic foot? Use 3.14 for π.

_____

Name _____

LESSON 13.4
**More Practice/
Homework**

ONLINE
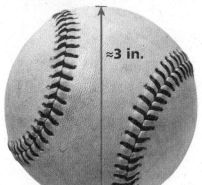
Video Tutorials and
Interactive Examples

Apply Volume

1. (MP) **Critique Reasoning** Eddie measures and finds the volume of the baseball shown. Does the approximate volume look correct? Explain.

$$V = \frac{4}{3}\pi r^3$$

$$\approx \frac{4}{3}(3.14)(3^3)$$

$$\approx 113 \text{ in}^3$$

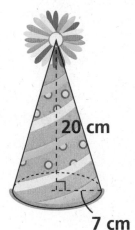

≈3 in.

_____

_____

_____

2. **Math on the Spot** Some party hats are shaped like cones. Use a calculator to find the volume of a party hat to the nearest hundredth of a cubic centimeter if the radius of the base is 7 centimeters and the height is 20 centimeters.

_____

_____

20 cm

7 cm

3. A grain silo is in the shape of a cylinder. The area of the circular roof is 803.84 square feet. If 13,665.28 cubic feet of grain fits in the silo, what is the height of the silo?

_____

4. A funnel in the shape of a cone has a diameter of 4 centimeters and a height of 9 centimeters. What is the volume of the funnel, to the nearest cubic centimeter? Use 3.14 for π.

_____

5. **Art** Ha-joon is a potter who makes sculptures of cylinders, spheres, and cones from clay. The diameter of each clay sphere, the diameter of the base of each clay cylinder and cone, and the height of each clay cylinder and cone are all 6 centimeters.

   A. Find the volume of the clay sphere, clay cylinder, and clay cone. Leave the answers in terms of π.

   sphere: _____   cylinder: _____   cone: _____

   B. How many clay spheres can Ha-joon make if he wants to use the same amount of clay as two clay cylinders? How many clay cones can Ha-joon make if he wants to use the same amount of clay as two clay cylinders?

   _____

Test Prep

6. A spherical fishbowl has a diameter of 4 inches. What is the volume of the fishbowl, to the nearest cubic inch? Use 3.14 for π.

_____

7. Alissa has an 8.2-inch-tall water bottle with a radius of 1.5 inches. Find the volume of the water bottle, rounded to the nearest hundredth of a cubic inch. Use 3.14 for π.

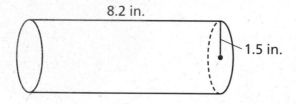

_____

8. A waffle cone has a volume of 31.25π cubic centimeters and a radius of 2.5 centimeters. What is the approximate height of the cone?

(A) 5 cm   (C) 15 cm

(B) 10 cm   (D) 30 cm

Spiral Review

9. Simplify.

$$\frac{7^4 \cdot 7^3}{7^5} = \underline{\hspace{2cm}}$$

10. Find the unknown side length of the right triangle.

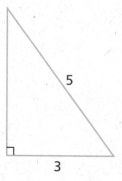

_____

11. Adrienne graphs the line $y - x = 7$. At what point will the line intersect the y-axis?

_____

Module 13 Review

Name _____

Vocabulary

1. Select all three-dimensional figures that have each characteristic.

	Cylinder	Cone	Sphere
A vertex	☐	☐	☐
A curved surface	☐	☐	☐
Exactly one circular base	☐	☐	☐
Two parallel circular bases	☐	☐	☐

2. What is the difference between the height and the slant height of a right cone?

_____

_____

_____

Concepts and Skills

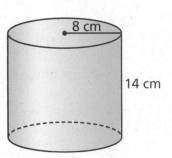

3. The cylinder shown has a radius of 8 centimeters and a height of 14 centimeters. What is the approximate volume of the cylinder? (Use $\frac{22}{7}$ for π.)

_____ cubic centimeters

4. A cylindrical water tank has a diameter of 10 feet and a height of 12 feet. To the nearest cubic foot, what is the volume of the water tank? (Use 3.14 for π.)

Ⓐ 942 cubic feet   Ⓒ 2261 cubic feet

Ⓑ 1884 cubic feet   Ⓓ 3768 cubic feet

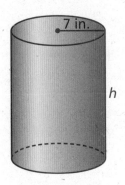

5. The cylinder shown has a radius of 7 inches and a volume of 2772 cubic inches. What is the approximate height h of the cylinder? (Use $\frac{22}{7}$ for π.) _____ inches

6. ⓂⓅ **Use Tools** A cone has a base radius of 8.2 meters and a height of 12 meters. To the nearest cubic meter, what is the volume? (Use 3.14 for π.) State what strategy and tool you will use to answer the question, explain your choice, and then find the answer.

_____

_____

7. A cone-shaped pile of sand has a base diameter of 7 feet and a height of 2.4 feet, as shown. To the nearest tenth of a cubic foot, what is the volume of the pile of sand? (Use $\frac{22}{7}$ for π.)

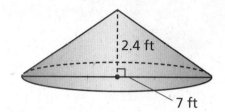

_____ cubic feet

8. A cone has a slant height of 25 centimeters and a radius of 20 centimeters, as shown. Which statements about the cone are correct? (Use 3.14 for π.)

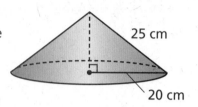

Ⓐ The cone has a height of 32 centimeters.

Ⓑ The height of the cone measures 15 centimeters.

Ⓒ The cone has a volume of about 314 cubic centimeters.

Ⓓ The volume of the cone is about 6280 cubic centimeters.

Ⓔ The cone has a base area of about 125.6 square centimeters.

9. A sphere has a diameter of 12 inches, as shown. To the nearest cubic inch, what is the volume of the sphere? (Use 3.14 for π.)

_____ cubic inches

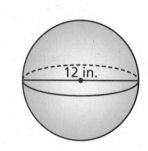

10. A spherical raindrop has a radius of 2.5×10^{-2} centimeter. What is the approximate volume of the raindrop? (Use 3.14 for π.)

Ⓐ 1.5×10^{-5} cubic centimeter

Ⓒ 4.9×10^{-5} cubic centimeter

Ⓑ 2.6×10^{-5} cubic centimeter

Ⓓ 6.5×10^{-5} cubic centimeter

11. A frozen yogurt stand has two types of containers. One is shaped like a cone, and the other is shaped like a cylinder. To the nearest cubic centimeter, how much greater is the volume of the cylinder-shaped container than the cone-shaped container? (Use 3.14 for π.)

_____ cubic centimeters

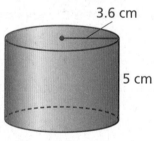

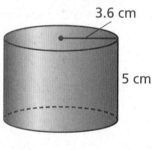

12. A paperweight is made from a solid sphere of aluminum. The radius of the sphere is 1.75 inches. The aluminum used to make the sphere weighs 1.56 ounces per cubic inch and costs $0.90 per pound. Select all statements about the paperweight that are true. (Use 3.14 for π.)

Ⓐ The sphere weighs about 14.4 ounces.

Ⓑ The weight of the sphere is about 2.2 pounds.

Ⓒ The volume of the sphere is about 16.8 cubic inches.

Ⓓ The sphere has a volume of about 22.4 cubic inches.

Ⓔ The aluminum used to make the sphere costs more than $5.

UNIT 1

MODULE 1, LESSON 1
On Your Own
5. They stay the same measure.
7. 2 inches 9. yes 11. 1 pair

More Practice/Homework
1. on the bottom 3A. yes B. no
5.

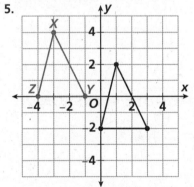

7. rhombus 9. the same size
11. $32.10 13. $\frac{1}{8}$, 0.125, or 12.5%

MODULE 1, LESSON 2
On Your Own
5. Building D 7. 60° 9. Opposite
sides are parallel and the same
length. 11. $(x, y) \rightarrow (x + 7, y + 1)$

More Practice/Homework
3. Figure E is not the same size
or shape as Figure C.
5.

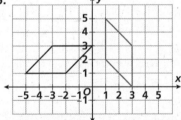

7. $(-3, 3)$; $(-1, 5)$; $(1, 4)$ 9. 0.05
or $\frac{1}{20}$ 11. 25 problems

MODULE 1, LESSON 3
On Your Own
5. 115° 9A. yes B. yes C. yes
11A. no; no B. yes; The right-
angle mark is in a different
location. C. yes; The right-angle
mark is in a different location.

More Practice/Homework
1. yes 3. no 5. A, C 7. D
9. 54 cm²

MODULE 1, LESSON 4
On Your Own
3. The size and shape of the
letter stayed the same. The V
now opens down instead of up.
5A.

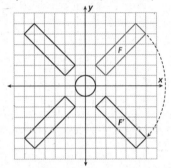

B. 90° clockwise about the
origin C. $(x, y) \rightarrow (y, -x)$
7. $(x, y) \rightarrow (-y, x)$ 9A. 90°
clockwise B. $(2, -1)$, $(5, -2)$, and
$(3, -6)$

More Practice/Homework
1. Figure B 3. $(3, -4)$, $(1, 0)$, $(4, 0)$
5.

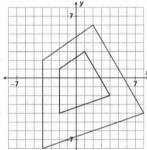

7. $(1, 1)$, $(5, 2)$, $(6, 4)$, $(4, 7)$, and
$(2, 3)$ 9. Figure 4 is a reflection
across a vertical line. Figure 2 is
a reflection across a horizontal
line.

MODULE 1, LESSON 5
On Your Own
3. no 5. Figure C 9. Possible
answer: I can use a ruler to
measure and compare the side
lengths. I can use a protractor
to measure and compare the
angles. 11. Figures 2, 4, and
5 are congruent to Figure 1.

Figures 3 and 6 are not
congruent to Figure 1.
13. Figure 1 15. Figure B

More Practice/Homework
1. Trace Figure 3 and place it
over my figure to show that
they match exactly in size and
shape. 3. no 5. a translation
3 units down 7. yes 9. C
11. $(4, -7)$, $(4, -3)$, $(9, -3)$
13. 1176 square inches

MODULE 2, LESSON 1
On Your Own
3. Left to right: reduction;
enlargement; reduction 5. no
7.

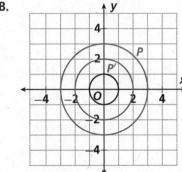

More Practice/Homework
3. no 5. B 7. reflection

MODULE 2, LESSON 2
On Your Own
3A. greater than 1 B. no C. no
5A. 3 B. $L'(21, 27)$; $M'(6, 15)$
C. $(x, y) \rightarrow (3x, 3y)$ 7A. $\frac{2}{3}$

B.

More Practice/Homework

1. Figure *B* 3. (7, −1)

5.

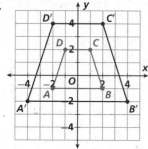

7. 30°, 60°, and 90°
9. rotation of 180° about the origin

MODULE 2, LESSON 3

On Your Own

3A, B.

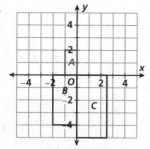

C. The flower beds are all similar.
5. Triangle *P* and Triangle *J*
7. Possible answer: dilation with scale factor 2 and center of dilation (0, 0), followed by a translation 1 unit left and 1 unit down 9. Possible answer: dilation with scale factor 4 and center of dilation (0, 0), followed by a reflection across the *x*-axis 11. (*x*, *y*) → (243*x*, 243*y*)

More Practice/Homework

1A, B.

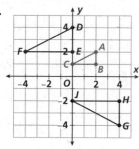

C. agree 3A. Possible answer: dilation centered at (0, 0) with scale factor 2, translation (*x*, *y*) → (*x* + 6, *y* + 2); not congruent; similar
B. Possible answer: reflection across the *y*-axis, dilation centered at (0, 0) with scale factor $\frac{1}{2}$, translation (*x*, *y*) → (*x* − 4, *y* + 4); not congruent; similar 5. B, C, D

7.

9. *A*′(−5, −2.5), *B*′(2.5, 5), *C*′(5, −10)

UNIT 2

MODULE 3, LESSON 1

On Your Own

3. 45°, 55°, 80° 5A. *x* + $\left(\frac{1}{2}x + 4\right)$ = 10 B. *x* = 4 C. 4 home runs D. 6 home runs 9. *p* = 1
11. *t* = 0.4 13. *n* = $-\frac{11}{7}$ 15. *b* = −4

More Practice/Homework

1. length = 39 feet, width = 9 feet 5. *a* = 3 7. *x* = 30
9. *x* = 7.5 11. C 13. 3 hours
15. $39,500 17. 45°, 55°, and 80°

MODULE 3, LESSON 2

On Your Own

3. yes; 3*x* + 2 = 3.5*x*; one solution
5. Alex is not correct.
7. infinitely many solutions
9. no solution 11. infinitely many solutions 15. infinitely many solutions 17. no solution

More Practice/Homework

1. no 3. Blake is not correct.
7. 1 9. 3 11. one solution; *x* = 4.2 13. C 15. 10.5*x* 17. C
19. 1 unit right and 2 units up

MODULE 3, LESSON 3

On Your Own

3A. *t* = 30 B. They are at the same height after 30 seconds.
C. 45 feet 5. Josh is 26 years old and Lynette is 23. 9. no
11A. *n* = 6 B. 6, 8, and 10
13. after 8 hours 15. 7 members

More Practice/Homework

1. for any number of games
3. 4.8 months 5A. 42 + 6*t* = 30 + 8*t* B. 2016 7. D 9. *m* = −3

MODULE 4, LESSON 1

On Your Own

5. no 7. 50°, 100° 9. 125°
13. *x* = 45

More Practice/Homework

1. *x* = 152.6 3. no

7.

Triangle	Unknown angle
1	90°
2	115°

9. 60 11. equal 13. one solution

MODULE 4, LESSON 2

On Your Own

5. yes 7. no 9. no 11. no

More Practice/Homework

1A. yes B. yes C. 22 ft 3A. 30
B. 60° 5. all similar 7. 8 oz
9. Possible answer: a rotation and a reflection

MODULE 4, LESSON 3
On Your Own
3. 112° **5.** ∠CBD **7.** no
9. alternate exterior angles
11. none; ∠3 and ∠5; ∠1 and ∠5; ∠3 and ∠4; ∠2 and ∠4

More Practice/Homework
1. 125° **3.** 115° **7.** B **9.** (−3, −4)
11A. $3w + 4 = 22$ **B.** 6 ft

UNIT 3

MODULE 5, LESSON 1
On Your Own
3. 2250 ft **5.** yes **7.** $k = 48$
9. $k = -3$ **11.** 15 cm **13.** 18 cm
17. $n = -4$

More Practice/Homework
1. They are similar right triangles. **5A.** $\frac{5.5}{8.25} = \frac{x}{22.5}$
B. 15 feet tall; 14.25 feet away
7. A **9.** −4 **11.** Store A

MODULE 5, LESSON 2
On Your Own
3A. lowered by $25 **B.** negative
C. $y = -5x$ **5.** $y = 3x$ **7.** $y = \frac{1}{3}x$
9.

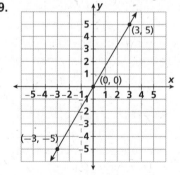

11. $y = -\frac{7}{3}x$ **13.** $y = -2x$

More Practice/Homework
1A. $80 **B.** $y = 20x$ **3.** $y = 5x$
5.

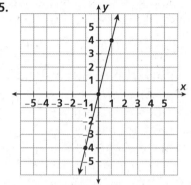

7. A **9.** 5000 **11.** $A'(-1, 4)$, $B'(-5, 6)$, $C'(-3, 10)$ **13.** $x = 5$

MODULE 5, LESSON 3
On Your Own
5. continuous **7A.** 0; 4; 12; 16
B.

Elevator

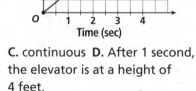

C. continuous **D.** After 1 second, the elevator is at a height of 4 feet.

More Practice/Homework
1A.

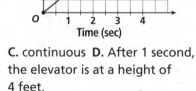

B. discrete **C.** 6 minutes
3.

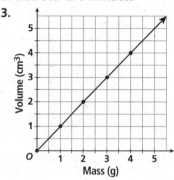

5. continuous **7.** $x + 32 + 30 = 180$; $x = 118$

MODULE 5, LESSON 4
On Your Own
3. yes; The ratios at each point are equal. **5.** 24 miles per hour; 16 miles per hour **7.** 40 miles
9A. 75 gallons per hour; 200 gallons per hour **B.** the rain barrel **11A.** 3 miles per hour
B.

Time (h)	Raj's distance (mi)	Peg's distance (mi)
0	0	0
1	2.5	3
2	5	6
3	7.5	9

C. 1.5 **D.** 4 hours

More Practice/Homework
1A. 1 bulb: $1.04; 3 bulbs: $3.12
B. $1.42 **C.** Hal's Hardware: $6.24; Sal's Supermarket: $8.52
D. Hal's **Hardware**; $3.42 less
3. ladybug **5.** muffins
7. the bumblebee **9.** $x = 2$

MODULE 6, LESSON 1
On Your Own
3A. $4; $7; $10; $13; $16; $19; $22
B. numbers of minutes greater than or equal to 0 **5.** 1 to 41
7. no

More Practice/Homework
1. whole numbers from 0 to 20
3.

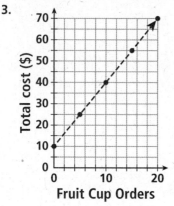

5. Possible answer: The section from $x = 0$ to $x = 1$ 7. B, D
9. 2 ft/s 11. any whole-number weight from 12 to 21 pounds

MODULE 6, LESSON 2
On Your Own
3. 2 vertical yards per horizontal yard 5. yes 9. $y = -3x + 5$; negative; does not pass through the origin 11. $y = -2x + 11$
13A.

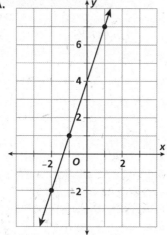

B. 3 units; slope C. no; 4
D. $y = 3x + 4$ E. yes

More Practice/Homework
1. Possible answer: $y = 3x + 2$ and $y = 3x - 2$ 3. Substitute the coordinates of the given point and the slope into the equation $y = mx + b$. 5. $y = 2x - 1$; y-intercept $= -1$

7. 3; rises 9. linear 11. -2; 3
13. yes 15. A 17. Distribute values on both sides of the equal sign. Then combine like terms. $y = -\frac{2}{5}$ 19. yes

MODULE 6, LESSON 3
On Your Own
3. Option 1 5. positive; The comic book becomes more valuable each year. 7A. where the line crosses the y-axis B. $10; starting value when comic book was purchased C. 2; Each year the value increases by $2.
D. $y = 2x + 10$ E. $60

More Practice/Homework
1. $2 per muffin; the cost per muffin 3. $25; cost per ink cartridge 5. $265 7. D 9. A, B
11. $-\frac{1}{5}$

MODULE 6, LESSON 4
On Your Own
5. 13; how many gallons of gasoline Bridget had when she started mowing 7. continuous
9. $0 \le y \le 13$; The amount of gas left in the mower must be between 0 and 13 gallons.
11. $y = -5x - 2$
13. $y = -5x + 38$

More Practice/Homework
1A. 1.5 B. $17.00 C. discrete
D. $y = 1.5x - 17$ E. all whole numbers from 0 through 150
F. $-17, or a loss of $17 G. $208
H. whole-number multiples of 1.5 from -17 to 208 3. $y = 5x - 9$
5. 12; 30 7. C 9. continuous
11. 10; 10

MODULE 6, LESSON 5
On Your Own
5. the cost of the charger; the price for each battery 7. 30 seconds 9. Jacey's program

13. 1; 5 15. Garage A: y-intercept is 5. The initial charge is $5. The slope is 2. Garage B: y-intercept is 7. The initial charge is $7. The slope is 1. The y-intercept is the initial amount charged. Garage B charges a greater initial amount. The slope is the rate per hour. Garage A charges a higher rate per hour.

More Practice/Homework
1. yes; All have the same slope and y-intercept. 3. -5; the initial amount spent to buy dog treats. 5. 2 dogs 7. 5 9. A 11. B
13. discrete

MODULE 6, LESSON 6
On Your Own
3. increases rapidly at the beginning; constant speed during the middle; gradually decreases near the end
11. from 0 seconds to 6 seconds
13. the ball staying at the same height as it rolls across the ledge 15. increases at a nonlinear rate

More Practice/Homework
3. Possible answer: Bicycle A slows down at a constant rate. Bicycle B slows down rapidly at first, then gradually comes to a stop. 7. A, B, C, E 9. Store A

MODULE 7, LESSON 1
On Your Own
5. The slope for Iceville is 1, so Iceville's hourly rate is $1 per hour. The slope for Super Skate is 0.5, so Super Skate's hourly rate is $0.50 per hour. 7. if skating more than 4 hours 9. The y-intercept for Plan P is 40. The fixed fee is $40. The y-intercept for Plan Q is 30. The fixed fee is $30. 11B. For both graphs, the slopes are 0.5,

so both charge $0.50 per mile. The y-intercept is 4 for XYZ Taxi and 5 for Quick ride, so they charge a different fixed fee. **C.** The graphs are parallel, so they will never cost the same amount for a given distance. **13.** At both shops, 4 ounces of frozen yogurt costs $3.25.

More Practice/Homework
1. The slope for both services is 1.5. Both services charge $1.50 per pound. **3.** Clean Machine **5.** D **7.** Both studios charge a monthly flat fee of $25 plus a charge of $10 per class.
9. $m\angle P = m\angle S = 110°$
11. infinitely many solutions

MODULE 7, LESSON 2
On Your Own
5A. disagree **B.** yes

More Practice/Homework
1A.

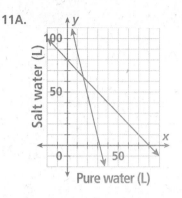

B. (−8, −8) **C.** Substitute (−8, −8) in each equation; both equations are satisfied.
3A. (1, 3) **B.** (4, 2) **5.** (4, −8)
7. $y = 50x + 20$ **9.** $x = 6$

MODULE 7, LESSON 3
On Your Own
3A. (10, 85) **B.** After 10 minutes, both drones are at a height of 85 meters.

5A.

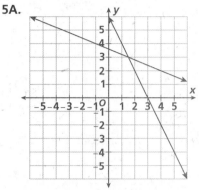

Possible answer: (1.5, 3)
B. (1.5, 3) **7A.** Quadrant II; The solution of the system, $\left(-\frac{1}{2}, 4\right)$, is in Quadrant II.
B.

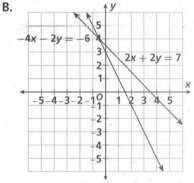

9. (−1, 6) **11.** $\left(\frac{1}{3}, -\frac{2}{3}\right)$
13. (0.5, 8)

More Practice/Homework
1. (4, 5); There are 4 trumpet players and 5 saxophone players in the jazz band.
3A. Possible answer: $y = \frac{3}{2}x + 5$
B. (−4, −1) **5.** D **7.** C **9.** (−6, 1)
11. $x = 15$; $m\angle 3 = m\angle 6 = 61°$

MODULE 7, LESSON 4
On Your Own
3. Quarters: 4, $1.00; Dimes: 11, $1.10 **5B.** no **7.** (2, 0.5) **9.** (14, 11)

11A.

Possible answer: (15, 65)
B. 16 liters pure water and 64 liters salt water

More Practice/Homework
1. 20 inches by 18 inches
3. Possible answer: He did not multiply the y-term in the second equation by −2; (1, 6). **5.** (−4, 0) **7.** (−1, 1) **9.** D
13. {−2, −1, 0, 1, 2}

MODULE 7, LESSON 5
On Your Own
5. infinitely many **7.** no **9.** none
11. one **13.** infinitely many
15. infinitely many solutions
17. no solution **19.** no solution

More Practice/Homework
1A. The system has no solution.
B. yes; They did not because the system has no solution. **3.** no
5. (0, 3) **7.** infinitely many solutions **9.** infinitely many solutions **11.** B **13.** infinitely many solutions; one solution; one solution; no solution; infinitely many solutions **15.** The candle starts at a height of 16 inches.

MODULE 7, LESSON 6

On Your Own

5A.

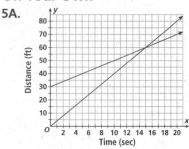

B. yes **7A.** $x + y = 90$ and $y = 2x + 15$ **B.** 25° and 65° **9.** no; The total number of questions on the test is needed. **11A.** $6b + 0.5g = 8$ and $30b + 7.5g = 60$ **B.** $b = 1$ and $g = 4$; Toni played 1 game of bowling and 4 holes of virtual golf. **13.** A sandwich costs $5.25 and a bowl of soup costs $3.50.

More Practice/Homework

1A. $x + y = 12$ and $6x + 9y = 88$; $x = 6.67$ and $y = 5.33$ **B.** 7 one-bedroom and 5 two-bedroom houses

3.

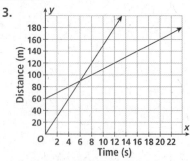

yes; after 6 seconds **5.** 17.50 **7.** 52 **9.** Triangles A and C
11. $y = -3x + 14$

UNIT 4

MODULE 8, LESSON 1

On Your Own

3. 6:30 p.m. **7.** nonlinear

More Practice/Homework

1A.

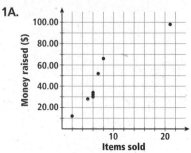

B. positive association; one outlier **3.** linear

5.

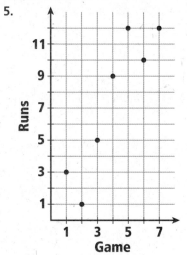

weak positive association
7. positive linear association; negative nonlinear association; no association **9.** (−2, 5)

MODULE 8, LESSON 2

On Your Own

3A. A trend line would be a good model. **B.** Possible answer:

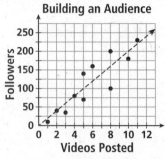

C. Possible answer: 400 followers
D. The estimate is made by extending the trend line beyond the data. That might change if new data are added.

More Practice/Homework

1A. The trend line is not a good fit. **B.** The new line will be less steep and it will move farther away from many of the original points. **3.** Possible answer: not necessarily; One of the data points below the line might represent an outlier, pulling the trend line down. **5.** If the outliers are on opposite sides of the trend line, they can pull in opposite directions. **7.** $x = 11$
9. $y = -2x + 3$

MODULE 8, LESSON 3

On Your Own

3A.

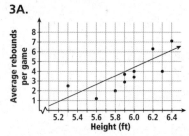

B. −22 **C.** It means that a person would get −22 rebounds if the person were 0 feet tall; no; This is not possible. **D.** Possible answer: It is possible that the tallest player gets the most rebounds, but it is also possible for a shorter player to get the most rebounds.

5. Possible answer: The more experience a person has with planting trees, the more trees the person can plant in a day.

9A.

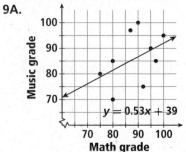

B. Possible answer: There is a weak positive association.

More Practice/Homework
1. Possible answer: Since the line trends down to the right, it shows that older people like the movie less. **3.** C **5.** yes **7.** D **9.** about 36% faster

MODULE 9, LESSON 1
On Your Own
3. yes

More Practice/Homework
1. Row 1: 51; 24; 75; Row 2: 119; 6; 125; Row 3: 170; 30; 200 **3.** C **5.** A **7.** $(2, -1)$

MODULE 9, LESSON 2
On Your Own
3A. Row 1: 0.03; 0.06; 0.09; Row 2: 0.21; Row 3: 0.76; 1
B. 0.24 **C.** 0.76 **D.** They add up to 1. **5.** $c = 1 - f$

More Practice/Homework
1B. 38%; The marginal relative frequency in the "Purple" column, which is 0.38, tells you this. **C.** 42%; The joint relative frequency for "Parrot" and "Red", which is 0.42, tells you this. **3.** D **5.** Row 1: 0.18; Row 2: 0.29; 0.13; 0.42; Row 3: 0.69; 1 **7.** $(-2, 2)$

MODULE 9, LESSON 3
On Your Own
3. $\frac{15}{30} = 0.5 = 50\%$ **5A.** 0.85 or 85% **B.** no

More Practice/Homework
1B. 0.4 or 40% **3.** D **5.** yes **7.** Bucket B

UNIT 5

MODULE 10, LESSON 1
On Your Own
7. $\frac{5}{11}$ **9.** They are irrational.
11. 0.0666...; $0.0\overline{6}$ **13.** $4\frac{3}{125}$
15. $-\frac{13}{33}$ **17.** $2\frac{16}{33}$

More Practice/Homework
1A. $\frac{32}{60} = 0.533333...$ **B.** rational
3. $45\frac{2}{15}$ hourly visitors
5. 0.037037037... ; $0.\overline{037}$ **7.** $-8\frac{29}{40}$
9. $1\frac{119}{225}$ **11.** $\frac{19}{33}$ **13.** D **15.** Row 1: 18; 48; 66; Row 2: 6; 48; 54; Row 3: 24; 96; 120 **17.** $3y + 5 = 4y - 30$; $y = 35$; $m\angle 1 = 110°$

MODULE 10, LESSON 2
On Your Own
5A. yes **B.** 5 ft; $5^3 = 125$
7. $\frac{2}{5}$; $\left(\frac{2}{5}\right)^3 = \frac{8}{125}$ **9.** $x = \pm 14$
13. yes; yes; Both are 0, since $0^2 = 0$ and $0^3 = 0$. **15.** 9
17. $x = \pm\frac{1}{7}$ **19.** $y = \frac{3}{5}$

More Practice/Homework
1A. 6 in.; $6^3 = 216$ **B.** 343 in³, 512 in³, or 729 in³ **3.** $y = \frac{4}{9}$
5. 17 **7.** $\frac{1}{10}$ **9.** $x = 7$ **11.** C
13. B **15.** $8\frac{2}{3}$ **17.** Acme Parking

MODULE 10, LESSON 3
On Your Own
7. 5.85 and 5.95; 5.9 **11A.** 4
B. 3.9 **13.** > **15.** < **17.** 6
19. 15 **21.** 8 **23.** $\sqrt{7}$ **25.** 7; 8
27. 2; 3 **29.** 2; 3 **31.** 7; 8
33.

$\frac{7}{4}$ $2.\overline{2}$ $(\sqrt{13}-1)$ $\sqrt{10}$
1 1.5 2 2.5 3 3.5 4

35.

$(\sqrt{48}-8)$ $(\sqrt{24}-5)$ $(\sqrt{60}-5)$ $\sqrt{17}$
-2 -1 0 1 2 3 4 5

37. $\sqrt{2}$; $\frac{10}{9}$; $(\sqrt{3}-1)$; $\frac{2}{3}$; $\frac{2}{9}$
39. $-3\sqrt{2}$; $(\sqrt{15}-7)$; $-\frac{12}{5}$;
$\left(3 - \frac{30}{7}\right)$; $(-6 + \sqrt{30})$ **41.** 1.05

More Practice/Homework
1. Kelsey's **3.** <
7.

$(\sqrt{22}-6)$ $(-5+\sqrt{25})$ $\frac{16}{5}$ $\sqrt{15}$
-2 -1 0 1 2 3 4

9. $(-\sqrt{45}+9)$, $\frac{12}{7}$, $(\sqrt{71}-8)$, $(\sqrt[3]{99}-5)$, $-\frac{8}{5}$ **11.** B
13. $-\sqrt{130}$, $-\frac{52}{5}$, $-3 -\sqrt{47}$
15. The relative frequency of owning a pet is about the same across the different music choices: 36%, 38%, and 35%. There does not appear to be a strong association.

MODULE 11, LESSON 1
On Your Own
3. Possible answer: The Pythagorean Theorem states that for a right triangle with legs a and b and hypotenuse c, $a^2 + b^2 = c^2$. **5.** 20 cm **7.** 24 m
9. 25 miles **11.** Ashley is not correct. The triangle is not known to be a right triangle.

More Practice/Homework
3. 25 in. **5A.** 12 yards
B. 72 yards **C.** The lengths of the leg and hypotenuse are 6 times as long. **D.** The length of the unknown side is 6 times as long.
7. A, D **9.** 10.6 **11.** -3, $\frac{10}{4}$, 2.7, $\sqrt{8}$

MODULE 11, LESSON 2
On Your Own
3A. $a = 7$ ft; $b = 24$ ft; $c = 25$ ft
B. 7; 24; 25; 49; 576; 625; converse of the Pythagorean Theorem; does **5.** yes **7.** no
9. yes **11A.** 4; 5 **B.** 6; 10
C. 24; 25 **D.** 9; 40

More Practice/Homework
1. 36; 77; 85; 1296; 5929; 7225; is; The square of *a* plus the square of *b* equals the square of *c*. **3.** Winston is incorrect because $25^2 + 36^2 \neq 64^2$. **5.** yes **7.** no **9.** not a right triangle; right triangle; right triangle; not a right triangle; right triangle; not a right triangle **11.** She did not use the correct formula for the Pythagorean Theorem. **13.** rational: 10, $3.\overline{31}$, $\frac{16}{3}$; irrational: 4.2123417...

MODULE 11, LESSON 3
On Your Own
3A. sidewalk route **B.** 11.9 m **5.** 10.77 m **7.** 28.8 **9.** 68.3 **11A.** Cone *A* **B.** 0.33 cm **13.** Since the internal diagonal is $\sqrt{12} \approx 3.46$ m, the longest rod that fits is 3.4 meters long.

More Practice/Homework
1A. 1336 km **B.** 553 km **3.** 7 in. **5.** C **7.** D
9.

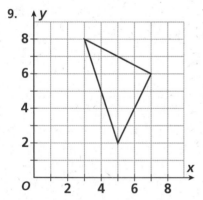

MODULE 11, LESSON 4
On Your Own
5. Point *E* **7A.** (−5, 2) or (4, 4) **B.** 9.2 units **C.** 20.2 units **9A.** (−5, 7) and (−8, −4) **B.** 11.4 units **C.** 25.4 units **D.** no **11A.** (1, 0.5), (5,3) **B.** 4.72 mi

More Practice/Homework
1. 4270 ft **3A.** (−2, −1) or (4, −4) **B.** 3 units; 6 units **C.** 6.7 units **D.** 15.7 units **5.** A **7.** C **9.** $x = 3.5$

UNIT 6

MODULE 12, LESSON 1
On Your Own
3A. 10^{11}; product of powers property **B.** 100,000,000,000 (one hundred billion) stars **5.** diameter of Milky Way disc; 10^{21} m **7.** distance from the Sun to Saturn, diameter of the Solar System, and diameter of Saturn **9A.** $2^2 \cdot 9^2$; $5^3 \cdot 8^3$ **B.** If $a \neq 0$ and $b \neq 0$, then $(ab)^m = a^m b^m$. **C.** $(3 \cdot 2)^5 = (6)^5 = 7776$; $(3 \cdot 2)^5 = 3^5 \cdot 2^5 = 243 \cdot 32 = 7776$ **11.** $\frac{1}{4}$ **13.** 65

More Practice/Homework
1A. 10^7; product of powers property, quotient of powers property **B.** 10,000,000 **3.** Katie; 175 more **5.** $\frac{1}{512}$ **7.** 81 **9.** A **11.** D **13.** $y = \frac{3}{10}$

MODULE 12, LESSON 2
On Your Own
5A. negative **B.** 1.7×10^{-8} cm **7.** Car B, Car D, and Car E **9.** 3 times as long **11A.** Possible answer: 1.099511628E12; $1.099511628 \times 10^{12}$ **B.** 1,000,000,000,000 **13.** 4.71×10^7 **15.** 9×10^{-10} **17.** 320,000,000 **19.** 0.00106 **21.** 8×10^9 is 40,000 times as great **23.** 2.4×10^{10} is 1000 times as great **25.** 1.54×10^8

More Practice/Homework
1. 7.5×10^{18} **3.** 186,000,000 **5.** 4.05×10^2 **7.** 6×10^{-14} **9.** 60,700,000 **11.** 0.000004 **13.** 2.8×10^{-4} is 20 times

as great than 1.4×10^{-5}. **17.** B **19.** A **21.** 7.4 cm

MODULE 12, LESSON 3
On Your Own
7. 1.58×10^5 vehicles **9.** 4.8×10^6; 4,800,000 people **11.** about 2.125 times as many **13.** 2×10^6 sheets **15.** 5 meters **19.** approximately 250 seeds **21.** 2.35×10^{-5} **23.** 1.15×10^7 **25.** 4.05×10^8 **27.** 2.542×10^5 **29.** no

More Practice/Homework
1. 8.1×10^5 students **3.** 2.8×10^{-6} kg **5.** 1.595×10^8 km² **7.** 7.89×10^5 **9.** 9.6×10^{-8} **11.** 2×10^1 **13.** 1.3×10^{-9} **15.** B **17.** 2.875×10^3 or 2875 attendees **19.** 5.8 units

MODULE 13, LESSON 1
On Your Own
5. 51.9 m³ **7.** Cylinder B **9.** 3 in. **11.** 10 mm **13.** 1.4×10^{12} mm³ **15A.** Possible answer: 248.2 cm³

More Practice/Homework
1. $432,180\pi$ ft³ **3.** 480 ft³ **5.** $V = \pi\left(\frac{d}{2}\right)^2 h$ or $V = \frac{\pi}{4}d^2 h$ **7.** 11 m **9.** B, C, D **11.** B **13.** 5.8×10^{-9}

MODULE 13, LESSON 2
On Your Own
3A. 63π cm³ **B.** 189π cm³ **5.** 16.6 m³ **7.** 204.7 cm³ **9.** 33π ft³ **11A.** 4 in. **B.** 12π in³; 37.7 in³ **13.** 301.44 cm³ **15.** 1059.75 mm³ **17.** no

More Practice/Homework
1. 7.8 m³ **3.** 59.3 cm³ **5.** 1017.4 ft³ **7.** $V = \frac{1}{3}\pi\left(\frac{d}{2}\right)^2 h$ or $V = \frac{1}{12}\pi d^2 h$ **9.** B, D, E **11.** 2.5; For each increase of 1 degree in the daily

high temperature, an additional 2.5 quarts of iced coffee are sold. **13.** 43.6 m^3

MODULE 13, LESSON 3

On Your Own

3A. $\frac{500}{3}\pi$ ft^3; 523.3 ft^3 **5.** 33.5 in^3
7. 20,569.1 m^3 **9.** 124.7 cm^3
11. $(1.7 \times 10^{-7})\pi$ m^3 **13.** 9.0 $\times$
10^{14} km^3 **15.** 1.6 $\times$ 10^{-9} ft^3
17. 3.1 $\times$ 10^{23} km^3 **21A.** $V =$
$\frac{1}{2} \cdot \frac{4}{3}\pi r^3 = \frac{2}{3}\pi r^3$ **B.** 1152π ft^3;
3617.3 ft^3 **C.** 62.4 m^3

More Practice/Homework

1. 4 cm^3 **3.** 1766.3 in^3 **5.** 248.3 cm^3
7. The student forgot to find the radius by taking half the diameter. **9.** A, C, D, F
11. Possible answer: The slope will be negative since the data have a negative association (as age increases, value decreases). **13.** no

MODULE 13, LESSON 4

On Your Own

3. 39,349π m^3 **5.** 2143.57 in^3
7. 396 ft^3 of water **9.** 4.19 $\times$
10^3 ft^3 **11.** 110,815,833 ft^3
13. no **15.** 1436.03 cm^3 **17.** 12 in^3
more **19.** 16 scoops

More Practice/Homework

1. no. **3.** 17 ft **5A.** 36π cm^3;
54π cm^3; 18π cm^3 **B.** 3 spheres;
6 cones **7.** 57.93 in^3 **9.** 49
11. (0, 7)

Interactive Glossary

As you learn about each new term, add notes, drawings, or sentences in the space next to the definition. Doing so will help you remember what each term means.

Pronunciation Key

ă	add, map	g	go, log	n	nice, tin	p	pit, stop	û(r)	burn, term
ā	ace, rate	h	hope, hate	ng	ring, song	r	run, poor	yōō	fuse, few
â(r)	care, air	hw	which	ŏ	odd, hot	s	see, pass	v	vain, eve
ä	palm, father	ĭ	it, give	ō	open, so	sh	sure, rush	w	win, away
b	bat, rub	ī	ice, write	ô	taught, jaw	t	talk, sit	y	yet, yearn
ch	check, catch	îr	tier	ôr	order	th	thin, both	z	zest, muse
d	dog, rod	j	joy, ledge	oi	oil, boy	th	this, bathe	zh	vision, pleasure
ĕ	end, pet	k	cool, take	ou	pout, now	ŭ	up, done		
ē	equal, tree	l	look, rule	ōō	took, full	ōō	pull, book		
f	fit, half	m	move, seem	ōō	pool, food	ōōr	cure		

ə the schwa, an unstressed vowel representing the sound spelled *a* in *above*, *e* in *sicken*, *i* in *possible*, *o* in *melon*, *u* in *circus*

Other symbols:
- separates words into syllables
' indicates stress on a syllable

A

My Vocabulary Summary

Addition Property of Equality [ə-dĭsh'ən prŏp'ər-tē ŭv ĭ-kwŏl'ĭ-tē] The property that states that if you add the same number to both sides of an equation, the new equation will have the same solution

Propiedad de Igualdad de la Suma Propiedad que establece que puedes sumar el mismo número a ambos lados de una ecuación y la nueva ecuación tendrá la misma solución

adjacent angles [ə-jā'sənt ăng'gəls] Angles in the same plane that have a common vertex and a common side

ángulos adyacentes Ángulos en el mismo plano que comparten un vértice y un lado

alternate exterior angles [ôl'tər-nĭt' ĭk-stîr'ē-ər ăng'gəls] For two lines intersected by a transversal, a pair of angles that lie on opposite sides of the transversal and outside the other two lines

ángulos alternos externos Dadas dos rectas cortadas por una transversal, par de ángulos no adyacentes ubicados en los lados opuestos de la transversal y fuera de las otras dos rectas

alternate interior angles [ôl′tər-nĭt′ ĭn-tîr′ē-ər ăng′gəls] For two lines intersected by a transversal, a pair of nonadjacent angles that lie on opposite sides of the transversal and between the other two lines

ángulos alternos internos Dadas dos rectas cortadas por una transversal, par de ángulos no adyacentes ubicados en los lados opuestos de la transversal y entre de las otras dos rectas

Angle-Angle Similarity Postulate [ăng′gəl-ăng′gəl sĭm′ə-lăr′ĭ-tē pŏs′chə-lāt′] Two triangles are similar if they have pairs of corresponding angles that are congruent

Postulado de Semejanza Ángulo-Ángulo Dos triángulos son semejantes si tienen dos pares de ángulos correspondientes y congruentes

association [ə-sō′sē-ā′shən] The description of the relationship between two data sets

asociación Descripción de la relación entre dos conjuntos de datos

axis [ăk′sĭs] A line of a coordinate plane that passes through the origin

eje Recta de un plano de coordenadas que pasa por el origen

B

base [bās] The number that is used as a factor when a number is raised to a power

base Cuando un número es elevado a una potencia, el número que se usa como factor es la base

Interactive Glossary

base (of a polygon or three-dimensional figure) [bās (ŭv ā pŏl'ē-gŏn' ôr thrē'dĭ-mĕn'shə-nəl fĭg'yər)] A side of a polygon; a face of a three-dimensional figure by which the figure is measured or classified

base (de un polígono o figura tridimensional) Lado de un polígono; cara de una figura tridimensional según la cual se mide o se clasifica la figura

bivariate data [bī-vâr'ē-ĭt dā'tə] A set of data that is made of two paired variables

datos bivariados Conjunto de datos compuesto de dos variables apareadas

C

center of dilation [sĕn'tər ŭv dĭ-lā'shən] The point of intersection of lines through each pair of corresponding vertices in a dilation

centro de una dilatación Punto de intersección de las líneas que pasan a través de cada par de vértices correspondientes en una dilatación

center of rotation [sĕn'tər ŭv rō-tā'shən] The point about which a figure is rotated

centro de una rotación Punto alrededor del cual se hace girar una figura

circumference [sər-kŭm'fər-əns] The distance around a circle

circunferencia Distancia alrededor de un círculo

My Vocabulary Summary

clockwise [klŏk′wīz′] A circular movement in the direction of the typical forward movement of the hands of a clock

en el sentido de las manecillas del reloj Un movimiento circular en la dirección típica de las manecillas de un reloj

cluster [klŭs′tər] A set of closely grouped data

agrupación Conjunto de datos bien agrupados

coefficient [kō′ə-fĭsh′ənt] The number that is multiplied by the variable in an algebraic expression

coeficiente Número que se multiplica por la variable en una expresión algebraica

conditional relative frequency [kən-dĭsh′ə-nəl rĕl′ə-tĭv frē′kwən-sē] The ratio of a joint relative frequency to a related marginal relative frequency in a two-way table

frecuencia relativa condicional Razón de una frecuencia relativa conjunta a una frecuencia relativa marginal en una tabla de doble entrada

congruence transformation [kŏng′grōō-əns trăns′fər-mā′shən] A transformation that results in an image that is the same shape and the same size as the original figure

transformación de congruencia Una transformación que resulta en una imagen que tiene la misma forma y el mismo tamaño como la figura original

congruent [kŏng′grōō-ənt] Having the same size and shape; the symbol for congruent is ≅

congruentes Que tienen la misma forma y el mismo tamaño expresado por ≅

© Houghton Mifflin Harcourt Publishing Company

Interactive Glossary

My Vocabulary Summary

continuous graph [kən-tĭn′yōō-əs grăf] A graph made up of connected lines or curves

gráfica continua Gráfica compuesta por líneas rectas o curvas conectadas

---

converse [kən′vûrs] Reverses the hypothesis and the conclusion of a statement or theorem

contrario Inverte la hipótesis y la conclusión de una declaración o teorema

---

coordinate [kō-ôr dn-ĭt, -āt] One of the numbers of an ordered pair that locate a point on a coordinate graph

coordenada Uno de los números de un par ordenado que ubica un punto en una gráfica de coordenadas

---

coordinate plane [kō-ôr′dn-ĭt plān] A plane formed by the intersection of a horizontal number line called the x-axis and a vertical number line called the y-axis

plano cartesiano Plano formado por la intersección de una recta numérica horizontal llamada eje x y otra vertical llamada eje y

---

corresponding angles (for lines) [kôr′ĭ-spŏn′dĭng ăng′gəls (fôr līns)] For two lines intersected by a transversal, a pair of angles that lie on the same side of the transversal and on the same sides of each of the other two lines

ángulos correspondientes (en líneas) Dadas dos rectas cortadas por una transversal, el par de ángulos ubicados en el mismo lado de la transversal y en los mismos lados de las otras dos rectas

---

corresponding angles (of polygons) [kôr′ĭ-spŏn′dĭng ăng′gəls (ŭv pŏl′ē-gŏn′s)] Angles in the same relative position in polygons with an equal number of sides

ángulos correspondientes (en polígonos) Ángulos en la misma posición formaron cuando una tercera línea interseca dos líneas

corresponding sides [kôr´ĭ-spŏn´dĭng sīds] Matching sides of two or more polygons

lados correspondientes Lados que se ubican en la misma posición relativa en dos o más polígonos

counterclockwise [koun´tər-klŏk´wīz] A circular movement in the direction opposite the typical forward movement of the hands of a clock

en sentido contrario a las manecillas del reloj Un movimiento circular en la dirección opuesta al movimiento típico de las manecillas del reloj

cube (geometric figure) [kyo͞ob (jē´ə-mĕt´rĭk fĭg´yər)] A rectangular prism with six congruent square faces

cubo (figura geométrica) Prisma rectangular con seis caras cuadradas congruentes

cube (in numeration) [kyo͞ob (ĭn no͞o´mə-rā´shən)] A number raised to the third power

cubo (en numeración) Número elevado a la tercera potencia

cube root [kyo͞ob ro͞ot] A number, written as $\sqrt[3]{x}$, whose cube is x

raíz cúbica Número, expresado como $\sqrt[3]{x}$, cuyo cubo es x

Interactive Glossary

cylinder [sil′ən-dər] A three-dimensional figure with two parallel, congruent circular bases connected by a curved lateral surface

cilindro Figura tridimensional con dos bases circulares paralelas y congruentes, unidas por una superficie lateral curva

D

data set [dā′tə sĕt] A set of information collected about people or things, often to draw conclusions about them

conjunto de datos Conjunto de información recopilada sobre personas u objetos generalmente con el objetivo de obtener conclusiones acerca de los mismos

denominator [dĭ-nŏm′ə-nā′tər] The bottom number of a fraction that tells how many equal parts are in the whole

denominador Número que está abajo en una fracción y que indica en cuántas partes iguales se divide el entero

dependent variable [dĭ-pĕn′dənt vâr′ē-ə-bəl] The output of a function; a variable whose value depends on the value of the input, or independent variable

variable dependiente Salida de una función; variable cuyo valor depende del valor de la entrada, o variable independiente

diameter [di-ɑm′i-tər] A line segment that passes through the center of a circle and has endpoints on the circle; or the length of that segment

diámetro Segmento de recta que pasa por el centro de un círculo y tiene sus extremos en la circunferencia, o bien la longitud de ese segmento

© Houghton Mifflin Harcourt Publishing Company

My Vocabulary Summary

dilation [dĭ-lā'shən] A transformation that enlarges or reduces a figure

dilatación Transformación que agranda o reduce una figura

discrete graph [dĭ-skrēt' grăf] A graph made up of unconnected points

gráfica discreta Gráfica compuesta de puntos no conectados

Distributive Property [dĭ-strĭb'yə-tĭv prŏp'ər-tē] For all real numbers a, b, and c, $a(b + c) = ab + ac$, and $a(b - c) = ab - ac$

Propiedad Distributiva Dados los números reales a, b, y c, $a(b + c) = ab + ac$, y $a(b - c) = ab - ac$

domain [dō-mān'] The set of all possible input values of a function

dominio Conjunto de todos los posibles valores de entrada de una función

E

elimination [ĭ-lĭm'ə-nā'shən] Algebraic process of eliminating a variable in a system of equations by combining the equations through addition

eliminación Procedimiento algebraico que consiste en eliminar una variable en un sistema de ecuaciones sumando las ecuaciones

Interactive Glossary

enlargement [ĕn-lärj′mənt] An increase in size of all dimensions in the same proportions

agrandamiento Aumento de tamaño de todas las dimensiones en las mismas proporciones

equivalent expressions [ĭ-kwĭv′ə-lənt ĭk-sprĕsh′əns] Expressions that have the same value for all values of the variables

expresiones equivalentes Las expresiones equivalentes tienen el mismo valor para todos los valores de las variables

exponent [ĭk-spō′nənt] The number that indicates how many times the base is used as a factor

exponente Número que indica cuántas veces se usa la base como factor

expression [ĭk-sprĕsh ən] A mathematical phrase that contains operations, numbers, and/or variables

expresión Enunciado matemático que contiene operaciones, números y/o variables

exterior angle (of a polygon) [ĭk-stîr′ē-ər ăng′gəl (ŭv ā pŏl′ē-gŏn′)] An angle formed by one side of a polygon and the extension of an adjacent side

ángulo extreno de un polígono Ángulo formado por un lado de un polígono y la prolongación del lado adyacente

Exterior Angle Theorem [ĭk-stîr′ē-ər ăng′gəl thē′ər-əm] The measure of an exterior angle of a triangle is greater than either of the measures of the remote interior angles

Teorema del Ángulo Exterior La medida de un ángulo exterior de un triángulo es mayor que cualquiera de las medidas de los ángulos interiores no adyacentes

F

function [fŭngk′shən] An input-output relationship that has exactly one output for each input

función Regla que relaciona dos candidates de forma que a cada valor de entrada corresponde exactamente un valor de salida

G

greatest common factor (GCF) [grā′tĭst kŏm′ən făk′tər] The largest common factor of two or more given numbers

máximo común divisor (MCD) El mayor de los factores comunes compartidos por dos o más números dados

H

height [hīt] In a pyramid or cone, the perpendicular distance from the base to the opposite vertex

In a triangle or quadrilateral, the perpendicular distance from the base to the opposite vertex or side

In a prism or cylinder, the perpendicular distance between the bases

altura En una pirámide o cono, la distancia perpendicular desde la base al vértice opuesto

En un triángulo o cuadrilátero, la distancia perpendicular desde la base de la figura al vértice o lado opuesto

En un prisma o cilindro, la distancia perpendicular entre las bases

hemisphere [hĕm′ĭ-sfîr′] A half of a sphere

hemisferio La mitad de una esfera

hypotenuse [hī-pŏt′n-ōos′] In a right triangle, the side opposite the right angle

hipotenusa En un triángulo rectángulo, el lado opuesto al ángulo recto

---

I

image [ĭm′ĭj] A figure resulting from a transformation

imagen Figura que resulta de una transformación

---

independent variable [ĭn′dĭ-pĕn′dənt vâr′ē-ə-bəl] The input of a function; a variable whose value determines the value of the output, or dependent variable

variable independiente Entrada de una función; variable cuyo valor determina el valor de la salida, o variable dependiente

---

indirect measurement [ĭn′dĭ-rĕkt′ mĕzh′ər-mənt] The technique of using similar figures and proportions to find a measure

medición indirecta La técnica de usar figuras semejantes y proporciones para hallar una medida

---

infinitely many solutions [ĭn′fə-nĭt-lē mĕn′ē sə-lōo′shəns] Occurs when every value of the variable makes a true mathematical statement, or if the graphs of two linear equations overlap and therefore intersect at infinitely many points

soluciones infinitas Occure cuando cada valor de la variable sea un enunciado matemático verdadero, o si las gráficas de dos ecuaciones lineales se superponen y por tanto se intersecan en puntos infinitos

input [ĭn′po͝ot′] The value substituted into an expression or function

valor de entrada Valor que se usa para sustituir una variable en una expresión o función

intercept [ĭn′tər-sĕpt′] The coordinate of the point where the line of the graph intersects an axis

intersección Coordenada del punto en el cual la gráfica interseca el eje

interior angles [ĭn-tîr′ē-ər ăng′gəls] Angles on the inner sides of two lines cut by a transversal

ángulos internos Ángulos en los lados internos de dos líneas intersecadas por una transversal

irrational number [ĭ-răsh′ə-nəl nŭm′bər] A number that cannot be expressed as a ratio of two integers or as a repeating or terminating decimal

número irracional Número que no se puede expresar como una razón de dos enteros ni como un decimal periódico o finito

isolate the variable [ī′sə-lāt′ thə vâr′ē-ə-bəl] To get a variable alone on one side of an equation or inequality in order to solve the equation or inequality

despejar la variable Dejar sola la variable en un lado de una ecuación o desigualdad para resolverla

Interactive Glossary

J

joint relative frequency [joint rĕl′ə-tĭv frē′kwən-sē] The frequency in a particular category divided by the total number of data values

frecuencia relativa conjunta La frecuencia en una determinada categoría dividida entre el número total de valores

L

least common denominator (LCD) [lēst kŏm′ən dĭ-nŏm′ə-nā′tər] The least common multiple of two or more denominators

mínimo común denominador (m.c.d.) El mínimo común múltiplo de dos o más denominadores

legs [lĕgs] In a right triangle, the sides that form the right angle; in an isosceles triangle, the pair of congruent sides

catetos En un triángulo rectángulo, los lados adyacentes al ángulo recto. En un triángulo isósceles, el par de lados congruentes

like terms [līk tûrms] Terms that have the same variable(s) raised to the same exponent

términos semejantes Términos que contienen las mismas variables elevada a las mismas exponente

line of reflection [līn ŭv rĭ-flĕk′shən] A line that a figure is flipped across to create a mirror image of the original figure

línea de reflexión Línea sobre la cual se invierte una figura para crear una imagen reflejada de la figura original

line symmetry [līn sĭm′ĭ-trē] The symmetry that a figure has if it can be divided into two parts that are mirror images

simetría axial La simetría que tiene una figura si se puede dividir en dos partes que son imágenes especulares

linear association [lĭn′ē-ər ə-sō′sē-ā shən] Two data sets have a linear association when their data values lie roughly along a line

assóciation lineal Dos conjuntos de datos tienen una asociación lineal cuando sus valores de datos se encuentran aproximadamente a lo largo de una línea

linear equation [lĭn′ē-ər ĭ-kwā′zhən] An equation whose solutions form a straight line on a coordinate plane

ecuación lineal Ecuación cuyas soluciones forman una línea recta en un plano cartesiano

linear function [lĭn′ē-ər fŭngk′shən] A function whose graph is a straight line

función lineal Función cuya gráfica es una línea recta

M

mapping notation [măp′ĭng nō-tā′shən] A rule used to express any type of transformation in the coordinate plane

notación cartográfica Regla utilizada para expresar cualquier tipo de transformación en el plano de coordenadas

marginal relative frequency [mär′jə-nəl rĕl′ə-tĭv frē′kwən-sē] The sum of the joint relative frequencies in a row or column of a two-way table

frecuencia relativa marginal La suma de las frecuencias relativas conjuntas en una fila o columna de una tabla de doble entrada

Multiplication Property of Equality
[mŭl′tə-plĭ-kā′shən prŏp′ər-tē ŭv ĭ-kwŏl′ĭ-tē] The property that states that if you multiply both sides of an equation by the same number, the new equation will have the same solution

Propiedad de Igualdad de la Multiplicación
Propiedad que establece que puedes multiplicar ambos lados de una ecuación por el mismo número y la nueva ecuación tendrá la misma solución

N

negative association [nĕg′ə-tĭv ə-sō′sē-ā shən]
Two data sets have a negative association if one set of data values increases while the other decreases

asociación negativa Dos conjuntos de datos tienen asociación negativa si los valores de un conjunto aumentan a medida que los valores del otro conjunto disminuyen

no association [nō ə-sō′sē-ā shən] Two data sets have no association when there is no relationship between their data values

sin asociación Caso en que los valores de dos conjuntos no muestran ninguna relación

no solution [nō sə-loo′shən] Occurs when no value of the variable makes an equation true, or when a system of two equations has graphs that never intersect because lines are parallel

sin solución Ocurre cuando ningún valor de la variable hace un ecuación sea verdadero, o cuando un sistema de dos ecuaciones tiene gráficas que nunca se intersecan porque son rectas paralelas

nonlinear association [nŏn-lĭn′ē-ər ə-sō′sē-ā shən]
An association between two variables in which
the data do not have a linear trend

asociación no lineal Una asociación entre dos
variables en las que los datos no tienen una
tendencia lineal

nonlinear function [nŏn-lĭn′ē-ər fŭngk′shən] A
function whose graph is not a straight line

función no lineal Función cuya gráfica no es una
línea recta

number line [nŭm′bər lĭn] A line used to plot real
numbers including integers, rational numbers,
and irrational numbers

recta numérica Recta que se usa para marcar
números reales que incluyen enteros, números
racionales y números irracionales

numerator [nōō′mə-rā′tər] The top number of a
fraction that tells how many parts of a whole are
being considered

numerador El número de arriba de una fracción;
indica cuántas partes de un entero se consideran

O

origin [ôr′ə-jĭn] The point where the x-axis and y-axis intersect on the coordinate plane; (0, 0)

origen Punto de intersección entre el eje x y el eje y en un plano cartesiano: (0, 0)

outlier [out′lī′ər] A point in a data set of ordered pairs that does not follow the overall pattern on a graph of the data set

valor extremo Un punto en un conjunto de datos de pares ordenados que no sigue el patrón general en un gráfico del conjunto de datos.

output [out′poot′] The value that results from the substitution of a given input into an expression or function

valor de salida Valor que resulta después de sustituir una variable por un valor de entrada determinado en una expresión o función

P

parallel lines [păr′ə-lĕl′ līns] Lines in a plane that do not intersect

líneas paralelas Líneas que se encuentran en el mismo plano pero que nunca se intersecan

perfect cube [pûr′fĭkt kyoob] A cube of a whole number

cubo perfecto El cubo de un número cabal

My Vocabulary Summary

perfect square [pûr′fĭkt skwâr] A square of a whole number

cuadrado perfecto El cuadrado de un número cabal

---

pi (π) [pī] The ratio of the circumference of a circle to the length of its diameter; $\pi \approx 3.14$ or $\frac{22}{7}$

pi (π) Razón de la circunferencia de un círculo a la longitud de su diámetro; $\pi \approx 3.14$ ó $\frac{22}{7}$

---

positive association [pŏz′ĭ-tĭv ə-sō′sē-ā shən] Two data sets have a positive association when their data values increase or decrease together

asociación positiva Dos conjuntos de datos tienen una asociación positiva cuando los valores de ambos conjuntos aumentan o disminuyen al mismo tiempo

---

power [pou′ər] A number produced by raising a base to an exponent

potencia Número que resulta al elevar una base a un exponente

---

preimage [prē′ĭm′ĭj] The original figure in a transformation

imagen original Figura original en una transformación

---

prime notation [prīm nō-tā′shən] Used to label transformed images by adding apostrophes to each letter label

notación prima Se utiliza para marcar imágenes transformadas agregando apóstrofes a cada letra

Interactive Glossary

principal square root [prĭn′sə-pəl skwâr rōōt] The nonnegative square root of a number

raíz cuadrada principal Raíz cuadrada no negativa de un número

properties of exponents [prŏp′ər-tēz ŭv ĭk-spō′nənt] Rules for operations with exponents

propiedades de exponentes Reglas de operaciones con exponentes

proportional relationship [prə-pôr′shə-nəl rĭ-lā′shən-shĭp′] A relationship between two quantities in which the ratio of one quantity to the other quantity is constant

relación proporcional Relación entre dos cantidades en que la razón de una cantidad a la otra es constante

Pythagorean Theorem [pĭ-thăg′ə-rē′ən thē′ər-əm] In a right triangle, the square of the length of the hypotenuse is equal to the sum of the squares of the lengths of the legs

Teorema de Pitágoras En un triángulo rectángulo, la suma de los cuadrados de los catetos es igual al cuadrado de la hipotenusa

Pythagorean triple [pĭ-thăg′ə-rē′ən trĭp′əl] A set of three positive integers a, b, and c such that $a^2 + b^2 = c^2$

Tripleta de Pitágoras Conjunto de tres números enteros positivos de cero a, b y c tal que $a^2 + b^2 = c^2$

Q

quadrant [kwŏd′rənt] The x- and y-axes divide the coordinate plane into four regions. Each region is called a quadrant

cuadrante El eje x y el eje y dividen el plano cartesiano en cuatro regiones. Cada región recibe el nombre de cuadrante

R

radical symbol [răd′ĭ-kəl sĭm′bəl] The symbol $\sqrt{}$ used to represent the nonnegative square root of a number

símbolo de radical El símbolo $\sqrt{}$ con que se representa la raíz cuadrada no negativa de un número

radius [rā′dē-əs] A line segment with one endpoint at the center of the circle and the other endpoint on the circle, or the length of that segment

radio Segmento de recta con un extremo en el centro de un círculo y el otro en la circunferencia, o bien se llama radio a la longitud de ese segmento

range (of a function) [rānj (ŭv ā fŭngk′shən)] The set of all possible output values of a function

rango (en una función) El conjunto de todos los valores posibles de una función

rate of change [rāt ŭv chānj] A ratio that compares the amount of change in a dependent variable to the amount of change in an independent variable

tasa de cambio Razón que compara la cantidad de cambio de la variable dependiente con la cantidad de cambio de la variable independiente

Interactive Glossary

rational number [răsh′ə-nəl nŭm′bər] Any number that can be expressed as a ratio of two integers

número racional Número que se puede escribir como una razón de dos enteros

real number [rē′əl nŭm′bər] A rational or irrational number

número real Número racional o irracional

reduction [rĭ-dŭk′shən] A decrease in the size of all dimensions of a figure

reducción Disminución de tamaño en todas las dimensiones de una figura

reflection [rĭ-flĕk′shən] A transformation of a figure that flips the figure across a line

reflexión Transformación que ocurre cuando se invierte una figura sobre una línea

relation [rĭ-lā′shən] A set of ordered pairs

relación Conjunto de pares ordenados

My Vocabulary Summary

relative frequency [rĕl′ə-tĭv frē′kwən-sē] The frequency of a specific data value divided by the total number of data values in the set

frecuencia relativa La frecuencia de un valor dividido por el número total de los valores en el conjunto

remote interior angle [rĭ-mōt′ ĭn-tîr′ē-ər ăng′gəl] An interior angle of a polygon that is not adjacent to the exterior angle

ángulo interno remoto Ángulo interno de un polígono que no es adyacente al ángulo externo

repeating decimal [rĭ-pēt′ĭng dĕs′ə-məl] A decimal in which one or more digits repeat infinitely

decimal periódico Decimal en el que uno o más dígitos se repiten infinitamente

right cone [rīt kōn] A cone in which a perpendicular line drawn from the base to the tip (vertex) passes through the center of the base

cono recto Cono en el que una linea perpendicular trazada de la base a la punta (vértice) pasa por el centro de la base

right triangle [rīt trī′ ăng′gəl] A triangle containing a right angle

triángulo rectángulo Triángulo que tiene un ángulo recto

My Vocabulary Summary

rise [rīz] The vertical change when the slope of a line is expressed as the ratio $\frac{rise}{run}$, or "rise over run"

distancia vertical El cambio vertical cuando la pendiente de una línea se expresa como la razón $\frac{distancia\ vertical}{distancia\ horizontal}$, o "distancia vertical sobre distancia horizontal"

rotation [rō-tā'shən] A transformation in which a figure is turned around a point

rotación Transformación que ocurre cuando una figura gira alrededor de un punto

rotational symmetry [rō-tā'shən-əl sĭm'ĭ-trē] A figure has rotational symmetry if it can be rotated less than 360° around a central point and coincide with the original figure

simetría de rotación Ocurre cuando una figura gira menos de 360° alrededor de un punto central sin dejar de ser congruente con la figura original

run [rŭn] The horizontal change when the slope of a line is expressed as the ratio $\frac{rise}{run}$, or "rise over run"

distancia horizontal El cambio horizontal cuando la pendiente de una línea se expresa como la razón $\frac{distancia\ vertical}{distancia\ horizontal}$, o "distancia vertical sobre distancia horizontal"

S

same-side exterior angles [sām-sīd ĭk-stîr'ē-ər ăng'gəls] A pair of angles on the same side of a transversal but outside the parallel lines

ángulos externos del mismo lado Par de ángulos que se encuentran del mismo lado de una transversal, pero por la parte exterior de las rectas paralelas

same-side interior angles [săm-sīd ĭn-tîr′ē-ər ăng′gəls] A pair of angles on the same side of a transversal and between two lines intersected by the transversal

ángulo internos del mismo lado Dadas dos rectas cortadas por una transversal, par de ángulos ubicados en el mismo lado de la transversal y entre las dos rectas

scale factor [skāl făk′tər] The ratio used to enlarge or reduce similar figures

factor de escala Razón empleada para agrandar o reducir figuras semejantes

scatter plot [skăt′ər plŏt] A graph with points plotted to show a possible relationship between two sets of data

diagrama de dispersión Gráfica de puntos que muestra una posible relación entre dos conjuntos de datos

scientific notation [sī′ən-tĭf′ĭk nō-tā′shən] A method of more conveniently writing very large or very small numbers by using powers of 10

notación científica Método que se usa para escribir números muy grandes o muy pequeños mediante potencias de 10

segment [sĕg′mənt] A part of a line between two endpoints

segmento Parte de una línea entre dos extremos

Interactive Glossary

similar [sĭm′ə-lər] Figures with the same shape but not necessarily the same size

semejantes Figuras que tienen la misma forma, pero no necesariamente el mismo tamaño

similarity transformation [sĭm′ə-lăr′ĭ-tē trăns′fər-mā′shən] A transformation that results in an image that is the same shape, but not necessarily the same size, as the original figure

transformación de semejanza Una transformación que resulta en una imagen que tiene la misma forma, pero no necesariamente el mismo tamaño como la figura original

slant height (of a right cone) [slant hīt (ŭv ā rīt kōn)] The distance from the vertex of a right cone to a point on the edge of the base

altura inclinada (de un cono recto) Distancia desde el vértice de un cono recto hasta un punto en el borde de la base

slope [slōp] A measure of the steepness of a line on a graph; equal to the rise divided by the run

pendiente Medida de la inclinación de una línea en una gráfica. Razón de la distancia vertical a la distancia horizontal

slope-intercept form [slōp-ĭn′tər-sĕpt′ fôrm] A linear equation written in the form $y = mx + b$, where m represents slope and b represents the y-intercept

forma de pendiente-intersección Ecuación lineal escrita en la forma $y = mx + b$, donde m es la pendiente y b es la intersección con el eje y

My Vocabulary Summary

solution of a system of equations [sə-lōō′shən ŭv ā sĭs′təm ŭv ĭ-kwā′zhəns] A set of values that make all equations in a system true

solución de un sistema de ecuaciones Conjunto de valores que hacen verdaderas todas las ecuaciones de un sistema

sphere [sfĭr] A round three-dimensional figure with a central point and all points whose distance from the center is less than or equal to the radius

esfera Una figura redonda tridimensional con un punto central y todos los puntos cuya distancia desde el centro es menor o igual que el radio

square (numeration) [skwâr (nōō′mə-rā′shən)] A number raised to the second power

cuadrado (en numeración) Número elevado a la segunda potencia

square root [skwâr rōōt] A number that is multiplied by itself to form a product is called a square root of that product

raíz cuadrada El número que se multiplica por sí mismo para formar un producto se denomina la raíz cuadrada de ese producto

standard (or decimal) form of a number [stăn′dərd fôrm ŭv ā nŭm′bər] A way of writing a number by using digits

forma estándar (o decimal) de un número Manera de escribir un número usando dígitos

Interactive Glossary

straight angle [strāt ăng′gəl] An angle that measures 180°

ángulo llano Ángulo que mide exactamente 180°

substitute [sŭb′stĭ-tōōt′] To replace a variable with a number or another expression in an algebraic expression

sustituir Reemplazar una variable por un número u otra expresión en una expresión algebraica

Subtraction Property of Equality [səb-trăk′shən prŏp′ər-tē ŭv ĭ-kwŏl′ĭ-tē] The property that states that if you subtract the same number from both sides of an equation, the new equation will have the same solution

Propiedad de igualdad de la resta Propiedad que establece que puedes restar el mismo número de ambos lados de una ecuación y la nueva ecuación tendrá la misma solución

supplementary angles [sŭp′lə-měn′tə-rē ăng′gəls] Two angles whose measures have a sum of 180°

ángulos suplementarios Dos ángulos cuyas medidas suman 180°

system of equations [sĭs′təm ŭv ĭ-kwā′zhəns] A set of two or more equations

sistema de ecuaciones Conjunto de dos o más ecuaciones

T

terminating decimal [tûr′mə-nāt′ĭng dĕs′ə-məl] A decimal number that ends, or terminates

decimal finito Decimal con un número determinado de posiciones decimales

---

transformation [trăns′fər-mā′shən] A change in the size or position of a figure

transformación Cambio en el tamaño o la posición de una figura

---

translation [trăns-lā′shən] A movement (slide) of a figure along a straight line

traslación Desplazamiento de una figura a lo largo de una línea recta

---

transversal [trɑns-vûr′səl] A line that intersects two or more other lines

transversal Línea que cruza dos o más líneas

---

trend line [trĕnd līn] A line on a scatter plot that helps show the association between data sets more clearly

línea de tendencia Línea en un diagrama de dispersión que sirve para mostrar la asociación entre conjuntos de datos más claramente. *ver también* línea de mejor ajuste

Interactive Glossary

Triangle Sum Theorem [trĭ′ăng′gəl sŭm the′ər-əm]
The theorem that states that the measures of the angles in a triangle add up to 180°

Teorema de la suma del triángulo
Teorema que establece que las medidas de los ángulos de un triángulo suman 180°

two-way relative frequency table [tōō-wā rĕl′ə-tĭv frē′kwən-sē tā′bəl] A two-way table that displays relative frequencies

tabla de frecuencia relativa de doble entrada Una tabla de doble entrada que muestran las frecuencias relativas

two-way table [tōō-wā tā′bəl] A table that displays two-variable data by organizing it into rows and columns

tabla de doble entrada Una tabla que muestran los datos de dos variables por organizándolos en columnas y filas

U

unit rate [yōō′nĭt rāt] A rate in which the second quantity in the comparison is one unit

tasa unitaria Una tasa en la que la segunda cantidad de la comparación es la unidad

V

vertex [vûr′tĕks′] On an angle or polygon, the point where two sides intersect; on a polyhedron, the intersection of three or more faces; on a cone or pyramid, the top point

vértice En un ángulo o polígono, el punto de intersección de dos lados; en un poliedro, el punto de intersección de tres o más caras; en un cono o pirámide, la punta

vertical line test [vûr′tĭ-kəl līn tĕst] A test used to determine whether a relation is a function: if any vertical line crosses the graph of a relation more than once, the relation is not a function

prueba de la línea vertical Prueba utilizada para determinar si una relación es una función. Si una línea vertical corta la gráfica de una relación más de una vez, la relación no es una función

volume [vŏl′yo͞om] The amount of space enclosed within a three-dimensional region; or the number of cubic units needed to fill that space

volumen La cantidad de espacio dentro de una región tridimensional; o la cantidad de unidades cúbicas necesarias para llenar ese espacio

X

x-axis [ĕks′-ăk′sĭs] The horizontal axis on a coordinate plane

eje x El eje horizontal del plano cartesiano

Interactive Glossary

x-intercept [ĕks-ĭn′tər-sĕpt′] The *x*-coordinate of the point where the graph of a line crosses the *x*-axis

intersección con el eje *x* Coordenada *x* del punto donde la gráfica de una línea cruza el eje *x*

Y

y = *mx* [wī ē′kwəls ĕm ĕks] The form for a linear equation that passes through the origin and has a *y*-intercept of 0

y = *mx* Ecuación que representa una ecuación lineal que pasa por el origen, la intersección con cada uno de los ejes es 0

y-axis [wī′-ăk sĭs] The vertical axis on a coordinate plane

eje *y* El eje vertical del plano cartesiano

y-intercept [wī-ĭn′tər-sĕpt′] The *y*-coordinate of the point where the graph of a line crosses the *y*-axis

intersección con el eje *y* Coordenada *y* del punto donde la gráfica de una línea cruza el eje *y*

Index

coordinate grid, 51, 56
  shapes on, 50–56, 57–64, 71–72, 73–74
coordinate notation, 15, 18, 35, 40, 74, 139–142, 192
coordinate plane, 227
  enlargements on the, 53
  graphing and labeling equations on the, 225–232
  graphing lines on the, 175, 180, 181–188, 233–240
  ordered pairs on the, 3, 15, 40, 74, 139–142, 186, 192, 380
  polygons in the, 4, 39, 41, 48, 58–64, 66–72
  Pythagorean Theorem in the, 389–396
  reductions on the, 50–56
  reflections on the, 21–28
  rotations on the, 30–36
  transformations on the, 6–12, 48
  translations on the, 14–20
corresponding angles, 22, 25, 66, 112, 115–130, 143, 248, 374
cube(s)
  edge length of, 346
  perfect, 348–352
  surface area of, 362
  volume of, 346, 407
cube root, 348–352, 353–360
  symbol for ($\sqrt[3]{}$), 348
  for zero, 350
cylinders, 432
  area of the base, 431
  height of, 431, 432, 433, 434, 435, 436
  radius of, 432, 433, 434, 435, 439
  volume of, 431–438
    formula for, 431, 432, 433, 434, 437

D

data
  interpreting linear, 295–302
  scatter plots in displaying, 279–286
  trend lines and, 287–294
  two-variable, 308
  in two-way frequency tables, 307–314
  in two-way relative frequency tables, 315–330, 332
data sets
  comparing, 307–314, 315–322, 323–330
decimals
  converting fractions to, 336
  repeating, 338–344, 361
  terminating, 338–344, 361
dependent variables, 172
diagrams. See under represent

diameter
  of cylinder, 431–438
  of spheres, 338, 359, 407, 464
dilations, 1, 66, 73
  algebraic representation of, 60, 61
  center of, 58, 60, 61, 73
  exploring, 57–64
  image of, 73
  scale factor for, 58–64, 140, 141
discrete graph, 156–161, 169, 200, 201
Distributive Property, 82, 103, 419, 424
division
  in equations, 80–88, 184–191, 260, 316–322, 339
  long, 336
  with scientific notation, 420, 421, 424, 425
domain, 174–180, 199–204, 221
dot plots, 278
drawings
  analyzing trend lines and, 287–294
  polygons in the coordinate plot, 4
  scale, 48, 249
  shapes with given conditions, 4

E

elimination, 250
  solving systems of linear equations by, 249–256
enlargements
  on coordinate plane, 53
  investigating, 49–56
equations. See also under represent; systems of equations
  linear
    applying, 95–102
    examining special cases, 87–94
    multi-step, 79–86
    in slope-intercept form, 182
    special cases, 87–94
    writing, 181–188
  multi-step, 79–86, 181–188, 224, 234–240, 242–248, 250–256, 258–264, 432–438, 440–446, 448–454, 456–462
  one-step, 78, 145–152, 336
  in problem solving, 75
  for proportional relationships, 145–152
  representing system of, by graphing, 225–232
  special cases of, 224
  using roots to solve, 364
equilateral triangles, 111, 363, 373
estimating, 234–240, 242–248, 249–256, 258–264, 266–272, 353
experimental probability, 28, 306

exponents. See also scientific notation
  laws of, 404–410, 427
  properties of, 403–410
expressions. See under represent
exterior angles, 109, 112–114, 131
  alternate, 124–130, 131
  same-side, 124–130
Exterior Angle Theorem, 110, 111

F

figures
  congruent, 37–44, 73
  similar, 65–72, 106
formula. See also under represent
  for pythagorean theorem, 366
  for the volume of a cone, 439–446
  for the volume of a cylinder, 431–438
  for the volume of a sphere, 447–454
fractions
  converting to decimals, 163, 327, 336, 337, 340, 342
  writing in lowest terms, 335, 339, 340
frequency
  conditional relative, 324
  joint relative, 317, 319
  marginal relative, 317–322, 323–330
  relative, 316
frequency tables
  constructing and interpreting, 307–314
  constructing two-way relative, 315–322
  interpreting two-way relative, 323–330
functions, 171–222
  comparing, 205–212
  constructing, to model linear relationships, 197–204
  domain of, 174, 175, 176, 177, 179
  graphing, 173–180
  interpreting rate of change and initial value, 189–196
  linear, 181–188, 221, 278
    writing equations for, 181–188
  nonlinear, 184, 213–220, 221
    describing and sketching, 213–220
  qualitative functions of, 213–220
  range of, 174, 175, 176, 177, 179
  vertical line test for, 176
  writing equations for linear, 181–196

G

GCF. See greatest common factor (GCF)
geometry. See also transformational geometry
  angles
    alternate exterior, 124
    alternate interior, 124
    complementary, 97, 105, 269

Index

Tables of Measures, Symbols, and Formulas

LENGTH

1 meter (m) = 1,000 millimeters (mm)

1 meter = 100 centimeters (cm)

1 meter ≈ 39.37 inches

1 kilometer (km) = 1,000 meters

1 kilometer ≈ 0.62 mile

1 inch = 2.54 centimeters

1 foot (ft) = 12 inches (in.)

1 yard (yd) = 3 feet

1 mile (mi) = 1,760 yards

1 mile = 5,280 feet

1 mile ≈ 1.609 kilometers

CAPACITY

1 liter (L) = 1,000 milliliters (mL)

1 liter = 1,000 cubic centimeters

1 liter ≈ 0.264 gallon

1 kiloliter (kL) = 1,000 liters

1 cup (c) = 8 fluid ounces (fl oz)

1 pint (pt) = 2 cups

1 quart (qt) = 2 pints

1 gallon (gal) = 4 quarts

1 gallon ≈ 3.785 liters

MASS/WEIGHT

1 gram (g) = 1,000 milligrams (mg)

1 kilogram (kg) = 1,000 grams

1 kilogram ≈ 2.2 pounds

1 pound (lb) = 16 ounces (oz)

1 pound ≈ 0.454 kilogram

1 ton = 2,000 pounds

TIME

1 minute (min) = 60 seconds (s)

1 hour (h) = 60 minutes

1 day = 24 hours

1 week = 7 days

1 year (yr) = about 52 weeks

1 year = 12 months (mo)

1 year = 365 days

1 decade = 10 years

Tables of Measures, Symbols, and Formulas

SYMBOLS

$=$	is equal to	10^2	ten squared
$\neq$	is not equal to	10^3	ten cubed
$\approx$	is approximately equal to	2^4	the fourth power of 2
$>$	is greater than	$|-4|$	the absolute value of -4
$<$	is less than	$\%$	percent
$\geq$	is greater than or equal to	(2, 3)	ordered pair (x, y)
$\leq$	is less than or equal to	$\circ$	degree

FORMULAS

Perimeter and Circumference

Polygon	$P =$ sum of the lengths of sides
Rectangle	$P = 2\ell + 2w$
Square	$P = 4s$
Circle	$C = \pi d$ or $C = 2\pi r$

Area

Rectangle	$A = \ell w$ or $A = bh$
Parallelogram	$A = bh$
Triangle	$A = \frac{1}{2}bh$
Trapezoid	$A = \frac{1}{2}h(b_1 + b_2)$
Square	$A = s^2$
Circle	$A = \pi r^2$

Volume

Right Prism	$V = \ell wh$ or $V = Bh$
Cube	$V = s^3$
Pyramid	$V = \frac{1}{3}Bh$
Cylinder	$V = \pi r^2 h$
Cone	$V = \frac{1}{3}\pi r^2 h$
Sphere	$V = \frac{4}{3}\pi r^3$

Surface Area

Right Prism	$S = Ph + 2B$
Cube	$S = 6s^2$
Square Pyramid	$S = \frac{1}{2}P\ell + B$

Pythagorean Theorem

$$a^2 + b^2 = c^2$$

200
NARROW-LOT
HOME PLANS

Stylish Plans For Houses Less Than 60′ Wide

HOME PLANNERS, INC.
Tucson, Arizona

Published by Home Planners, Inc.
Editorial and Corporate Offices:
3275 West Ina Road, Suite 110
Tucson, Arizona 85741

Distribution Center:
29333 Lorie Lane
Wixom, Michigan 48393

Rickard D. Bailey, President and Publisher
Cindy J. Coatsworth Lewis, Publications Manager
Paulette Mulvin, Senior Editor
Amanda Kaufmann, Project Editor
Paul D. Fitzgerald, Book Designer

Photo Credits
Front Cover: © Andrew D. Lautman
Back Cover: © Andrew D. Lautman

First Printing, September 1993
10   9   8   7   6   5   4   3   2

Printed in the United States of America.

ISBN softcover: 1-881955-06-0
ISBN hardback: 1-881955-10-9

On the front cover: This handsome Nantucket Cape home, Design
AA2493, serves as the vacation home for Charles and Catherine
Talcott. Located on Lake St. Clair, Ontario, Canada; Builder: Yves
Frenette Construction, Stoney Point, Ontario; Landscaper: Boardwalk
Gardens, Tilbury, Ontario. For additional information about
this design, see page 40.

On the back cover: The rear of Design AA2493 shows an expanse of windows—perfect for enjoying the views of the lake. Inside, a cathedral ceiling and soaring windows lend a feeling of spaciousness to the gathering
room.